Female Masculinities and the Gender Wars

Female Masculinities and the Gender Wars

The Politics of Sex

Finn Mackay

I.B. TAURIS
LONDON • NEW YORK • OXFORD • NEW DELHI • SYDNEY

I.B. TAURIS

Bloomsbury Publishing Plc

50 Bedford Square, London, WC1B 3DP, UK

1385 Broadway, New York, NY 10018, USA

29 Earlsfort Terrace, Dublin 2, Ireland

BLOOMSBURY, I.B. TAURIS and the I.B. Tauris logo are trademarks of
Bloomsbury Publishing Plc

First published in Great Britain 2021
Reprinted 2021 (three times)

For legal purposes the Acknowledgements on p. viii constitute an extension
of this copyright page.

Cover design by Adriana Brioso
Cover image: Vicent: SILENCE EQUALS DEATH, Paris, 2004, by Del LaGrace Volcano

A catalogue record for this book is available from the British Library.

A catalog record for this book is available from the Library of Congress.

ISBN: HB: 978-0-7556-0664-1
PB: 978-0-7556-0663-4
ePDF: 978-0-7556-0665-8
eBook: 978-0-7556-0666-5

Typeset by Deanta Global Publishing Services, Chennai, India
Printed and bound in Great Britain

To find out more about our authors and books visit www.bloomsbury.com
and sign up for our newsletters

This book is dedicated to
My father
Roderick Beattie Mackay
1951–2015

And

My friend, Greenham Woman
Helen John
1937–2017

Contents

Acknowledgements

First, I would like to acknowledge my cat companions, Isambard and Solomon. They bring me spontaneous joy every day and have slightly taken the edge off successive Covid-19 lockdowns. Along with my wife and our son, these two complete our little family. Finishing this book during the pandemic has been a difficult process, battling around childcare and work. It has not been easy, but here we are, and once the shock recedes, I think we will be proud that we managed.

I would also like to thank Tomasz and Nayiri and all the team at Bloomsbury, for their initial faith and constant enthusiasm. Thank you to Professor Jack Halberstam,Professor Esther Newton, Del LaGrace Volcano, Professor Kimberlé Crenshaw, Campbell, John Stoltenberg, Juno Roche and all of those who either looked over and/or reviewed the book; including those who were enthusiastic and encouraging but did not have time to review it in the end. It is such an overwhelming honour to have my heroes read my work and I treasure these reviews. I cannot explain how moving it was when they started to come in, I am incredibly grateful. My colleagues in my team in Sociology at UWE Bristol are always a support, fun and inspiring, and a major reason why I love working there; a special shout out to my office wife Dr Michal Nahman. Thanks also to all the colleagues at UWE who keep everything going, those in the HAS office who booked desks for me to get some quiet and head space away from working at home, particular shout out to Emma Jefferies and Sheri Pitteway, also those in the cleaning and facilities team in our department who are always great but especially now, and to those in the coffee shop who I see far too often! Thanks are also due to all my friends on Twitter, from whom I learn so much and keep up with what is happening all around the world.

Sadly, during the pandemic, the ceaseless attacks on and lies told about trans people in our media have only increased. I would like to take this opportunity to point out the real effects this has on trans men, trans women, transgender people and their families. The gender wars are not an item on a Gender Studies reading list; they are real battles, with real casualties. Trans women and trans men respond and persist with honour, dignity and patience, and it is enraging because they should not have to. They should not have to deal with the fallout of a culture war in which they have been made easy scapegoats to detract from the actions of a monstrous government that is burning down the remnants of what civil society is left after over a decade of ideological cuts. The fact that our media is awash with conspiracy theories about trans lives, in the face of this, should be a national shame.

Sometimes, when discussing gender wars, people will accuse those that disagree with them of being on the wrong side of history. When I look through history, I see familiar sides; I see conservatives, religious fundamentalists and traditionalists on one side, and I see queers, and trans people and gender benders on the other side. This whole book is against binary approaches; it is about how many things can be 'true' at once, and how real life happens in the grey areas. Yet, when I see the lines that are drawn, I know which side I choose. I stand with the queers every time because they are my people and because I am one of them.

We know what the other side is capable of, with their strange alliances on all the bridges they are willing to cross; this is no time to be burning ours. It is likely that this book will not please everyone from any particular vantage point on the gender wars. No doubt it will attract criticism for not going far enough or for going too far. I remain convinced that there are areas of agreement in the middle, there are similar visions of a better future and we have to try to keep heading towards it, together.

Introduction

Despatches from the wrong sides of history

In a way I have been researching this book my whole life, because I have been studying masculinity for as long as I can remember. Like many queer people, I realized the sociological separation of sex and gender early on, and in that space was where I made my home. I have always been interested in the in-between identities, the not quite one or another, the individuals who, for various reasons, don't quite fit. Today, there are more categories than ever to choose from, for sex, gender and sexuality identities, but still relatively little tolerance for those who don't choose one and stick to it. This mirrors our political and social context, which is dominated by a with-us or against-us approach, in which potentially liberating debates about our changing landscape of previously fairly fixed labels and identifiers have been turned into a war. It is a war that has real consequences for people's basic human rights, to family life, to freedom of movement, to employment, to parenting and, even, to life itself; and all the while, different sides are screaming this over a battlefield, telling the other they are on the wrong side of history.

These are the so-called gender wars. If you have been anywhere near social media recently, you are likely to have encountered them; high-profile celebrities and public figures have joined in and also furthered mainstream awareness of debate and disagreements around gender identities and trans rights. In the summer of 2020 the famous British children's author J. K. Rowling, for example, departed from wizards and owls to start blogging about the rights and wrongs of trans and transgender movements; mainly the wrongs from her perspective, which she describes as gender critical (GC), a term often used by campaigners focussing particularly on the exclusion of trans women in some or all women-only spaces. British newspapers from left to right have also covered this topic, and it has taken up airtime on several news and cultural documentaries in the UK, for example, on BBC and Channel 4. In the UK, as well as other European countries and the United States, the issue is further popularized by attention to so-called culture wars and dismissive suggestions by politicians and media that trans rights are part of a generational move to 'snowflake' identity politics. Many people may only have fleeting awareness of such controversy and be unsure of what terms and labels mean, feeling unable to take any one side or another, but not wanting to offend anyone. If you are one of this majority in the middle, then, hopefully, you will find this book useful in providing some of the background about how this issue has come to prominence, explaining why it is often so controversial and defining some of the common terms you may hear.

For many of us these debates are personal though, and it is impossible to remain neutral. Trans men, trans women and transgender people are having to watch their basic human rights being put up for debate on an almost daily basis. Trans people are seeing themselves scapegoated in an increasingly bizarre array of things, from anti-vaccine protests to conspiracy theories about Big Pharma and Artificial Intelligence as well as profoundly antisemitic conspiracy theories. In the United Kingdom, the United States and other countries too, it is difficult to avoid seeing headlines or comment pieces about trans youngsters, the rights and wrongs of gender-neutral toilets, debate about who should be allowed in changing rooms or statistics about referrals to gender identity clinics. My perspective on this is from a UK standpoint, and my research is UK and US focussed; the narratives and activism in both these countries are often similar and mutually informative. These two countries actually share activists and activist groups as well, particularly those arguing for trans exclusion, as I shall explain later. Policy and commentary in the area of sex and gender are fast moving and changing; it is difficult to keep up with, even here in my home country of the UK, with Celtic nations often differing in approaches. This is another reason for keeping my focus on where I am most familiar. The findings and arguments presented here are therefore from this particular standpoint and location. In this book I will platform voices from queer and transgender masculine subjects that are taken from my 2017 survey research with over 200 responses from all over the UK, including the Celtic nations and from both rural and urban locations. I use the term 'transgender' in this book as the umbrella term which the influential scholar Susan Stryker has defined as:

 'all identities or practices that cross over, cut across, move between, or otherwise queer socially constructed sex/gender boundaries' (Stryker, 1994: 251). The current gender wars, or trans debates or trans questions, or whatever we call them, mainly consist of a ceaseless media focus on the medical responses to trans young people, the conflicts over whether women's spaces should be inclusive of trans women or not and conspiracy theories about alleged trans agendas. All of this is often simplified in the media into a battle between feminists and trans people, particularly between trans women and one school of feminism, which I personally subscribe to and have been researching for many years, and that is Radical Feminism. The popular term TERF, standing for trans-exclusionary radical feminist, is used to describe any anti-trans or anti-trans-inclusion viewpoint or campaign, whether it is from someone who describes themselves as a feminist of any kind or not, let alone whether they actually are a Radical Feminist.

Stuck in the middle with me

Many of those struggling in the gender wars, and many of those watching all of this unfold, whatever their own opinion on the matters that arise, have unquestioningly taken on the received wisdom about the roots of this increasingly fierce fight, and the homogenous framing of Radical Feminism. As is always the case, things are not as simple as they are presented. Not all Radical Feminists are trans-exclusionary, and not all those who are transphobic or trans-exclusionary are feminists, far from it; and much of Radical Feminist theory was presciently queer and radically trans-inclusive. Some Radical Feminists are even trans themselves. It is therefore not always possible to pick a side in this skirmish; some of us have roots in both camps. I am a long-standing feminist activist. I have identified as and with Radical Feminism since my teens, because that is the political theory that most closely matches my own political standpoint; not that I agree with all that has come from that school or strand of feminism. Putting my politics into action I have organized and campaigned for women's liberation alongside other social justice activism for peace and socialism. I founded the London Feminist Network in 2004 and revived the London Reclaim the Night march against all forms of male violence against women. My career has included working in the women's sector, against domestic abuse and for organizations such as Women's Aid. As a teenager I lived at a women's peace camp, inspired by Greenham Common. I have also been active in building and maintaining queer social spaces from my early twenties and spent several years in London immersed in the queer scene. Identifying as a butch lesbian for some of the time, as well as trans butch in some settings, I am used to communities where sex, gender and sexuality are organized very differently to the mainstream sex-gender rules, and I have seen and benefited from the potential that flourishes within those alternatives. Butch is a term that describes a sexuality and gender identity, usually understood to apply to lesbian or bisexual masculine women. For Black lesbian and queer women or masculine queers, the term 'stud' is commonly used, in place of butch, as the latter is more associated with White communities. The phenomenon that such terms describe is a universal phenomenon, with varied and wonderful names all over the world; and I will introduce you to all of this further in Chapter 6. Suffice to say, I have a stake in both sides of the current gender wars, I have skin in this game, and I find myself in the middle, yet again in between categories. From this vantage point I hope to guide you through some of the military history of this current supposed culture war, correcting some of the myths that are thrown from both trenches and contextualizing where it all came from and where we might go next.

Post-trans landscape

The current backdrop for this book is one marked by a growing awareness of the fluidity and flexibility, rather than fixity, of sex, sexuality and gender – a backdrop I will refer to as a post-trans landscape. By using this term, I certainly do not mean to suggest that all trans rights have been won and that thus movements for the human rights and recognition of trans women and trans men, and transgender people more broadly, are redundant. The reality, of course, is far from the case. However, while perhaps still widely misrepresented and misunderstood, there is undeniably an increasing visibility, including in mainstream media, of the lives of trans men and trans women and gender diverse people. These lives are receiving new attention, but they are not new. Trans people have been organizing in the UK, for example, for decades, long before the current attention. In her collection *Trans Britain* (2018), Christine Burns documents this activism, allowing trans organizers to archive and report on the history of their movement, from transgender groups in Manchester in the early 1970s to legal campaign groups like Press for Change, founded by Professor Stephen Whittle in 1992. From America, the trans activist and academic Susan Stryker also outlines over a hundred years of transgender history in her classic text *Transgender History* (2017). The mainstream visibility that we see today, while far from holistic, does add to the apparent generational shift in attitudes towards categories previously presented as unquestionably fixed. The fact is that for many young people today, gender, sexuality and even sex are at least up for debate, and often, a moveable feast. This more questioning and fluid context is what I refer to with the term 'post-trans landscape'.

The actress Laverne Cox's appearance on the cover of *Time* magazine in May 2014 was referenced by that magazine as a so-called 'trans tipping point'. Not long after, in the summer of 2015, Caitlyn Jenner was featured in *Vanity Fair*. In 2018 a series of programmes with the title 'Genderquake' were screened on the British terrestrial television channel, Channel 4. This included a fly on the wall documentary bringing together young individuals of diverse sex, gender and sexuality identities, including trans women, a non-binary young person and one trans man. Accompanying this there was also a live, studio debate including celebrity activists for trans rights: the model Munroe Bergdorf and Caitlyn Jenner. These examples are of course some of the most famous examples of trans lives, from the United States and the United Kingdom, and it cannot be, and has not been, ignored that those enjoying most visibility are often those with arguably particularly privileged lives and who embody gendered body ideals, in this case of femininity. As the scholar Hannah Rossiter has asserted, 'The last few years have seen a significant rise in the visibility of trans women such as Carmen Carrera, Laverne Cox, Caitlynn Jenner, and Janet Mock, who are all conventionally physically attractive and very feminine' (Rossiter, 2016: 87).

A 2015 survey of 1,000 thirteen to twenty-year-olds by a US marketing intelligence firm reported that 56 per cent of the youth respondents knew someone who used gender-neutral pronouns such as 'ze'. On sexuality, just over half, 52 per cent stated that they did not define as exclusively heterosexual (Innovation Group, 2016). This cohort of digital natives, those born approximately between 1995 and 2003, often labelled in marketing language as 'generation Z', appear to be embracing sex, sexual and gender diversity in even greater number than the older millennials (those who entered higher education, training or career in the early 2000s). Recent research with children in UK schools has found over twenty-three different terms in use for gender identity, for example:

> One significant theme was children and young people's expanding gender vocabulary: 23 different terms for gender identity were used by participants in our research. Many participants were also advocates for the rights of sexual minorities and trans people, and were highly critical of gender inequalities. They often saw these rights as 'modern' or 'twenty-first century' and as important aspects of their sense of self and values, identifying themselves as more progressive than earlier generations. (Bragg et al., 2018: 4)

Gender ideology and other conspiracy theories

These shifts have not been without friction, as I have introduced earlier, and there are some fierce kickbacks to such changes, from across political spectrums, left and right.

It should be noted that these have been going on for some time. The Catholic Church began mobilizing specifically against shifts towards more fluid understandings of gender and gender identity as far back as the mid-1990s, when feminist organizations brought language around gender mainstreaming and gender equality to the fourth World Conference on Women in Beijing, for example, in 1995. Pope John Paul II wrote a letter to the then United Nations (UN) secretary general Mrs Gertrude Mongella, emphasizing the complementarity but difference of women and men, and of masculinity and femininity. This was emphasized again in the *Declaration of Interpretation of the Term 'Gender' By The Holy See* (Beijing, 15 September 1995), in the Pope's *Letter to Women* in Beijing again, and also in the Lexicon, from the Pontifical Council for the Family, *Lexicon: Ambiguous and Debatable Terms Regarding Family Life and Ethical Questions* (2003). In October 2015 the Relatio Finalis or final report from the Synod of Bishops to the Holy Father, Pope Francis on *The Vocation and Mission of the Family in the Church and in the Contemporary World* made clear that gender follows sex like soul and body. 'According to the Christian principle, soul and body, as well as biological sex (*sex*) and socio-cultural role of sex (*gender*), can be distinguished but not separated' (Relatio Finalis 2015: 58; emphasis in original). More recently, guidance aimed at schools and educators brought together these standpoints on sexuality and gender and specifically critiqued and warned against 'gender ideology' and 'gender theory'. In *Male and Female He Created Them: Towards a Path of Dialogue on the Question of Gender Theory in Education* (2019), the Congregation for Catholic Education warns that a dangerous gender theory is undermining marriage and the family, destabilizing sacred differences between men and women and indoctrinating children to believe that sex, sexuality and gender are matters of individual choice.

The terms 'gender theory', 'genderism' and 'gender ideology' have all entered into public debate on trans and transgender rights, often being used in the current gender wars by 'anti-gender' right-wing religious groups, as well as by right-wing governments (Graff & Korolczuk, 2018a; Kuhar & Patternotte, 2017; Grzebalska, 2016). 'The anti-gender discourse effectively mobilised groups, associations, and organisations belonging to the Catholic militancy, along with radical right parties and groups' (Lavizzari & Prearo, 2019: 431). These terms and similar language are also used by some GC and feminist groups; indeed, this terminology may have influenced the term 'gender critical' in the first place, or arguably at least popularized its use. However, many trans-exclusionary Radical Feminists and GC feminists point out that they use this term very differently from how the Christian right and right-wing states will utilize it. Writing for Woman's Place UK on Viktor Orban's transphobic, misogynistic and homophobic decrees in Hungary, the socialist feminist Jayne Egerton asserts that 'our respective analyses have so little in common' (2020). Egerton highlights that for GC feminists, the term 'gender-critical' (GC) means to critique any approach that serves to 'conflate sex with gender and deny the material reality of sex-based oppression. This is a far cry from the definitions shared by the growing "anti gender" movements in Central and Eastern Europe' (Egerton, 2020). Sadly though, groups of Conservatives, Christian right organizations and feminists do sometimes work together on questions of trans rights and inclusion, and I shall go on to give a couple of examples of this (Moore & Greenesmith, 2021; Correa et al., 2018; McRobbie, 2018).

In the United States, right-wing conservative Christian fundamentalist groups like the Family Research Council view gender ideology as a third wave of an assault against the heterosexual nuclear family, the first wave being the feminist movement and the second being the gay liberation movement (O'Leary & Sprigg, 2015). Attending for the third time in October 2017, Donald Trump became the first sitting US president to speak at the Values Voter Summit in Washington, DC, run by the Family Research Council. The 2017 Summit saw a panel on 'Transgender Ideology in Public Schools: Parents and Educators Fight Back' at which an activist called Meg Kilgannon, director of Concerned Parents and Educators of Fairfax County, asserted that lesbian, gay and bisexual or LGB rights had taken hold in American schools and that attacking the trans community was the only way to fracture and break this hold, believing that there is less public support for trans rights and that this could unseat the LGBT movement as a whole. 'Gender identity on its own is just a bridge too far', comforted Kilgannon. 'Divide and conquer. For all its recent success the LGBT alliance is fragile, trans activists need the gay rights movement to help legitimise them' (Kilgannon, 2017). Kilgannon went on to promote coalition building wherever possible, praising the group Hands Across the Aisle, founded in 2017 by lesbian activist Miriam Ben-Shalom and Christian anti-choice activist Kaeley Triller-Haver (Triller, 2019), communications director of a group called Just Want Privacy, who campaign to reverse policies allowing trans men and trans women to use the bathroom that matches their identity.

Hands Across the Aisle is a coalition of Christian women, feminist women and anti-trans-inclusion campaigners, including one British member, the founder of a successful anti-trans-inclusion group called Standing for Women (HATA, 2018). 'Who knew we agreed on so much', Kilgannon said in 2017, reassuring the audience that lesbians and feminists all share their view that gender identity is bad and explaining that it can be seen as a form of lesbian eugenics to erase masculine lesbian girls. This is our first indication of the importance and presence of the figure of the masculine female; it is one often invoked and utilized as a reference point in the current gender wars. As I will go on to explore, this is just one reason why masculine lesbian genders and masculine queer female identities need to be centred and allowed to speak for themselves, rather than being weaponized as pawns in someone else's game.

Right-wing conservative Christian fundamentalist groups like the Heritage Foundation have also hosted numerous conferences and panels on gender ideology – for example, a fringe event at the 2019 Committee on the Status of Women (CSW), which was titled 'Gender Equality and Gender Ideology: Protecting Women and Girls' (CSW63 Side Event). Anti-trans-inclusion feminist organization the Women's Liberation Front (WoLF) have participated in events with the Heritage Foundation, and they describe themselves as a Radical Feminist organization. For example, they collaborated at a conference on 16 February 2017 on 'Biology Is Not Bigotry: Why Sex Matters in the Age of Gender Identity' with Mary Lou Singleton from WoLF; And again, on 28 January 2019, for example, at a panel debate on the inequality of the Equality Act, concerned at moves to outlaw discrimination on the grounds of sex and gender identity (SOGI), with Jennifer Chavez and Kara Dansky for WoLF (Dansky now works for the Women's Human Rights Campaign). The anti-trans-inclusion activist and founder of Standing for Women in the UK, Mrs Kellie-Jay Keen-Minshull, known on social media as Posie Parker, attended that meeting in Washington, DC, as an audience member and also conducted some direct action of her own. A few days later, on 30 January 2019, Mrs Keen-Minshull and another British anti-trans-inclusion campaigner, filmed and broadcast themselves on Facebook live while interrupting Sarah McBride in a meeting on Capitol Hill. McBride is a prominent activist for trans rights in the United States and is press secretary for the HRC or Human Rights Campaign. The two activists are heard in the video accusing McBride of not caring about lesbians receiving mastectomies, of hating women in general and of ignoring women in a male fashion (Braidwood, 2019).

In 2019 WoLF also collaborated with the Heritage Foundation, the Family Policy Alliance and other groups to produce a parent resource guide, *Responding to the Transgender Issue,* published by the Minnesota Family Council, an affiliate of Alliance Defending Freedom and Focus on the Family, which was founded by the influential evangelical Christian, James Dobson. All these groups are against same-sex marriage and abortion. Focus on the Family, for example, founded a long-running gay conversion conference titled Love Won Out. Speaking at the fortieth anniversary celebration for Focus on the Family, former US vice president Mike Pence described James Dobson as a 'friend and a mentor' going on to enthuse the audience and assure them they had an ally in Donald Trump (Pence, 2019). WoLF also worked with another conservative Christian group, Concerned Women of America, to host a lobby outside the Supreme Court on 8 October 2019 supporting the dismissal from employment of a trans woman, the late Aimee Stephens, seeking to transition in her workplace, Harris Funeral Homes, who were defended in their legal fight by Alliance Defending Freedom (*R.G. & G.R. Harris Funeral Homes Inc. v. Equal Employment Opportunity Commission*). A famous British feminist activist and lesbian rights activist Linda Bellos also flew from the UK to attend the event. These two countries have much interaction on the gender wars, sharing both activists and activism it seems. WoLF have worked on other legal cases, trying to attack trans rights through the courts, together with far-right conservative Christian groups, such as the Family Policy Alliance, for example, a lobbying arm of Focus on the Family, filing an Amicus Brief with them in 2017 in the case of a young trans man, Gavin Grimm, taking his school through the courts to provide him with access to the bathroom that matched his identity as a man (Gloucester v. G.G).

None of this has done much to separate the wedding of feminism with anti-trans viewpoints of course, although groups such as WoLF do receive criticism from feminists, especially those on the political Left, for aligning themselves with wealthy and well-connected homophobic, right-wing anti-abortion conservative groups. Such criticism appears to have little effect though, as groups like WoLF believe the Left and mainstream feminism has abandoned them in their fight against gender ideology, which they believe is the most dangerous threat to women's rights today. From that framing, it is vital to make coalitions wherever is possible, and the ends justify the means. It is important to make clear, right at the start of this book, and as I shall argue throughout, that this is not a position I support. For the record, as far as I can see, the tragedy is that we all share a much greater enemy, and that enemy is the religious right and associated conservative forces, what Graff and Korolczuk define as 'illiberal populism' (2018: 798). A movement which is 'inherently anti-elitist and anti-expert, hostile to individualism and minority rights, which are the core tenants of liberal democracy' (2018: 798). As Wodak (2015) elaborates, this form of populism is rooted in ideology based on 'a nativist concept of belonging, linked to a chauvinist and racialized concept of "the people" and "the nation"' (Wodak 2015: 47). Whatever we call it, it is growing across Europe and North America. This threat is fascist, and it is masculinist nationalism. This enemy is the anti-choice, pro-natalism, White supremacist forces that are seeking to build their own version of Margaret Atwood's nightmarish vision of Gilead, in fact rather than fiction, across Europe, the United States and other parts of the world. They must not succeed.

UK consultation mobilizes gender wars

Here in the UK the shifting sands in the terrain of terminologies and policies on gendered and sexed identities have come increasingly into the public eye, accompanied by increasing backlash. This was partly due to the Westminster government's public consultation, in 2018, on the Gender Recognition Act (GRA) 2004. The review concluded in September 2020, with the government deciding to make no changes, but to reduce the costs of a Gender Recognition Certificate (GRC; Truss, 2020). The Women and Equalities Select Committee followed this up in October 2020 with an enquiry into whether the government's conclusions were adequate, hearing evidence from those with different perspectives on reform of the GRA. The 2018 review of this act had followed the initial Women and Equalities Select Committee transgender equality inquiry back in 2015, which resulted in a report suggesting urgent updating of the GRA. The then minister for women and equalities Nicky Morgan promised to 'tackle unnecessary bureaucracy and to assess the need for medical checks contained within the 2004 Act' (Morgan, 2016: 5). Trans rights organizations, lesbian, gay, bisexual, trans, queer, intersex or LGBTQI+ and allies groups around the country agreed and organized to campaign in favour of reforms to this act, particularly the proposals for self-identification. The consultation asked about reforms that would remove the costly, invasive and time-consuming need for medical authorization before a GRC, with amended sex marker, could be issued. The Conservative government noted themselves, however, that many trans people did not bother pursuing this route currently, probably partly because of the aforementioned barriers. Their national LGBT survey for the Government Equalities Office in 2017, the largest survey of lesbian, gay, bisexual and trans or LGBT life ever conducted, found that around 12 per cent of trans respondents had secured a GRC.

Just as campaigns began or stepped up in support of trans rights and to lobby for liberalizing reforms to the GRA 2004, so too new organizations set up to work against such moves. This included several GC or gender-abolitionist feminist, lesbian separatist and lesbian feminist groups who took this opportunity and began far-reaching lobbying and activism against reforms relaxing the existing bureaucratic and medical processes. Such groups have protested, disrupted and picketed Stonewall and Pride (Ditum, 2018c) events, for example, conducted billboard campaigns and imaginative media stunts. They have experienced protest in turn, with public meetings by groups such as Woman's Place UK having venues cancelled at the last minute and being subject to large and noisy direct action outside events that do go ahead. To avoid this, such groups often arrange pre-meeting sites and avoid advertising venues in advance. This was the case with one of the early groups to emerge against liberalizing the GRA 2004. Set up in July 2017 by Venice Allen, We Need to Talk ran a series of information events to raise awareness about the UK consultation. In September 2017 women waiting to go to a London meeting of We Need to Talk were assembling at Speaker's Corner in Hyde Park, central London. Protestors aiming to disrupt the meeting were also there and one of those protestors assaulted a woman waiting for the meeting. Protestors also accused GC activists of filming them without consent, and of holding one protestor in a head lock. GC activist Maria MacLachlan was struck by a young protestor and video footage of that incident was widely shared. The case later went to court in April 2018 and the protestor was found guilty of assault. In March 2020 a meeting of Labour members opposed to Labour support for recognition of gender identity and in defence of what they called sex-based rights was disrupted by protestors using smoke bombs. This was in an area of London in close proximity to a residential tower block of flats called Grenfell Tower, the site of a horrific fire on 14 June 2017 that took seventy-two lives and is widely seen as an act of corporate manslaughter. This protest tactic was seen as an insensitive move and the organizing group, London Bi Pandas, later apologized, confirming that they should have put more thought into the action and been mindful of the local residents so recently affected by the traumatic fire.

The point to take from such examples is that the warlike phrasing that is often used about the gender wars is not entirely an over-dramatization, as these sorts of incidents demonstrate. This is not an abstract debate; it has become highly charged and often physical; meetings are stopped, venues withdrawn, attendees threatened, jobs lost and cases have even ended up in court. While protest is a political right for those on all sides, it is hard to support this when it turns to physical violence or the complete blockading of political meetings from taking place at all. Self-organization and political assembly are also a political right, as long as such gatherings do not move into hate speech that promotes or incites violent hate crime or violence of any sort. However, reaction is inevitable in the current environment, especially when some feminist and GC groups and individuals are against not only reform of the GRA 2004 but the whole existing system for legal recognition and protection of trans men and trans women – in a continuation of a fight that was declared within feminism decades before (Hines, 2020; Jeffreys, 2018; Hines, 2017). As I set out at the start of this chapter, this historic and long-running battle is now at the stage of what some scholars in the field of gender and sexuality studies have described as a war: 'The dispute between some self-identified feminists and trans persons, trans women especially, and trans supporting feminists has erupted into a full-scale ideological war. Once at the level of conflict, officially undeclared, we have moved into the territory of "you are either with us or against us", with real threats against real people – from both sides' (Watson, 2016: 246). While this quote refers to a long-running skirmish as being officially undeclared, this will, perhaps, not seem the case to feminist activists who have been barracked up against just these arguments for a long time, since the 1960s and 1970s.

Turf wars

It has been noted before (Enke, 2018; Awkward-Rich, 2017; Williams, 2016) that these gender wars are often fought over the turf or territory of women's self-organized spaces and movements. These are the grounds of the so-called TERF struggle. TERF is a label put onto anyone who voices transphobic views, or standpoints against trans inclusion in any spaces, but particularly in women-only spaces. Feminist activist Viv Smythe is widely credited with having first coined the term, or at least put keyboard to internet and forever immortalized the acronym. In 2008 Smythe was running an introductory blog on feminist facts; when it reached a larger following, discussions inevitably emerged over whose facts were being represented as true, and whose were being erased. In a debate over differing views on the famous women-only music festival at Michigan, which I will explain in Chapter 3, the acronym TERF was utilized to avoid posters having to write out the whole descriptor for a particular standpoint within some elements of Radical Feminism (Smythe, 2018). The very need for this term, within feminist communities, has now been completely overlooked; the need for a discerning term arose because not all Radical Feminists agree on trans inclusion or exclusion. There is no one homogenous Radical Feminist stance on trans inclusion, as I will go on to argue in this book.

Fights, conflict and struggles over who can or cannot be allowed entry to women-only spaces and on what grounds are not a new invention. Nevertheless, it seems important to repeat this, because it is often suggested that the feminism of the Second Wave in the United States and the United Kingdom, which is my focus in this book, was implicitly and irredeemably transphobic to its core and was by nature trans-exclusionary. Widely critiqued as a racist, homophobic, classist and transphobic period of activism, Second Wave is a term used as a chronological referent point as well as an ideological label. Simply chronologically it is used to describe the uprisings of feminist activity and visibility that occurred during the emergence of many New Left social justice movements from around the 1960s to the 1980s across the Western world. The common accusation or charge is that these Second Wave feminists who went before us were unconcerned with power relationships between women, and only concerned with barricading the Women's Liberation Movement or WLM to anyone who did not look like the norm in the mainstream – White, educated, middle-class, heterosexual. This is not true, of course, and even a cursory look through any archive, such as the Feminist Archive in the UK, for example, illustrates that Second Wave feminists were diverse, and also profoundly and urgently aware of power relationships between women and were trying to address those issues transparently. 'The second wave of women's liberation in the 1970s was made up of many currents, including women of colour, socialist feminists, and others, who fought for an understanding that all women don't face identical oppression. Many white women within the movement recognised the necessity to be on the frontlines against racism' (Feinberg, 1998: 52). Simplifications of that herstorical moment also erase the presence and contributions of Black women's feminist movements and scholarship, working-class women's activism and theory, lesbian women's self-organization and also trans women active and influential in feminism. The WLM of that era did not manage to eradicate the structural inequalities of racism, homophobia or transphobia, for example, inside its movement or without, nor has any so-called wave of feminism since, though more recent waves often define themselves favourably against the perceived failures of past activism (Baumgardner & Richards, 2000). What herstory shows is that debate about the inclusion of trans women in feminism has been long-running and that some groups and organizations were in favour and were working with trans women, while others were not (Williams, 2016). The takeaway point here is that trans women were involved in the foundational and legacy-building Second Wave of feminism, and that some feminists, including Radical Feminists, were supportive of working alongside trans women in that movement.

Then, as now, there were Radical Feminists reflecting on power relationships, solidarity and differing life histories and organizing together with trans women. Then, as now, there were also Radical Feminists, often also lesbian feminists, lesbian separatists or separatist feminists, who took what is now called a GC or gender-abolitionist stance, and who viewed the growing medical and legal advancements in the 1980s and 1990s, around sex reassignment surgery and interventions, as just the medical institutionalization of gender stereotypes. Those are truisms and should not be glossed over or denied. But, the mythology of the gender wars today frequently weds all Radical Feminism to transphobia; in fact, the two have become synonymous, and all feminism and feminists are arguably now suspect. Sometimes, those uncritically accepting this mantra have a sense of where this mythology stems from, and names like Janice Raymond and Michigan are touchstone citations. I shall introduce you to this history here in this book, detailing the infamous work of Raymond (1989) in Chapter 2 and, in Chapter 3, the saga of the lesbian feminist rite of passage that was the Michigan Womyn's Music Festival. While there is much to critique, the unquestioning merging of Radical Feminism with transphobia deflects attention from the much larger structural threats which endanger both feminists and trans people alike.

If it were only Radical Feminists that trans people had to worry about, then their worries would be severely decreased. Radical Feminists are not a majority in government, nor are they dominant in major medical companies, insurance multinationals or chief executives of the National Health Service or NHS in the UK. Donald Trump, implausible former president of the United States, is not a Radical Feminist. Yet, he barred trans people from the military, many with years of exemplary service in that career; he promoted rules for entry to public toilets, based on birth sex, regardless of whether individuals have been living as trans men and trans women for decades, and he allowed medical providers to refuse to provide trans surgery, he furthered freedom to practice prejudice for those who wish to refuse healthcare, or even goods and services to trans people purely on the grounds of them being trans. Across Europe the growth of the nationalist right includes vocal lobbying against LGBTQI+ rights, utilizing language from the Catholic Church and warning against what it calls gender ideology. These forces of sex and gender conservatism have never been good for women or minorities, and any feminists who assume that their enemy's enemy is their friend do so at their own, and everyone else's peril. As we saw in the quotation from Kilgannon, different factions on the trans-critical side of the gender wars, while mainly focussed on controlling and often restricting the lives of trans women in particular, often invoke the figure of masculine females or butch lesbians, weaponizing these identities to suggest that a trans agenda is erasing lesbians and coercing them into becoming trans men from a young age. Masculine female queer or lesbian people are then in a slightly contradictory position in these debates; being secondary in focus to trans women, the most feminine of whom are most likely to be platformed by the media, and being without queer or trans masculine figureheads, and being regularly spoken about while rarely given space to speak for themselves.

Female masculinity on the map

British media loves to fuel and fan the flames of the gender wars. The terrain of this battle is often full of stories about children being forced to transition too young, as trans men or trans women, and later regretting those interventions. Often the figures used in such media coverage are young female-bodied people, masculine individuals who we are told were really, all along, just tomboys or just lesbians or just butches. Sometimes these sorts of labels are shamelessly manipulated by those who care less about young butches or queers and mainly about attacking trans people. It seems everyone is very suddenly concerned about butch lesbians and female masculine queers, especially heterosexual commentators, yet mostly the mainstream remains completely ignorant about our actual lives and identities. 'Lesbians face a fight for their very existence,' wrote journalist Janice Turner for *The Times* in July 2019; Turner is married to a man and mother to two sons. She bemoans that butch swagger is being transed out of young lesbians who turn to transition purely because of homophobia and misogyny. 'Because if a lesbian is seen as a second-class woman – or barely a woman at all – why wouldn't girls surrender the fight and take testosterone' (Turner, 2019). Turner writes that 'butch girls now stand alone' going on to cite increasing referrals to gender identity clinics as 'the erasure of lesbians' (2019). In a blog about why she takes a GC stance, author J. K. Rowling discloses that thirty years ago she may have transitioned to live as a trans man, to escape the 'sexualised scrutiny and judgement that sets so many girls to war against their bodies in their teens' (2020). She states that she felt ambivalent about being female: 'I've wondered whether, if I'd been born 30 years later, I too might have tried to transition. The allure of escaping womanhood would have been huge' (Rowling, 2020). Passionate about LGB rights since its strong support for homophobic Clause 28, *The Telegraph* covered the launch of a new LGB organization in 2019, the LGB Alliance UK. The Alliance was set up in frustration with Stonewall, the UK's national LGBTQ+ rights group, for failing to respond to charges of putting trans people before the concerns of lesbian, gay and bisexual people. *The Telegraph* journalist quotes LGB Alliance co-founder Bev Jackson: 'Young lesbians in particular are suffering; experiencing huge social pressure to transition to male if they do not conform to traditional gender stereotypes' (Swerling, 2019). 'At last!', shrieked the *Daily Mail* in September 2020, 'Teachers are told to stop pushing tomboys to change their gender just because of the way they like to dress or play' (Owen & Heale, 2020). 'Thank God they didn't make this tomboy trans' is the headline in another article in *The Times*, interviewing a psychotherapist about her concerns that gender non-conforming children are being wrongly diagnosed as transexual (Kinchen, 2018). While identifiers like butch and gender non-conforming (GNC) are being utilized in such discourse regularly, the people who actually identify as butch or GNC are rarely heard from, let alone those who blend available categories or identify as trans and butch or transgender butch, for example, or transmasculine.

Masculine female people are being given a narrative about who they are, which is allegedly naive potential victims of transing who need protecting, all the while there are ironically no masculine female role models in the media at all, and no celebration of female masculinity, lesbian masculinity or trans masculinities, and no trans men. Mainstream media is cheerleading for tomboys, yet the reaction to gender non-conformity in children appears to be waiting any revolution, with bullying, discrimination, hate crime and everyday hostilities still very much in evidence. In addition, certain strands of feminism, the very same strands that are now often situated on the trans-exclusion side of the gender wars, have ironically long demonized butch lesbians, accusing them of aping patriarchal masculinity and fetishizing sexism; I shall explain this in more detail later in this book. For these reasons I have focussed my analysis of the gender wars from the perspective of those very figures, centring female masculinities and transgender masculinities for a change. We have a useful perspective on these debates; just as we are often between certain identities, we also fall between the cracks of available discourses on current so-called gender culture wars and panics. We have an investment in camps which are described as warring and discrete. From this perspective there are no easy answers to today's gender questions, and there should be less picking sides and more sharing of common ground. That is my aim in this book.

Seizing the means of masculinity

As I have introduced briefly at the start of this chapter, I have always identified as and with masculinity for as long as I can remember; from the available gender models in society, that was the one I was drawn to. I therefore have never felt like I crossed from one expected gender to another possible gender, and thus I do not formally use the term 'transgender' for myself. The word 'trans' means to cross, as in words like 'transport', or 'transnational'. Thus, to trans gender would mean to cross the socially constructed lines of gender, or to cross identify with a gender that one originally did not or was not able to. That is not my story. Another reason I do not formally use the word 'trans' for myself is because I personally think that legally, socially and medically transitioning to live life as a trans man or a trans woman is significant and so I reserve the term 'trans' for those who are trans men or trans women. People who have crossed the lines of sex are individuals who, in the past, would have been called transexual, meaning literally cross-sex. That term is now considered pathologizing though, overly medical and is widely seen as out of date. Queer professor extraordinaire Jack Halberstam has introduced the term 'trans' with an asterix added, trans* – to highlight that this contains a multitude of identities and to encourage and celebrate the fluidity of gendered and sexed terminology (2018a). All acts of naming and identity claims are of course deeply personal, and everyone has their own unique perspective on this and will have their own personal preferences.

I consider myself quite gender conforming; the gender I most conform to just happens to be masculinity, as it is quite conventionally recognized and understood. For these reasons I cannot formally label myself as transgender, trans, GNC or non-binary (NB); they just don't feel like they fit, although I certainly identify with many of the criteria for those terms. I'm a butch lesbian but not in the sense of being a woman-loving woman, or a woman-identified woman in the way that so many proud butch lesbian women inhabit and honour that identity. I will explore these identities more in Chapter 7. I have come to settle on queer, or queer butch as an identifier, acknowledging the many, often contentious, political and ideological attachments to that term. This is a new development for me, as previously I rejected the term 'queer' due to my opposition to various political stances that are often associated with queer politics, particularly legal and policy responses to the industry of prostitution. I was always excited by and have enjoyed studying queer theory since my first degree in women's studies in the 1990s, however, and recently the normative conservatism at work in the context of the gender wars has ironically pushed me more towards this label as a personal identifier. While I certainly do not agree with all of the political stances often attached to queer, it is a fluid term that is not defined by any sex, sexuality or gender. It encompasses that which is outside the sex/gender/sexuality conservative norm – the rigid binary assumption that everyone will be either male, masculine and heterosexual or female, feminine and heterosexual. Like many people, not only those who would consider themselves LGBTQI+, I have never been able to fit into those rules, mainly because my gender identity was never viewed by others as congruent with my sex at birth, although it felt perfectly natural to me.

Climbing the tomboy family tree

From as way back as I can remember I watched, noted and copied how the men around me, and those in films and books, looked and behaved. How they sat, how they walked, how they wore their shirts, how they rolled up their sleeves, how they ate, drank and smoked. I knew precisely how belts should be worn and which way round the buckles should go; I knew the right side for shirt buttons and that a gentleman should never fasten up a waistcoat all the way down. Growing up in rural Scotland, in a poor farming community, I never had much opportunity to practice such sartorial delights, and the irony is that the boys I knew and grew up with could not care less about style rules for masculinity. The men I knew were rarely in anything but boiler suits, and my own father lived in putty stained jeans and a fleece. My mother told me once that my dad bought a new shirt only twice in his life, and wore it straight out of the packet, first to visit me in hospital when I was born and then to attend my wedding. My dad was a quiet soul, practical and competent at pretty much everything, from cooking and cleaning to installing new windows or building a roof. He showed me that men can be as kind and caring as the next person; a natural baby whisperer with a solitary, grumpy edge, he wasn't a saint, but he was never a stereotype. It is right that I should start this book about masculinities with my own father, and that's where those of us with dads, for better or worse, first learn about who and what men are meant to be, the fiction and the reality. For some of us, we take these examples and are drawn to a masculinity that we were never expected to have, never taught and never schooled into. We pick and mix from the available models around us and we make an identity that suits. At best such a bespoke, hybrid identity is tolerated, but for many it is brutally supressed, just as their brothers are having it brutally enforced. For too many boys, masculinity is groomed through stereotypical gender rules, the first lesson of which is not to be feminine (Roberts, 2018; Frosh, Phoenix & Pattman, 2002); I will discuss all this in more detail in Chapter 5. This is a book informed by the masculinities of those people who were not born with bodies sexed as male, who aren't men and who were never supposed to find a home in the masculinity they now make their own, and own. These individuals have had many names, always and forever and all over the world: tomboys, butches, dykes, transgender, studs, he-she, bulldagger.

I was what you would call a tomboy. For a long time I thought I was a boy, or rather, I just never wasted much time contemplating whether I was or not. I considered myself the same as the boys I hung around with. Everything they did, I did, and I dressed as they did and looked similar to them. Then I began to realize I probably wasn't male like boys were male. I have memories of sometimes wondering before I went to sleep if I would wake up the next day and be male bodied, because then it would match who I was. Such a physical transformation did not seem out of the question when I was about seven or eight; and I would not have been surprised if it had happened one morning. Eventually, I realized I was not male and probably would never be, but this didn't have to stop me from being a boy, so I carried on boy-like. I grew up with the only child around, a boy my age, and we lived like siblings. From dawn till dusk we played armies, made rafts, climbed trees and pursued adventures to avoid being caught and called for farm duties or to stack wood.

In the summer holidays I would sometimes leave the countryside for the city, spending weeks at a time with my grandmother and grandfather in Nottingham in the Midlands of England. For several of those summers I lived as a boy, making little gangs with other local boys and getting into trouble. I must have been about nine or ten at this time. I had short, white blonde curly hair and a red baseball cap my grandma had brought back from Perth, Western Australia, and it was the only baseball cap I had. I can still remember it like a picture. It had a black swan on the front and I wore it every day. I would go for tea at my friends' houses, and their mothers would call us down to eat, shouting up the stairs with a carefree: 'boys, teas ready'. I have distinct memories of this jarring, not because I knew it wasn't true but because I knew they would not believe it was true if they knew I wasn't male. It never occurred to me that I was being anything but my honest self, but I was aware even then that nobody else would see it that way. I was perceptive enough to understand that it would be seen as lying. As I was quite an honest and worthy child, that felt difficult. The majority of readers may be unfamiliar with such experiences; I would ask you to imagine something you experience as core to yourself, in a natural and seamless way, being viewed by others around you as a lie – a stigmatized, vulgar lie for which you know you are expected to feel shame. It makes the everyday business of just being yourself – self-conscious; this is a feeling that may be familiar to many queer people, to many lesbian, gay and bisexual people. It is a sense of observing oneself as you know others will see you, tailoring and tweaking appearance, mannerisms and speech in response. What conflicted was the awareness that my life would be considered performance, rather than just my life. I much preferred being called 'he' and being known as a boy, because that meant I could carry on being me in the ways that I felt were natural and unthinking. Being any other way would have been a performance. Yet people like me did not have the luxury of unthinking self-expression, or not for long into childhood anyway. There is a common assumption that female children are tomboys because they want to play with boy's toys and enjoy physical activity. I didn't want to be a boy so that I could enjoy the freedom of boys; I already had that freedom.

When I reached my teenage years, I had to get to grips with the idea that I might be a lesbian, as I had always mainly been attracted to girls. I say mainly, but it was hard to separate being attracted to boys with wanting to be them. However, the label of lesbian was not appealing, and it felt too specialized and niche. I did not feel special or different but of course as everyone was growing up into teenagers around me, now I was being forced to realize that I was different, very much so. When I was about eleven or thereabouts, I remember having a conversation with one of my friends, who knew I was female by that time. We were in my grandma's house watching the original Total Recall on VHS; although then it wasn't the 'original', it was just Total Recall and there was only one. This of course was highly illegal, as the film was an 18 rating; unfortunately my dear grandma has now passed so there's no worries of her being reported to the social for retrospective safeguarding issues. My friend was called Mehboob and he was a bit younger than me; he lived round the corner with his family and his sisters. We were laughing at the scene where one of Arnold Schwarzenegger's friends makes out with an alien woman who has three breasts. Mehboob was saying he'd know what to do with three breasts and he stood up wiggling his hands around and then dancing about in the front room singing. I can remember his face, his shiny school trousers and tank top, and his lovely Nottingham accent. He asked me why I didn't just stop telling people I was a boy, and just be a 'lemon' instead; this was how kids talked about lesbians in those days, and he used it purely as a describing word, as did I. I explained to him that it wouldn't feel right because if I was to get a girlfriend, I would not want to be with a girl who wanted to be with a girl, because I wasn't a girl. I would have to find a girl who wanted to be with a boy who was a kind of boy like me. I remember him nodding and accepting this completely in that way that young people are so good at accepting other people's truth, being not yet cynical, and hopefully with little reason to be. I did not know then about femme lesbians, I did not know the word 'butch' either, and I wouldn't even learn that word until I was eighteen. I hoped that there were girls out there who wanted boys like me, but I had no language for it. Later I would understand identity terms like 'lesbian', 'butch' and 'trans'.

The absence of seamlessness

I read the late Leslie Feinberg's *Stone Butch Blues* when I was around eighteen and finally felt validated, learning that the way I was had a name, and a history. Here was a character who was female bodied, but regularly lived as a man, a character who also inhabited lesbian spaces, but who didn't quite fit in any of these spaces. I recognized a lot of myself in that character, in Feinberg's Jess. Throughout my life I have questioned whether I should pursue a path to transition as a trans man. In my twenties I signed up to the FTM (Female to Male) London Network newsletter, and looked into hormones and surgery. I identified myself as trans or as a trans butch in some queer spaces. Dissatisfaction with stereotypical masculine gender norms and sexism in some of those communities though, an overt focus on medical transition, my own feminist politics and health concerns put me off such a path. As time has progressed, I have led a happy life in between such categories, enjoying some of the freedoms and space that this brings. I have certainly learnt a lot from being an insider-outsider in the categories of man and woman. At various points I made a decision to stay in the classification I am in, and to stay in the body I have, as it is. This hasn't always been easy. I did not pursue transition for many reasons due to health and politics, but a lack of desire for a more male-defined body was not one of them. This may be far removed from the experiences of most readers of this book. Sex dysphoria is hard to explain to those who have never had it; it is also different for every individual, and I can of course only speak to my own experiences. It is also important to underline that everyone's relationship with their body is complex and often troubled. This is unsurprising in our hyper scrutinizing and objectifying consumer society. Sex dysphoria is often wrongly conflated with gender dysphoria, and while they obviously are interconnected, I personally feel they are not exactly the same. For some people, the latter can be addressed with a haircut or a change of clothes, or a new nickname, which, in such a binary sex-gender society like ours, will often lead to an assumption of the sex considered normative for that gender expression. If you look and act recognizably feminine, other people, especially in brief, passing exchanges, will likely assume you are female. If you look and act recognizably masculine, in turn, people will likely assume you are male. This is the phenomenon known as cultural sex, and I outline what this means in Chapter 1.

While being read as one sex or the other can be shaped by gender expression, one's outward gender expression does not actually change one's embodied physicality, including bodily characteristics which are sexed by society. To have sex dysphoria, for me personally, is to feel like one's sexed bodily characteristics are not well fitting, or just do not sit right. Like a collar or waistband that always chafes, or the shoes that rub. But then imagine you know you cannot easily change clothes; you probably have to get used to them, so you learn to live with them. This is not the same as desiring to be thinner or fitter or more conventionally good looking by whatever standards of hotness are trending. Almost everyone will experience those painful desires, to different degrees; indeed, the beauty industries for men and women depend on such feelings and play their part in constructing them too. But sex dysphoria is an absence of seamlessness; it is the jolt when you catch sight of yourself in a mirror or check out new clothes in a changing room and your sexed bodily characteristics are not what you expect or see in your mind's eye. Since puberty started to change my body as a teenager, I have tried to hide those changes. I untucked shirts and wore trousers loose to try to hide my hips and waist; tight vests and tee shirts under shirts helped to flatten my chest. Most women will have the experience of becoming aware of their sexed body via the imposition of sexual harassment from boys and men (Barter et al., 2009; Renold, 2002), that was not my experience and that was not why I sought to hide those features, though this is a common assumption made about masculine female people as well as trans men.

It should be noted that while it is an offensive and patronizing assumption to suggest that all trans men are trans men due to experiences of abuse, it cannot be assumed that trans men or butch lesbians or masculine of centre (MOC) individuals have not experienced violence and abuse. Sadly, trans men are not immune to sexual violence; butches, queer females, MOC or GNC female people are not immune to sexual violence and sexual abuse. Indeed, misunderstanding and erasure of such communities serve to hide the risk factors faced, which certainly do exist. These populations are vulnerable to male sexual violence as masculine-identified female people may be more likely to move in male-only friendship circles, to consider themselves outside of the male gaze and to not see themselves represented in popular imagery of victims of male violence, which usually portray recognizably feminine women. In addition, being in a minority group which is often stigmatized can contribute to risk-taking activities, early experimentation with recreational drugs or alcohol, or the use of these to self-medicate. Added to all this, we know that crimes of sexual violence are unlikely to ever be reported to authorities; for those trans or transgender individuals who may struggle to accept the sexed physicality of their body, it may be challenging to verbalize the sexual violence that was perpetrated against that body. None of this is to suggest a hierarchy of victims of male sexual violence, or to claim that transgender or GNC victims are somehow more affected; it is just to point out the differences in responses, which will influence help seeking, and which should be considered by those services providing support to victims of sexual violence.

Fortunately, and perhaps partly because I often got read as a male child, I did not experience sexual harassment and did not become aware of my bodily sexed physicality through such an imposition. I am aware that this is rare, and lucky. I just felt that the sexed features of my body did not match who I was, and I was aware of that from early on. While many women are likely unhappy with their breasts, or the appearance of their genitalia, or dissatisfied with their hips or thighs, they likely do not wish they had physical bodily features that are sexed as male. Everyone experiences this differently and there are different degrees of liveability; for some people the sexed features they were born with are not liveable, or are even unbearable. Some people therefore seek changes so that they can go beyond just surviving in their body, and can actually thrive. For me, living with a degree of sex dysphoria means there is no seamlessness in something that feels, and which society treats as, fundamental.

Camping in between – perspective on the gender wars

I socialized in queer social spaces and networks and in my late twenties met many other butches and bois, some of whom identified as trans butches or transgender butches, as well as many trans men. We used male terms for each other and masculine gendered terms of bonding and affection such as brother, bro and dude. I always found it difficult to fix on one term to call myself, even as the available terms for sexuality and gender identity have expanded beyond what any of us could have imagined back then. There are now more labels than ever, but I still don't feel like any of them describe me precisely. The label of queer butch is one that I would use if I was asked to pick a flag, but things like badges, pronouns and categories are not so important to me now. In the course of a day I can be referred to as 'son' while getting on the bus, 'mate' in a shop or 'Miss' while queuing in the bank. I do not care which pronouns people use for me and I'm accepting of male or female pronouns because neither feel comfortable, for different reasons. In queer spaces I prefer male pronouns, but outside of those spaces I am aware that would be seen as performative. Then I'm taken back to that disjointed feeling I described from my childhood, where one's normal behaviour becomes self-conscious because it is seen as abnormal by others. Politically, I will never deny my femaleness, or my roots in women's, feminist and lesbian communities and for me womanhood is a political identity and that is the way I relate to it. I am a political woman, in the way people commonly (mis)understand political lesbianism. Politically, as a feminist, it is important to make that claim and step up for womanhood. For all these reasons it is easier to let people choose what pronouns they use for me; I have friends who never refer to me as anything but 'he', friends who see me as in between and others who just see me as a different kind of woman.

Living a life forever in between categories, being read as a male youth, a trans man, a lesbian or being asked by complete strangers what I am or if I'm a boy or a girl gives one an intimate perspective on the social construction and maintenance of sex and gender norms. One becomes painfully aware of the gender rules, when one isn't seen as playing by them. Sometimes it can be easier to be read as male, which may be safer, than being outed as not what people thought and then facing violent homophobia or transphobia as a result. Sometimes it is necessary to be seen as female, in women's toilets, for example, or other women's spaces and then it becomes necessary to emphasize that and make it obvious in ways one usually would not. I have been studying the workings of sex and gender all my life, not least to stay safe and alive. It was then a privilege to focus my academic research on those who forge an identity in between categories like butch and trans, in between categories like man or woman. My aim in my work, and partly in this book, is to highlight that such identities exist at all, in a climate where thoughtless binary thinking is the standard and where one is expected to be clearly one thing or another, or be forever unintelligible. There is still scarce language for lesbian gender identities overall, for masculine women, for butches or for masculine lesbian gender in Black communities, like studs or AGs, the latter being an American term, short for aggressives. There is scarcer language still for queer trans/butches or those who identify as MOC, or as GNC or NB. Yet, on the other hand, we are inhabiting a period in history where masculine lesbians in particular are being pushed to the fore and namechecked by the various forces of sex and gender conservatism which are uniting to try to stall and reverse rights for trans men and trans women.

Surveying the borders

My survey research conducted in 2017 was on the subject of lesbian and queer masculinities in the UK, and asked for participants over eighteen years of age who identified as or with labels like butch, stud, GNC, NB, masculine female, trans or transgender. The survey was anonymous and thus I have given pseudonyms to all the participants who I quote in this book. It was not simply a tick box survey; I used open text boxes, with unlimited space, to allow respondents to describe for themselves their own relationships with sex, gender and sexuality labels and identifiers. The research was unfunded and had to be conducted in my scholarly activity time during the summer holidays; it received ethical clearance from my university faculty ethics board. I expected to receive approximately 30 responses, and so I was thrilled when I received over 200 and eventually closed the survey at 247 responses. I had shared the survey to LGBTQI+ groups, using social media, email and personal contacts in some organizations. It received responses from all over the UK, including from those in both rural and urban locations. However, the responses were not representative of our glorious and diverse LGBTQI+ population, and there are two main weaknesses with the survey research. First, the responses are from overwhelmingly White respondents, thus Black and global majority queers or studs are not well represented. Had I been able to acquire time and funding, I would have much preferred to conduct interview research, and physically visit social spaces, clubs and networks, including those where there were a majority of Black and Asian queers, for example. The majority of respondents identified as White English, British or European, with eighty-five respondents ticking this response. Not every respondent chose to answer this question, only 183 filled in this section. Nine identified as mixed or dual heritage, and sixty-two chose to write their own ethnic identity, which included a variety of mainly European nationalities. As a White British researcher I have to take responsibility for this weakness of the data gathered, and it is important to emphasize to readers that, as is so often the case, the majority of voices platformed here are from White respondents. The stories presented here then are just one part of a much richer story. Second, the majority of respondents were around the middle-age bracket, with most being between thirty-five and fifty years old, which misses out precisely the younger generations who are at the forefront of generational change and supposedly much more fluent in sex, gender and sexuality fluidity. While the survey undoubtedly had limitations, it brought to light experiences from communities who are not usually listened to, and it highlights the need for further insider research from all corners of the gender debate. Certainly, this research is just a beginning, but it is nevertheless a significant beginning, and platforms vital testimonies and perspectives that everyone turning to the gender question needs to hear.

Platforming these voices I will explore questions about whether sexuality and gender are innate, what masculinity is and could be and what that particular gender means to those who are told they are trespassers in it, copies of it or failed women or men. The increasing public focus on and awareness around the lives of transgender people and trans women and trans men also leads to a situation where anyone non-gender conforming is likely to experience the assumption that they are on route to an identity as a trans man or trans woman, further enforcing binary and linear possibilities for gender exploration and expression. This again is ironic, because while panic ensues about enforced trans identities and so-called transing, anyone not seen as sex and gender congruent will experience misreading, mis-sexing and resulting hostilities all of which apply pressures and force of their own. While different sides shout at each other that they are on the wrong side of history, the actual history of trans inclusion in feminism, and feminist theory on trans inclusion, is sidelined. In this book I will argue that the popular wedding of Radical Feminism with transphobia is wrong, and that early Radical Feminism was presciently and profoundly queer in its approach to sex and gender.

A bunker mentality that demands adherence to certain mantras, in either camp, closes down debate that certainly needs to happen, but seems further and further away. Trans women are women is the answer to the question of whether trans women are women, but it isn't the only question we need to ask. The tragedy is that sides are being fought for at all, by communities which should have no sides, because we all share a greater enemy, and that is the forces of racist right-wing nationalism seeking to impose reactionary sex and gender conservatism on everyone. I will also argue in this book that the real barrier to trans inclusion and to the further progression of trans rights is not feminism; it is in fact that which feminism has always fought against, and that is sexualized male violence. It is the epidemic and normalized backdrop of everyday sexualized male violence against women, children and marginalized men that is both the oppression all women have in common and the barrier to trans inclusion in everyday life.

1

Let's talk about sex and babies

What's logical about biological sex?

It is common to see queer activists, commentators and writers arguing that biological sex is a spectrum, and therefore that anti-trans campaigners should not focus on categorized biological sex at birth as defining what sex, let alone what gender, people will become in their future lives. Chase Strangio is a lawyer with the ACLU who in 2019 worked with Aimee Stephens in the influential Harris Funeral Homes case in the Supreme Court of the United States (R.G. & G.R Harris Funeral Homes v. EEOC) to defend rights for trans women and trans men to transition in their workplaces without discrimination. He wrote in *Slate* in 2016 that there is no such thing as a male body. He asserted that 'all components of sex from genitals to hormones to chromosomes exist on a spectrum rather than as a binary' (Strangio, 2016). Trans activist and writer Riley J Dennis in a series for the online magazine *Everyday Feminism* argues that 'sex isn't as simple as male or female, and the idea of a binary biological sex is often used to undermine the validity of transgender people's identities' (2016). In their 2017 book, scholar and activist CN Lester, on the subject of what sex is, suggests that 'we are better served by an idea of a sexual continuum than by the prison of two separate and opposite categories' (2017: 64).

Many activists and scholars would not use the language I have used here, language such as 'biological sex'. Increasingly, activists and social justice organizations will use phrases such as 'sex assigned at birth' and sometimes people will use acronyms like AFAB or AMAB, standing for assigned female at birth or assigned male at birth. Stonewall, the leading organization for LGBTQ+ human rights in the UK, defines that sex is 'assigned to a person on the basis of primary sex characteristics (genitalia) and reproductive functions' (Stonewall, 2021). Such phrasing is used to avoid talking in what are seen as more limiting and binary terms about 'birth sex'. This careful use of language is to highlight that the male or female sex of babies is announced, or assigned to them, merely after a cursory glance at genitalia at birth; or it is declared from the sight of a sonogram scan while the foetus is still in the womb. Activists rightly point out that whatever designation they are given at birth, human beings may go on, in their futures, to identify as a different sex, or none at all. In addition, a minority of people have what are called variances of sex development, this is also called intersex. It is important to note that being intersex, that is being born with atypical sex characteristics, is not the same as being trans, transgender or NB, though of course, some intersex people may also identify as NB or transgender: 'Intersex/DSD is not synonymous with being non-binary, and whilst some people may be non-binary, intersex people can also be female, or male' (Anick, 2020). Scholar of NB identities, Dr Surya Monro, also underlines that intersex must not be conflated with trans or NB, because 'this is a different phenomenon . . . intersex people have congenital sex variances that are pathologized and they are usually subject to medical interventions as infants/children to force their conformity to gender binaries, whereas endosex trans people seek to transition later in life' (Monro, 2019: 129). Endosex is a term used to describe people born with typical male or female sex characteristics, those who are not intersex. Figures from research led by biologist Anne Fausto-Sterling suggest that up to 1.7 per cent of the population globally are intersex; this is a significant population and would suggest that variances of sex development are as common as red-haired people. However, this figure includes variances that not all scientists or medical clinicians recognize as intersex, such as conditions called Klinefelter syndrome or Turner syndrome, which affect fertility; and the 1.7 per cent figure is not universally accepted, with some putting the figure at a much lower 0.018 per cent (Sax, 2002). It is also hard to gather accurate figures because of the differing definitions and classifications, as intersex activist Anick explains: 'It's also worth pointing out that there are no accurate statistics on how many people are impacted by DSDs because definitions vary within law, medicine, and culturally' (Anick, 2020).

Human bodies may have a combination of so-called male chromosomes or hormones, but external so-called female genitals. Or, sometimes, babies may appear to have combinations of features, what used to be called 'ambiguous genitalia', which is rare, and is still, horrifically, often 'corrected' in non-medically necessary surgeries that will affect the individual for the rest of their lives (Koyama, 2003). Global human rights and advocacy organizations led by and for intersex people have been challenging such practices for decades, groups like the Organization Intersex International and InterAct in the United States. Prior to this, activist Cheryl Chase founded the influential, Intersex Society of North America, ISNA, in 1993, which thrived with many successes and law changing achievements until 2008. International Intersex Forums have been meeting since 2011 and the UN has spoken out against forced sterilization and medically unnecessary genital surgeries, for example. Sometimes intersex features are visible at birth; sometimes they emerge during puberty or later on in life if people decide to pursue becoming parents. But, in many human bodies, not only those showing variances of sex development, scientists have pointed out that classifying sex as either one or other clear binary category is often much more difficult than most people assume. 'The science is clear – sex is a spectrum', writes molecular biologist Liza Brusman from the Scripps Research Institute in San Diego, the United States: 'just like gender isn't binary, our biology isn't binary either: it, too, exists on a spectrum. In fact, many people's bodies possess a combination of physical characteristics typically thought of as "male" or "female"' (2019). There are hormonal, chromosomal and reproductive differences within the group classified as female, and within the group classified as male, not only between these two defined groups.

Neurosexism

Anne Fausto-Sterling proposed in 2000 that there was no need for birth-sex categorization to be listed on documentation such as driving licences, and that visible characteristics such as height, eye colour or more detailed identification validation tools such as fingerprint scanning were surely more applicable and useful. There are currently growing calls that it may indeed be time to remove sex markers from birth certificates and other such identification altogether; this was the focus of a three-year UK Economic and Social Research Council research project from 2018 to 2021. The project investigated the decertification of sex in all official documentation in England and Wales, to remove sex and gender from classifications dealing with legal personhood. In America now, at least ten states, from Arkansas to Vermont, offer the option of having 'X' listed under the sex marker on identification cards and drivers' licences, instead of the usual M or F. In the summer of 2019 records acquired by *USA Today* found that over 7,000 Americans had taken up this option. During the 2018 consultation on the UK GRA, several of the questions dealt with possible alternatives to listing birth-sex categorization on official documents, in efforts to acknowledge those who identify as NB, or who otherwise do not wish to be classified by sex as male or female, or who do not identify as men or women nor wish to be boxed into either binary category (Darwin, 2020). In 2017 the UK Government Equalities Office (GEO) conducted a survey into the lives of LGBTQ people in the UK, with over 100,000 respondents, of which 6.9 per cent identified as NB.

Feminist scholars have contributed much to the research on human sexed characteristics and highlighted the often gendered, racist and phallocentric naming, classifying and construction of these characteristics. Science, much as it may like to portray itself as such, is no more lacking in bias than any other form of research. As the feminist researchers Liz Stanley and Sue Wise point out in their classic 1983 book on research methods, it is impossible both to do research and not to do research from the medium of one's own experience. What this means is that nobody, not even a scientist, can stand apart from the world they study; they are a part of it and have their own views and life experience of what they investigate. Because gendering is so fundamental to most of our societies, it is perhaps not surprising that biased language slips into classifications about everything from hormones to cells. You can read about this in books from neuroscientists such as Gina Rippon in her book *The Gendered Brain* (2019) and from the psychologist Cordelia Fine, who unpicks myths about sexed and gendered behaviours and traits, what she has called 'neurosexism', in *Delusions of Gender* (2010). Testosterone, for example, despite being present in both men and women, is often referred to as the 'male hormone' or, worse, the 'male sex hormone'. This is a history of sexing the body, which has been researched by Fine in her 2017 book *Testosterone Rex*, as well as by Katrina Karkazis and Rebecca Jordon-Young in *Testosterone: An Unauthorised Biography* (2019).

The development of secondary sex characteristics, human sexual attraction and attractiveness, propensity to interpersonal violence, risk-taking behaviour and sex drives have all been frequently reported, including in scientific research, through the use of highly gendered language which reflects social stereotypes of masculinity and femininity more than any innate and naturally occurring behaviours. This is a kind of self-fulfilling research, which sets out with the assumption that men have higher sex drives than women, are more competitive or more comfortable with risk, for example, and then looks for biological reasons in men to find out why this is the case. The results are then used to further the belief that men are more competitive, aggressive, risk-taking and have higher sex drives than women. Sometimes, in these sorts of narratives, this is partly put down to the steroid hormone testosterone. It is not unusual to hear people blame testosterone for all sorts of things, disruptive behaviour in boy children, for example, men's participation in extreme sports, or for higher crime rates among men. I have heard many parents talk about the immaturity of their boys, or the tantrums of their boys, at toddler age, and then blame this on spurts or sudden increases of testosterone. This is, in fact, a common-sense reasoning from my degree students too, and also from guests and attendees at debates or panels on feminist theory or women's rights. It seems to be a widely held belief that men are more aggressive, violent and need sex more than women because of high levels of testosterone.

Nuerosexism, mentioned earlier, is the belief in a brain sex – or more correctly, brain gender – and it is a common popular ideology. It is the suggestion that men and women have different brain structures that dictate stereotypically masculine or feminine behaviours. We should immediately note the conflation of sex and gender here, and when you see such stories or studies about 'brain sex differences' or 'sex in the brain' assertions about hardwired differences, look out for the examples given. The examples of these differences are often stereotypically macho or stereotypically feminine behaviours; this tells us only about gender roles and cites behaviours which are not proven to be the sole biological preserve of one sex or another. In other words, they are describing gender stereotypes, not necessarily physical bodily differences between males and females (sex), and they are arguing that these stereotypes (social) are biologically driven. Again, the parents among you will not be strangers to such beliefs; they are voiced in playgroups, playgrounds and parks, as well as in many parenting manuals. These messages will tell you that boys and girls are just wired differently. Many parents think boys are naturally more physical than girls, and that they will enjoy physical play, while girls won't. I've conversed with parents who explain that boys are bound to be more pushy than girls because of their natural differences; all the while toddler girls are in our faces screaming and shoving their way around. I've been told by fellow parents that girls just mature faster than boys, and need less attention, aren't so boisterous, will learn faster and can be left on their own more. This sort of sexist popular psychology, or science of stereotypes, is unfortunately very common, as scholar of anti-gender discourse Agnieszka Graf explains:

> People want the family and gender roles to be a space of predictability, of naturalness and community, and there is a strong demand for any talk about gender in the public sphere to confirm their preconceptions. For a long time, I have studied popular cultural discourses about gender in Poland and the United States, and it is astonishing how pop sociobiology is filled with endlessly repeated stereotypes. No matter how many times these ideas are debunked, the books that promote

them are best sellers. Women are monogamous, men are polygamous. Women are caring, men are competitive. It's all in your brain. All your preconceptions are true. (Graf, 2018)

A lot of this popular psychology or pop science, which makes its way into the public sphere, is usually received from news reports and clickbait headlines, via gendered language that often relies on Darwinian assertions about sexual selection and the mating practices of non-human animals. You can read more about this in the robust and accessible work by Oxford University professor of language and communication, Deborah Cameron, such as in her 2007 book *The Myth of Mars and Venus*, for example. The ideology of sexual selection asserts that female animals are commodities which male animals want, in order to pass on their genes through breeding all over the place; thus, male animals will compete for the attention and approval of female animals, who will then choose the most impressive specimen for mating. This explains why male species are often more colourful than females, they need to be, in order to attract attention and find mates. This theory, often from carefully selected species of non-human animals, is then lifted wholesale onto human animals, with all sorts of suggestions and generalizations following from it. Such as that, men have to be funnier than women to make women laugh so that women will be attracted to them – 'Men are funnier than women, study claims', reported the BBC news in 2019, highlighting coverage of international research summarized in *Psychology Today*. Such as that, men will pursue wealth, career and status because they are not motivated, as women naturally are, to focus on childcare and childrearing instead. In a Channel 4 news interview with Cathy Newman in 2019, the psychologist Jordan Peterson asserted that the gender pay gap is a result of innate, hardwired differences between women and men, what he called 'ineradicable differences'. These differences mean women will choose flexible caring and people-oriented work, and especially work that fits around raising children, whereas men are more hardwired to be interested in things and systems. He provided, as proof of this, the example of Scandinavian countries that have committed themselves to equal opportunities in law and yet still have mainly female nurses and male engineers. Another popular belief is that men struggle to be monogamous because they are biologically driven to spread their genes around as many women as possible – 'Evolution May Explain Why Men Are More Likely To Cheat', bleated a report in *Forbes* magazine in 2018. The article goes on to explain that the so-called sexual pursuit area of men's brains might be up to two and half times larger than that in women's brains. Other common stereotypes, such as that women are better at multitasking, for example, may be widely recognized as stereotypes, but they are still quite persuasive and the danger when stereotypes become common knowledge is that they can also be assumed to be common sense, underneath the jokes and banter we will all be familiar with. 'Women "better at multitasking" than men, study finds', documented a BBC news headline in 2013, summarizing a study from the *BMC Psychology* journal. The story we are told again and again is that women are the caring sex, and also, the choosing sex, and men must compete to be chosen through a variety of means.

The science of gendered brains, and hardwired gender roles, has been challenged by psychological researchers such as Cordelia Fine, and neuroscientists like Gina Rippon and Lise Eliot, and by the psychiatrist Vernon Rosario, for example, although such critical perspectives are far from universally accepted, in fields of science or in society in general. Professor Lise Eliot, from the Chicago Medical School, warns against viewing sex differences in the brain as proof of sex differences in behaviour or personality. In her book *Pink Brain; Blue Brain* she argues that there are indeed differences, including physical size differences, but that these do not carry the meanings researchers often like to attach to them. Indeed, the subtitle of her book is *How Small Differences Grow into Troublesome Gaps and What We Can Do About It*. It is difficult to neutrally explore differences when the effects of gender are assumed to be proof of natural differences. The possible dangerous circularity of neurosexist beliefs should be obvious, as I introduced earlier; this is because they are often based in gender stereotypes, and then researchers go looking for proof of those gender stereotypes. I would argue that we should be asking, instead, how and why certain behaviours have been defined as masculine and male in the first place, and others as feminine and female. Why is risk-taking seen as masculine? Why is having casual sex with numerous partners seen as masculine? How many is 'numerous', and who says? Why is revelling in physical play masculine? Why is enjoying maths or being good at reverse parking seen as masculine? Why is raising children feminine? Why is emotion feminine? We should also question how we could separate out differences in human behaviour when it would be so difficult to find a control group who were not subjected to gender stereotyping, often since in the womb? If girls were raised completely differently, for a generation or two, would they show more interest in playing with trucks and bricks, and if boys were raised completely differently, would they show more interest in babies and dolls? When researchers go looking for hormonal, brain or cellular 'causes' for such gendered behaviours, they are looking in the wrong place; what such studies tell us is the gender bias of the researchers, and nothing more.

Quantum sex

Consciously aiming to avoid such stereotyped thinking, scientists such as the influential Anne Fausto-Sterling (2000) and Susanne Kessler (1998) have researched the performative acts of the scientific sexing of the human body, and particularly have researched the medical responses to infants born with what are called variances in sex development, or what are sometimes called intersex features. Fausto-Sterling points out that, from a medical perspective, there are several different features which are sexed in humans and which can be used to classify sex characteristics as male or female. These are usually gathered into five headings, chromosomes, genes, hormones, internal and external sex organs and secondary sex characteristics such as breasts and facial hair. Studies of cells, genes and gene mapping are all showing the variances of human bodies and the interplay of these with environment, personality and culture. Psychiatrist and medical historian Vernon A Rosario summarizes this interplay, referring to what he calls 'quantum sex', an acknowledgement of the complexity of human bodies and the difficulty of reducing this to a two-sex model. Although he believes that the future of such scientific research will lead to a gradual ejection of the binary model, he nevertheless posits that, whatever names they are given, or whether they are named at all, human bodies do generally coalesce into two different groupings based on the measurable characteristics which are currently sexed and which are linked to reproductive function and capacity: 'I am not suggesting that sex is not primarily bimodal—with two curves corresponding to two typical functional outcomes, male and female' (Rosario, 2009: 278). However, as it seems that human beings are made up of many features that could be called male or female, with more and more complex variations being identified every day, it could be argued that such features should not be sexed at all: 'Whether biologists and medical experts have focused on sex-determining molecules, chromosomes, hormones or internal or external genitalia, it has not been possible to agree upon a categorical definition' (Fausto-Sterling, 2019: 530). Perhaps then, instead, they should just be seen as human features, and certainly not as the defining make-up of singular sexes of which there are only two, let alone with the added assumption of binary social roles. As philosopher Dr Asa Carlson explains, reading the classic feminist work of linguistics and philosophy professor, Sally Haslanger (2000) – reproductive, sexuality and sexual normative ideals are social. It is then important to question the social necessity of sex and sexing: 'To debunk sex does not necessarily have to imply the denial of facts about anatomy etc., but might, for example, mean to make visible how the sex categories depend on social practices' (Carlson, 2010: 69). We should perhaps ask the question posed in 1993 by famous feminist theorist Christine Delphy, when she queried – 'why sex should give rise to any sort of social classification' (Delphy, 1993: 3). Arguably, it should not.

Most of us will perhaps never know our chromosomes, genetic or hormonal make-up. Many people assume their reproductive system and fertility will work as 'normal'. The normative assumptions about the assumed primacy of heterosexuality and heterosexual reproduction should not go unnoticed in all of this, and it matters. Some people will find out that so-called 'normal' reproduction needs extra intervention or that it may not be possible to conceive or carry children in certain ways, but people do not usually find that out until they try to have children. Unfortunately, due to the social constructions of femininity and masculinity that we are investigating in this book, such discoveries concerning fertility can carry levels of shame, stigma and self-blame, partly because ways of conceiving and birthing children are gendered in our society and seen to define 'normal' manhood and womanhood. In many cases though, in the general day-to-day life, most of us probably understand sex as either male or female, with genitalia and reproductive capacity being the common defining features of sex. Bodies with a penis and testicles and the presumed ability to produce sperm are seen as the defining features of being sexed as male. Bodies with a vulva, vagina, breasts and the presumed ability to carry a baby in the womb are seen as the defining features of being sexed as female.

Cultural sex

It is interesting that our cultural understandings of sex as male or sex as female are so dependent on genitalia, because in our culture we wear clothes that hide our genitalia and we do not know what genitalia most people around us have, aside from intimate partners, children or dependent family members, for example. We probably don't give it much thought. In social life and regular interactions, we mainly focus on gender presentation, role and display; and from that we assume that people's genitalia will be congruent with the social gender role we decipher them to have. This detective deciphering work is based on the commonly understood, current cultural cues of gender, as in masculinity or femininity. Facebook may have over fifty gender categories but I don't think most people use those when they make a snap judgement about another person they are just meeting at work, on the bus, or interacting with in a customer service capacity. We use sexed pronouns of 'he' or 'she' based on gender presentation, we ascribe social role, attached stereotypes and assumptions about that person based on that reading; all of that unfolds without us knowing or even thinking about the individual's genitals, because that is irrelevant in most daily interactions in most workplaces and consumer practices. This is the phenomena of what is called cultural sex or cultural genitals as Susanne Kessler and Wendy McKenna described in their 1978 classic *Gender: An Ethnomethodological Approach*. This sex/gender attribution process is the secondary assuming of sexed genitals, based on the primary reading of gender presentation. Philosophers such as Professor Judith Butler (1993) then continued to popularize this approach, pointing out that gendering brings sex into being because sex is gendered, and vice versa. To be human is to be sexed, the first question asked of a newborn concerns whether the sex is male or female; the following categorization will then shape the life of the baby, which most of us will recognize. But the reading of certain bodily features, or signs, is also itself a cultural and political process. As Christine Delphy has argued, 'society locates the sign which marks out the dominants from the dominated within the zone of physical traits' (Delphy, 1993: 5).

The signs on the body, the shape and form of genitals, are first constructed as important signs designating personhood into one or the other recognized categories of 'human' and are then read as such, with corresponding schooling commencing in either masculinity or femininity. This process of reading those features is not a neutral process; therefore, as Delphy argued, it is not enough to say that masculinity and femininity is obviously cultural and social, but the sexed features of the body are not: 'When we connect gender and sex, are we comparing something social with something natural, or are we comparing something social with something which is also social (in this case, the way a given society represents 'biology' to itself)?' (Delphy, 1993: 5). In this way, although the genitals are there, and are obviously features of the human body, whatever form they take, the decision to read them in certain ways, or indeed, *to read them at all*, as designations of personhood is a distinctly cultural and political position. As the foundational and inspiring French Radical Feminist Monique Wittig argued, in an essay originally penned in the late 1970s, sex differences are social differences, rooted in economics, politics and ideology.

For there is no sex. There is but sex that is oppressed and sex that oppresses. It is oppression that creates sex and not the contrary. The contrary would be to say that sex creates oppression, or to say that the cause (origin) of oppression is to be found in sex itself, in a natural division of the sexes pre-existing (or outside of) society. (Wittig, 1992: 2)

The human body has been defined by powerful institutions in ways that serve racism, sexism and heterosexism to the favour of those in power who are the ones doing the defining.

Enlightening sex

Philosophers, scientists and religious leaders have classified human bodies into rank for millennia, this is not news; this has been perpetrated with idealized versions of White, European male masculinity at the top of a hierarchy, with men being defined by the mind rather than their body. This is what can be referred to as a Cartesian dualism of mind over body, heralding from the famous French philosopher and mathematician Rene Descartes and his work in the 1600s. His statement, 'I think, therefore I am', is now printed on everything from mugs to tee shirts, but it symbolizes a brutal and bloody mind/body split, which perhaps characterizes what is called Enlightenment thought and which has not favoured women. Women, as a class, have been constructed as closer to nature, as more connected to the body than men, ruled by menstrual cycles and hormonal fluctuations that men escape, and thus men are presumed to transcend these weighty trappings of the body. Women and the matter of the body are on the wrong side of the dualisms that divide mind and body, man and woman, culture and nature and reason and emotion; women are constructed as illogical, over-emotional and irrational. Freed from the gross, fleshy, anchoring matter of the physical body, men (of certain race and class at least) are thus able to pursue the matters of the mind instead, developing their intellect, producing great works, starting wars and running countries. Eco-feminists such as Vandana Shiva and Maria Mies have critiqued such philosophy extensively and persuasively, documenting its ramifications in every area of life. It has been labelled as a masculinist, racist, imperialist and patriarchal project to normalize and justify the exploitation of women and all 'others' (those defined as somehow less than human, or other, compared to the human defining them) including Black and global majority populations, first nation or indigenous peoples, the natural resources of the earth and non-human animals.

The human body is thus far from neutral, it does not just simply exist, and it cannot simply just be. As feminist cultural theorist Elizabeth Grosz has highlighted, 'the body, or rather, bodies, cannot be adequately understood as ahistorical, precultural, or natural objects in any simple way; they are not only inscribed, marked, engraved, by social pressures external to them but are the products, the direct effects, of the very social constitution of nature itself' (1994: x). It is difficult to argue with the social constructionist theories that posit the body as incapable of existing *a priori* to the cultural understandings of what the body means; and I would not argue with them. We mustn't forget that so-called 'neutral' science and medicine in the West has for centuries presented philosophical beliefs about human bodies as scientific fact. Human bodies have been brutally abused to develop and 'prove' those facts, look, for example, at the early beginnings of formal medicine in the West, where enlightened medical men made their careers on the bodies of enslaved people. Read and weep at the shocking history uncovered in the work of history Professor Deirdre Cooper Owens (2017), for example, detailing the development of gynaecology as a profession. This began with the torture of enslaved Black women, vivisected by young White men wrestling for power and prestige in the new medical industries they had created. The neutral scientific revolution in the West was anything but. It has furthered racist beliefs about the superiority of White European's brains and hereditary intelligence, the animalistic nature of Black men and women, the base sexuality of Black women, portrayed as 'jezebels', as Professor Hill-Collins points out (2000: 81), the natural hysteria and fragility of upper-class White women compared to White men and many, many more such harmful ideologies.

Judith Butler said that to be sexed as female or male at birth is to be humanized, indeed is to be seen as human at all and is part of a set of rules governing binary sex, sexuality and gender organizing, the 'heterosexual matrix', that constructs this system while claiming to simply describe and observe it: 'Sex not only functions as a norm, but is part of a regulatory practice that produces the bodies it governs' (Butler, 1993: 1). I am not saying that the physical body is purely a social construct that would disappear overnight in a puff of smoke if we all started defining human beings differently (climate change is a far greater threat to human existence than queer theory!). But, certainly, we would all see and understand human bodies differently if we attached different meanings, or no meanings at all, to material features such as genital shape, size and methods of reproduction.

Gender, sex and racism

While many of us are used to a binary organizing of sex and gender, this has not always been the case around the world, and alternatives are often highlighted to underline that the Western binary sex/gender schema, what Professor Maria Lugones calls the 'modern/colonial gender system' (2008: 2), should not be assumed to be normal, natural or biological. Genital differences were also not the primary organizing sign in all cultures throughout history; they did not dictate role, position or inheritance, for example (Boellstorff et al., 2014). Writing about Southwest Nigeria from the 1860s to the 1960s, and the impact of British occupation and exploitation during colonialism, Professor of Sociology Oyeronke Oyewumi notes that 'the nature of one's anatomy did not define one's social position' (1997: 13). In the precolonial period she studied, social rank was based on age, which denoted seniority and a male person was in no way inherently senior to a female person based purely on anatomy. Social status was also relational and shifted depending on interactions. Some people will also point to communities and cultures which recognized diversity in gender presentation and role and where this wasn't seen as dependent on the biological genital and reproductive features of the body at birth. This is partly what leads to the common suggestion that the imposition of sex and gender binaries on humans is imperialist, colonialist and a controlling mechanism of the Western powers from the Global North. As the scholar Veronica Sanz points out, 'at the turn of the eighteenth century in Europe, the two-sex model became the foundation of a new social order' (2017: 3). Dan Irving in 'Trans/Gender' asserts that the 'sex/gender binary system and discourses governing normative gender performance are integral to settler colonialism. . . . The normative discourses of gender that privileged European colonizers were shaped through colonizers' projections of their own fears onto Indigenous peoples' (Irving, 2019: 116). European colonial enforcers, Western explorers and later anthropologists have attacked, reduced and simplified various examples of the diversity of sexed and gendered roles and lives. Unable to see beyond assumptions of binary, hierarchical and oppositional sex and gender roles, as being the bedrock of 'civilized' heterosexual sex and reproduction, such other lives were categorized as deviant; as homosexual inverts who were feminized men or masculinized women, as homosexual people in prostitution or as pitiable hermaphroditic eunuchs occupying an unnamed void between normal women and men.

Historically, in parts of Albania, Montenegro and Kosovo, for example, young female people in a family were sometimes allowed by their community to take on the role of a man, for example where a father and brother had died or where otherwise there was no male heir to become the head of the family, provide for and defend the family and community. These were roles that were not culturally appropriate for young women. Andrea Young has documented this tradition in her 1999 book on Albanian sworn virgins or burrnesha who had to take a pledge of celibacy to take on their new role. This was in the context of a profoundly patriarchal and patrilineal culture, and it was about gender role, not sex. The point was that the biological sexed features of the individual's body were overlooked, were excused and ignored on this occasion for the sake of keeping those patriarchal norms in place. The sworn virgins did not have to alter their genitals in order to take on their role.

In her 1987 book *Male Daughters, Female Husbands*, Professor Ifi Amadiume documents the flexibility and utility of sex and gender labels and roles in the Igbo communities of a town called Nnobi in South Eastern Nigeria. Professor Amadiume explained that although there were terms for men and women, there was also a third person singular term, 'O', which stands for male and female; the term 'ya' replaces what would be 'his' or 'hers' in English language, thus everyday speech is not so gendered. Nor is man used as a default term to signify all humans, and the term 'mmadu' means humankind. Igbo society was built around roles linked to ownership of land and family lineage. There were separate roles for men and women, but it was possible for women to become recognized as 'male daughters' in the place of a son, for example. They could then inherit agricultural land; the daughter would be a replacement, where there was no male heir to take on the father's 'obi' or family line and property belonging to it. Female husbands referred to the title system, whereby an industrious, successful woman could take on wives. The lack of sexed language allowed for the polygamy system to apply flexibly to either husband and wives groupings or wife and wives groupings, which were industrial units. The wife and the co-wives worked together; new wives joining the group brought even more wealth, and these woman to woman marriages could be very successful. However, Professor Amadiume underlines that this was nothing to do with sexuality, and that it should not be confused with lesbian identity or relationships: 'Such interpretation of, for example, the cases cited in this book would be totally inapplicable, shocking and offensive to Nnobi women, since the strong bonds and support between them do not imply lesbian sexual practices' (1987: 7). Nor was it concerned with biological sexed characteristics. The roles and titles did not signify any bodily transition, and it was more a transition of role and title.

In December 2019 the magazine *Vogue*, in Mexico, featured a cover model from Southern Mexico's muxe population, a term for a recognized third-gender individual and role, long recognized in the indigenous Zapotec population. This is the first time an individual from a third-gender community has been on the cover of *Vogue* magazine anywhere in the world. Much is made of historical studies of Native North American, first nation Two-Spirit people, previously known with the European colonialist term 'berdache', but having many different names in different tribal languages, as explained by Two-Spirit activist and writer Jen Deerinwater: 'The names used varied based upon the language spoken and the tribal traditions. Nádleehí, Winkté, Niizh Manidoowag, Hemaneh, Asegi are just a few of the names our ancestors were known as' (Deerinwater, 2017). In recent years writers and activists from those communities themselves have had to decry the uninformed usage of their terms and tokenistic reference to their traditions by outsiders who do not understand them or try to wrongly conflate them with lesbian, gay or bisexual sexual identities (Bowen, 1998). The term 'two-spirit' is also used as a catch-all term, which critics acknowledge is a starting point, but itself can act to limit the diversity of sex and gender expression and roles. In the *Introduction to Queer Indigenous Studies*, Qwo-Li Driskill and the collective of editors note that there is a danger that the term 'inevitably fails to represent the complexities of Indigenous constructions of sexual and gender diversity, both historically and as they are used in the present' (2011: 3).

Based on my external understanding this tradition was again mainly about gender, not sex, nor, necessarily, sexual orientation; the biological genital and reproductive features of a human being were not seen to dictate destiny in terms of gender role and presentation, nor sexual orientation or intimate relationship. Someone with features that would be sexed as female could take up arms, traditional masculine dress or traditional men's positions in community decision making or ritual, for example, as well as taking on particular roles as a Two-Spirit, such as ambassador or healer, which was widely considered a sacred identity. Likewise, someone who was a male-bodied Two-Spirit could take on roles and positions usually undertaken by women in the community, as well as the particular and specific roles accorded to a Two-Spirit person. The name itself refers to the combination of spirits, including masculine and feminine in one, to make one unique spirit who defies Eurocentric sex and gender binaries (Fertig, 2009). As Gary Bowen explains, 'Native terms overlap in meaning with terminology used by the dominant society, they are not identical because Native concepts of gender and identity differ in significant ways from the dominant culture'

(Bowen, 1998: 65). Once again, this is not about sex specifically or narrowly; it is about gender. In fact, the reason for the difference, for the special, recognized and respected status in the first place was that Two-Spirit people were sexed as female but taking on masculine roles or dress or blending these in their Two-Spirit identity. Or, Two-Spirits were sexed as male but taking on female roles or dress, or blending and combining these. This was a distinct status, which varies across tribal traditions, involving the blending or crossing of gender roles (Barker, 2017). Being male bodied and taking on masculine roles and dress, for example, would *not* be different or noteworthy, but it was seen as *just one* of the possible relationships between sex and gender role, and there were, and are, more than just two in many cultures.

As Professor Oyeumi points out, interpretations of such social organizing, from outside, are always going to be partial, because they are rooted in particular views of sex and gender: 'Because gender is pre-eminently a cultural construct, it cannot be theorised in a cultural vacuum' (1997: 21). Such variety in social organizing exists and persists, despite Spanish, British, French and other colonizing countries from the late 1400s in the so-called 'age of exploration' or 'age of discovery' up to the seventeenth century, trying very hard to wipe out such identities and roles, in what Professor Deborah A Miranda has called a 'gendercide' (2010). Often sacred individuals and roles were viewed as deviant, when these colonialist powers discovered, not new lands, but new territories and peoples to occupy, exploit and erase. It is not snowflakeism to acknowledge this; it is just one bloody fact of European and Christian history, among many such examples. It is certainly, arguably, a relatively recent Western project to force an Enlightenment style hierarchical dualism onto everything, including social gender roles and sex and gender identities and relationships. As scholar Naomi Scheman describes, colonialism and the imposition of racialized and gendered hierarchies grows from 'a world view which believes in the absolute superiority of the human over the nonhuman and the subhuman, the masculine over the feminine . . . and the modern or progressive over the traditional or savage' (1993: 186). The history of global Western colonialism is one of the export and expansion of this ideology, which necessitated a violent suppression of any other. This cannot be denied, as theorist Veronica Sanz identifies, 'Victorian ideologies and European colonialism legitimized differences between the sexes and the races' (2017: 4). Sanz then argues that what is called 'biological sex' 'is a circular network that reproduces itself precisely because it has no clear referent' (2017: 4). The trans activist, historian and scholar Susan Stryker has also argued for this interpretation, pointing out the racist and sexist history of the science of sex difference, and arguing that what is referred to as the sex of the body is actually made up of numerous features 'that can and do, form a variety of viable bodily aggregations that number far more than two' (2006: 9).

Spectrum sex

I suggest that the focus within some queer activism on scientific proof of the spectrum of sex in particular is somewhat contradictory, however, given the critiques of the history of science, discussed earlier in this chapter. Queer activism has always questioned the production of privileged knowledge that seeks to define, control and contain varied human features, practices and preferences of sexuality, gender identity and sex identity. Not least, in the medical responses to intersex infants, the medically unnecessary genital mutilation of intersex infants, forced sterilization of intersex and trans people, the gatekeeping of access to services from gender identity clinics on the condition of sterilization, the denial of fertility treatment or fertility assistance to lesbian or gay couples or trans women and trans men, and no doubt many more such brutal examples that could be added. I have to ask then, what we think will come of turning to science and medicine to prove that there are, for example, perhaps actually 720 variations of human sexed features, and that humans share this in common with the creeping, animal-like, yellow blob fungus, *Physarum polycephalum*, put on display in the Paris Zoological Park in October 2019. Humans are not creeping yellow blub mushrooms, nor are we seahorses where exclusively it is the male of the species who carry and birth young, nor are we clownfish where males can spontaneously change their sex and reproductive features to take on the position of a dominant female fish. Most humans are born with a penis and testicles or a vulva and a vagina. Most babies start life in a womb, usually in a woman or sometimes a trans man, usually their mother or parent. Sometimes life starts in the womb of a surrogate, who may be assisting another family, or, due to the nature of contemporary capitalism and the ancient exploitation of women's reproductive labour, this can and does also take place under an exploitative context, and often in the poorest parts of the world. Whatever the context surrounding it, birth is a process whereby eggs are fertilized by sperm to produce a human foetus, either through penis-in-vagina intercourse or through clinic-assisted or self-insemination. Combinations of this appear to have been going on for a long time, all around the world, at all times in history as far back as we know – babies begin as foetuses in the womb, and they are born with a vulva and vagina or a penis and testicles, and in a minority of cases intersex features. None of this, however, indicates universal human approaches to the meaning of those genitals, let alone to the organization of roles and relationships based on them.

Sex that matters

The features of genitals at birth do not need to be singled out as defining labels at all or labelled as anything. No more than we may call out a baby's weight at birth and define the individual by that for the rest of their life, referencing it in official documents and using it to suggest appropriate future careers, clothing or sexual relationships. The idea would seem ridiculous. However, we still have to acknowledge that physical features of the body such as reproductive systems, genitals, hormonal cycles and puberty are all bodily experiences that matter. Professor of Sociology Oyeronke Oyewumi points out that just as it is wrong to classify differences in roles and behaviours between men and women as natural or biological, which is a form of essentialism, it would also be wrong to write off the significance of bodily differences between men and women, not least in childbirth. Feminism, she states, would be wrong to insist 'that all observed differences are social fabrications' (1997: 36). These bodily differences matter for health reasons for a start. They matter for how we may become parents if we choose to do so. They matter for how we may have sex and the various forms of sexual pleasure we may experience. They matter for how we may experience our bodies in the world and how facilitative that world is to bodily functions such as menstruation and the bodily state of pregnancy, for example. The same can be said of all bodily features; there is no argument for prioritizing genital or reproductive features.

We certainly do not need to separate the world out into two categories of human beings by their genitals at birth and have this lead to social, cultural, economic and political destinies. Sex is indeed used to organize and govern human beings, within most power structures, but that political process does not erase the fact of the embodied experiences such as those above. Fausto-Sterling suggested provocatively and rather with her tongue-in-cheek in 1993 that there might be at least five human sexes, or combinations that could be identified and used to classify sexed groups, intending to highlight the inadequacy of the binary two-sex and only two-sex model to fully reflect the diversity of human sexed characteristics. To the categories of male and female then, she creatively added 'herms' people born with testes and ovaries, 'merms' those born with testes but also aspects of what is called female genitalia as well, and 'ferms' those who have ovaries but also some aspects of what would be categorized as male genitalia. To return to my earlier point, the question is though, what would be the goal of really and seriously pursuing such a science of quantifiable typologies and spectrums of classifications anyway? If we accept the errors and violence of binary thinking, and we reject the practice of shaping the futures of human beings by the physical shape of their genitals and their internal reproductive capacities, then surely adding yet more categories cannot be a goal; indeed Fausto-Sterling asserted similar, rallying against medical industries and attempts 'to flatten the diversity of human sexes into two diametrically opposed camps' (2000: 23). Arguably, any pursuit of such typologies, by medical and psychiatric industries, or by those campaigning against them, would simply give rise to those who would say that they have been assigned to the herms, to take Fausto-Sterling's ironic taxonomy, based on their bodily chromosomal or hormonal make-up, but in terms of their identity, they feel more like a ferm, or they experience more in common and a better fit with those who are classified as female. My point is that humans are diverse, and perhaps always will be, no matter the amount of labels we keep applying, as indeed Butler cautioned: 'When some set of descriptions is offered to fill out the content of an identity, the result is inevitably fractious. Such inclusionary descriptions produce inadvertently new sites of contest and a host of resistances, disclaimers, and refusals to identify with the terms' (Butler, 1993: 221).

If the meaning of sex is a social construct, what does it mean?

I agree with the theorists who argue that the meaning of sex is a social construct. But, as with all social constructs, these meanings are also experiences. As with all social constructs they are embodied, and they have bodily effects. I suggest that we cannot have it both ways. If we acknowledge that the meaning of sex is culturally constructed, then this behoves us to acknowledge the current cultural meanings put onto sex and the effects those meanings have. The meaning of sex leads to the experience of sex and influences our experience of our own bodies as sexed, as well as our experiences and interpretations of other people's bodies as sexed. This is why I part company with the theorists and activists, like those who I quoted at the start of this chapter, who argue that the currently sexed features of the body should be ignored, in place of the primacy of gender identity and gender presentation. Susan Stryker, for example, in *The Transgender Studies Reader*, argues that governments, state services and wider society do 'violence to transgender people by using genital status, rather than public gender or subjective gender identity, as the fundamental criterion for determining how they will place individuals in prisons, residential substance abuse treatment programs, rape crisis centers, or homeless shelters' (2006: 10). She argues that different combinations of sexed bodily characteristics, whether on trans bodies or intersex bodies, and different combinations of gender presentations and gender identities, should all ideally be seen as both 'morally neutral and representationally true' (2006: 10). Arguing for a future where genitals are not seen to represent or dictate social roles such as that of woman or man, husband or wife, father or mother, for example, famous scholars McKenna and Kessler urge us to jettison biological rulebooks: 'As long as the sex/gender distinction remains, as long as biology is seen as the bedrock on which gender rests, there can be no deep understanding of the central point we were making' (McKenna & Kessler, 2000: 69).

Beyond this binary, we would speak easily and seamlessly of women's penises or men's wombs, trans men would not be barred from listing themselves as the father of the children they carry and birth, lesbian trans women who happened to have penises would not be seen as any less of a lesbian nor their partners be suspected of really being straight. There would be no understanding of penises as male or vaginas as female, because these would just be seen as bodily features that any body may have, in many possible combinations. As I will explore elsewhere in this book, some people, in some parts of their life at least, inhabit such a world already, as they have these identities validated and read by their partners, friends and peers. In many queer spaces, relationships and friendships self-definition is the accepted norm; sexed bodily features and genitals can exist in the imagination as much as in the flesh, and can be enjoyed and experienced on a different level because of this. For the record, I think moves towards such a world would be progressive moves, bring it on, as far as I'm concerned. The influential feminist theorist Christine Delphy emphasized that in order to move towards non-hierarchical futures, we have to be able to imagine what they would be like, and I think that imagining a world where the genital or reproductive features of the body are culturally neutral is a very important and revolutionary project. Critiquing feminists who do not follow through on their analysis of gender roles as foundational to sexist, patriarchal society, Delphy complains that too many are wedded to the notion of gender difference, to an ideology of role and behavioural differences between two human groups called women and men.

All feminists reject the sex/gender hierarchy, but very few are ready to admit that the logical consequence of this rejection is a refusal of sex roles, and the disappearance of gender. Feminists seem to want to abolish hierarchy and even sex roles, but not difference itself. They want to abolish the contents but not the container. They all want to keep some elements of gender. Some want to keep more, others less, but at the very least they want to maintain the classification. Very few indeed are happy to contemplate there being simple anatomical sexual differences which are not given any social significance or symbolic value. (Delphy, 1993: 6)

Well, here is one feminist who is very happy to contemplate the latter, and as I will discuss later in this book, I actually believe this is, and has to be, the fundamental goal of Radical Feminism; as indeed many Radical Feminists have argued, such as Kate Millett, Shulamith Firestone and Andrea Dworkin. This will be addressed further in Chapter 2.

Sex rank

However, as I have been arguing all along in this opening chapter, the meaning of sex may well be socially constructed but it is also materially experienced. We cannot pretend the current hierarchy of sex rank does not exist, with all the corresponding power relationships between women and men and all the different values attached to the types of bodies that are seen as men's bodies and women's bodies. Why is it that menstruation is not neutral but is often a source of shame and stigma? Why is it that many girls and young women are raised from young girlhood to fear and avoid men and to see male bodies as a threat? This is because, in a context of sex rank where being male and a man is seen as being superior, inferiority is read on and through the body, and it is also socialized into the body. There are common bodily gender stereotypes that many of us will be familiar with, such as women and men sitting differently, eating differently, walking differently and talking differently. This is what we could refer to as the habitus of gender, using theory from the famous sociologist Pierre Bourdieu (1930–2002), who studied how social classifications have material and bodily effects; social inequalities act upon the body, and they are not just abstract theories. He explored this in the frame of social class, pointing to how poorer, working men would eat, walk, style their facial hair and experience their body very differently to richer, upper-class men who did not have to work in manual labour and were socialized very differently. We can also observe that gender socialization has a real, embodied, physical effect; it causes a gendered habitus. In the Western world, for example, being feminine is about being small, taking up little space, listening rather than talking, walking with small steps, sitting with one's legs crossed, eating delicately and in small bites or finger held portions, speaking quietly and not dominating space. These are physical and bodily acts; the body becomes schooled in gender and starts to perform these gendered acts as second nature, so much so that they become seen as nature, which is what we are told they are in the first place, and thus the nexus of gender goes full circle.

Because women are seen as more attached to and ruled by their body and bodily functions, they are assumed to be baser than men, and this includes in matters of sex and sexuality. Women's bodies represent sex and sexuality, and they are constructed as the site of sex and reproduction and thus the recipient of men's agentic sexual drives – which pop science tells us is a natural and universal masculinity, as illustrated by earlier discussions in this chapter. This matter is raced; indeed matter is raced, by which I mean the physical matter of the body. The sex and sexuality of Black women, indigenous and first nation women, for example, was not seen as fragile in the way White women's sexuality was seen. As Oyewumi argues, Western culture is marked by what she calls a bio-logic, the primacy of observable physical differences, and the racist and sexist essentializing of those differences: 'Thus, in the colonial situation, there was a hierarchy of four, not two, categories. Beginning at the top, these were: men (European), women (European), native (African men), and Other (African women). Native women occupied the residual and unspecified category of the Other' (1997: 122). Black women were construed as even closer to nature, even more base and animal-like. Unfortunately, this is not history; an example could be seen in the higher rates of maternal mortality for Black women. Official confidential enquiries into maternal deaths and morbidity in the UK from 2014 to 2016 found that Black women are five times more likely than White women to die during pregnancy or childbirth (Knight et al., 2018). These shocking statistics arguably raise questions about institutional racism in health institutions, a-priori racist assumptions about Black women's health, well-being, pain thresholds or cultural viewpoints, for example, and a lack of Black and global majority staff in senior positions in the NHS and related health settings. White women's sex and sexuality has been pathologized for millennia too, but it was not constructed in the frequently animalistic way that Black women's sexuality has been constructed and is often still represented, particularly for White women in higher socioeconomic groups; thus there are important differences here that should not be generalized.

What such treatment has in common is that women's sexuality, and sexual agency (or lack of it), was always seen as different to men's, and that difference, in a founding and foundational way, often equalled the difference between predator and prey. Women were, and are, sexually objectified, and this objectification is classed and raced as well; this happens in media, culture, film, advertising and all throughout our society. While constructed as sexual objects for male judgement, women are also made responsible for managing such judgement and attention – at once told to take it as a compliment but also to tread carefully and protect themselves in such interactions. The rank contradictory onslaught of such social messages cannot help but have powerful effects. Women are told to aim for sexual attention from men and make themselves pleasing to men in order to attain it; but women are also told that men's attentions can potentially be dangerous and thus they should take precautions to ensure those attentions do not become personally threatening, nor should they entice or provoke sexual violence. From girlhood we are taught, as I was taught, to be careful of strange men, to turn down lifts or drinks from strange men, cover drinks with special drink stoppers when out in clubs, and to smile and placate men rather than escalate situations involving unwanted attention. This is the type of 'safety work', as feminist legend Professor Liz Kelly termed it, which Dr Fiona Vera-Gray has detailed and explored in her (2018) book *The Right Amount of Panic*. The reason I am bringing safety work into this chapter discussing definitions of biological sex is to illustrate the current problems with arguments for ignoring the significance of bodily sexed features in place of gender identity and role.

Male violence and the cultural meanings of sex

Readers will notice that we are several thousand words into a chapter answering the question of what is biological sex, a question that to many people should be answered in a few words. The short answer would be that sex is male or female, based on genital features and reproductive capacity. I hope it has become clear throughout this discussion here that biological sex is actually a lot more complicated than that. Not only is it medically and scientifically complicated, but it is also socially complicated by the fact that most people do not know the genitals or hormonal make-up of others, and we base assumptions about biological sexed features on the presentation of gender and gender role. The theory of cultural genitals is not a theory; I would suggest it is a common everyday practice to deduce sexed bodily features on the basis of gender presentation as either recognizably masculine or feminine. Nonetheless, secondary sexed characteristics, such as height, facial hair, musculature, hip size, tone of voice, breasts, waist size and much more, are all also gendered as stereotypically masculine or feminine and they are also used to assume biological sex. Although there are differences in secondary sexed characteristics between women and between men, as well as between women and men, most of us probably assume that someone who is tall, broad shouldered, narrow hipped, without breasts, with facial hair and with a deeper toned voice is male and a man. This is borne out by the amount of scrutiny and challenge that masculine butch lesbians and MOC queer individuals have to face when they try to use women's toilets or women's changing rooms, for example – as I will chronicle later in Chapter 8 on queering female masculinity. When these individuals do not emphasize female secondary sexed characteristics or when they are tall or muscly, they will frequently be assumed to be male men and not appropriate to be in women's spaces. Being read as a man comes with different sets of repercussions of course depending on how one's race, class and age are read. Being read as a man will differ depending on what type of man one is seen as by others in public settings; not all men are equal. Black queer individuals, MOC or stud or AG individuals, for example, will likely have to deal with different sets of challenge to White queers, if they are read as Black men, or Black male youths in a context of structural and often deadly racism. Queer individuals who may be routinely read as younger than their years may experience being followed round shops by security guards or questioned by police, for example. Being read as a male teenager can result in being subjected to the pecking scrutiny that is the patriarchal pecking order and finding oneself challenged to fights by male teenagers, for example. These sorts of mis-sexing experiences are not just the preserve of queer or lesbian individuals either, tall women or women who are very fit and muscly or who have a deep-toned voice, of any sexual orientation or gender identity, may well be familiar with such scrutiny, assumptions and challenges in women's toilets and changing rooms, for example.

Our snap judgements about the sex of another person are based on such readings, including the reading of secondary sex characteristics. Trans women who are tall, broad shouldered, narrow hipped, or who have a deep-toned voice or who have small breasts or facial hair, may well be assumed to be men. Just as non-trans women who are tall, broad shouldered, narrow hipped or have a deep-toned voice pitch or who have small breasts or who have facial hair may well also be assumed to be men. In women's spaces these types of assumptions will not be pleasant; this level of scrutiny is unsettling and challenge can be frightening. Unfortunately, women are not immune to bigotry, to prejudice, nor are women immune to committing verbal and physical harassment. I am not suggesting that any of this is a good state of affairs; I am just pointing out one of the possible reasons for its occurrence, a reason that I feel does not get enough acknowledgement or attention and that was one of my motivations for writing this book and adding my perspective to the gender wars.

There is a context to women's fears and defensiveness about people they assume to be men sharing their intimate spaces, whether those people identify as men or not. Bodies with features that are stereotypically sexed as male will be assumed to be men. This can equal threat and the need for caution. It is not really gender presentation that is the issue here; someone could present as feminine, but if their secondary sexed characteristics are assumed to be male, then that will ring alarm bells to women who have been socialized into a lifetime of hypervigilance, and schooled into policing their surroundings and spaces for potential threat, often subconsciously. There is also the fact that some men have been using their bodies as weapons against women for centuries, too many women today have experienced this. Too many men use their, on average, greater height, musculature and strength to violently control and abuse women. From the England and Wales Crime Survey 2018 it is estimated that one in five women and one in twenty-five men have experienced sexual violence – defined as rape, sexual assault, indecent exposure or unwanted touching. The component in the survey enquiring about experiences of sexual violence was introduced in 2015 and since then there has been no discernible change in these figures. This type of male violence is sadly commonplace, and most women will have experienced it at some time, or have close friends and relatives who have. In rape, men use their penises to commit sexual violence against women by violently penetrating their vaginas, often causing physical external and internal injury to these genital areas. Such experiences are embodied experiences and that must not be erased, as well as being cultural experiences too, shaped by archetypal ideology about the sexuality and value of women and men. The latter will affect how such all-too-common experiences are reported, shared, spoken of, responded to, believed or not; and all of that will affect the embodied experience in turn, shaping the pain both physical and psychological. It is not feminists, of any school, who have constructed women as victims; perpetrators have done that, and they do it every time they victimize a woman; they do it every time they use their body to harm a woman's body. Indeed, it is true that the body and biology are not neutral, and for women, male bodies are seen as a threat, and they have been constructed as such in the mythology around men's dominance but they are also physically experienced as such. Women have good reason to believe that this threat is real. This matters, and it does not get discussed nearly as often as it should in debates on everything from unisex toilets to refuges. The meaning of sex is culturally constructed, and the current cultural meanings of male sex characteristics are loaded; they freight power, threat and danger.

Given that women are taught to be careful around men, manage interactions with strange men, avoid being on their own or in vulnerable situations with strange men and take steps to protect themselves from men's potentially negative attention, while being pleasing and attracting positive attention, but not in any way going too far as to provoke negative attention, it is no wonder that women may be anxious around men – or people they assume are men. Women then have good reason to scrutinize others in women's spaces and perhaps especially in intimate and vulnerable spaces. The important point here is that this is not necessarily motivated by homophobia or transphobia; it could simply be motivated by a lifetime of cultural conditioning that tells you to look out for men and view them as a potential threat. This level of cultural conditioning and resulting hypervigilence is not going to disappear overnight, and it has not disappeared in the context of the so-called gender revolution because there has been no sex revolution. That is, there has been no revolution between the sexes, no revolution in the power relationships between men and women. The enemy of gender revolution is sexualized male violence against women.

What then, can we conclude, is biological sex? Within patriarchy it is the current cultural understandings that place meaning on genital and reproductive bodily features – and what they mean is rank. Currently, there are two main sexed categories, female or male, and this categorization happens at birth based on whether a baby has a vagina and a vulva – female; or a penis and testicles – male. There is no reason to label babies by their genital features, and there is no reason to separate out society into two types of human, male or female, and binary division always equals hierarchy, which is what this separation serves and brings into being. Like most feminists, I look forward to a society where genital features do not confer humanness, let alone rank. When sex marker no longer confers rank, there will be no need for the sex marker. Genitals and reproductive capacity should not be important other than for health, sexual intimacy, pregnancy and parenting; they need have no other value or significance, and this is not to say that the value and significance are not important, nor that it should not be treated as important. But we are not in such a world yet, and we cannot pretend that we are. Going forward, I support efforts against sex-segregation throughout society; I see this as a feminist aim, and such moves would make life easier for all non-gender-normative people, whether they identify as trans or not. This project should start with the places where it can be done with the least impact, such as public toilets, or on forms of identification. Gender stereotypes are not naturally occurring, and gendered behaviour differences between women and men are not biological; they are but social consequences of inequality. If we got rid of the inequality, then we could look forward to a situation where the shape of bodies does not matter in the ways we are discussing here, because the shape of bodies would not symbolize threat, nor delineate rank and superiority. One way towards this admittedly grand aim is to start levelling out women and men wherever we can, and to dismantle systems, including in the built environment, that treat us as different species and in that segregation create fear, mystery, division and fascination around each other's binary lives and our assumed binary bodies. I propose this project as a feminist concern because feminism is about building revolutionary change, rather than forever building gated communities from the worst of men's presumed natural excesses.

In Chapter 2 I will explore some of the feminist understandings of sex and gender, their construction, impact and cost. Because trans-exclusionary feminist positions have been most associated with Radical Feminism, I shall specifically focus on this school of feminism. It is also the school of feminist theory and activism that I am most familiar with and most drawn to. Radical Feminism shares the same general aims as all schools or strands of feminism, such as equal rights for women and men under the law, in employment and in domestic caring work, for example. If Radical Feminism can be distinguished from other schools of feminism, it is arguably by four main points of focus. First, Radical Feminism asserts the existence of patriarchy, that is, a system of male supremacy with male dominance in mainstream positions of power and authority in society. Second, this type of feminism promotes women-only organizing and women-only leadership as a vital and empowering tactic of any social justice movement. Third, there is a recognition of sexualized male violence against women, children and marginalized men as being a keystone of women's oppression. Lastly, there is an extension of this analysis of sexualized male violence to include the prostitution and pornography industries. As feminism is a broad social justice movement, there are varying strands within it of course, all with differing and sometimes conflicting views on the origins, purpose and meaning of sex and gender. I will outline the roots of some of these disagreements, the herstory behind the current so-called TERF standpoints, and argue that much of Radical Feminism is actually compatible with a trans-inclusive stance. Indeed, Radical Feminism has influenced much of what we now call queer theory, which emerged in the 1990s in lesbian and gay studies, as a reaction to the sidelining of lesbian concerns, a homogenizing focus on gay men and a lack of attention to the intersecting power relations within LGB communities.

2

Feminist revolution now

What is the Radical Feminist
stance on trans inclusion?

The current gender wars are not a new invention. They did not begin with the UK consultation on the GRA in 2018. They did not begin with gender-critical organizing on the UK parenting forum Mumsnet, although that is a significant site of lobbying and information sharing for GC feminists and GC activists. Gender-critical is a term used by those who are critical of what they call gender ideology or trans ideology and who are, in the main, opposed to liberalizing laws around sex and gender recognition and opposed to the inclusion of trans women in many women's spaces. The current gender wars were not invented by philosopher Judith Butler in the 1990s. They are also not an invention of feminism, of any type, though they have a long history within feminism and are informed by a legacy of theoretical and practical conflict and disagreement. Feminism is a social justice movement, and, like all social justice movements, it works within and is influenced by the society it seeks to improve; it does not and cannot exist in a vacuum. Thus, feminism is impacted by power relations between women and has always, with differing methods and varying levels of progress, attempted to at least acknowledge that and aim to reduce that impact. This has always included attention to power relationships along the social fractures of race, social class and sexuality for example. Cherrie Moraga in 1981, in the classic Black feminist text *This Bridge Called My Back*, urges the importance of acknowledging such tensions, rather than denying them or simply wishing they would go away. Unity is fragile and has to be continually produced, as she states: 'Within the women's movement, the connections among women of different backgrounds and sexual orientations have been fragile, at best' (Moraga, 1983: 30). Of course, building unity and acknowledging the workings of power have never been easy. Although I will focus on it here in this book, the issue of inclusion within feminism is much bigger than trans inclusion, and, perhaps, the focus on the latter is a part of much larger and older attempts to wish problems away, and shoot the messengers who point them out. Such as the alienating and destructive prevalence of racism and classism within feminism of all strands. But, as Moraga asserts, we must not stay silent, for this is part of the problem. We cannot pick teams and shout at each other from the wrong sides of history; we need to create a language of dialogue and contextualize our differences and resistances, making room for mistakes along the road. 'We need a new language, better words that can more closely describe women's fear of and resistance to one another; words that will not always come out sounding like dogma' (Moraga, 1983: 30).

Any peruse through a history of the Second Wave will show that, contrary to some ageist anti-feminist stereotypes, the activists involved then were well aware of power differences between women and the need to redress these somehow; indeed they were often a source of conflict, what I have termed feminist faultlines (Mackay, 2015). Needless to say, the movement of that period did not manage to eradicate such power relationships; they did not end racism or classism or homophobia in the movement, far from it, but nor have any waves since. The same is true of differences between women on what was sometimes called the transsexual question or transvestite issue, which arose during the Second Wave. Second Wave is used as a chronological reference, to pinpoint the visible uprisings of feminist activity that spread across Western democracies from the 1960s to approximately the late 1980s. During that historical moment, feminists were disagreeing over the inclusion or exclusion of trans women in women's groups, collectives, communes and businesses. This fact illustrates the complexity within feminism over the matter of differences between women; it also does, and should, trouble simple takes that maintain any suggestion of a singular feminist position on trans inclusion.

Increasingly, in the public sphere, feminism in general has unfortunately become suspect for transphobia, and in particular, the school of feminism called Radical Feminism has almost become synonymous with transphobia. It has got to the stage where transphobia is considered some sort of product of Radical Feminism or foundational tenet of this strand of feminism. GC feminists, GC activists, transphobic conservatives and anti-trans campaigners are subsumed into Radical Feminism, not least under the term – TERF, whether those individuals identify as a feminist, Radical Feminist or not. Nuances such as the differences between political lesbianism, cultural feminism and separatism, or the differences between GC and gender-abolitionist viewpoints do not flow easily or untrammelled into the so-called gender debates in the mainstream. There is undoubtably a level of misogyny, sexism and ageism which fuels the blanket ridicule, dismissal and wilful ignorance about just what Radical Feminist theory even is, and what it isn't. Second Wave has become a dirty word, an insult in many circles, and Radical Feminism emblematic of an out of date, politically incorrect and prissy feminism which will not be mourned when it dies out. However, a politics and theory as strong as Radical Feminism, a politics and theory that is truly radical in the revolutionary sense, will never die out; and in fact, its influence can be seen in much queer theory and activism today, proving, time after time and decade after decade, its prescience and relevance.

Much classic Radical Feminist theory had standpoints on sex and gender that we might now say bear similarity to queer theory, and this work was profoundly forward thinking, although it would obviously not have been termed as queer theory in the 1960s and 1970s, before the academic field and term 'queer theory' had even emerged. To look at just a few limited examples, there are influential Radical Feminist theorists such as Andrea Dworkin, Shulamith Firestone and Kate Millett, all from the United States, who were hopeful about research into the social construction of sex roles. They deconstructed gender, wrote positively about androgyny and concluded that biological sex is not as binary or as fixed as had been assumed. The French Radical Feminist Monique Wittig, for example, is quoted extensively in Butler's classic *Gender Trouble* and enables much of that theorizing. If all Radical Feminist theories were exclusively anti-trans and all Radical Feminist activism anti-trans-inclusion, then there would have been no need for any specific term to distinguish activists who supported trans inclusion from those who did not. That term, well used today, is, of course, TERF – trans-exclusionary radical feminist. The acronym has become so widely shared in social media activism and mainstream journalism that it has become almost a void, as it is applied to anyone expressing transphobic, prejudiced, bigoted or otherwise exclusionary views about trans men, trans women and all transgender and trans people. It is applied to those who are not feminist activists and would never identify themselves as feminists; it is put onto those who may be feminists but are certainly not Radical Feminists; it has become a shorthand for transphobic, and mostly applied to women, although I have seen the related adjective 'terfy' applied to men also.

As outlined in the Introduction to this book, the label 'TERF' appears first to have been used in the early 2000s. An Australian Radical Feminist blogger and journalist, Viv Smythe, is widely credited with being the first person to use it, in 2008, in an online blog about introductory feminist theory and frequently asked questions. In a piece addressing debates over reactions to the Michigan Womyn's Music Festival in the United States, which I explain in more detail in Chapter 3, Smythe used the acronym – TERF. This was simply to avoid having to write the description in full, every time she wanted to reference Radical Feminists who were against the inclusion of trans women in some or all of women-only spaces (Smythe, 2018). Interesting, and highly relevant to my perspectives on the whole of the gender wars, is the fact that in her original blog in 2008, Smythe actually suggested that some of those women taking that TERF stance might be better referred to as separatists, or TES, meaning trans-exclusionary separatists. This speaks to older conflicts from the Second Wave, between Radical Feminism and what became known as cultural feminism – and the accusations of essentialism that are made against both strands, but particularly unfairly and incorrectly against the former. I will introduce you to some of this history in this chapter and will explain some of the important differences between Radical Feminism, lesbian feminism, lesbian separatism and cultural feminism. Although Smythe was perhaps the first person to use the term TERF on an internet site which lasted long enough for people to find it and notice, she herself acknowledges that the disagreement it identified, and perhaps even the shorthand label itself, had been around beforehand.

Trans women of the Second Wave

It is vitally pressing to write back into feminist herstory the fact that, whatever stance other feminists took on the matter, trans women were present and involved, including in key roles, in the foundational and legacy-building Second Wave of feminism in the

United States and the United Kingdom. Professor of History and Gender and Women's Studies at the University of Wisconsin-Madison in the United States Finn Enke urges us to consider such complexities of feminist history and asks: how did so-called

> '1970s feminism' enter collective memory as the exclusionary thing, distinct from the experiences, labour and critiques by feminists of colour, trans and queer people of the same era? And why, when existing nuanced narratives might invite us to deeper analysis, are stories of exclusion and abjection so magnetic? More to the point, how might we highlight the mixings in the past and simultaneously envision a less polarized present? (Enke, 2018: 10)

Then, just as is the case now, there were Radical Feminists who worked with and organized alongside trans women.

Less well known in the terrain of the gender wars are names like Beth Elliott, an American musician and activist who was heckled on stage at the 1973 West Coast Lesbian Conference in Los Angeles, held at UCLA in April of that year. Elliott was one of the organizers of the conference, and a former member and vice president, in the San Francisco chapter, of the US national lesbian group the Daughters of Bilitis, which published the lesbian periodical *The Ladder* from 1965 to 1972. Beth Elliott was a lesbian feminist, a folksinger booked to perform at the conference, and she also happened to be a trans woman. Some delegates at the conference, which was attended by over a thousand women, lobbied against Beth Elliott performing. A group from San Francisco called the Gutter Dyke Collective had prepared and brought printed leaflets to give out to delegates, informing attendees about a new trend in the movement, the trend of men deciding they are women who then 'invade and drain' the lesbian community (McLean, 1973: 36). When it came time for Beth to perform, she was booed and heckled aggressively by sections of the conference. Kate Millett called for peace, and other well-known feminist activists such as the writer and historian butch lesbian Jeanne Cordova, who was then an editor of the journal *The Lesbian Tide*, tried to calm the situation and eventually a vote was held among the delegates on the conference floor as to whether Beth should continue to perform. The vote was won in favour, and most accounts suggest it was won by a large majority (Cordova, 2000). Beth performed a short set and then left the conference, which is unsurprising after such an experience. The next day, Saturday, at the conference, feminist activist and writer, founding member of the New York Radical Women Robin Morgan adapted her keynote speech to include reference to this incident. She spoke out against the presence of an infiltrator and gatecrasher, who she referred to as a man in drag, a transvestite, a male-bodied transsexual and a man, stating that Beth Elliott, although she did not name her, on principle, as she stated she did not want to give Beth any more publicity, was not a sister and did not deserve to be given female pronouns or included: 'No, I will not call a male "she"; thirty-two years of suffering in this androcentric society and of surviving, have earned me the name "woman" . . . he dares, he dares to think he understand our pain? No, in our mother's names and in our own, we must not call him sister' (Morgan, 1977: 180).

TERF roots

This speech is one highly pertinent example of the background to the modern gender wars that we find ourselves in, because it crystallized publicly the growing question around the inclusion of trans women in feminism, and it dramatically introduced around 1200 lesbian and feminist activists to some of the main arguments that still rumble on today. Including the familiar arguments that trans women are motivated by a desire to invade women's spaces, and that this is the mentality of a rapist: 'I charge him as an opportunist, an infiltrator, and a destroyer – with the mentality of a rapist' (Morgan, 1977: 181). This in an infamous point from Janice Raymond's famous book of course, as I shall explain in more detail later; Raymond asserted that all trans women rape women's bodies, by appropriating women's bodies and identity (1979). In this early speech we can also see often repeated arguments used today in the gender wars against trans inclusion. Arguments such as that trans women claim to be women purely so they can seduce lesbian women: 'It is, one must grant, an ingenious new male approach for trying to seduce women' (Morgan, 1977: 171). There are also the common arguments that trans women uphold and reinforce the harmful gender norms of femininity: 'How many of us will try to explain away – or permit into our organisations, even – men who deliberately reemphasise gender roles, and who parody female oppression and suffering' (1977: 180). Or, for example, there are the arguments that trans women should organize separately and cannot be accepted as women because they have not been treated as women and girls since birth: 'If transvestite or transsexual males are oppressed, then let them band together and organise against that oppression, instead of leeching off women who have spent entire lives as women in women's bodies' (Morgan, 1977: 181). Gender abolitionists such as the lesbian feminist Janice Raymond further promoted and publicized these views, bringing them to a much larger stage in her infamous publication, continuing these refrains that trans women are metaphorical rapists of women's spaces, who lack the lifetime of female socialization that defines womanhood, and who are defenders of dangerous gender norms. The gender abolitionist, lesbian feminist Professor Sheila Jeffreys has published similar more recently and seems to maintain in her current campaigning that trans women are parasitical, take over women's bodies and seek easy access to lesbians and other women for their own perverse sadomasochistic agenda.

In 1973, in her keynote speech at the West Coast Lesbian Conference, Morgan also raised the argument that transvestism, trans identification and the art of drag by drag queens, all of which she conflates as one throughout her speech, are all the same as the racist portrayal of blackface by White people: 'We know what's at work when whites wear blackface; the same thing is at work when men wear drag' (Morgan, 1977: 180). This too is another argument still being perpetuated today. In 2014 the GC Canadian Radical Feminist Meghan Murphy wrote an article for the online magazine and podcast, which she founded, *Feminist Current*, asking why drag isn't seen the same as blackface, by liberals and by members of the LGBTQ community. In 2019 the GC philosopher, Professor Kathleen Stock OBE, writing for *Standpoint* magazine, asked why blackface is evil but drag is not. I suggest, then, that the US West Coast Lesbian Conference of

1973 is significant for many reasons. It was a flashpoint for conflicts that were already familiar to many active organizers in the Women's Liberation Movement and for organizers and members of lesbian and lesbian feminist communities; it introduced those conflicts to many more feminists, who then took that information back to their own lesbian and lesbian feminist networks across America; it also highlights that by the beginning of the 1970s there were clearly different approaches to the inclusion of trans women, with some groups involving trans women as sisters and others not.

As well as Beth Elliott's contribution, another trans woman, Sandy Stone, went on to be so influential with her reply (1991) to Janice Raymond's 1979 book *The Transsexual Empire*. Stone had been a member of a feminist, women-only music production company called Olivia Records and living as part of their lesbian collective. Olivia was founded in Washington, DC, in 1973 by five activists, Ginny Berson, the musician Meg Christian, Judy Dlugacz, Kate Winter and Jennifer Woodul (Morris, 2015). The Olivia collective actually supported Sandy Stone years later, by paying towards her sex reassignment surgery. Stone was a key member of the company, designing and building their sound systems and production technology as well as being a recording engineer. The collective stood by her as complaints and threats began to be targeted at Olivia due to their trans-inclusive stance; this included violent threats, plus plans for a boycott by the late 1970s. Eventually, Stone's position there became untenable and she left to join academia with well-known cultural theorist, Professor Donna Haraway in 1983 (Stone, 2018). Much of this history is lost when all Radical Feminism is branded a TERF project, as the trans historian and editor of the fantastic online resource the *TransAdvocate* Cristan Williams has highlighted herself: 'Lost in these popular representations of radical feminism is its long and courageous trans inclusive history' (Williams, 2016: 255).

There was a slight irony to the debacle over Robin Morgan's disavowal of the inclusion of Beth Elliott and her storming critique of the conference organizers in 1973, demanding, as she did, an apology for divisiveness and for insulting every woman present. It is perhaps complicated by the fact that Robin Morgan's own attendance and her star status as an invited keynote speaker at a lesbian conference was not without some controversy. Morgan, who had identified as bisexual at her first ever Consciousness Raising (CR) group, was at that time in a relationship with a man, a man she referred to as a faggot-effeminist, with whom she had a child, describing their parenting as both biological and nurturant. In a footnote to her edited speech, reproduced in her collection of essays, *Going Too Far*, first published in 1977, she provides a definition of faggot-effeminist: 'A self-descriptive term evolved by those radical homosexual men who, after helping to found the Gay Liberation Front, broke with it because of its oppression of women and effeminate men' (Morgan, 1977: 174). Although self-defining as bisexual and stating that this was an accurate description of her situation, she chose to politically define herself as a lesbian in the *New York Times* in 1968. Morgan defined herself as a lesbian because she defined herself as a lover of women, a lover of the community and people of women; in this sense she argued that all women are lesbians: 'I identify as a Lesbian because I love the People of Women and certain individual women with my life's blood' (1977: 174). Her speech referenced Goddess worship, the Sapphic tradition of women's intellectual and creative life and women's spirituality movements in the Wiccan tradition; she also referred to herself as a witch. She actually closed her speech with an invitation to the Goddess, which is used in circles, covens or meetings of followers of those Goddess and Wiccan religions – Blessed Be; indeed. There is much in her speech that could be classified as less Radical Feminism and more cultural feminism.

The cultural turn: What on the goddesses' earth is cultural feminism?

In her history of American Radical Feminism, *Daring to Be Bad*, Professor of History and Gender Studies Alice Echols asserts that Radical Feminism was usurped by cultural feminism from around 1973. It should be noted that her work was controversial and heavily critiqued by Radical Feminists who accused her of misrepresentation and using selective quotations from classic feminist works. Their argument was that while Radical Feminists may celebrate women's community building and practices and state that these should be expanded, this was never framed by them as being necessary due to biological differences between women and men. Radical Feminists saw differences between women and men, generally, as a socially constructed divide. Professor Echols blames what she sees as the transition from radical to cultural feminism on the conservative backlash in the United States, a backlash against feminism and all social justice movements that exploded at that time. In addition, she blames the various splits and schisms within the Women's Liberation Movement itself, primarily the so-called lesbian-straight split. Echols argues that the allure of cultural feminism was based partly in its potential to heal, rise above and move forward from this particular feminist split or faultline. This was a division that had been aggressive and highly destructive, not least from the early days of the movement in 1966, when Betty Friedan, founder and first president of the National Organisation for Women (NOW), famously referred to lesbians in the movement as the lavender menace. In her 1973 speech, Robin Morgan frequently mentions the lesbian-straight split, but she argues that this is not the real issue at stake at all. The real issue, she states, is whether women collaborate with the patriarchy or not, whether they adopt what she called 'male styles' or not and whether they carry in their hearts a passion for the gynocratic world that would run on the power of women. 'Not the Lesbian-Straight Split, nor the Lesbian-Feminist split, but the Feminist-versus-Collaborator Split' (Morgan, 1977: 185). This idea of a gynocratic future is fundamental to what some see as cultural feminism; it describes the liberation of what was called the female principle, with activists like Roxanne Dunbar, founder of American feminist group Cell 16 in 1968, calling for female liberation rather than women's liberation. Such standpoints were referred to by their critics at the time as female cultural nationalism. Critics such as the famous feminist psychoanalyst Professor Juliet Mitchell, in the UK, wrote an early article with Rosalind Delmar on women's liberation in Britain in 1970; there the authors warn against aggrandizing or promoting so-called feminine attributes: 'Re-valuations of feminine attributes accept the results of an exploitative situation by endorsing its concepts' (1970: 38).

Alice Echols also highlights another early paper, which she sees as an embryonic expression of cultural feminism in the United States. This is the 'Fourth World Manifesto', which was jointly written by a group of feminist women, including Barbara Burris and Kathleen Barry, for a conference in 1971. In that paper, the fourth world is a world made in the image of the female culture, defined not as a class in the political sense, but as a caste – 'the female is defined by her sexual caste status' (Burris, 1973: 331). Theorists such as Professor Sheila Jeffreys continue to define women as a sex caste to this day, whereas the terminology used by many Radical Feminists is sex class in a political sense, although Jeffreys does utilize both framings in her work. In her 2014 book *Gender Hurts*, for example, Jeffreys notes that female pronouns (she/her) are a form of honorific address, for members of the sex caste of women, who have survived the oppression that comes with that membership. In 1971, Burris and her colleagues thought that political class divisions, along with all other power differences between women, including racism, were a distracting invention of the male Left; they called for women to reclaim their female culture, a culture that prioritized love, emotion and intuition. The late Ellen Willis, music critic, journalist and theorist, in her 1984 essay on 1960s Radical Feminism and feminist radicalism, proclaims cultural feminism as antithetical to Radical Feminism.

> The great majority of women who presently call themselves 'radical feminists' in fact subscribe to a politics more accurately labelled 'cultural feminist'. That is, they see the primary goal of feminism as freeing women from the imposition of so-called 'male values' and creating an alternative culture based on 'female values'. Cultural feminism is essentially a moral, countercultural movement aimed at redeeming its participants, while radical feminism began as a political movement to end male supremacy in all areas of social and economic life, and rejected the whole idea of opposing male and female natures and values as a sexist idea, a basic part of what we were fighting. (Willis, 1984: 91)

Jane Alpert's 1973 publication 'Mother-Right' is another founding example of cultural feminism, of its maternalism, pronatalism, essentialism and in general its wild differences from every premise of Radical Feminism. It brought together many such views and existing tendencies of the time, but it was widely shared, so it served to publicize and validate these essentialist approaches. It was actually heralded by feminist leaders such as Robin Morgan herself, who Alpert credits as an inspiration.

> For centuries feminists have asserted that the essential difference between men and women does not lie in biology but rather in the roles that patriarchal societies (men) have required each sex to play. . . . However, a flaw in this feminist argument has persisted: it contradicts our felt experience of the biological difference between the sexes as one of immense significance. (Alpert, 1973: 5–6)

Alpert, the former radical leftist, who had been an associate of American far left group the Weathermen, goes on to explain that women's creativity and power spring from the biological potential of pregnancy and childbirth. Writing of prehistoric matriarchies and Goddess worship, she argues that female power is sacred and divine, and is in the genes of all women, whether or not they have been pregnant or birthed children. As she asserts, 'the inner power with which many women are beginning to feel in touch and which is the soul of feminist art, may all arise from the same source. That source is none other than female biology: the capacity to bear and nurture children' (Alpert, 1973: 8). Alpert believes that women's psychic qualities, the qualities that from ancient times have been associated with women, such as empathy, intuitiveness, inventiveness, protection of others, emotional responses and nurturing abilities are not, in fact, ancient patriarchal stereotypes, but the real and essential inner power of all women. The way forward then, as far as cultural feminism believes, is to make these female principles the overarching principles of all humankind, to end all oppression and build truly humane societies into the future.

Writers such as the lesbian feminist Professor Mary Daly arguably further promoted such views, reinforcing the links between women and spirituality, women and pacifism and women's closer spiritual links to the fate of the earth and non-human animals; this sort of message can perhaps be seen in her 1973 classic *Beyond God The Father*. In 1973 Barbara Burris added a postscript to 'The Fourth World Manifesto', when it was reproduced in the collection *Radical Feminism*, edited by Anne Koedt, Ellen Levine and Anita Rapone. This clarification from Burris suggests some disillusionment with how their manifesto had been received and used: 'This "Manifesto" was never intended to be a glorification of the female principle and culture. It was never intended to imply that women have more "soul" than men or that women are inherently more human than men' (1973: 355). Burris seems to warn against the essentialism of cultural feminism; she critiques feminists for branding any behaviour or activity they disagree with as male, or male-identified, and concludes that neither womanly or manly traits, within the current unequal state of patriarchy, are going to be the values that engender freedom: 'It would be a tragedy if women were to make our oppressed state into a virtue and a model of humanity and the new society' (Burris, 1973: 357).

Cultural feminism and the de-sexing of lesbianism

Another unfortunate feature of cultural feminism was arguably its de-sexing of lesbianism, and its re-definition of lesbianism not as a sexual orientation, and not about sexual acts and sexual relationships, but about political and spiritual bonds between women. This of course was one of the reasons for its appeal, given the prior mentioned tensions between lesbians and heterosexual women in the Women's Liberation Movement at that time – the gay/straight split. In the cultural feminist outlook, it was not men that were a problem per se and it was not a problem necessarily if women lived with or sexually partnered with men; the problem was male values and male principles. As long as one avoided those, and became woman identified and loved women politically, then this was lesbianism in its political and pure sense. This was what Robin Morgan voiced in her 1973 speech at the lesbian conference on the West Coast, and some elements of these viewpoints can arguably be seen in the passionate arguments for lesbian feminism from theorists such as Sheila Jeffreys, Mary Daly and also Janice Raymond, who of course continues to be so pivotal in today's narratives of the gender wars. In 1989 in an article in *Women's Studies International Forum*, Janice Raymond decries the de-politicization of lesbianism and the adoption of what she calls 'male-power modes of sexuality' (p 149) such as femme-butch relationships and identities. As I set out in the Introduction to this book, butch lesbians have long been subjected to suspicion and derision in some feminist spaces, accused of copying sexist patriarchal male practices. I think those of us in the butch camp have reason to be slightly suspicious of modern feminist claims to solidarity with tomboys and butch lesbians, as I will go on to explain in this chapter. In the article 'Putting the Politics Back into Lesbianism' Raymond argues for a lesbian sexuality that is rooted in imagination, not popular fantasy, and she defines lesbian feminism as women's equality with ourselves:

> It defined equality as being equal to those women who have been for women, those who have lived for women's freedom and those who have died for it; those who have fought for women and survived by women's strength; those who have loved women and who have realised that without the consciousness and conviction that women are primary in each other's lives, nothing else is in perspective. (1989: 152)

In her 2018 book on the history of lesbian feminism, Sheila Jeffreys defines lesbian feminism similarly, as a rush of female energy that can be found in women-only spaces. Quoting the late Mary Daly on the creative gynergetic flow, she imagines this energy as a flame, a woman-loving high, noting that it is usually irresistible: 'Some women resisted the flame, but many saw no reason to' (2018: 60).

Scapegoating butches

Travel back in time to 1973 again and we can see the beginnings of this trail being blazed. Morgan, in her speech to the thousands of lesbian feminists present, proclaimed that women's love for each other is not a male love; it is not the love of the male principle or male values. Rather, it is an ancient, spiritual, holy and sacred love, a transcendental love of the mind, a wellspring, one which is not debased by genital responses.

> Every woman here knows in her gut the vast differences between her sexuality and that of any patriarchally trained male's – gay or straight. That has, in fact, always been a source of pride to the lesbian community, even in its greatest suffering. That the emphasis on genital sexuality, objectification, promiscuity, emotional non-involvement, and course invulnerability, was the male style, and that we, as women, placed greater trust in love, sensuality, humour, tenderness, commitment. (Morgan, 1977: 181)

It is no coincidence to me that Morgan singled out butch lesbians for criticism in her speech. Underpinning her theme and her desire to reframe lesbianism as the political stance of spiritual woman-loving, she scapegoats butch lesbians as examples of the male style and male values in women; neatly discrediting a long-standing community of actual lesbians and indeed those most visible lesbians who had received so much of the brunt of societal homophobia only to be excluded again by many elements of the Second Wave feminist movement. Morgan references what she calls 'the butch bar dykes', cruising for 'a cute piece', who, 'in escaping the patriarchally enforced role of noxious femininity, adopt instead the patriarch's own style, to get drunk and swaggering just like one of the boys, to write of tits and ass as if a sister were no more than a collection of chicken parts' (Morgan, 1977: 182).

Dispiritingly, such prejudices and simplistic generalizations about butch lesbians were fundamental to much theorizing of the Second Wave and indeed continue to the present day, as I subject to interrogation and critique in the second half of this book. These stereotypes were encountered by many of the young butches and queers who responded to my survey research, noting hostility in both lesbian and feminist spaces. This is yet another reason why butch lesbian history and butch, stud and masculine lesbian or queer voices must be put back into the debate around the current gender wars.

The de-sexing of lesbianism meant that, like Morgan, any woman could identify as a lesbian – indeed be a purer and holier lesbian than the collateral damage embodied by the butch lesbians or any other lesbians whose sexual practices were casual, genital, indifferent 'male styles'. Thus, this pure and spiritual lesbian-loving had nothing to do with having sex with other women; instead it was a form of political and cultural separatism, as Ellen Willis recounts.

> To complicate matters, many of the feminists who 'converted' to lesbianism in the wake of lesbian separatism did so not to express a compelling sexual inclination but to embrace a political and cultural identity; some of these converts denied that lesbianism was in any sense a sexual definition, and equated their rejection of compulsory heterosexuality with 'liberation' from sex itself, at least insofar as it was 'genitally orientated'. In this atmosphere, lesbians who see freedom to express their unconventional sexuality as an integral part of their feminism have had reason to wonder if the label 'male identifier' is any improvement over 'pervert'. (Willis, 1984: 104)

It should be noted that Robin Morgan later acknowledged that she had perhaps misrepresented lesbianism, after having serious lesbian relationships of her own, she spoke in interview in Off Our Backs in 2001 and said maybe the way she had used the label of lesbian in the past had been superficial (Morgan, 2001).

Radical Feminism is not cultural feminism

Most of those who identify with Radical Feminism today refute that their feminism is anything to do with cultural feminism and obviously refute any charges of essentialism. It is true that the two are often simplistically joined, with commentators mistaking all Radical Feminism for particular cultural feminist arguments. Writing in his book on masculinities for example, the well-known gender scholar James Messerschmidt provides a summary on the history of Radical Feminism, and he asserts that Radical Feminists built a position that 'led to a celebration of an alleged essential "femaleness" and a denunciation of an avowed essential "maleness"'. He goes on to suggest that for all Radical Feminists, 'everything, from the workplace to the bedroom, that is "female" is good and everything "male" is bad' (2018: 7). This is a shocking simplification and reduction; it is one that is all too common. He even cites in his references for these claims the work of Alice Echols, who herself made clear that the revolutionary potential of real Radical Feminism was robbed by cultural feminism. Even trans-exclusionary lesbian feminists such as Professor Sheila Jeffreys do not argue that masculinity and femininity are essential, or that everything female or done by females is good; far from it. In her arguments for strategic lesbian separatism, Jeffreys cautions against withdrawing from the world and retreating into a blinkered standpoint where wider society cannot be seen and critiqued and where lesbians and lesbian practices are out of bounds for critique: 'It can become a dissociation from the world, such that the context in which certain practices and ideas originated in male supremacy is forgotten, and anything done or thought by a lesbian can be supported' (Jeffreys, 2003: 24).

It should be noted that both Raymond and Jeffreys champion lesbian feminism in particular, with Jeffreys of course being the founder of revolutionary feminism. This is a uniquely British school of feminism that Jeffreys founded at the 1977 national Women's Liberation Movement conference, that year held in Islington, London, UK. There she presented a paper on the need for revolutionary feminism and against the liberal takeover of the movement, and she wrote that feminism was becoming a sort of toothless Tupperware party or bland Townswomen's Guild, because the righteous anger against men as an oppressor class was being discouraged to make the movement palatable to the masses. Despite this history, both these writers and activists have become associated with Radical Feminism more broadly. Obviously they do come from that tradition, but the fact of their own political standpoints as lesbian feminists is often erased or glossed over. Indeed, their work is often taken as proof that Radical Feminism overall is intrinsically transphobic. The journalist Katelyn Burns, writing for *Vox* magazine on the UK TERF wars, describes both Jeffreys and Raymond as Radical Feminists and proclaims Janice Raymond's infamous book as the defining work of TERFism for example: 'In 1979, radical feminist Janice Raymond, a professor at the University of Massachusetts wrote the defining work of the TERF movement' (Burns, 2019).

The TERF empire: First strike

Let us turn then to the most widely cited text. American professor of women's studies and medical ethics, the radical lesbian feminist Janice Raymond, who studied with the feminist philosopher and theologian, the late Mary Daly, wrote a book called *The Transsexual Empire: The Making of the She-Male* in 1979. Whether most of the troopers in this current gender war have read the book or not, time and again Raymond is held up as a TERF poster girl, representing and homogenizing a whole generation of feminist dinosaurs it seems the world would rather see extinct. Professor Sally Hines, chair of sociology at the University of Sheffield, notes that 'The stance of what has recently become to be known as a TERF (trans exclusionary radical feminist) perspective is evident in the much cited 1979 book by Janice Raymond, 'The Transexual Empire' (Hines, 2017: 2). Raymond was not the first or the only lesbian feminist to critique trans recognition and inclusion though, as I have introduced earlier, but, as poet and academic Cameron Awkward-Rich credits, this work has perhaps had the most significant and long-lasting effect.

> The tension between lesbian separatist and trans communities has its roots in the women's movement of the 1970s and 1980s, best demonstrated by the conflict surrounding the publication of Janice Raymond's The Transexual Empire: The Making of the She-Male, which she first published in 1979. While Raymond was not the first to critique transsexuality in the name of feminism, her work has had the most significant effects on our cultural landscape. (Awkward-Rich, 2017: 827)

Indeed, Raymond's work played a part in Sandy Stone's departure from Olivia Records, as Raymond not only sent drafts of her manifesto to Olivia Records but personally critiqued the collective in her published book, accusing Sandy Stone of patriarchal practices and of splitting women's movements. Professor Patricia Elliot acknowledges that the widespread awareness of the book and its association with Radical Feminism has led to a climate where all feminism is suspected of transphobia, a climate 'in which all non-trans feminist critique of trans theory is associated with the explicitly transphobic work of Janice Raymond, thus tainting all critical endeavours before they can be considered carefully' (Elliot, 2004: 14).

It is certainly not difficult to find transphobic statements in Raymond's book; it is often violently visceral, pruriently describes the bodies of trans people and medical interventions and ultimately accuses trans women of being, however knowingly or willingly, dupes in some monstrous patriarchal erasure of female-born women. In among all that, it does also contain some commentary, which is surprisingly not that different to the commentary that some trans activists were also making at the time, particularly in the sections dealing with the burgeoning medical industry around emerging gender identity clinics in universities in the United States and the science of sex reassignment. What must be noted here, however, is the importance of identity; it matters that the trans women and trans men who critiqued the medical industry of that period did so from a position of personal experience. Their experiences spoke to others who were also going through similar, whereas Raymond was commenting on this from the sidelines and blatantly speaking over those who were actually going through it.

It could be argued that Raymond's main argument in this most famous book at least was not so much with trans people themselves though, but with the medical industry; indeed, this is the toxic empire that she refers to. This is actually recognized and underlined by some of her critics. Queer heroine and trans activist Kate Bornstein allows that 'Raymond's book is a worthwhile read, chiefly for its intelligent highlighting of the male-dominated medical profession, and that profession's control of transexual surgery' (1994: 46). Author and academic Patrick Califia comments that the 'bulk of Raymond's book is taken up with a determined attempt to paint the medical doctors and therapists who provide the hormones and surgery that make sex-reassignment possible as an evil empire of high-tech agents for the patriarchy' (Califia, 1997: 96). British Sociologist Carol Riddell, in her popular and widely shared critique, originally from 1980, of Raymond's book and her politics, observed similarly: 'Janice Raymond attacks the sex-researchers as the evil-intentioned instruments of patriarchal sex-role coercion' (Riddell, 2006: 151). Indeed, guilty as charged, this is exactly what Raymond does assert: 'The role of the gender identity clinics and the medical psychiatric establishment in general in reinforcing sex-role stereotypes is a significant one' (Raymond, 1980: 91).

Many trans men and trans women, speaking from their own experiences during the 1970s and 1980s, actually made similar observations about the medical establishment (Heyes, 2018). Sandy Stone, for example, who wrote perhaps the most famous riposte to Raymond, ingeniously titled *The Empire Strikes Back: A Post-Transexual Manifesto*, recounted that in the United States, the gender identity clinics – when assessing trans women – often made stereotyped judgements about who could best 'pass' as a feminine woman, and then, concerned with performing 'successful' interventions, would police who was able to receive them: 'The clinic took on the additional role of "grooming clinic" or "charm school" because, according to the judgement of the staff, the men who presented as wanting to be women did not always "behave like women"' (Stone, 1991: 291). Providing the perspective of a trans man, Zachary I Nataf wrote in 1996 that many might recall how gender conservative the gender clinics were in the UK as well: 'The gender clinics reinforce conventional, conservative, stereotypical gender behaviour and notions of an unambiguous, fixed and coherent gender identity, although the experiences of most transgendered people is that identity actually evolves and changes' (1996: 20). Theorist Talia Mae Bettcher notes the irony of 1990s queer theory evolving to actually arrive at many of Raymond's points, albeit from different directions.

> To be sure, there is a perverse sense in which the emerging transgender politics of the nineties endorsed many of the points that Raymond herself had made. There was agreement that the medical model of transsexuality serves to perpetuate sexist norms, and that transsexuality is not a pathological condition but arises, rather, as a consequence of an oppressive gender system. There was even agreement that bodily dysphoria, which motivates surgical intervention, would disappear in a culture that had no gender oppression. (Bettcher, 2016: 412)

Contrary to popular belief, Professor Raymond does not make a biological argument for womanhood as such, not in her most famous publication; that is, she does not state that what makes someone a woman is purely their reproductive capacity or genitalia. This is actually a common critique thrown at all Radical Feminism, which is frequently accused of being essentialist, as I have pointed out earlier. Raymond does, however, state that what makes someone a woman is being treated as a woman because of their female sex characteristics at birth, their internal reproductive system and external genitalia. She argues that what women share in common is the experience of being treated as women in patriarchal society, usually from before birth, what she calls the 'total history of what it means to be a woman or a man, in a society that treats women and men differently on the basis of biological sex' (1980: 18). Gender, as in masculinity and femininity, is not rooted in biology in this analysis, a stance that is shared by queer theorists, as well as by both gender abolitionist and GC feminists. This feature is often overlooked, in order to make the popular claim that Radical Feminism in general is essentialist, or even, that it is a form of biological determinism.

Diane Richardson highlights this misconception, writing in the collection *Radically Speaking: Feminism Reclaimed*, edited by Diane Bell and Renate Klein (1996). 'One of the most common misreadings of radical feminist thinking is that it is essentialist; that it locates the source of women's subordination in female biology and/or male biology' (Richardson, 1996: 143). In a recent 2019 collection on the workings of power in everyday practices, scholar of Human Rights and Sexuality Studies Dan Irving summarizes the gender wars as a conflict between trans-exclusionary Radical Feminists and trans feminists; he wrongly presents Radical Feminism as, generally, fundamentally essentialist: 'Radical Feminists' arguments are rooted primarily in biological determinism. Womanhood is defined for them by the interconnection between genitalia and other visible signifiers of female embodiment and gender socialisation as women' (Irving, 2019: 113). It is often suggested that Radical Feminist politics and theory define the role of women in society as being based on possessing a female reproductive system and female chromosomes for example. Professor Sally Hines summarized in 2019 that 'Raymond's claim is that gender is an expression of biological sex, the latter of which is chromosomally dependent', and Hines goes on to describe Raymond's position on, as she sees it, 'the fixity of sex and gender, fiercely denying the gender identities and expressions of trans women and men' (Hines, 2019). Hines charges Raymond with explicit biological essentialism; 'From this premise, gender and sex are locked into each other and secured at birth' (Hines, 2019). Scholar of bioethics at the University of Sydney, Australia, Kathryn Mackay, in an article on ectogenesis, also sums up what she calls the TERF standpoint, or 'TERF argument, and those like it, which claim that anyone who has or ever has had a penis cannot be a woman is evidence that genitalia has special importance among certain groups in deciding a person's gender identity' (Mackay, 2020: 3). However, such essentialist views would actually be an anathema to all Radical Feminist scholarship, including from Raymond's own lesbian feminist perspective, as she clearly spells out in her own work: 'One of the primary tenets of the women's movement has been that so-called gender identity differences are not natural nor immutable' (Raymond, 1980: 64).

Gender is not sex

Gender is certainly not fixed in sexed bodily features, let alone fixed at birth in the Radical Feminist perspective because gender is not considered natural or biological, and gender is definitely not seen as an expression of biological sex; as if any Radical Feminist would assert that female equals a natural femininity or that male equals a natural masculinity. As a purely social construction gender is not something considered to be present and innate at birth; it can only be made. Bodily sexed characteristics are indeed seen as fixed and generally unchangeable in Raymond's classic book, but it is a misreading of Raymond to suggest or speculate that she also considered gender to be innate and born. Raymond, as a gender abolitionist, did not believe that anyone was naturally or biologically gendered, and indeed she would advocate for everyone to give up gender roles and refuse to participate in the institution of gender. In fact, her rallying against the medical industry was because she felt it entrenched and further institutionalized gender. From such a standpoint the problem would not be a person sexed as male at birth who wished to participate in femininity, nor a person sexed as female at birth who wished to participate in masculinity; the problem would be masculinity and femininity full stop, for anyone. For Raymond, the medical, pharmaceutical and psychiatric industry is stepping in to enforce congruent sex and gender norms for trans people, and in turn shore up the foundations of those norms for everyone, whether trans identified or not. Indeed, Raymond added that every gender-conforming person shared the ideology of gender with trans people, and she asserted that every feminine woman was also doing this work and was therefore a transsexual too in so far as they shored up the patriarchal creation of femininity. Raymond acknowledges that such an extremely sex- and gender-normative society will produce trans people. For her it is inevitable, in a conservative, binary sex and gender system, that there will be people who do not wish to fit into the sex and gender role they are presented with from birth. In fact, Raymond sees so-called cross-sex and cross-gender identification as simply normal human presentation, and she thinks human beings naturally possess a vast array of personalities and characteristics, which do not depend on sex. She believes the medical empire is a death strike to that diversity.

The empire strikes out

Perhaps my reading here is too simple, too fluffy a version of Raymond's early declaration of war in the ongoing gender wars. Plus, any close analysis of Raymond's broader points in her book may matter less now, because the battles seem only to increase in intensity and range every day, mission creeping into all areas of life, from toilets to sports to summer camps. Most often, what we see in mainstream coverage and in social media activism is people fighting over who is a woman and who is not a woman. We can see this, for example, in the UK-based campaigns such as those from Fair Play for Women, or from Standing for Women and its founder Mrs Keen-Minshull, as well as from other outspoken anti-trans-inclusion media campaigners such as Catholic activist and anti-abortionist Caroline Farrow, who is the campaign director of an organization called CitizenGo. It is significant of course that there are less public battles over who is a man and who is not a man; the sexism in this silence is yet to be fully acknowledged. But this particular battle line, over who is or isn't a woman, has a long history, as we have seen from the influential US lesbian conference in 1973 outlined earlier, and from Sandy Stone's experience at Olivia Records and her life in lesbian feminist collectives. From the UK there are early examples of the effect of such battles too, with groups also reporting being split over this issue, incidentally highlighting, yet again, that there wasn't one line on trans inclusion, and that trans women were involved in the Second Wave WLM from the early days both in the UK and the United States. Sadly, trans-exclusionary feminists were then able to use the occurrence of disagreement to further their charges that trans women were divisive splitters and full of attention-seeking male entitlement. As just a couple of examples from the archives attest, the conference papers for a Rad/Rev (revolutionary feminist and Radical Feminist) conference in Leeds, Yorkshire, UK, in September 1979 include a paper responding to the question of 'transsexuals in the women's liberation movement' by activist Lal Coveney. The paper concludes that trans women will always be men, and that they cannot be women because being a woman is based on lifelong experience of being treated as such, from birth. 'It needs to be stated loud and clear that being a woman is a long-term experience, and one that isn't summed up by a collection of female genitalia with some clothes draped over them' (1979: 1). Repeating similar arguments to those outlined already in this chapter, Coveney notes that trans women cannot be trusted, and she also charges trans women of caricaturing women through appropriating femininity. This was being popularized at the time of course in Raymond's book, such views are also a lasting legacy from Morgan's arguments conflating racist blackface with the identity of trans women: 'These beings represented the male caricature of me, and I did not feel sorry or sisterly, I felt undermined and hostile' (Coveney, 1979: 1).

However, in another example, a 1985 article in *Spare Rib* magazine, which was the British feminist periodical from 1972 to 1993, titled 'Are You a Real Woman?', contributor Rosalind A Tubb notes that her CR group happens to have a trans woman as a member. Tubb critiques feminists who would seek to bar her trans sister and accuses them of being just like patriarchal men who decry what and who women can be. She states that she knows she is a woman, and she knows her colleague is a woman too: 'I am a woman, not because of my body, but because I define myself as one' (1985: 8). These territorial disputes, clearly circulating for several years, are covered in depth in Raymond's 1979 book of course and they informed what came after. As many of her critics have rightly drawn attention to, Raymond does indeed argue that trans women are not 'real' women. It is easy to see why readers would take issue with her language on this matter:

> No man can have the history of being born and located in this culture as a woman. He can have the history of wishing to be a woman and of acting like a woman, but this gender experience is of a transsexual, not of a woman. . . . Surgery may confer the artifacts of outward and inward female organs but it cannot confer the history of being a born a woman in this society. (Raymond, 1980: 114)

Such a stance is clearly dated, partly because of course we now have decades of influence from queer theory, much of it feminist informed, suggesting that surely nobody knows what it is to be a 'real' woman or man. When it comes to these social roles, practically everyone is trying to fit into received stereotypes about what is womanly or manly, what is feminine or masculine, and then trying to match up to those ideals. Incidentally, Raymond herself acknowledges that these roles are constructed.

Despite her commendable calls for human diversity and expression however, which she makes frequently in the 1979 book, Raymond does not appear motivated to make the world an easier place for transgender or trans expression; rather, she is only motivated to get rid of sex and gender roles altogether. Her aim, as a gender-abolitionist feminist, is to abolish gender as a sex rank system. Therefore, Raymond does not advocate anyone taking up, reclaiming or aggrandizing sex and gender roles, whether that be a trans person or any person. She is a gender abolitionist, and applies that to all; she believes everyone should be free of gender; there is no room for playing, queering, fucking with or reclaiming gender in this standpoint. Whatever one's view on that gender-abolitionist perspective, at least Raymond is consistent; she applies her view to all individuals, however they may identify, as trans men, trans women or transgender or queer or even as adult human females.

The elimination of male privilege and the sex distinction itself: Radical Feminists rap sex and gender

Janice Raymond's work has helped to seal the link between Radical Feminism and trans-exclusionary feminist positions, but she is not the only lesbian feminist theorist to have written about sex and gender or on trans women in feminism. Raymond's position and that of similar anti-trans-inclusion scholar Professor Sheila Jeffreys have always been somewhat contentious within feminism, and their position on this question, and many other areas, represents only one strand within feminism. While influential and important, they certainly don't reflect a homogenous standpoint in Radical Feminism; in fact, there are many other different and opposing views that come from within Radical Feminist theory and activism. Most Radical Feminists agree that there isn't one singular definition of Radical Feminism anyway, just as there is no one agreed definition of feminism in general. This openness has its downsides of course; for one thing it enables capitalism to exploit feminism as a brand, in order to sell more products to women. It enables women in mainstream power, responsible for policies that directly negatively impact on women disproportionately, to claim that they are feminists, simply because they are women in politics or women in business for example. It is as if we collectively think so little of women and women's potential, that any woman who has a lot of money, or a senior position in business, must somehow be leaning in on her feisty feminist mission, rather than just having a lot of money, or being able to play the game in the mainstream corporate world for example. However, this openness of the definition of feminism is also a strength, and a fluidity, which is inspiringly oppositional to the sort of fixed dogmas that have always been the enemy of all feminisms, such as the many religious and conservative ideologies that have sought to define and confine women and women's potential; defining women as mothers, singularly, and confining women to the home and domestic sphere alone. The term 'radical' in Radical Feminism can be taken to mean going to the root of issues, not addressing symptoms alone but trying to find the causes of inequality and then rendering those obsolete. Radical Feminism grew out of women theorizing their own lives and struggles, in what became known as CR. It is a feature of Radical Feminism that any political theory should grow out of practice, the practice of women's daily lives and the challenges that are put in the way of that.

Two famous Radical Feminists, the American writers Kate Millett and Shulamith Firestone, for example, have argued in their classic works that the aim of feminist revolution must be the erasure of sex difference itself as an organizing principle. Unlike Raymond, they made these arguments without focussing on scapegoating trans women. In fact, there is plenty of Radical Feminist theory that argues that sex is not destiny, and that sex at birth should not be a marker of human beings or a marker of human separation into two distinct categories or genders. I would suggest this is a staple of most Radical Feminism which has, like feminism generally, long fought against the political ideology of appropriate roles for women and men, justified by claims to biological suitability or functionality. The late, great artist, writer, activist and scholar Kate Millett made this point overtly: 'Whatever the "real" differences between the sexes may be, we are not likely to know them until the sexes are treated differently, that is alike. And this is very far from being the case at present' (Millett, 1970: 29). Similarly, Firestone argued, 'the end goal of feminist revolution must be, unlike that of the first feminist movement, not just the elimination of male privilege but of the sex distinction itself: genital differences between human beings would no longer matter culturally' (Firestone, 1970: 19). The Radical Feminist Ti Grace-Atkinson also argued this overtly back in 1969: 'I believe the sex roles of both male and female must be destroyed, not the individuals who happen to possess either a penis or a vagina, or both, or neither' (2000: 86). Other famous Western Radical Feminists such as the late Andrea Dworkin and the stateswomanly legal scholar Catharine MacKinnon have made similar arguments. The former, just as Raymond also argued, acknowledged that any fiercely policed binary gender society would inevitably produce those who did not, could not or would not fit in to it, and so would seek to shift or exist between the allowed boxes and labels. In fact, to be human was considered by definition fluid, and therefore it was human not to fit into inhumane constraints and labels: 'Transsexuality can be defined as one particular formation of our general multisexuality which is unable to achieve its natural development because of extremely adverse social conditions' (Dworkin, 1974: 186). Of course, many feminists may argue that we cannot know what stance or position Dworkin would take on the modern gender wars because this feminist legend is no longer with us (Stoltenberg, 2020), all interpretations of her work in the current context are just that, an interpretation; certainly, there will be feminists who disagree with my take on it here.

Well known and admired in Radical Feminism for her tireless activism against the pornography industry and for the rights of women working within it, Andrea Dworkin argued that in a rigid sex/gender binary society, or 'state of emergency' as she called it, sex reassignment surgeries must be a human right, provided for free by the community. She wrote that 'every transsexual has the right to survival on his/her own terms. That means that every transsexual is entitled to a sex-change operation, and it should be provided by the community as one of its functions. This is an emergency measure for an emergency condition' (Dworkin, 1974: 187). Dworkin also speculates that in an androgynous, pansexual, NB future, trans identity may occur less frequently. She envisions that 'community built on androgynous identity will mean the end of transsexuality as we know it. Either the transsexual will be able to expand his/her sexuality into a fluid androgyny, or, as roles disappear, the phenomenon of transsexuality will disappear and that energy will be transformed into new modes of sexual identity and behaviour' (Dworkin, 1974: 187). Raymond has been critiqued for similar expressions, with the assertion often being made that Raymond argues for trans women to be mandated out of existence, to be made extinct. Writing in *The Guardian* in 2011, author and journalist Roz Kaveney summarizes that 'Radical feminist Janice Raymond desired to "morally mandate transexuality out of existence"' (Kaveney, 2011). However, if we return to the context of this quote, from the appendix of her 1979 book, what Raymond is suggesting is arguably more similar to Dworkin; she is asserting that polarized gendered society should be eradicated and that beyond that, in a future society, there would be no desire to gender one's body with hormones and surgery because gendering would no longer be practised by anyone. Therefore, the medical and surgical industries around this would cease to exist, an endpoint that Raymond welcomes. Unlike Dworkin, Raymond does indeed argue that sex reassignment surgery should not be freely available or funded, and she does class it as unnecessary mutilation. On her own website she clarifies this herself: 'I did not then or now believe that federal or state funds should subsidize transsexual surgery for anyone because, in my view, it is unnecessary surgery and medical mutilation' (Raymond, no date). As I said at the opening of this chapter, it is not difficult to find bigotry and prejudice against trans people in her book, and it is entirely unsurprising that so many have critiqued it for just that.

The theorist Andrea Dworkin also wants to see an end to the gender binary and to the institution of heterosexuality, but she advocates for the growth of androgyny and pansexuality as a political stance to eradicate power relationships in society; 'if we can create androgynous community, we can abandon power altogether as a social reality —that is the final, and most important, implication of androgyny' (Dworkin, 1974: 191). She also notes that binary sexed bodily characteristics may not be as fixed as we presume: 'We are, clearly, a multi-sexed species which has its sexuality spread along a vast fluid continuum where the elements called male and female are not discrete' (Dworkin, 1974: 183). She ponders whether things like height and musculature may be less polarized by birth sex in an equal society for example, and she prophecies that scientific research will continue to find more similarities and commonalities, than differences, between male and female sexed bodies: 'We can presume then that there is a great deal about human sexuality to be discovered, and that our notion of two discrete biological sexes cannot remain intact' (Dworkin, 1974: 181). This is the polar opposite stance to more cultural feminists who believe not only that there are only two biological sexes and that they are immutable but that arising from this biology there are also two roles or two ideologies, with the aim of that version of feminism being to reclaim and assert the female principle. Instead, Dworkin urges us towards a future that, she says, is almost unimaginable in the context we inhabit now, 'the process of destroying particularized roles and fixed erotic identity. As people develop fluid androgynous identity, they will also develop the forms of community appropriate to it. We cannot really imagine what those forms will be' (Dworkin, 1974: 189).

Recently the impressive law professor and feminist shero Catharine MacKinnon, who worked with survivor and activist Andrea Dworkin for many years, not least in feminist campaigns against the pornography and prostitution industries, has clarified that she aggressively does not care about the so-called gender wars and that she is not bothered in the slightest if a trans woman happens to be using the toilet in the next bathroom cubicle: 'Many trans women just go around being women, who knew, and suddenly, we are supposed to care that they are using the women's bathroom. There they are in the next stall with the door shut, and we're supposed to feel threatened. I don't. I don't care. By now, I aggressively don't care' (MacKinnon, 2015). Other well-known feminists, not just Radical Feminists, have made similar clarifications. The famous co-founder of *Ms.* magazine, for example, Gloria Steinem, writing in *The Advocate* in 2013, affirmed the self-identification and rights of trans people.

> So now I want to be unequivocal in my words: I believe that transgender people, including those who have transitioned, are living out real, authentic lives. Those lives should be celebrated, not questioned. Their health care decisions should be theirs and theirs alone to make. And what I wrote decades ago does not reflect what we know today as we move away from only the binary boxes of 'masculine' or 'feminine' and begin to live along the full human continuum of identity and expression. (Steinem, 2013)

I have argued throughout this chapter that Radical Feminism is often unfairly misrepresented, simplified and assumed to be inherently transphobic and trans-exclusionary. In addition, Radical Feminism is often mistaken for or conflated with lesbian feminism, separatism or cultural feminism, which are all quite different strands, tendencies and different schools of thought. Generally speaking, much of Radical Feminism grew out of left-wing organizing, anti-war and anti-racism movements, when women within those groups realized that the Left needed radicalizing on women's rights and that women's leadership was vital to all progressive social movements for positive change. While Radical Feminism recognized the importance of women-only self-organization, particularly in male-dominated social justice movements blighted by sexism, it was not a retreatist separatist movement. Separatism was a separatist movement and involved women strategically creating women-only lives as much as possible, for example, living in women's communes, setting up women-only businesses and social venues – sometimes more permanently, for example, in the women's land movements. Obviously, there was crossover, as Radical Feminists were present in many of those endeavours, along with feminists and lesbians of differing political standpoints; but living a separatist life was not a hallmark or necessity of Radical Feminist theory. The creation as well as sustenance of women-only organizing and services was, however, a key concern for Radical Feminists, but, even as lesbian feminist Sheila Jeffreys maintains, this was always a tactical separation; it was not an escapist withdrawal from the world, and it sought to change the world (2003). Janice Raymond argued for the same strategic approach and both sought to distance themselves from any form of cultural feminism: 'The dissociation that I criticise is not that of women coming together separately to then affect the 'real' world. Rather, it is a dissociation that proclaims a withdrawal from that world' (Raymond, 1986: 25).

Lesbian feminism was concerned with a strategic or tactical separatism, as Professor Jeffreys has documented, and the creation of lesbian-only and women-only social and cultural spaces, accommodation and businesses, as well as being active in the creation of feminist infrastructure more generally, for all women, not least in the refuge movement, in which many lesbian feminists were influential. For lesbian feminists, being a lesbian was not simply a sexual or romantic identity, but a political identity. Lesbian life and activism made that strategic separatism possible, and many lesbian feminists chose not to interact with men at all in day-to-day life. However, this did not usually extend to full-time separatist living, and in fact, many lesbian feminists were critical of what they saw as a lifestyle move, because for them creating lesbian-only communities was a political act, to be pursued in the present revolutionary moment and was about building a future, not dropping out. Lesbian feminism is often confused with what is called political lesbianism, and there probably is some degree of overlap here. Indeed, lesbian feminists were influential in theoretical critiques of heterosexuality, as indeed were Radical Feminists generally – debates which took place in the wider Women's Liberation Movement, and which were often considered controversial.

For example, the Leeds Revolutionary Feminist Group and their infamous pamphlet on political lesbianism in 1979, which was later published by OnlyWomen Press under the title *Love Your Enemy?* (1981). Lesbian feminism and lesbian separatism was also critiqued by Black feminist groups, who pointed out that Black lesbian women worked together with Black men against racism, and with Black men in anti-racist movements, all the while tackling sexism in those movements too. Perhaps a most famous critique of lesbian separatism comes from the Black feminist lesbian statement produced by the Combahee River Collective in 1977 in the United States: 'As we have already stated, we reject the stance of Lesbian separatism because it is not a viable political analysis or strategy for us. It leaves out far too much and far too many people, particularly Black men, women, and children.' Particularly relevant for my focus in this book, the Combahee statement also critiques biological determinism, pointing out that biology does not produce gender or gender roles; for example, it does not cause the types of violence so often connected to and defined as masculinity:

> We have a great deal of criticism and loathing for what men have been socialized to be in this society: what they support, how they act, and how they oppress. But we do not have the misguided notion that it is their maleness, per se – i.e., their biological maleness – that makes them what they are. As Black women we find any type of biological determinism a particularly dangerous and reactionary basis upon which to build a politic. (Combahee River Collective, 1977)

Political lesbianism was sometimes less about lesbianism and more about prioritizing separatism as a political act. It may have better been termed political separatism for example, as it did not concern itself with sex or romance between women, or sex and romance at all, but rather the prioritization of women and the withdrawal of all energies, domestic, caring, financial and sexual, from men. Lesbian feminists often believed that such a move would form the bedrock of feminism generally, and that for feminist revolution to happen, women had to withdraw physically and psychically from men. The Leeds group underlined that to choose political lesbianism was not to choose to have sex with women necessarily; they pointed out that celibacy was a valiant option.

Radical Feminism is not cultural feminism and does not see men and women as different species with innate and immutable traits. Radical Feminism always maintained that revolutionary change was possible because individuals were capable of change and that there was nothing biological about the prevalence of male sexual violence. Men as a group were constructed as a political class, and as an oppressor class on the axis of sex inequality, but this was seen as political and not nature. The aim of Radical Feminism then was to remedy the impact of, reduce the extent of and eventually remove patriarchy from power. Women-only organizing and leadership was a tool to pursue this aim, but not an end in itself, and there was always an assumption that old class allegiances can be extinguished, progressive men would rebel, and that both men and women had more in common to gain from an egalitarian future. It is for these reasons that I am a Radical Feminist.

The history of Radical Feminist organizing is one that clearly includes trans-exclusionary positions; but it also includes trans-inclusive theorists and organizations. Lesbian feminists and Radical Feminists who promote trans exclusion often do so on the grounds, as discussed earlier, that womanhood is defined by being sexed as female at birth, and, as a result of that designation, being treated as a woman, all of one's life, in a world where that means second class. In a world of male supremacy, women's labour is exploited, including their bodily labour in terms of birthing and rearing children. Women's bodies are sexually objectified and exploited. Women's bodies are used in patriarchy, but they are not used because they have female bodies; they are used because women are made inferior within patriarchy. Women whose bodies cannot get pregnant are still used and exploited. Women who do not experience sexual violence are still used and exploited in other ways, at work, in the domestic sphere and many more. My point is that it is not because of biology that women are oppressed; patriarchy did not spring from the ether the moment the first humans stood up and wandered the earth, displaying their genitals and sexed characteristics. Having a body with a penis or with a vagina is not like mother nature's political sorting hat that separates the rulers from the ruled. These bodily features have been constructed by society to symbolize rank; it is important to remember that they do not have to be seen this way. As I outlined in more detail in Chapter 1 on the construction of biological sex, I would assert that Radical Feminism is truly revolutionary in asking us to reformulate how we understand and see 'sex'. The body will not disappear if we do, and bodies still need specific health responses for example, including responses to reproductive systems, pregnancy and birth, but the meanings of the body could change. This is what Radical Feminist theorists like Andrea Dworkin and Shulamith Firestone are asking us to imagine.

Radical Feminism is compatible with trans inclusion. We follow in the footsteps of those women who upset Robin Morgan by calling Beth Elliot their Sister at the West Coast Lesbian Conference way back in 1973. Those conference organizers like Barbara McLean who stated: 'No. We do not, cannot relate to her as a man. We have not known her as a man' (1973: 36). Those women like Patty Harrison and Robin Tyler who rushed to the front of the stage to defend Elliot in 1973. Those women who took Sandy Stone as one of their own in their lesbian communes and the women's music business in Olivia Records during the Second Wave. There will be many more such cases. The fact that letters to *Spare Rib* for example, articles in newsletters and periodicals, or conference papers from national feminist conferences, point to trans inclusion being an agenda item in local groups and CR groups indicates that some groups were trans-inclusive. Feminism is not a lineage marked by universal trans exclusion. This is a history that demands much more concern and focus. No doubt it has not received it because neither women nor trans communities in general are seen as worthy subjects, nor history-making agents, but indeed they are.

Sex at birth is sex class forever

Many of the arguments we hear in the gender wars today against trans inclusion also hinge on a definition of womanhood that requires being categorized as female from birth and being treated as such for a lifetime. Women's experience of and resistance to sexism and male violence is one thing that all women share; I would agree with this. In fact, I think that in all our diversity, under all manifestations of patriarchy around the world, women and all those sexed as female at birth share in common our experience of and resistance to sexism. However, as I will explore in this book, on a daily basis this experience is often dictated by how we are categorized by others, based on gender presentation, and by our ID and paperwork items of formal identification when we require services, healthcare or we apply for jobs for example. Having an M for male or an F for female on our identification can be the difference between getting or keeping a job or not, between getting paid a higher wage or not. Being seen as a woman in the world can result in sexual harassment or violence; it can result in marginalization at work or exclusion. Such experiences are also raced and classed; racism and class discrimination impact on not only victimization but on resources and responses which shape and constrain freedom and healing from victimization. Perpetrators of sexual violence do not usually stop to take a hormone count, map our genes or even require our genitals to be exposed.

This means that trans women who are read as women in the world will be subjected to all of the above too. In addition, they may also be subjected to transphobia as well, where their trans status and history is known. In public life many trans women will sadly be no strangers to sexual harassment. In fact, high-profile trans women in the UK, such as Munroe Bergdorf (2017), for example, have spoken openly about experiencing stalking and rape. The American author Julia Serano has also written about her experiences of harassment and attempted date rape (2017). We also need to take into account that, regardless of people's views on the matter, trans men and trans women are going through transition at younger ages. This can be what's called a social transition, changing one's name and using different pronouns, or using medical interventions to suppress the effects of puberty and then perhaps taking what are called cross-sex hormone treatments or pursuing surgery from when legally recognized as an adult, which in the UK is from eighteen years of age for example. This changing demographic of trans men and trans women does call into question definitions of womanhood that require lifelong experiences of being treated as a woman; how long is lifelong? What of trans women who transitioned decades ago and have lived a lifetime as women? What of young adults who transitioned socially from childhood and then with medical interventions from their late teens? Is a decade of being treated as a woman enough to recruit someone into the 'woman' camp? Or five years, or two?

If womanhood is defined by having sexed as female genitals or secondary sexed characteristics, then surely all post-operative trans women would be automatically included. Those opposed to trans inclusion may then raise a point about male privilege. Trans women, even if they were never comfortable with the designation, were for a time, in early life, treated by the world as boys and/or men. This may have led to receipt of some perks of patriarchy, benefits along the lines of increased wages, lower risk of early experience of sexual violence, promotion in the world of work, years available in which to build up experience in male-dominated fields and such like. No doubt this is the case for some trans women, particularly those women who came out as trans and then transitioned later in life. But, like anyone else, trans women are not a homogenous group. The British journalist Paris Lees acknowledges her different upbringing, for example,

> I am not a woman in the way my mother is; I haven't experienced female childhood;
> I don't menstruate. I won't give birth. Yes, I have no idea what it feels like to be
> another woman – but nor do I know what it feels like to be another man. How can
> anyone know what it feels like to be anyone but themselves? (Lees, 2013)

While many trans women were not brought up as girls, although this is changing today, as mentioned earlier, this does not have to be taken as proof that all such individuals sailed through life with seamless male privilege. It stands to reason that individuals who rejected the roles imposed on them from an early age would have been punished for doing so; as writer and activist Celeste West highlights, 'While it is clear some trans women benefit from some elements of male privilege before transition, others are unable to fit well enough into the proscribed gender role to be able to do so' (2013).

Homophobia and transphobia blight the lives of young people who reject sex and gender norms, even today, regardless of how those young people actually define or identify themselves. That includes violence, sexual violence and rape, peer and family rejection. If we focus on lived experience of sexism and resistance to that, then surely trans women are woman enough to be brought into the ranks of womanhood. If we acknowledge that women are more than whatever reproductive system and capacity they may have or not have, more than whether or not they menstruate, more than whether or not they give birth, then I would suggest that the 'more' is precisely what feminism stands for. Feminism is the political unity of women under conditions of patriarchy. Thus, all those who are treated as women by patriarchy should have a place in that unity. Definitions of female classification may focus on our bodily features, but all women, not only trans women, have varying relationships with their bodily features and indeed with their bodies. This is the focus of the second half of this book where I look at female masculinity, queer and lesbian gender.

Sisterhood is political; not biological

It is ironic that trans people are sometimes accused of trying to erase the category of sex and pretend that sexed bodily features don't exist, when trans people who transition go through such a lot to change and shape the sexed features they were born with, into a more liveable body. As author Julia Serano argues, 'I can assure you that trans people are highly aware of biological sex differences — the fact that many of us physically transition demonstrates that we acknowledge that sexually dimorphic traits exist and may be important to some people!' (Serano, 2017). For some feminists, sex at birth is sex forever. The persistence of sexed chromosomes and DNA in the body is often invoked as physical proof of the impossibility of changing sex – as I explored in detail in Chapter 1. Even when it is acknowledged that sexed features and genitals can be changed and are therefore not immutable, sex class is seen as fixed at birth and a sex-class change is impossible in this reading. Feminists who take that fixed stance are unlikely to change their minds on this issue. For the rest of us, I suggest it is important to think about the myriad of ways that sexism and unfair treatment in patriarchy impact differently on all different types of women. This includes the intersections of racism, class oppression, homophobia, failure to accommodate illness and disability or cater to caring responsibilities for example. Feminism has always been painfully aware of difference between women, even when it tried to pretend it wasn't there in order to construct an imaginary village, and an aspirational united but respectable front. As feminists, we need to consider in what ways intersectional exclusions, sexism and unfair treatment under patriarchal rule affect and include trans women, because it undoubtably does. For me, Sisterhood is political, not biological.

In this chapter I have already mentioned some of the roots of the current feminist versus trans gender wars, Raymond's book and also the Michigan Womyn's Music Festival. This event crops up frequently in commentary on Radical Feminism and trans exclusion; it is often cited as proof of the innate transphobia of Radical Feminism generally. It is a significant part of the history of the gender wars, yet the story told of that festival is not always the whole story, or the whole truth. I was fortunate to attend the festival myself, and I have my own perspectives on what it meant and symbolized. In Chapter 3 I shall introduce you to the background of this festival, explaining how it has become so central to the trans question in feminism and arguing that even here, there was still no monolithic feminist standpoint on trans inclusion or exclusion.

3

The day the music died

Michigan, myths and the ground zero of terfdom

Michigan Womyn's Music Festival began in 1976, the spirit of certain kinds of feminism made flesh in earth and pines; the Second Wave lesbian feminism of The Land thrived and jived its way through forty tumultuous decades, dancing over many feminist faultlines in the process, before finally faltering and closing in 2015. The festival was initially founded and produced by lesbian feminist activist Lisa Vogel, her sister and friends, along with an occasional collective ranging in number from three to six. The festival was run as a private business, with profits put back into the expansive running costs, on 651 acres of land that Vogel now owns near Grand Rapids, Oceania County in rural Michigan, the United States.

There is not another festival like it, and perhaps now, there never will be again. I was privileged to attend Michigan or MichFest, as it is known, in 1998. A sacred pilgrimage in certain feminist communities, travelling to Michigan and staying on 'The Land' is an experience to treasure and one to recount with pride. The festival lived up to all its legends, beginning on the road trip there, as we started to notice more and more trucks and cars with women's symbol stickers and rainbow flags on the bumpers. On route, in among the prolific sprouting of front yard billboards bearing biblical quotes next to monumental crosses, there would also be gas stations with rather incongruous signs reading 'welcome womyn' in between the fuel prices and 'last stop for ice' adverts. Everyone got out of their trucks to socialize in the line waiting to enter the festival to park, and, on hearing we were 'festie virgins', old-timers had tips about where to camp and what bands to see that year.

Although I travelled home with several new CDs and managed to see the Indigo Girls live, the music was less significant than the whole atmosphere. The vibe of the place reminded me strongly of my experiences living at a women's peace camp but multiplied by thousands and several hundred acres. From the approach to the site onwards, the achievements and potential of women were awe-inspiring and inspirational. There were women fixing scaffolding, climbing up lighting and sound rigs, wiring electrics; there were women laying gravel paths for wheelchair access, women driving forklifts and diggers. Even today, this would still be remarkable; maybe on their own these things don't sound that radical, but put all together in one place, where everywhere you looked there were huge structures and infrastructure installed and maintained by women; it was quite something. I would go so far as to say it was empowering, though I hate that term and the hollow buzzword it has come to be. MichFest, although not perfect, as nowhere is, was an example of women's power. Whatever people may think about the politics of the leadership of the festival, it was an example of women's power; and for hundreds of thousands of women it was a powerful experience. It was an intriguing and motivational snapshot of what women are capable of, not only in the physical building and maintenance, but in the constructing of community over those hot summer weeks – a whole city, up from the dust and earth, every year for forty years. Of course, many would say, and did argue fiercely, that what women are also capable of is constructing borders, recreating exclusions and inequalities, just like in the world outside the festival gates; and the most famous, and perhaps most final of these tremors, was the feminist faultline around the inclusion of trans women at the festival, and the inclusion of trans-identified people in general.

The expulsion

At the 1991 festival, festie Nancy Burkholder was attending her second MichFest with a friend, Laura Ervin; she stayed no longer than a day. As night fell, Nancy was asked to leave and was escorted off the site on the grounds that she had been identified as a trans woman, and because the land was reserved for 'natural', womyn-born womyn-only (Burkholder, 2013). Nancy responded that nowhere in the tickets or programme was there a rule that trans women were not allowed. She informed the festival officials that there had always been and was still other trans women at the festival; she asked the women who questioned her to go and confirm this stance with the festival directors, and, in an interview for the *TransAdvocate*, she reports that they went to ask the organizing team and came back to her to clarify that 'they had indeed verified that transsexuals were not allowed at the festival' (2013). It is not clear though that this was a unified or well-publicized view of all those involved in organizing the festival, let alone of all those attending. In an interview with Jocelyn Macdonald for the online lesbian/bi magazine *AfterEllen* in 2018, Lisa Vogel recalls that the woman in charge of security at the gate, who handled the incident and actually had to escort Burkholder off the site, did not agree with the womyn-born-womyn policy herself, 'but some womyn at the gate were bugging out about this womon's presence, this trans womon's presence. And one thing led to another' (Vogel, 2018). Vogel recounts that Burkholder's ticket was refunded, and she was accommodated in a nearby hotel that the festival used for artists who were performing. This incident drew public attention and hostility to the long-running, though loose, largely undefined and, until August 1991, unacted trans-exclusionary womyn-only policy of Michigan. It was the only time that the festival formally expelled a festie guest on the grounds of being a trans person.

Trans exclusion wasn't an agreed policy of the festival; it was not as if all festival attendees took a vote every year and came up with this stance and agreed it in a wombonly circle of decision-making consensus. As Vogel herself acknowledged, there was a diversity of views, among the festival workers and in the attendees; most people, she said, couldn't care less either way and were happy to overlook the issue and attend the festival without getting involved in the debate: 'I think people were all over the board. The Festival community is not monolithic. And nothing about the festival community demanded a certain adherence to a particular point of view to be whole within the community' (Vogel, 2018). In another first-hand interview from a different perspective, a friend of Nancy Burkholder's, radical lesbian feminist activist Janis Walworth recounts the events of 1991 and what followed. As soon as she found out what had happened to her friend, Walworth was determined to take action at the festival itself that year, to let everyone know that this had unfolded in their name, and to address this incident of exclusion. It is important to remember at this time that this was pre-internet and smartphone. News and messages had to be shared on large wooden message boards, with cards, marker pens and pins being the SMS of the day.

Walworth stated that most festie goers were completely unaware that a festie had been expelled, and that the great majority were unaware there was even any such policy to expel trans attendees, 'there apparently was a policy, which was never promulgated in any significant way. Although, the festival organizers apparently understood that the phrase "womyn-born-womyn" was meant to exclude trans women, other people didn't necessarily understand the meaning the festival gave to that phrase' (Walworth, 2014). One of the festival organizers had indeed publicly expressed concerns about trans inclusion in women's spaces much earlier however, several years before. An archived letter to a feminist newsletter called *Sister: West Coast Feminist Newspaper* (June–July) in 1977 addressed the women's music collective of Olivia Records and critiqued the collective for allowing a trans woman, Sandy Stone, to work with them as a sound engineer and producer, accusing the collective of hiding her identity, and expressing the view that many women in the women's music business would not want to work with her. The letter was signed by MichFest founder Lisa Vogel.

Growing out of the 1970s Second Wave Women's Liberation Movement in America and the burgeoning cultures of women-only organizing, lesbian feminism and separatist living, the festival sought to create a space in contrast to mainstream society, one where women could dance in the dark, sleep under the stars, sunbathe naked and flirt and have sex with other women, all with total freedom and validation, without the fear of reprisal, and without the fear of male violence (Morris, 1999). The women-only stance, logo or banner was then a key part of building this oppositional space, the spelling of women without the word 'men' – womyn – was itself an acknowledgement of this agenda and a signifier of lesbian and separatist feminism. As years went on though, and cultures changed, it is debatable whether most guests associated the Fest with particular kinds of feminist politics; for many women it was a women's outdoor music festival, and it was enjoyed and appreciated on that basis, without any sense of pressure to understand, let alone sign up to, certain niche kinds of politics. The 'womyn-born-womyn' label and name of the festival began as, and was, however, a political term, and a term that already assumed something of a degree of insider knowledge, a community of understanding and a shared sense of meaning around the title and the mission, for most of the regulars at least. Under scrutiny, however, and from outside the festival community – as well as within – the term came to be seen as an essentialist policing, and a cruel, transphobic reference to anatomy rather than politics.

The grounds of Camp Trans

Queer, gay and trans communities rallied around the initial publicized incident of Nancy's expulsion at Michigan, once people returned home and news began to be shared. For the remainder of the festival in 1991 meanwhile, Nancy's friends on site were doing their best to raise awareness about what had happened. Janis Walworth remembered going around The Land just telling everyone she met; she and Nancy had attended the festival the year before without any incident, and most people were appalled that a festie woman had been expelled and chucked off the site. As Walworth explained in an interview with Cristan Williams, 'I spent the rest of my time at that festival talking to people and just letting them know what had happened. And most people I talked to were horrified.' As soon as they got home, Walworth and the rest of Nancy's friends began raising awareness of the incident as much as they could: 'After the festival, we began a letter-writing campaign, writing gay newspapers and stuff like that, just to make sure that people knew' (2014). There was a small gathering outside the festival entrance the next year in 1992, and Walworth and her friends took literature on site to distribute and to display on information tables. Walworth wrote up and printed fliers about 'Gender Myths' with facts and corrections of misrepresentations about trans women. They stuck these up on the walls of portaloos and gave them out to festie attendees; they also created badges to give out, emblazoned with the slogan 'Friend of Nancy'. In 1992 Walworth and her friends also distributed a survey, to as many festies as they could, canvassing opinion on trans inclusion. In a 2014 interview for the *TransAdvocate*, she explains why she felt this was important: 'I felt like we could sit there and hand out literature all day, but we didn't really have any basis for doing a real protest without knowing what our support-base was' (Walworth, 2014). To the joy of feminist archivists everywhere, Walworth has kept her survey templates and the breakdown of responses for posterity and for feminist herstory. She reports that 633 responses were collected that year, with 73.1 per cent responding yes to trans inclusion and 22.6 per cent responding no; the remainder were not sure or did not answer the question.

In 1993 she and her friends returned to do similar, including several trans women in their group. However, they were eventually asked to leave the festival by security, allegedly for their own safety. Apparently, some responses to their presence had not been favourable, and they had agreed among themselves prior that if the festival asked them to leave, they would not resist. They had their camping equipment ready to go, and so they left and set up over the track from the festival entrance. Huge banners were painted and hung up, so that nobody coming or going from the festival would be able to miss them. Workshops were held and many festies came out from the site to attend them; festies also brought food, flowers, water and gifts to the camp. The next year, it was decided to return to the same spot, as it was so visible, across from the festival gates, and in 1994 Camp Trans was formally born. It emerged from the many queer movements that were just becoming strong at that time, in real space and then, later, in the new frontiers of cyberspace; and so, the battle lines between and within some queer and feminist circles, sketched out in the historic skirmishes in the 1970s, now crept into ever more aggressive and polarized positions. These positions then actually took up physical posts, turning the political debate into tangible, tactical territories, as queer activists, in a fine and tested tradition of civil disobedience, took their opposition to the very gates and established Camp Trans in protest, almost right opposite the entrance to MichFest.

Camp Trans for humyn born humyns

It was in 1994 that writer and activist Riki Anne Wilchins thought up the name Camp Trans, and nearly thirty people of all ages pitched up on public camping ground near Vogel's land, along with other high-profile writers and activists, including Leslie Feinberg and Minnie Bruce Pratt. Camp Trans sought to inform festies of the exclusionary entrance policy and protest at the transphobia of the womyn-born-womyn stance. Their banner along the front of their camp read – For humyns-born-humyns. Janis Walworth and her friends continued their awareness raising work on The Land too, attending workshops inside the festival. They were regularly escorted and provided with security by groups of Lesbian Avengers and also leather dykes from the Twilight Zone camping area. The Lesbian Avengers founded in America in 1992, taking a direct action approach to campaigning for LGBTQI+ human rights and inspired by the grassroots activism of gay liberation campaigns like ACT-UP; they put lesbians and lesbian concerns to the forefront, in a wider gay community where women often felt sidelined. I would suggest that it is no coincidence that support for Walworth and her friends at the opposite camp came from these quarters, given the history of the so-called lesbian sex wars.

The 'sex-wars' is a simplistic term used to describe a faultline in lesbian and feminist communities between those who theorized sexual practices such as femme-butch relationships, BDSM and the production of lesbian pornography as sexist and patriarchal and those who were seeking to create and celebrate these emerging cultures and communities. Much lesbian feminist theory as well as Radical Feminist theory and activism was profoundly against femme-butch sexuality, as I have already introduced in earlier chapters. These schools of feminist theorizing were also against sadomasochistic sexual practices; indeed they often even suggested that femme-butch identities and relationships are inherently perverse and sadomasochistic. These particular groups of sexual outlaws were therefore used to being constructed as deviant and were well versed in navigating exclusion and opposition, within lesbian communities and spaces. The presence of groups and individuals openly into practising BDSM was not universally supported at festival, for example (Kaplan, 1996). Although, I would point out that Walworth's memories of Lesbian Avengers and leather dykes walking protestors around The Land demonstrate that Lesbian Avengers and leather dykes were present and established at the Fest, I suggest that this only further indicates the diversity and complexity of the MichFest community. The situation was far more nuanced than a simple one side against the other, even though the two camps were literally pitched that way physically. For example, contained within MichFest was The Twilight Zone campground, known for public sex and BDSM. Although, its location itself was a physical representation of its outsider and outlander status, it was separated off from other camping grounds, partly because it was often loud and partly because it was not suitable for children or younger guests. It is interesting that this particular feminist faultline was accommodated on The Land, despite tensions and differing views among festies on BDSM in lesbian communities. Workshops were held annually on safer sex and consent, including in consensual BDSM sexual practices, and these were not kept secret but were included in printed festival programmes.

When it came to Camp Trans, from the early days the MichFest organizers and MichFest collective members, and Vogel herself, seem to have responded and debated numerous times with Camp Trans. This apparently included taking part in workshops and generally, on occasions, a mutual and usually respectful dialogue did appear to be beginning to be established, and maybe it would have grown – though MichFest did not revoke its womyn-born-womyn policy. Vogel reported as much herself, remembering that people went back and forth and that nobody was denied entry, 'everybody from Camp Trans came in. My partner of 20 years was in that group that came across the road, so I know first-hand from her too. Now, that part of the story is never told. No one says, "they didn't stop us from coming in". No one bothers to mention that' (Vogel, 2018). It appears then, according to varying reports, that there was a to and fro between attendees at both camps, Camp Trans and The Land, with guests from both attending workshops at the other site and seemingly trying to listen to each other and understand concerns on both sides of the track.

Michigan and the queering of gender

Over the following years, Camp Trans grew, running until 2012 and becoming a symbol and focal point for the wider and burgeoning trans rights and liberation movements. The Michigan festival itself became singled out for protest, with artists and guests being encouraged to boycott the event and musicians and LGBTQ organizations signing public petitions against it, for example, through an organized boycott titled Equality Michigan. To this day, Michigan is still shorthand for feminist trans exclusion and remains an important symbol for the presumed and protested natural transphobic tendencies in feminism, and specifically the feminism of previous generations. Michigan is often held up to justify attacks and blanket dismissal of such generations. Yet the queer and feminist work those generations did there to blaze a trail for so much that came after has left a legacy that I would argue all of us benefit from. Writing in the *New York Times*, feminist theorist Dr Sophie Lewis identified MichFest as a specifically TERF festival and celebrated its extinction. 'In America, however, TERFism today is a scattered community in its death throes, mourning the loss of its last spaces, like the Michigan Womyn's Music Festival, which ended in 2015' (Lewis, 2019). MichFest intermittently released public statements clarifying that women of many and varied gender identities had always attended and continued to attend the festival. Reflecting on the journey of the festival and the attacks it received, Vogel pointed to this diversity:

'It's made up of everybody, just everybody. But they overlooked the radically inclusive community. Because they don't care about the radical gender expression of womyn. Michigan was the most radically diverse group of womyn that you could find in one space' (Vogel, 2018).

Lisa Vogel argued that the festival was not popular in mainstream LGBT fields anyway, not at any point, even before it became a focus for protest against trans exclusion; because it was seen as an embarrassment she suggests, as a hangover from 1970s Women's Lib, and as old and grey as the women who presumably attended. Vogel also notes that gay male communities were regularly exclusive in their events, with no protest in return, 'all kinds of things happen within the gay male community that is exclusive of trans people, that is exclusive of womyn, that is exclusive of, for example, anyone except bears. They have complete autonomy of whoever they want to include' (Vogel, 2018). Regular events at MichFest testify to the gender diversity on display, and included communal festivities such as the annual Butch Strut for example, seen as a carnival of female masculinities (Browne, 2009). Trans men at various stages of medical, hormonal or social transition also attended the festival; some of these testimonies are recorded in valuable, herstorical archives collected first hand by Geographer Kath Browne, at the 2006 festival. 'As trans men, butch lesbian identities and other expressions of female "masculinities" are part of Michfest's past and present. . . . To exclude trans men would be unthinkable for many' (Browne, 2009: 550).

My own memories of the festival, years before Browne's research, also contain many meetings with transmasculine people and trans men, as well as festies with beards, festies with top surgery; I would assert that festies who identified as trans were not a rarity, even then. As my friend and I queued at and then entered the festival gates in 1998, nobody asked us how we defined our sex, currently or in the past, I can recall no signs stating conditions of entry and we were not given any paperwork clarifying who was welcome and who was not. As festie virgins we were taken to an orientation tent and shown a video which covered practicalities, such as maps and car parking procedures. The video mainly informed us about the different camp sites available to choose from, and their diverse flavours so to speak, from quiet family areas, to the secluded BDSM party zones where one should be prepared for an anything goes ethos. I remember nothing in that orientation session about what type of women should attend and what type of women should turn around and go.

This point was made regularly in public statements by Vogel and the MichFest collective themselves, which can be read as pleas to the queer community to politically support the womyn-only stance. In a 2006 press release from Vogel, for example, cited by Browne (2009), there is a call to 'sisters in struggle', and a request to 'the transwomen's community to meditate upon, recognise and respect the differences in our shared experiences and our group identities even as we stand shoulder to shoulder as women, and as members of the greater queer community' (2009: 548). Statements such as this confirmed that only womyn were welcome; those who understood this meaning and lived that meaning were asked to honour it, for one week of the year and allow the space to be created and to thrive. The festival collective and production company, We Want the Music (WWTM), asserted time and again that nobody would be judged at entry, let alone frisked or asked to display their genitals or produce a birth record in order to prove their sex. Recalling this, in 2018 in a letter to a UK organizer of the Queer Up North festival, Vogel insisted again:

> I can say with certainty that we did not at any point attempt to ascertain who was or was not a natal woman. . . . We did say and meant that our intention was to create a safe space focussed on womyn who were born womyn, who experienced a girlhood (in all of our diversity), and who still lived their lives identified as a woman. . . . The onus was then up to anyone to decide how to support and respect that intention. (2018)

In another interview that same year in *AfterEllen*, Vogel reiterated that everyone was well aware that trans people had always attended the festival, 'we do not question anyone's gender. We are well aware that trans women and trans men attend the event, and they attend as supporters, not detractors of the female-centred space' (Vogel, 2018). However, over the years this was all interpreted by many Camp Trans activists and allies as simply a form of reactionary don't ask, don't tell policy, similar to that much critiqued policy in operation at that time in the US military and applying to lesbian, gay and bisexual recruits: 'Despite the fraught arguments that (re)create womyn, entry to Michfest is not policed. Respect is requested but nobody is asked about their sexed herstory as a condition of attendance at the festival. Rather many trans activists claim that Michigan operates a "don't ask, don't tell policy"' (Browne, 2009: 544).

The penis invasion

Then, in 1999 an alleged incident occurred which further soured whatever fragile attempts at dialogue may have or could have been budding and unfolding. Protestors from Camp Trans apparently entered the MichFest site, aiming to raise issues in workshops which took place as part of the festival; these were on many and numerous subjects from safe sex to star signs. As part of their presence-making protest they used the communal showers; these are outdoor shower stands, where festies shower naked together; indeed public nudity is so common at Michigan as to be almost a prerequisite for attendance. These protestors have been described in accounts of that year, as being one post-operative trans man and one pre-operative trans woman among others, including some teenage protestors. Allegations of such protests, their intent and methods, as well as suggestions of sabotage and intimidation carried out by Camp Trans protestors, it should be noted, are disputed and denied by other accounts. Some of the responses from festies on site were allegedly violent and threatening to the young protestors (Williams, 2020). In the folklore of this particular event, regardless of how the individuals involved identified themselves or who else was in that group of protestors, or how it even happened or unfolded, what has got widely reported from this incident, and become received history, is that there was a 'penis protest' on The Land, that is, the MichFest site. This incident is often referred to in literature surrounding Michigan as 'the invasion' (Mantilla, 2000; WWTM/Vogel press release, 1999). 'The display of a penis in the female showers problematically perpetuated the association of all trans people (men and women) with what is read as a male embodiment, the penis. Such an invasion runs counter to the Michfest (feminist) ethos of communal living, safety and celebrations of female embodiments' (Browne, 2009: 549).

Some festies complained to workers and asked for complaints to be lodged with the WWTM Collective formally; news of the protest quickly spread around the festival, and many felt that the principle of safe women's space had been wilfully breached (camptrans.com, 2000). Writing the next year in the feminist magazine *Off Our Backs*, Karla Mantilla upholds that such an action breached women's safe space and also displayed an ignorance around why that safe space is so important to many women. She asserts that if the protestors 'had any real understanding of what it is to be a woman in patriarchy they would have respected, not violated, women's space, and they would have understood what a horrific violation it would be for a woman to be confronted with a strange naked biological male, penis and all, when she herself is unclothed and vulnerable' (Mantilla, 2000: 5). In an interview with Ricki Anne Wilchins, discussing this incident, published on the, no longer live, CampTrans2000 website, Wilchins expressed surprise and alarm at the reaction from some festival attendees. Linking this to what she sees as aggressive man-hating elements at MichFest, she remarks that 'the big uproar from the separatists was that there were "penises on the land"' (camptrans .com, 2000). She then explains how the men from the portaloo company are treated when they have to access the festival to service those facilities, noting, 'there is that much hostility towards men in some parts of the festival' (camptrans.com, 2000). The male sanitary staff entered on the back of flatbed lorries and were escorted from each portaloo location by a festie worker, who walked slowly in front of the lorry while ringing a bell shouting loudly: 'men on the land'. This practice was to alert festies to the presence of men on The Land, so that those attendees who did not want to see, or come into contact with men while they were at the festival, did not have to. I remember witnessing this myself, waiting to cross one of the dusty tracks and observing the bemused and, it seemed to me, rather alarmed faces of the men sitting on the back of the truck watching the scenes of the festival slowly unfold before them.

Wilchins's take on this does seem a rather unfair and reductionist account of attendee's reaction to the naked protest conducted by people with penises; however those individuals protesting may have identified themselves. First, it is not possible to know whether those festies who complained even identified as separatists; as I have discussed elsewhere in this book, separatism is a political stance, with a long and bold history and, arguably, should not be used as some kind of throwaway insult or assumed to be a slur. Second, those attending the festival elect to do so, knowing and perhaps because the entire event is women-only; it could be the case that those attendees were not expecting, nor amenable to seeing, people with penises naked in communal showers. This doesn't necessarily mean that people with all sorts of bodies had not long been attending the Fest. We must remember that trans men, queer festies and trans women had long been attending Michigan anyway, with no such penis protests being recorded at any other time, until this particular alleged incursion by Camp Trans. It could be the case that trans women attending Michigan prior were mainly post-operative trans women (acknowledging that, in the United States in particular, this would be a minority of women able to afford surgery and recovery), or that trans women and trans men, fully aware of the controversy surrounding entry policies, and aware of the ethos of the festival, chose not to join in the frequent public nakedness that defined the festival site. As tensions grew, any such individuals on The Land may also have chosen not to do so for fear of drawing attention to themselves, suggesting that for such guests the site was not exactly a safe and liberating space. Non-sex and gender-normative people are sadly used to having to hide ourselves, to risk assess before simple activities like going to the toilet or buying clothes in a store. It is ironic, perhaps, that MichFest advertised and prided itself on being one rare site where this would not happen; yet we could assume that over the years, guests with bodies that were not recognizably sexed as female may well have been covering up. It is also the case that when people understand they are different from the majority, they are often not exactly clamouring to put themselves forward and into the spotlight, precisely because of the hostile scrutiny and responses often received.

Michigan and safe space

It must also be acknowledged that MichFest was nevertheless a liberating place for many, arguably the majority of attendees, and was a special, almost sacred site, felt and experienced by many attendees, in all their diversity, to be a place of healing, recovery and re-empowerment. There were numerous events and workshops, for example, for womyn who had survived domestic abuse, rape, sexual assault and other forms of male sexual violence against women. There were workshops on rejoicing in female bodies and genitalia, understanding and nurturing female bodies, how to rebuild sexuality and sex after abuse and much more. For those womyn survivors, the forms of violence that they experienced were often perpetrated against them by men with sexed as male bodies, men who chose to use their penises to harm them and violate their sexed as female bodies and their bodily integrity. It was not those festie womyn who constructed the penis as a weapon in some abstract sense or out of an ideological commitment to lesbian feminist separatism. It was the choice of men who committed criminal acts of violence to use their bodies as a threat and a weapon, against women – women who then saw and used MichFest as one place of healing and emboldening recovery from those particular forms of violence. It should not need saying that those men who choose to rape and abuse have weaponized the penis, not feminists; and they are supported by foundational societal systems and millennia of religious and philosophical myth which represents men as all-powerful and uses the phallus as a symbol of that power, dominance and aggression. Yet it does seem to need saying. It is sadly and surely understandable why some women may not want to be around men, or those people they perceive as male bodied, as long as male violence remains at the horrific levels at which it stands.

I have addressed this issue at several different points in this book, and many of the tensions that play out on the turf of the gender wars come back to the meaning of sexed as male bodies. The lesbian feminism of places like Michigan was part of a movement of activism to reduce and respond to male sexual violence against women. In the face of such an institutionalized and normalized occurrence, the statistics and the body count have tragically not reduced at all, and thus the activism continues. Many sections of feminism, especially newer generations, are using and building now on the legacy of feminist and queer theory and activism to reformulate meanings of sex, gender and sexuality, to broaden and open up that movement and to aim their fire at sex/gender conformity more fully. This is admirable and has great potential. Meanwhile, however, as we have not yet achieved the feminist revolution, for too many people the male body continues to have specific meanings, and it means threat and violence. This will be difficult to change as long as it remains reality for so many women and children.

Trans-inclusive womyn's space

The collaboration of lesbian feminist politics and dyke culture is, however, clearly not incompatible with trans inclusion, when an open and honest policy and leadership is taken from the start. This was in fact happening alongside MichFest, often with the same people taking part as guests, managers, performers and workers. One musician who performed at MichFest went on to set up her own trans-inclusive music festival for example, Radical Feminist and lesbian Robin Tyler. Robin acknowledged the sensitivities involved and the lesbian separatist herstory behind exclusion at MichFest and places like it. She reinforced that Michigan was a place for survivors of sexual violence and was known for being so, and said she understood that people were therefore sometimes sensitive about who was included, but she believed that safe spaces could still be built and people could learn together and overcome differences of all kinds: 'I understand people being victimized and sexually abused. . . . For all people – trans or not – the idea is that we're working on getting better. These places are about getting better. We have to work on getting better so that we don't oppress other people' (2016).

Of course, it could be countered that survivors of male violence have plenty of work to do the rest of the time, out in the real world, and that if people want to seek out a place for female-bodied people only, once a year, they should be able to have that option. There is also a question mark over why survivors should be called upon to do this sort of personal growth and work around the borders of womankind and the bodily morphologies that can be included within. There is also, arguably, a question mark over whether a gated, outdoor music festival is the right space in which to do that work challenging borders, particularly at a festival with a rare history of being womyn-only and womyn-centred, which almost all other events were not. However, Tyler recounts how the West Coast Women's Festival which she organized, and which was regularly attended by around 3,000 women, also had workshops for survivors and that these were held without ever having any complaints or concerns being raised about the festival space being trans-inclusive. As leaders and producers, the organizing team were clear from the start that the space was trans-inclusive; they personally introduced and welcomed trans women working on the team, pointing out their contributions, and all of this seemed to set the tone, with guests apparently not really seeing it as an issue. Another organizer from that particular festival, a Radical Feminist Dyke, Jan Osborn, confirms this, stating that the trans-inclusive stance was not an issue for them, and that they had many women attending who attended MichFest as well, plus workers on the crew who also worked at both festivals. This indicates that for many festie women, the idea of a trans-inclusive festival was not a problem personally, and it suggests something about the culture and leadership of Michigan in particular, that made an active choice to take the trans-exclusionary stance and then stick to it.

Jan Osborn emphasized the importance of reflecting on the different backgrounds of all women, and the varying levels of power and privilege that exist between all women:

> we ALL have privilege in some areas and are oppressed in others. Okay, so some trans women spent time trying to live as men before they transitioned and maybe they benefited from male privilege, but that isn't any reason to discriminate against trans women. It's just another way that we have to be conscious about the privilege we might have. I mean, I'm white and that means that I need to conscious of that privilege. (2016)

MichFest itself, although diverse, was still predominantly a White festival, and The Land included a Women of Colour stage and area, clearly designated for Women of Colour only. This space was to acknowledge the need for some room that was not White dominated, in a country and society scarred by White supremacy. This did not solve racism at the festival, nor could it of course; Lisa Vogel actually recalled how problematic it was that many White women attended who never, in the rest of their lives, socialized with any Black women at all and were suspicious of Black lesbian women in particular. Talking about gender diversity at festival, she noted that White women were often more likely to report studs or butch Black lesbian women to festival stewards and insinuate that they must be trans or that they must be a man on The Land.

> And white womyn were not used to being around a diversity of black womyn. So much so that when I was approached, my first question would be, 'what is the person's skin colour?', and then, if they said black, I wouldn't even bother taking it any further, I'd just say, 'sister, you know, I think you need to check yourself.' (Vogel, 2018)

The existence of the Women of Colour space illustrates another feminist faultline that was accommodated at Michigan, in addition to the faultline rippling out from the lesbian sex wars. This was, of course, the conflict around racism in the women's movement and the often lacklustre response from feminism as a whole in addressing its own complicity in this societal inequality. This is just one example of what feminist political scientist Professor Mieke Verloo calls the interfering inequalities – the structural inequalities that pervade the very social justice movements that are trying to eradicate them. Author and academic Emi Koyama (2006) in an essay on the unspoken racism of the trans-inclusion debate also highlights the presence of the Womyn of

Colour space at festival, outlining differing views from the festie community on what this model might mean for the possibility of trans inclusion. For some this simply raised the question of why such a space couldn't similarly be provided for festies who wanted a female-born or womyn-born-womyn room to breathe, without then defining, delineating and limiting the life histories of all women welcome on all of The Land in general. However, a key difference here is that the Womyn of Colour tent provides sanctuary from the Whiteness and racism of the festival site as a whole; there are inequalities between women on the grounds of racism, and all White women benefit from racial privilege simply because we are White. In order to argue for trans-exclusionary protected space on similar grounds, non-trans festies would need to argue that they were structurally oppressed by trans women and thus needed room to breathe for once, in a context of institutionalized supremacy of trans women. Such a situation is, of course, fiction. If that model and line of argument was to be taken forward though, it would have perhaps made more sense to have such a space set aside on The Land for trans women, who could self-organize and recuperate, acknowledging that not everyone on the festival site was an ally. Then the festival as a whole could have been open to all women, including trans women; but, as we know, that did not happen and the trans-exclusive policy persisted, even as the boycotts grew louder and larger.

The norming of MichFest

Another complaint from some MichFest workers and attendees was that the existence of Camp Trans and the way it presented itself in contrast to Michigan, by default constructed those within the festival gates as gender normative. As I have stated earlier, this was refuted by many attendees and in many reflections and accounts of the Fest, who all recounted the gender and body diversity on display every year. In 2018 Lisa Vogel emphasized the importance of Michigan in showcasing women in all their diversity: 'I can't tell you the hundreds of letters I read over the years of women saying, "I never felt comfortable with my appearance until Michigan." And that's simply because we saw the diversity of womyn' (2018). In a 2001 article titled 'Sex, Lies and Feminism' Croson argues that Camp Trans attempted to position itself as radical by positioning MichFest as conservative. From my own personal archives, the advert for Camp Trans 1999, for example, referred to the Michigan festival womyn as 'gender police' and ended with a call to join Camp Trans instead and to 'Be there or be square. Or maybe just gender-normative' (camptrans.com.1999). Croson argues that in this sort of framing, only the individuals at Camp Trans are allowed to be gender different or gender minorities, erasing the rainbow of diversity that had become a defining feature of MichFest. 'Transgender activists claim they are "gender" minorities within the presumptively "gender normal" women who attend Festival. . . . If such adherence to norms existed as a regular practice, every woman would be heterosexual, married and having babies' (Croson, 2001: 6).

At the 1999 MichFest, organizers actually distributed a statement to festies in attendance, reminding attendees that gender diversity was a feature of the festival and should not be questioned. Like everything, this particular issue was also raced, as in the aforementioned example, where Vogel recounts how Black lesbian butches or studs were more likely to be questioned by White women and reported to festival stewards.

> It was really clear that here we were; we had this womyn-only space and womyn were getting confused – if they didn't know butch womyn or bearded womyn or black womyn, then they were IDing sisters as men. And so really our original focus on this started out as: we don't want here to be any place where a woman is questioned. Cuz we're questioned about our womonhood all the time. I mean, I'm a butch womon; I've been questioned. (Vogel, 2018)

The fact that by 1999 the festival had to start giving out reminders to festie attendees not to question other guests about their gender diversity or gender diverse appearance indicates perhaps how toxic relationships had become with Camp Trans across the road. It was unfortunate that, because of the festival boycott and the continuing protests of Camp Trans and growing awareness about this conflict, suspicions were raised on The Land, which then ironically made it even harder for gender diverse festies to relax and enjoy the space as they had in the past. No doubt used to being scrutinized and questioned about their sex and gender in the mainstream, non-gender-conforming festies now had to contend with such questioning on The Land too, as suspicions festered. Mantilla gives us an insight into this culture of suspicion: 'One of the most important things women get from going to Michigan is the feeling of complete safety from men and patriarchal rape culture. Now that safety has been eroded. Now, even if a man isn't there, there in our minds is the possibility of violation – that a male could be there' (2000: 5). In the statement distributed at festival to attendees in 1999 with the warning about questioning others, Vogel urged that 'Michigan must remain a space that recognises and celebrates the full range of what it means to be a womon-born woman. Butch/gender ambiguous womyn should be able to move about our community with confidence that their right to be here will not be questioned' (1999).

Gender diverse attendees were also apt to be suspected of being protestors with Camp Trans. At the 2000 MichFest, there were protests again as Camp Trans brought its resistance onto the site. It is reported that eight young queer activists were evicted from MichFest after standing up one evening in the packed dining tent and holding aloft signs declaring their various identities as boy, FTM, trannieboy, boydyke and intersex for example (CampTrans2000). By 2000 Camp Trans had renamed itself GenderCamp2000 and then press released that hundreds of MichFest attendees stood with these eight young protestors for over an hour, until festival security had to be called to break up the protest and expel the activists. Quoted in the press release that I have saved in my own archives from GenderCamp is one activist noting that the entrance policy for MichFest was not only unfair but also unrealistic and outdated as, they suggest, many people on The Land would not be able to honestly define themselves as a womyn-born-womyn anyway. Acknowledging and accepting the gender diversity of a large proportion of MichFest attendees, but using this to discredit the entrance policy, the activist asserts: 'Half the women in there are butch, boy, or FTM identified and wouldn't be able to say they were 'womyn-born womyn' if asked' (CampTrans2000).

Michigan for women in all their genders

In 2018, in a letter responding to an article about the Queer Up North Festival in Manchester, England, UK, Vogel maintained and emphasized yet again that gender diversity was valued at MichFest. She wrote: 'The festival had the broadest spectrum of gender presentation of womyn you could find anywhere on the planet, and for all the gender variant sisters run out of bathrooms and cursed in the street, we were adamant that no one's gender would be questioned on the land' (Vogel, 2018). Accounts such as these were fired back and forth across the access road separating Camp Trans from MichFest throughout the late 1990s and into the early years of the new millennium. Over this time, artists who performed there were boycotted and critiqued; and several went public about refusing invites on the grounds that the festival was transphobic, including the long-running festival fixtures the Indigo Girls in 2014. As Vogel noted in 2018, Michigan became widely seen as 'the ground zero of terfdom', and even the tens of thousands of diverse festies who attended could not dent that epidemic narrative. In 2015 the festival finally closed; Vogel herself was ready to leave, and the festival was becoming more and more expensive to run and the negative attention was just one thorn in the side within a changing climate, with demand for more mainstream and corporate events the norm. Big corporates wouldn't sponsor a lesbian-feminist-themed festival and nor were the festival organizers interested in courting such support; they wanted to be able to keep the festival running in the way it had always been, but increasingly found this was not possible. 'Michigan was one of the few iconic, steeped-in-radical-feminism organizations that still existed after forty years. Still committed to maintaining the same value system always. A lot of folks may have morphed into something that mimicked the mainstream ways of doing things and I was never interested to do that' (Vogel, 2018).

Michigan and the future of The Land

In 2017 a non-profit organization in Michigan secured federal status as a charity. We Want The Land Coalition (WWTLC) – a nod to the name of the business that ran MichFest: WWTM – raised funds to make an initial down payment and buy The Land, for $1,500,000 in April 2017, when Lisa Vogel finally sold the 651 acre site of the former festival. The coalition will pay the purchase price off in instalments, contracted to 2025, during which time Vogel will still be the formal real estate owner. Having shouldered the costs, personal and financial, underwriting insurance, laying out infrastructure investment for sewerage, water and power to the site, haggling with Shell Oil to drive a hard bargain for gas rights under the land and being ultimately responsible for the bottom line at Michigan for decades, Vogel could have perhaps sold the site on the open market for much more. In 2016 Vogel noted in an online forum discussing the fundraising for the site, that she estimated it could fetch upwards of three million dollars. It was not uncontroversial that Lisa was selling the land, or that she was entertaining the option of selling it to a private investor, but she gave WWTLC an extended time period to raise the money; she worked to ensure a conservation easement for the site protecting it from commercial development, and she helped to organize fundraisers for the WWTL Collective herself. These efforts of the community then paid off, securing the land for women and girls into the future. The new collective made The Land available and open for events from Autumn 2019, running various fundraising activities to make their regular payments, such as their Be The We campaign, involving womyn setting up giving circles and organizing social events that publicize and raise money to secure The Land. On their website, WWTLC state that all women and all women's groups will be welcome to hire the land for their own private events. They clarify that they will not define who is and who is not a woman, and that the land is available to all women, including trans women:

> WWTLC's vision is that opportunities exist for all kinds of events to occur on The Land, with all kinds of definitions and intentions, including explicitly biologically female-only events; explicitly transwoman-only events; and others. WWTLC will not define or determine who is female, woman, or girl with regard to who participates in or hosts events on The Land. Rather, our mission is to hold space for the possibility of gatherings and events for women and girls which exemplify all of the differing philosophies and definitions held passionately by our community. (WWLTC, 2018)

In 2020 the events offered on The Land ranged from a sobriety healing week in the woods to a mystical womxn's magical festival.

Perhaps this is a fitting end to the MichFest story, an ending that is also a beginning. This new beginning takes its departure point from a complicated and tumultuous stance, one that had tried to define the parameters of womyn, and now it starts afresh. In conclusion, I admire Lisa Vogel and the team for keeping their festival going; organizing such an event is certainly no mean feat. It is no exaggeration to say it was life changing and life saving for many women. It was an earthly embodiment of certain feminist tendencies, lesbian feminist and separatist feminist tendencies. Controversial though they always were, for different reasons, and as even more controversial as they became in more recent years, these are nevertheless significant and influential strands of feminist thought, history and activism. They are motivations that made things happen, that set up refuges, that started helplines, that ran shelters, that bought land and built world famous music festivals for women, giving jobs, careers, qualifications, promotion and experience to women in so many male-dominated areas. Those politics have a place, and they had a place in Michigan. In the various interviews and letters and press releases from Vogel and the collective, it always seems like they were happy to point out and emphasize the reality of sex and gender diversity on The Land. They acknowledged that trans men regularly attended and that trans women often attended too, and that this was all enveloped into the labrys tattooed bosom of the festival community, while still, on the face of it, maintaining a spiritual commitment to, and centring womyn-born-womyn, meaning women sexed as female from birth. As they themselves therefore seemed to be insisting, the attendance of trans men, queer-identified people and a minority of trans women guests did not detract from the ethos of the festival, the vibe or the sense of belonging and ownership for those who valued and came back for the lesbian feminist tradition of it all. The question I have to ponder on is whether it would have been so terrible then to just quietly change the policy and formalize that attendees could define womanhood for themselves, as long as they respected the traditions the festival came from and could hold and honour that for that one long weekend. On the other hand, it was a privately run music festival, which was a full-time job to bring into being every year, and, as trans exclusion is indeed one strand within lesbian feminist and separatist history, if the organizers wanted it to stay that way that was of course their prerogative. As I have argued elsewhere in this book, self-organization is a political right; if women assigned as female from birth want to organize and run their own festival once a year, I do believe that is their right.

Personally, I was just as excited and inspired by Camp Trans as by MichFest, not least at the founding involvement of Leslie Feinberg, who has long been a hero of mine. As I spelled out at the start and have returned to frequently in this book, feminist and trans liberation is not reducible to two warring camps – not even when they are under canvas, and literally at two camps! There is much in common, and many individuals in common, who have skin and soul in both sides. I recognized many of my own people, so to speak, both at Camp Trans and at Michigan as well; but I did not, and still cannot, agree with the politics of trying to shut down the MichFest festival. Lesbians and lesbian feminists were never the all-powerful baddies they are portrayed as, and are hardly a powerful group in society, nor do they dominate space, media or culture anywhere in the world and never have. They are under attack from the very same forces that attack trans and queer people, from conservative states, nationalist governments, pro-natalist fascism, religions and the misogynistic and homophobic right-wing. Feminism generally, and in particular any kind of Radical Feminism, let alone lesbian feminism, was, even at the height of MichFest, unrepresented in mainstream culture. Over the decades that the festival ran, lesbian feminists were witnessing their herstoric web of womyn's bookshops, businesses and music labels disappearing; I did not support trying to erase yet another key part of that lesbian feminist legacy. While I clearly do not agree with much of the theory of lesbian feminism, and I was uncomfortable personally about the stance of trans exclusion, MichFest was a tradition for certain strands of feminism, and I do not think there is much to be gained from speeding or celebrating the extinction of our predecessors, to which many of us owe a debt. However, now that particular era has ended, for many reasons. The new beginning stakes a claim to this piece of land, a claim that stands firm on fluid borders, a claim that solidifies the natural topography of difference and diversity. Whether this will heal those rifts and fractures that map across this corner of America remains to be seen. Undoubtedly, the legacy of MichFest is one that should be honoured, and there would be no better way to keep it alive than with the continued, everlasting presence of all the diverse communities that make up and give meaning to this label of womankind.

This chapter has explored the roots of some of the feminist tensions around the definitions of sex and gender. It should be clear that these are not just abstract debates; they are not a product of naval-gazing in privileged feminist spaces. These feminist faultlines have impacted the creation of feminist infrastructure, spaces, communities and movements. They have split feminist groups, events and sadly, friendships; and they are still doing so. Now that I have covered some of this history, from Janice Raymond's infamous book, and the beginnings of trans-exclusionary lesbian feminism in the Second Wave, to the demise of MichFest, I will now focus on how these struggles are playing out today. The theory of lesbian feminism, lesbian separatism and perhaps some elements of cultural feminism can arguably be seen today in some of the GC and gender-abolitionist battles against trans inclusion. In Chapter 4 I will explore just what these terms mean and the differences between them.

4

Abolition and the critical turn

Critiquing gender-critical feminism

On and off social media, it is not uncommon for people who are critical of trans inclusion to refer to themselves as 'gender critical' or 'GC'. This term has grown up in the conflict of the gender wars; it is a term that would probably not have been used by feminist activists of the Second Wave, perhaps because it didn't need saying. Most feminist theory then, particularly Radical Feminism, was inherently gender-critical, and assumed to be so, because it critiqued stifling gender norms for women and set to work at taking these apart, in every area of life from pay packets to trouser pockets. Radical Feminism in particular was committed to critiquing gender because a primary tenet of that school of feminism was that gender, as in masculinity or femininity, is not biological but is a social construction used to impose and enforce sex rank. This position was outlined earlier in Chapter 2. From approximately the late 1960s and into the 1980s, across Western democracies the WLM of the Second Wave took on, tackled and trashed laws and policies which actively discriminated against women because they were women. The Second Wave WLM brought an end to laws that had made discrimination against women legal, in employment, property ownership and financial autonomy, for example. Later on in that truly revolutionary period, there was a term used in the women's movement that was similar to today's 'gender critical', but arguably not with exactly the same meanings – that term was 'gender abolitionist'. This latter term has made a bit of a comeback too, but gender critical or GC is much more often used today and is probably more well known in the context of the current gender wars. GC is a term and a self-descriptor that activists will use for themselves; it is not a term put onto them, unlike the widely popular label, TERF.

What is gender critical?

GC politics have been in the mainstream press in the UK and many other countries for several years now, particularly since coordinated mobilizations against proposals by the UK government to liberalize the Gender Recognition Act 2004; these mobilizations emerged around the public consultation on this matter in 2018. The Conservative government, under Theresa May who was prime minister from 2016 to 2019, pledged their commitment in 2017 to remove unnecessary bureaucratic barriers and intrusive checkpoints from the legal Gender Recognition process set out in the current 2004 Act. Being trans was not an illness the government pointed out, and reiterated that it should no longer be seen as such, seeking to de-medicalize the process and allow individuals to apply for a Gender Recognition Certificate without the need for any medical diagnosis, meaning that individuals would self-certify that they are a trans man or trans woman. Several other countries have a process allowing individuals to transition without a medical diagnosis of gender dysphoria, such as by legal statutory declaration, in Ireland (2015), Portugal (2018) and Norway (2016), for example (Zanghellini, 2020). A public consultation on reform began in the UK on 3 July 2018 and was concluded with the Westminster government's response in September 2020. Many new groups were formed to mobilize against what they called self-ID being brought into any new legal Gender Recognition Act – groups such as Fair Play for Women, Standing for Women, Women's Place UK and We Need to Talk.

There were suggestions in the public consultation on the 2004 Act that concerned removing the need for a medical diagnosis of gender dysphoria as a requirement to legal recognition as a trans man or trans woman; but there was no discrete question on whether respondents were for or against 'self-ID' (King et al., 2020). Opponents saw any such changes as creating a free-for-all where individuals could change their legal sex classification on a whim, and then change back again. Opponents feared that men with criminal intentions against women and children would change their legal sex to female in order to access single-sex spaces to perpetrate sexual violence, and then simply change back again. Other fears were that men who had a sexual fetish about inhabiting women's private spaces would transition in order to permanently inhabit those spaces. Relaxation to the criteria for medical diagnosis and evidence of living as a trans man or trans woman for at least two years, which was bizarrely called the 'real-life test', all of which is judged by an anonymous gender recognition panel, was seen by many as simply giving a green light to predators. Opponents to liberalizing the 2004 Act stated that even if a change to self-ID did not result in numbers of predators manipulating the law, it may make it legally impossible to bar or question anyone who might be a man in women-only space, effectively removing the right to women-only single-sex spaces, making them default unisex and making them unsafe in general.

As it stands, places like clothing store changing rooms and public toilets are not policed; trans women and trans men are understood to be able to use the spaces that align with how they identify, and being a trans man or trans woman is a legally protected characteristic in the Equality Act 2010 under gender reassignment. The Code of Practice alongside the act suggests that in the provision of goods and services, trans men and trans women should be treated as the gender (it means sex) they have transitioned to. In the Equality Act, gender reassignment (unfortunately legal and policy terms often conflate gender and sex) is one of the nine protected characteristics; this protection begins as soon as an individual announces they are intending to transition, socially, legally, medically or however they choose. There is actually no requirement to have had any medical intervention. It is illegal to discriminate against someone on the grounds that they are pursuing or have pursued what is called gender reassignment. Thus, there is already a form of self-ID in place, because individuals self-identify as trans and are then protected under the Equality Act 2010; no evidence is required and a Gender Recognition Certificate (GRC) is not a requirement. A GRC is not needed to access public toilets or clothing store changing rooms, for example. A GRC enables the issue of a birth certificate with amended sex marker, which can help to streamline all identity documents and avoid invasions of privacy for trans men and trans women.

A GRC specifies that for all purposes someone must be treated as the sex they are now legally recognized as under the Gender Recognition Act 2004, but there are limits to this, as legal scholar Professor Alex Sharpe explains: 'Thus the scope of legal gender recognition is delimited in relation to competitive sport, parental status in the context of existing children, succession, peerages, and particular gender-specific offences' (2020: 551). There are allowances for exceptions in single-sex settings such as those concerning the women's sector; these are detailed in the 'Equality Act 2010 Statutory Code of Practice: Services, public functions and associations' (2011):

> If a service provider provides single-sex or separate sex services for women and men, or provides services differently to women and men, they should treat transsexual people according to the gender role in which they present. However, the Act does permit the service provider to provide a different service or exclude a person from the service who is proposing to undergo, is undergoing or who has undergone gender reassignment. This will only be lawful where the exclusion is a proportionate means of achieving a legitimate aim. (2011: 197, para 13:57)

The Equality Act 2010 (Schedule 3, paragraph 28) specifies that on a case by case basis, where there are valid reasons for doing so, it may be possible for a service or provision to be exempt from treating someone as the sex they are legally recognized as through their GRC, and/or be able to treat someone differently/refuse a service on the grounds of them being a trans person, with or without a GRC. This different treatment has to be a proportionate means of achieving a legitimate aim; otherwise, it could be classified as discrimination. In the explanatory notes alongside the act, an example given of where this may be legitimate is in the provision of a group counselling session for women who have been subject to male sexual violence. Excluding a trans woman from that space would, it was suggested, be proportionate if it was felt that inclusion would negatively affect non-trans women members. There is a lot of ambiguity around such directions and many in the women's sector, as well as the Equality and Human Rights Commission (EHRC), have repeatedly argued that the government must produce clearer guidance, to protect trans people and the services they may need, as well as to give authority and clarity to single-sex services where they feel it is necessary and proportionate to exclude trans people. While giving evidence to the Women and Equalities committee on reform of the GRA, on the 9th December 2020, Professor Stephen Whittle OBE emphasised that these current protections are adequate, and highlighted that trans people should not be penalised for the crimes some violent men choose to commit: 'we should not be looking to address any issues around predatory men by marginalising a small community, which itself is all too often victimised by predatory men. We are totally understanding, as a community, of the issues raised by gender-critical feminists, because we are also victims' (Whittle, 2020).

There are widely held concerns among GC organizations that non-trans women and girls will be forced to stop using public women's spaces and communal intimate spaces for fear that these will effectively be unisex and that one might be observed by a man or person believed to be a man, which brings anxiety: anxiety which is not unjustified – as I explored in Chapter 1. Opponents to liberalizing the GRA also feared that non-trans male fetishists could use the law to perpetrate voyeurism and abuse in women's intimate spaces, facing off any challenge with the retort that they identify as a woman so must not be questioned or ejected. Readers will notice that most of these objections do not actually centre trans women; they are concerns around non-trans men utilizing changes or flexibility in law and policy to harass, intimidate and abuse women and girls. It is also rather ironic that the concerns raised as resulting from liberalizing the GRA process would not actually change the situation as it currently stands, because however easy or difficult it is to gain, a GRC is not required to be protected as a trans person on the grounds of gender reassignment under the Equality Act 2010 (Finlayson et al., 2018).

Sometimes opponents argue that trans women will be just as likely as non-trans men to commit sexualized violence against women and children, due to their sexed as male biology at birth and/or their male socialization for an unspecified number of influential years. These sorts of arguments circulate widely in the gender wars and are frequently cited, hinted at or otherwise used to mobilize transphobic responses. It is sometimes suggested that all trans women are inherently a threat to women and girls and should not be in intimate spaces for women and girls. Needless to say, there is no evidence to suggest this is true (Sharpe, 2020; Zanghellini, 2020; Hasenbush et al., 2019). It is clearly an offensive, demonizing and pathologizing generalization, made all the more offensive by the fact that trans women also fear and are affected by sexualized male violence. While undoubtably the unusual suspects in sexual violence, trans women and non-trans women do sometimes commit intimate partner violence, rape or sexual assault; this should not be denied, but nor should such a minority of cases be used to generalize about entire populations as if by their nature they are pathologically threatening and dangerous. It is also the case, unfortunately, that some opponents to trans inclusion argue their standpoint by suggesting that all trans women actually have what is called autogynephillia, an unproven and wildly offensive philosophical theory from sexologist Ray Blanchard. The theory suggests trans women sexually fetishize the female form and thus seek to create that form permanently in their own body for the purpose of sexual arousal (Serano, 2020). As activist, writer and researcher of Cis Studies, Mallory Moore asserts, the theory of autogynephillia, AGP, as it is known, is 'a theory of transsexuality by and large inherited from a century of sexological pathologisation of all forms of sexual "deviance" from a heterosexual and cisgender norm' (Moore, 2020). Whatever particular standpoint, theoretical framing or objection was taken to moving to self-ID; many creative campaigns against it began to emerge in the public sphere in the UK, including on community message boards such as Mumsnet in the UK, which is an online message board aimed at mothers, parents and carers. It is the UK's largest parent's network and boasts approximately ten million visitors per month. It is a vital source of information, solidarity and advice sharing for parents, undoubtably indispensable for many and particularly for new parents. It has also become a popular site for GC activism and networking.

Two Mumsnet members, Amy Desir and Hannah Clarke, launched an eye-catching campaign called Man Friday, where supporters self-identified as male on Fridays in publicity stunts and entered men-only areas. One target was the Hampstead men's swimming pond in London in May 2018, which received a fair amount of press attention and public interest in photos of women wearing fake beards and mankinis being escorted away by police (Hardy, 2018). GC politics have also made it into the courts several times in the UK, garnering a great deal of media coverage; indeed, the UK media seemingly have a particular interest in issues surrounding trans rights, and it is often far from sensitively addressed. One such legal case was brought by the social policy researcher and financial expert Maya Forstater, who took her employer to an Employment Tribunal in November 2019 after her contract was not renewed by her employer. This followed her expressing what she described as her GC views on social media; her case was not successful, but at the time of writing an appeal is likely to go ahead in 2021. Another case, in February 2020, initially resulted in another loss for GC campaigners, the case of Kate Scottow who was found guilty of misusing communication networks to cause annoyance and anxiety to another woman, Stephanie Hayden. Hayden had brought the case after Scottow had repeatedly used male pronouns to refer to her, made unfavourable comments about trans women and called her 'a pig in a wig' in one instance. However, in December 2020 Scottow's conviction was overturned at appeal, where the Judges decided that the right to offend others was part of free speech. In February 2020, former police officer Harry Miller took to the courts and won, with his complaint about how the police mistreated him after he had retweeted allegedly transphobic material, particularly an excruciatingly hateful so-called limerick about trans women. The court agreed that the police had overstepped the mark, turning up at Miller's workplace and warning him off social media for committing what the police had called, non-crime hate incidents. In court, Justice Julian Knowles accused the police of Orwellian censorship and suppression of free speech. Miller's case resulted in a new organization called We Are Fair Cop, who seek to campaign for those who are questioned, reported to or threatened by the police for, as they see it, critiquing trans ideology and expounding GC views.

Frequently, when GC is used as a descriptor of an individual's politics, it will often be in the context of feminist or Radical Feminist theory, but not always. Not all GC activists are women; some are men, and not all are feminist. Sometimes, GC activists will also label their own politics as Radical Feminist and some GC activists are of course Radical Feminists. Unfortunately, however, these two standpoints – GC and Radical Feminism – have been conflated in much popular understanding to the point of meaninglessness. Too often any anti-trans, or anti-trans-inclusion, or GC positions are seen as some sort of textbook Radical Feminist position. However, GC activists are not the only people with a critical and suspicious stance on trans inclusion; conservative and religious movements have been targeting trans and queer communities for several years now, stepping up their propaganda in response to increased recognition and public awareness around gender and sexuality fluidity. As I explained earlier in this book, the trans community are being used and abused in order to split the LGBTQI+ movement and erode public tolerance for sexuality, gender and sex diversity. Many of those individuals, particularly those in positions of power and authority, who are vocally anti-trans-inclusion, and against increased recognition for trans liberation movements or trans rights, are not feminist in any way, let alone Radical Feminist, and would never align themselves with that stance.

Gender identity does not exist

So, what does it mean to be GC? In her submission to the London Central Employment Tribunal in November 2019 policy and financial expert Maya Forstater defined her position as one that recognizes the immutability of biological sex and the existence of only two biological sexes in humans, these being male and female, acknowledging variances of sexual development in a minority of cases – topics that I covered and introduced in Chapter 1 on the construction of biological sex. In addition, Forstater defined that her GC stance does not recognize gender identity and does not believe this exists, while acknowledging that some people do believe in it. Forstater's GC stance is not a Radical Feminist one, and she has publicly stated that she does not identify as a Radical Feminist. Her defence was that other people's belief in their gender identity should not coerce her to believe in it, nor should it trump biological sex or force her to respond to people as if it does (Forstater, 2019). This is actually a good summary of the meaning of a GC position in practice. The GC academic, philosophy Professor Kathleen Stock from the University of Sussex has also provided a definition of this position in academia specifically:

> Broadly speaking, gender-critical academics argue that there are problems, either conceptually or practically or both, with the legal and social prioritisation of the notion of gender identity over categories such as sex. They also tend to be critical of gender, understood as distinct sets of social stereotypes – 'femininity'; 'masculinity' – attached to the sexes, arguing that these are contingent, harmful, and should not be perpetuated. (Stock, 2019a)

In this definition we can see a familiar crossover with Radical Feminist understandings of socially constructed gender roles as power relationships, as I explained in previous chapters. In this quote gender is recognised mainly as a set of stereotypes and for many GC campaigners, the idea of gender identity is but a dangerous fiction.

Forcefully arguing this point in the UK is a GC group called the LGB Alliance, which formed in London on 22 October 2019 in response to dissatisfaction with lack of answers from Stonewall, UK, on critical questions about trans inclusion and to counteract what they saw as widespread public confusion as to the meanings of sex and gender. The LGB Alliance believe that the protected characteristic of sex in the UK Equality Act 2010 is being erased. They believe that lesbian and gay gender non-conforming children are being subjected to conversion therapy when they are referred to gender identity development services; that homosexuality is under threat from trans inclusion because lesbian and gay trans people cannot be contained in the bracket of same-sex relationships; and that trans identities among young people are caused by social contagion. This group, like many GC organizations, states that gender is a social construction, and in the run up the disastrous UK 2019 General Election, they published twelve questions for supporters to put to prospective members of Parliament in all political parties. These included points on what they refer to as a dangerous 'gender identity doctrine', such as the suggestion that children are being taught people can have many different gender identities.

The LGB Alliance also campaigned around the Scottish government consultation on the Gender Recognition Reform (Scotland) Bill, which ran from December 2019 to March 2020, being put on hold during the Covid-19 lockdown in the summer of 2020. Included in the Scottish draft bill, similar to what was proposed for England and Wales, were proposals to ease the process of gender transition by removing the necessity of a medical diagnosis, and enabling individuals to self-identify as trans after a minimum of six months living in their preferred sex identity, with a required three-month reflection period and an age limit of at least sixteen years old at which point someone could start the process of applying for a Gender Recognition Certificate. The LGB Alliance fundraised and ran national adverts in the mainstream Scottish press, warning of what they perceive as the dangers of easing the GRC process, suggesting it will result in a 'gender free-for-all', whatever that means. These adverts were featured as full pages in *The Herald* and *Scotland on Sunday* in January 2020, with the headline 'Press pause on the gender recognition bill'. On 6 March 2020 another full-page advert ran in the *The Scotsman*, under the heading 'Self-ID gives predators the green light' urging people to respond critically to the consultation before it ended on 17 March.

Sex is real and gender is oppression

For many GC activists, masculinity and femininity are not only social constructs; they are oppressions and are therefore not identities. GC activists are critical of the idea that there is such a thing as gender identity. To them, women and men are simply sex descriptors, of whether one was born female or male. Anything on top of that is purely personality perhaps, preferences or, especially in the case of women, harmful conditioning into sex role.

A GC political stance asserts that having a female body at birth means one is put into the sex class of girls and women to receive different, inferior treatment to those classed as boys and men, who, in turn, are put into the superior sex class of men, due to their male bodies at birth. This inferior treatment perpetrated upon women from birth includes sexual objectification, sexual harassment and sexual violence from men, which several of my respondents raised as a universal female experience and one that bonded women together as women. Women's inferior treatment was therefore seen as inseparable from being labelled female at birth.

GC activists do not support language such as that of 'sex assigned at birth' because they believe sex is observed at birth and is an immutable fact. As discussed earlier, this was a key point in the unsuccessful November 2019 Forstater tribunal. Forstater made it clear that, for her, from her GC perspective, no human being can change their biological sex from one to another. She argued that this was a scientific fact, as well as being her belief and that it should therefore be protected as a belief. In late December 2019 the judge ruled that her beliefs could not be so protected, because they could involve the harassment of another individual, for example through persistent use of sexed pronouns that were opposite to that which an individual used for themselves and/or were in their official documentation and state classification. In the case of an individual with a Gender Recognition Certificate in the UK, for example, a trans woman is legally recognized with female terms and a trans man is legally recognized with male terms. The judge pointed out, therefore, that refusing to accept this legal status could not be classed as a protected belief and could in fact shift into criminal harassment and even a hate crime.

The judge was careful to point out in his summary that the claimant was obviously free to believe that gender identity is a fiction, and free to believe that trans people should not be referred to or considered as the sex they identify or are legally recognized as; he summed up too that individuals are also free to campaign against liberalization of the GRA and for female-only women's spaces if they so wish. I do not agree with much of Maya Forstater's position, nor the way she expresses it, but neither can I support the actions of her employer, when they refused to renew her contract, if this was based only on her Twitter conversations and personal blogs. It is not clear whether the employer pursued disciplinary measures first, or investigated the potential impact on colleagues and clients from the expression of views that some saw as transphobic. Generally speaking, I do not support campaigns to have people sacked, or campaigns to seek out and complain to their employers, to find and share their private details online, to have them arrested or to get groups banned from public meeting rooms and places. It is unfortunate that such occurrences are not rare within the battlefield of the gender wars, and it is deeply sad that this situation has become so brutally polarized in the first place. I have long been disturbed at the current rush to turn to litigious and criminal state interventions.

Womanhood, in the GC perspective, is defined by birth sex and by membership of the female sex class from birth. While some GC activists may acknowledge that sexed characteristics on the body can be changed, through hormones and surgery for example, sex class status is not seen as changeable and remains as the sex one was categorized at birth. A major claim of GC activists is that biological birth sex is nearly always immediately obvious, and that in the case of trans men or trans women, while it may be polite to refer to such individuals as the sex they identify, it will still be obvious which sex they were at birth. In this analysis, sex at birth is sex forever, and also, importantly, sex class at birth is definitely sex class forever – even if one changes one's bodily sexed characteristics. For many GC activists then, trans women, including post-operative trans women with sexed as female primary and secondary sex characteristics, would be viewed in this analysis as permanent members of the male sex class. In turn, trans men would be seen as permanent members of the female sex class, when trans men are mentioned at all, that is, because this group, and trans masculinities in general, is often marginalized and ignored. Part of my motivation for writing this book is to bring trans and queer masculinities into this so heated battlefield, because the experiences of these individuals can serve to trouble some of the limited binary positions that have so far been staked out. It is also an important contribution because trans women, transgender women and trans feminine people are far from the only casualties in the gender wars, although it is these individuals who so often bear the brunt.

The transing and erasing of lesbians

There is seemingly a widely held concern that trans men are simply naive and manipulated gender non-conforming lesbians who have been led astray by the so-called trans cult or trans cabal. This pressure is considered to be a form of lesbian erasure, making a lesbian identity less and less likely as a valid choice, echoing debates around what is called 'butch flight' that I address in later chapters of this book. Butch flight refers to a concern in the lesbian community that butch or masculine lesbians will be lost to a trans identity, resulting in a declining lesbian community. Queer theory is often singled out too, as being a cause of what GC activists see as a trans trend. This so-called trend is also seen as being responsible for the rape of lesbians, and it is suggested that trans women transition to rape lesbians, or otherwise pressure lesbians sexually. We can see here the familiar arguments from 1973 still being so influential. In addition, it is asserted that lesbian women who are vocal about not being attracted to trans women will be shamed into silence by accusations of transphobia. By most GC standpoints there can be no lesbian trans women or gay trans men anyway, because sex at birth is sex forever, and because homosexuality is defined as opposite sex desire and relationships – opposite birth-sex desire and relationships that is. Trans women and trans men who identify as lesbian or gay and who are partnered with non-trans partners, by GC ideology, are always and forever the opposite sex to their sexual partners, therefore by these standards cannot be homosexual.

The language common in GC discourse frequently makes reference to 'transing', 'trans cabal', 'trans ideology', 'gender ideology' and 'trans cults'. It is phrasing that may sound extreme or dramatic to readers unfamiliar with the gender wars, but, as I've introduced before, this is only the tip of the iceberg.

Sex not gender

Several of the survey respondents in my research used the phrase 'adult human female'. This is from the campaign in 2018 led by anti-trans-inclusion campaigner Mrs Kellie-Jay Keen-Minshull, known on social media as Posie Parker, who is founder of the organization Standing for Women, which created and funded black-and-white street billboards and tee shirts with the slogan 'woman = adult human female'. Mrs Keen-Minshull is not a Radical Feminist and has said several times that she does not identify as a feminist either.

Sex not gender has become a familiar refrain on social media more widely and in the gender wars in particular. This even became a hashtag on Twitter and is frequently on placards and banners at GC events. From this perspective only sex matters. Prominent anti-trans-inclusion theorist Professor Sheila Jeffreys explains it succinctly: 'it is on the basis of biological sex that women are subordinated. Female foetuses, for instance, are aborted in some countries and communities, not because they have a gender but because of their sex, whereas gender is a social construction which can only be created after birth' (2014b: 43). Sex is a description of bodily features, not an identity; and gender is just stereotypes, therefore also not an identity.

GC is critical of essentialism

GC campaigns are frequently charged with being essentialist. I would suggest that this, in fact, is one of the main critiques of GC feminism; sometimes, it must be said, unfairly. While I have much to disagree with in GC narratives, I can also see that it is frequently misrepresented and simplified. One of the main ways it is simplified is in the accusation that anyone holding GC views, or anyone branded a 'TERF', is motivated to stop trans women, trans men and trans people from pursuing their own gender identity. For example, writing an opinion piece in the *New York Times* in February 2020, the author Juliet Jacques accuses those she refers to as coming from a 'so-called radical feminist tradition' of upholding 'the conceit that trans and nonbinary people should not determine their own gender identities'. Perhaps this is just trouble with semantics, but many self-defined GC activists would deny that there is such a thing as a gender identity in the first place, and second, would promote that individuals should present however they please, be that culturally construed as masculine or feminine, regardless of their biological sex at birth. There is no problem with individuals presenting as masculine or feminine – gender. The GC issue is with individuals identifying as a sex other than that which they were labelled at birth. I would posit that there is plenty to disagree with in lots of GC viewpoints, around assertions of 'gender ideology' for example, without reducing and misrepresenting them and their stance.

Prominent GC journalists and academics have also been clear to emphasize their anti-essentialist politics. In 2018, journalist Sarah Ditum wrote for *The Economist*, 'Feminism offers the radical proposition that what you like, what you wear and who you are should not be dictated by your chromosomes, hormones or any other marker of biological sex' (2018a). This is usually a foundational stance of GC positions, which also, importantly, has much in common with Radical Feminist theory, as I argued earlier in Chapter 2. GC activists are thus not default essentialists, and I suggest it is a mistake to label them as such, as GC academic Dr Rebecca Reilly-Cooper has noted: 'The reason we come to feminism is because we feel that gender is an oppressive hierarchy that limits our potential, and we want to be liberated from the demands of femininity, which is just the expression of female submission' (2015).

However, those who refer to themselves as GC are not necessarily against the sorts of personal expression that may be seen by society as gendered in terms of outward presentation, like clothing, styling or beauty practices for example. Outward presentation and clothing choices are often seen in GC narratives as personal preference and expressions of personality, albeit in a context where there is obviously pressure on women to fit in and look a certain way for all sorts of reasons; this is an important element that I shall return to later in this chapter. On sex roles, although I have pointed out that it cannot be generalized that all GC activists will be essentialists, sometimes GC activists do appear to promote the idea that some aspects of attitude and behaviour may be linked to sexual difference and therefore may never disappear entirely. The GC academic Callie Burt notes that not all GC activists take the same view on the significance of sex differences, but asserts that many will share her view: 'One can (and I do) believe that females may show some biological tendencies or dispositions that differ from males, on average (e.g., less physical aggressiveness)' (Burt, 2020: 22). At a conference in 2020, Professor Stock argued that 'feminism should acknowledge that the interests of women and men are not exactly the same. Men and women are two different kinds of people, with some shared needs and interests, but also many competing ones, and I assume that in any culture it is likely to be that way' (2020). Stock went on to clarify that she does not support gender-abolitionist feminism, describing this as fantasy:

> Nor I think should feminism aim for 'gender abolition', which again, I think of as a kind of basically liberal fantasy: the complete abolition of masculinity and femininity, stripping us back to our supposedly rational core. Yet masculinity is the set of the cultures of men, and femininity the set of cultures of women, and apart from it being impossible to abolish these cultures in any case, there are many valuable aspects of both. (Stock, 2020)

I have also conversed with some GC activists who do believe that being female does, generally speaking, involve a desire to be a mother and to care for children and that this is likely to be different for male people or less of a desire for male people. These views are certainly not rare in feminism generally, as they are not rare in society generally either. Sometimes, at their more extreme, they take the form of what has been called cultural feminism, as I explained in Chapter 2, and they can also be found in some expressions of Eco-Feminism and women's spirituality movements. It would be another generalization to assume this cultural feminism is always present or motivating in such movements though. Certainly, there are many Priestesses of Goddess Circles out there, and activist peace women, and Eco-Feminists who do have a full analysis of the dangers of gender essentialism and do not pursue their activism because they believe women are inherently different to, let alone better than, men.

Some of those GC activists who do focus on differences between women and men though, whatever the relationship of those differences to nature or nurture, may feel that these sorts of differences between women and men are precisely the sorts of things that should be celebrated. In particular, differences around caring, nurturing and the psychological impact of knowing that one is of the sex theoretically capable of carrying a child in pregnancy, even if one cannot or chooses not to. GC campaigner and philosopher Dr Jane Clare Jones has written on the 'patriarchal devaluation about what female people are and what female people can do' (2019). While pointing out that biology is not destiny, she calls out the negative, patriarchal propaganda, or 'masculinist hogwash', which devalues what female bodies can do, in terms of pregnancy, childbirth and childrearing. Jones underlines the importance of rejecting suggestions that motherhood is just 'bovine-passivity', in favour of acknowledging motherhood as 'an active and axiomatically creative endeavour' (Jones, 2019). It can be regularly observed in mainstream society that many people, of all political persuasions or none, consider some sorts of differences between women and men, around nurturing role, caring, providing and childbirthing role, to be features that make women different to men.

Toilets that matter

One of the more base and frustrating areas where possible innate differences between women and men also get publicly discussed is in the context of the so-called bathroom debates (Martino & Ingrey, 2020; Riggle, 2018; Bender-Baird, 2016). In the United States the bathroom bill debate has very real and dire consequences; some conservative states are trying to stop trans men or trans women from using sex segregated public toilets at all, and young trans students have had to take their schools to court, for example, just for the right to use toilet provision like any other pupil. In Virginia, Gavin Grimm finally won a four-year battle in 2019 against his local Gloucester county school board for discriminatory trans bathroom bans, for example. In the UK fierce disagreements over so-called gender-neutral toilets have played out in the press, particularly concerning schools. 'Girls are skipping school to avoid sharing gender neutral toilets with boys after being left to feel unsafe and ashamed', reads a *Daily Mail* headline in the UK in October 2019. 'Unisex toilets put girls at risk of period shaming', documented the *Independent* in February 2019, reporting on research into school toilets in Wales. The Westminster government launched a toilet consultation at the end of 2020, to canvass views on unisex toilets, signage and amounts of toilets available. Meanwhile, increasing public panics about trans-inclusive public toilets are leading to gender non-conforming lesbians being even more frequently challenged or thrown out of women's toilets (Maurice, 2021). This was the case for sixteen-year-old Ny Richardson in Hull, Northern England, UK, who was thrown out of a branch of McDonalds in 2016 after staff accused her of going into the wrong toilets – the women's (Webb, 2016). This is such a common experience among gender non-conforming women and masculine lesbians that it was raised by almost every masculine respondent to my survey; I shall shed light on such experiences later in the second half of this book, in the chapters on butch experience and queer masculinity.

Many people invoke differences between women and men, cultural, biological or both, when arguing against sharing unisex toilets. It is often assumed that men, in general, have different standards of personal hygiene for example, and that this is just one of the many grounds why women's toilets must remain women-only, or rather, for only women sexed as female from birth – with safety for women from sexualized male violence and voyeurism being the main and more serious concern.

In discussions about the merits of what are wrongly called 'gender-neutral toilets' but are really unisex single-occupancy toilets, it is not unusual to hear claims that mixed sex toilets, as compared to women-only toilets, will become dirtier and smellier if men are routinely using them. As the GC group Woman's Place UK emphasize on their website, 'Women and girls want separate cubicles because of issues of noise, smell, privacy and fear of potential attack' (WPUK, 2018). They acknowledge that unisex toilets are increasingly being established as part of efforts towards inclusion, but argue that this does not include women – 'under the pretext of inclusion, all these changes are removing from women the right to privacy, dignity and safety' (WPUK, 2018).

Obviously, it is not only GC organizations like Woman's Place UK making such objections. On 29 March 2020 a headline in the *Mail on Sunday* newspaper screeched: 'ban male-bodied trans women from ladies' toilets, says Equality Minister' (Owen, 2020). The minister in question was Baroness Berridge, director of the Conservative Christian Fellowship, who argued that trans women had no place in such places. In the lockdown summer of 2020, rather than responding to the global call to make Black Lives Matter, the Conservative government, under the helm of Liz Truss, minister for women and equalities, hinted to the press, in the form of *The Sunday Times*, that the government would take some sort of national control of toilets and force local authorities to ban trans women with male anatomy from women's public toilets (Shipman, 2020). Earlier that year, in February 2020, Conservative peer Lord Lucas had begun a debate in the House of Lords on single-sex toilet provision in public buildings; complaining about 'woke' culture he passionately argued that a unisex toilet would make women feel unsafe and impinge on their natural needs around menstruation, for example. He knew what he was talking about because he had been in some unisex toilets in the Department for Education at Westminster, and described them as deeply unpleasant.

Covering this debate, Caroline Ffiske for the London-based online news site *The Article* supported the stance of Lord Lucas and bemoaned the loss of female camaraderie in the ladies. All women want their women-only loos, she writes, for safety and privacy, and also another reason: 'That is, camaraderie. It has been frayed of late. I sometimes feel that the more we have pushed for equality between the sexes, the more we have loosened bonds within them. Though none of us would want to go backwards, there is some loss in that.' However, she goes on to say: 'But it isn't all gone. One of the places female camaraderie emerges is the female toilet. At nightclubs, young women sit on the sinks and share make-up (or they once did)' (Ffiske, 2020). Conservative peers like Lord Lucas shouldn't even have to table such debates; Ffiske warns, nobody, least of all Conservatives, like interfering in the lives of individuals and would rather that morals and manners led the way. In reality of course, the law and the state interfere in the lives of individuals every day, in fundamental and often negative ways. Not least in the lives of LGBTQI+ people in terms of if they can marry, if they can have children or be parents, if they can retain custody of their children, if parents can refuse surgical interventions for infants with variances of sexual development and in what cases, whether religious groups can provide gay conversion 'therapy' or not, whether school materials should acknowledge lesbian and gay families or not, if they can be legally recognized as a mother or father to their own children, or whether trans men and trans women have a right to paperwork that matches the life they are living.

Arguments for separate toilets for women, rather than unisex toilets, may just seem like common sense to many readers. Indeed, when I have had conversations with people at conferences, festivals or debates where I am speaking about these sorts of issues, most people will tell me that obviously women need their own space because men are just dirtier and will urinate on the toilet seat and floor, and generally not clean up after themselves. We may have all seen evidence to support such generalizations, but that does not mean that this unfortunate situation is biologically dictated, nor does it mean that the current state of affairs cannot be changed. Personally, I am appalled at the frequent suggestion that women need separate toilets from men to protect our dignity, and I note the Victorian tone to such a term. I am bemused as to why women need protection from smells and noises that men may make which are somehow unique to their male biology, as if the acts of urination and defecation, by anyone, including women, will not carry the potential for smells and noises. I will always rail against such generalizations whenever I hear them, because every time we accept these generalizations as truisms we delay progress, because we hold back change. Rather than setting a low bar, we must accept that men are not biologically messier or dirtier than women and that this is purely a social construct. Men's learned and condoned helplessness does not benefit women, who, as mothers and primary carers, often spend a great deal of precious time cleaning up after men and boys. We must start from the assumption that men have just as much ability to keep shared spaces clean, and then demand that they do.

Although some GC activists do use such stereotypes about men's personal habits and hygiene standards compared to women, their stance, in theory, is critical of all imposed gender stereotypes – that is, the stereotypes imposed on people from birth based on their physical sex characteristics. These are the gender stereotypes we will all be familiar with, and which most of us, especially feminists, will strongly disagree with. These are the supposed natural norms that limit us all, for example: that women are not good at science or can't park cars, or that boys are better with spatial awareness and are more competitive and aggressive than girls. GC activists do not subscribe to these sorts of sexist gender stereotypes, and therefore they seek to neutralize them, critique and challenge them in themselves and others. As I mentioned earlier, and will now return to, this stance does not necessarily have to extend to gendered personal expression such as clothing and personal grooming though, which is often put down to personal choice and personality, nor is anyone saying it has to. The philosopher and GC activist, Professor Kathleen Stock, makes the latter point clear in some of her writing: 'I don't care what anyone looks like, how they dress, what they do to their body' (Stock, 2018). However, it is, I would argue, noteworthy that it does not follow that a GC activist will be critical of their own, or others, personal choices to present as a feminine woman by wearing make-up, high heels, dresses, having long hair or shaving their body hair, for example. For some GC activists then, though obviously not all, GC is a stance that is critical of gendering on the inside, in terms of beliefs about oneself and one's ability, but not necessarily on the outside, in terms of gendered appearance.

There is no gender, and personality is personal, not political

It may appear to readers that this standpoint is fair enough; we can't escape society after all, we are brought up wearing certain clothes and we have varying beauty and grooming practices imposed on us. Dress requirements in workplaces still frequently require women employees to wear feminine clothes or very feminized uniforms for example, including staff make-up guidelines for female staff, or being pressured to wear high heels at work. Fashion in general is far from unisex, despite the occasional, overpriced 'gender-neutral' baggy grey sweatshirt, and women may feel they have no choice but to buy clothes that are tailored a certain way, either so they fit their bodies more comfortably and/or so they can be seen in a sexist society as professional or appropriately feminine. As GC philosopher Dr Rebecca Reilly-Cooper notes, 'Wanting to abolish the oppressive and limiting effects of gender does not mean that radical feminists want to stop anyone expressing their personality in the ways that they enjoy. Feminists do not wish to ban make-up or high heels, or to prevent girls from playing with dolls and dressing up like princesses' (2015). Aside from the fact that there are certainly feminists who would like to ban high heels and would seek to stop girls being dressed up like princesses, there is also the point that just because these things are the norm, and it is often easier to do them rather than stand out by refusing to do them; this should not mean they are out of bounds for question and critique.

It is interesting that being GC is not widely seen as necessitating personal critique of one's own gender presentation and gendered presentation. Maybe the political is indeed personal; maybe one can reject what society says girls and women should be like, while still looking like what society says girls and women should look like. The two are certainly not mutually exclusive, nor am I suggesting they should be. However, this acquiescence to gendered presentation was never the stance of Radical Feminism, far from it. This is why it's so interesting, as I highlighted at the beginning of this chapter, that these two terms are often, perhaps wrongly, linked together – GC and Radical Feminism. The proclaimed sheroes of anti-trans-inclusion feminism have been radical lesbian feminists and revolutionary feminists who were gender abolitionists; not gender critics, but proud gender refuseniks who eschewed beauty practices and theorized femininity as male violence against women.

Abolition not critique

For example, let's start at the top. The prolific revolutionary feminist, lesbian feminist writer and anti-trans-inclusion activist Sheila Jeffreys has consistently defined beauty practices such as make-up and the shaving of body hair, or fashions such as high-heeled shoes, as forms of sadistic, sexist cruelty against women under patriarchy. In her 2005 book *Beauty and Misogyny* she argues that the United Nations should include such beauty practices in the formal definition of harmful traditional and cultural practices. She considers beauty practices as a distinctly Western example of this, which, she proposes, has been conveniently ignored due to racism, Western imperialism and sexism implicit in the state architecture of institutions like the UN. Jeffreys ticks off the policy requirements to define Western beauty and fashion industries as harmful cultural practices: 'damaging to the health of women and girls, to be performed for men's benefit, to create stereotyped roles for the sexes and to be justified by tradition' (2005: 3). She is exasperated at the lack of progress since the Second Wave of feminism in the 1970s across the Western world, pointing out that during that period women used consciousness raising or CR to reflect on the limited set of imposed options from which they made certain choices. Women analysed why exactly they felt they had to wear make-up or shave their legs, or wear restrictive feminine clothing. From this ground-up political theorizing came standpoints rejecting beauty practices and adopting this rejection as a feminist political act. Jeffreys is disappointed that this process has not continued but has, in fact, gone backwards. Jeffreys dedicates her 2005 book to her partner, for her persistence in a lifetime of resistance to beauty practices. The very notion of 'beauty' was viewed by feminists such as Jeffreys as a patriarchal construct and nothing more than an oppression of women.

However, according to Professor Jeffreys, it is thanks to liberal feminism and postmodern thinkers such as the philosopher Judith Butler (who incidentally seems to get blamed for almost everything, like a Raymondesque she-devil for the 'other side' of the gender wars) that beauty practices have got more extreme and are sold as empowering, totemic signifiers of women's free choice, liberated sexuality and equal place in the world. Of course, Jeffreys argues they are the very opposite. She states that the wearing of make-up, for example, displays women's inequality compared to men: 'It could be that the wearing of makeup signifies that women have no automatic right to venture out in public in the West on equal grounds with men' (2005: 34). Practices like tattoos, ear piercing or belly button piercings are also analysed. At an Andrea Dworkin memorial conference, which I spoke at, held at Ruskin College, Oxford University in 2006, Jeffreys made beauty practices the focus of her speech. She spoke about piercing, for example, belly button piercings: 'Now women are supposed to show their navels and have them pierced. So men are getting the sadomasochistic satisfaction of women's pain and piercing just when they are walking round the street, sitting on the bus, and so on and so on' (2006). In fact, most of Jeffreys's theorizing on the political position of women in society links to sadomasochism sooner or later. Tattoos are sadomasochistic acts of self-harm for example, particularly practised by marginalized communities like lesbians and gay men – an assertion that hasn't aged well, considering the now normalized prevalence of tattoos and body art on mainstream celebrities, including those from privileged backgrounds. High heels, which she describes as torture instruments, are visible signs of harm to women and eroticize women's vulnerability compared to men, providing men with a sadomasochistic sexual thrill at the sight of it; Jeffreys chose a picture of a high-heeled shoe for the front cover of her 2005 book.

Compulsory heterosexuality and political lesbianism

As a lesbian feminist, Jeffreys has also written about political lesbianism and lesbian separatism; in fact, she was one of the authors of the famous conference pamphlet on political lesbianism produced by the Leeds Revolutionary Feminist Group in 1979, which became the OnlyWomen Press publication 'Love Your Enemy? The Debate Between Heterosexual Feminism and Political Lesbianism', published in 1981. Political Lesbianism is often popularly misunderstood as enforced sexual relationships with other women. However, it never actually meant this, as the writers of the documents in question made clear. These papers are in public records and can be returned to and consulted for clarity, for example, through the Feminist Archive in the UK, based at two sites in Bristol and Leeds. Political lesbianism is actually about focussing all one's energies on women and the women's movement; it is a sort of political prioritizing and political loving of women, as I discussed earlier in Chapter 2. It therefore involves removing one's energies from men, individually and as a group, those energies being domestic, political, cultural, financial, sexual and so on. The aim was then to redirect these energies to women and the WLM; it was nothing to do with having sex and there was no taboo on celibacy, which was seen as a valid option for women who did not desire to have sex or sexual relationships with other women for whatever reasons. Nobody, least of all lesbians, were suggesting that currently heterosexually oriented women should be forced to pursue sexual and romantic relationships with lesbian women, realizing the heartbreak and hurt that could come from such dictates.

It must be noted that the radical lesbian feminist women of that political period were experimenting with all sorts of new cultures and lifestyles; they created lesbian communes, they raised children communally, and they practised non-monogamy. As Professor Jeffreys herself asserts, 'Though genital connection might not, for some, have formed the basis for their identity, an enthusiasm for passionate sexual relationships certainly marked the lesbian feminism of that period' (Jeffreys, 2003: 22). Although, Jeffreys goes on to explain that passionate friendships can be lesbianism too, and that sex may be unimportant or insignificant in political woman-loving. However, the accusation of de-sexualization of lesbianism was a common critique of political lesbianism at the time, informing those who sought to suggest that lesbian feminism had become too much like cultural feminism. I believe that this remains a valid critique, and it is unfortunate that those promoting the political act of prioritizing women adopted the term 'lesbian' to describe this political stance, when, perhaps, the term 'separatism' would have been more accurate. 'Separatism' is the term used for feminist or lesbian separatism where women build communities and ways of living, as much as possible, separate from men; in so doing they prioritize women's knowledge and skills, building networks of women in all professions and trades, for example. As I have highlighted in previous chapters in this book, this has a proud herstory in feminism, and is profoundly radical. Whether permanent or temporary communities they are powerful because they illustrate what women are capable of, and they take control of practical and manual skills that, in many countries, women have historically been barred from and which would be necessary for revolutionary social change between the sexes.

Although Sheila Jeffreys is often referred to as a Radical Feminist and aligns herself with these politics too, it is important also to remember her claim to revolutionary feminism. Professor Jeffreys praises revolutionary feminism for what she labels 'tactical separatism', this was not an escapist essentialism, she argues, but an insider-outsider position, where the revolutionary lesbian feminist 'manages to live in the world men have made, whilst working to change it from a separate base in women's friendship and culture' (2003: 25). Jeffreys became a lesbian herself in 1973 and has always expounded that heterosexuality does not have to be a permanent condition. In *Unpacking Queer Politics* (2003) she called again for a political critique of heterosexuality, branding this institution as private slavery for women: 'Thus, for women in particular, the "private" world of heterosexuality is not a realm of personal security, a haven from a heartless world, but an intimate realm in which their work is extracted and their bodies, sexuality and emotions are constrained and exploited for the benefits of individual men and the male supremacist political system.' Therefore, she goes on to assert that 'Transformation of the public world of masculine aggression, therefore, requires transformation of the relations that take place in "private". Public equality cannot derive from private slavery' (2003: 146). Similarly, another famous gender abolitionist, Janice Raymond, author of *The Transsexual Empire* (1979), whose work we explored in more depth in Chapter 2, has also espoused the urgency of a more political and politically conscious lesbianism, highlighting that male sexuality is intimately bound together with power and that therefore heterosexuality can never be equal: 'there are positive advantages in status, ego, and authority for men in the ways they have exercised their sexuality. Women cannot uncritically bracket this analysis in order to revel in the joy of sex' (Raymond, 1989: 151).

For many GC activists today, Professor Sheila Jeffreys's work in particular, theorizing the trans rights movement as a men's fetishistic, sexual rights movement is highly regarded and often quoted. Since moving from Australia back to the UK, Jeffreys has involved herself fully in the movements and mobilizations against trans inclusion in women's and feminist spaces and against any proposed liberalization or updating of the current UK Gender Recognition Act 2004, for example. Jeffreys is a co-author of the Women's Human Rights Campaign Declaration on Women's Sex Based Rights, launched in March 2019. In September 2017 she spoke at a meeting for the GC group Fair Play for Women, where she suggested that trans women want to use women's toilets because it gives them an erection and they seek to invade women's spaces for sexual thrills. She has spoken with Mrs Keen-Minshull at several events organized by a group called We Need to Talk, who campaigned and mobilized public information exchanges against liberalization of the UK Gender Recognition Act and encouraged people to critically respond to the consultation – events such as one titled 'Inconvenient Women', on 13 June 2018 in London at Camden Town Hall. Earlier that same year, on 14 March 2018, at their fifth meeting, Jeffreys spoke at an event on 'Transgenderism and the War on Women' also organized by the group We Need to Talk. This was held in a committee room, the term for a generic meeting room that can be booked by MPs for speakers, briefings and functions, in the Westminster Houses of Parliament, this one was booked by Conservative MP David Davies. Incidentally, this location is important because I have seen it reported in numerous sources, especially in the United States, that this meeting was before the Westminster Parliament, and that Jeffreys herself addressed Parliament, which was not the case. For example, in an article explaining the rise of anti-trans 'radical' feminists, in *Vox*, journalist Katelyn Burns reported in 2019 that Jeffreys went before the UK parliament: 'Australian radical feminist Sheila Jeffreys went before the UK parliament in March 2018 and declared that trans women are "parasites", language that sounds an awful lot like Trump speaking about immigrants' (Burns, 2019). While I disagree with Jeffreys on a great deal, it is important to be clear on the facts, and she did not have an audience with parliament at this event. In her speech at this gathering Jeffreys stated that trans women are parasitical in that they occupy the category of woman, rendering it meaningless and erasing female-born women from public life and space.

Radical to the roots: Gender abolition

In her 2014 book *Gender Hurts* Jeffreys argues that gender abolition is a key and fundamental goal of Radical Feminism. She underlines that this project cannot be about just critiquing gender here and there, or critiquing some parts of it, but must aim for taking the whole thing apart. Jeffreys argues for gender abolition, not GC stances:

> Radical feminist theorists do not seek to make gender a bit more flexible, but to eliminate it. They are gender abolitionists, and understand gender to provide the framework and rationale for male dominance. In the radical feminist approach, masculinity is the behaviour of the male ruling class and femininity is the behaviour of the subordinate class of women. Thus gender can have no place in the egalitarian future that feminism aims to create. (Jeffreys, 2014a: 42)

Jeffreys would likely urge all women to give up femininity, despite the pressures to perform it, and to abolish all gender and to give up heterosexuality as well. Just because some GC feminists agree with Jeffreys on her views on trans rights, it obviously doesn't have to follow that they will subscribe to all her views, like those outlined earlier on gender abolition or those illustrated earlier on the beauty industry or the evils of heterosexuality.

However, as I have stated throughout this book, I think the conflation of GC feminism with Radical Feminism is misleading for many reasons, the gender-critical-versus-gender-abolition stances being just one. There is arguably a certain irony in proponents of GC approaches to trans rights disavowing any need to assess their own subscription to feminine gendered norms and presentation, or to heterosexuality, or to highly gendered, status claims based on being a mother or wife, for example. Although controversial among trans-exclusionary activists, including feminists of different types, one of the leaders of anti-trans-inclusion activism in the UK, Posie Parker, places great value on gendered status categories such as mother and wife; she could also be described as very feminine presenting. Mrs Keen-Minshull identifies herself on her own website under the header 'Woman, Mother, and Wife' and corrected a doctor she was debating on Sky News on 26 September 2018, when he referred to her as 'Ms', reasserting that she was married and should be known as 'Mrs'. She is the only UK member of the US anti-trans organization Hands Across the Aisle, founded by lesbian activist Miriam Ben-Shalom and Christian conservative anti-abortion campaigner Kaeley Triller-Haver.

One reason that I take issue with the personal staying personal is the recent trend of some GC activists to claim that everyone is non-binary, or to make jokes about having a 'gender-free' identity, to belittle the whole idea of gender identity in the first place. Interviewed by journalist Tara John for CNN in April 2020, the co-founder of the LGB Alliance, Kate Harris, stated that 'There is no evidence in the world that gender identity exists' (John, 2020). It could be argued that as the extremes of the gender binary are an impossible fiction of idealized Barbie and Ken dolls, nobody is the embodiment of these norms and thus everyone is indeed non-binary. As Reilly-Cooper explains for herself in *Aeon* in 2016, 'despite possessing female biology and calling myself a woman, I do not consider myself a two-dimensional gender stereotype. I am not an ideal manifestation of the essence of womanhood, and so I am non-binary. Just like everybody else.' In a speech in London for the group We Need to Talk, in June 2018, Professor Sheila Jeffreys asked the audience whether anyone there would say they had a gender, or would like protection to express it, whatever it was; clearly she was bemused as to what gender identity may be, other than the imposition of false gender norms. Writing in 2018 the journalist and GC activist Sarah Ditum wrote: 'There is no such thing as gender identity' (2018b).

Whether purely social or not, as I discuss throughout this book, many people do indeed experience gender as a fundamental part of their identity. This includes feminine women and masculine men, the majority of whom go to great lengths to express their gender through their dress, behaviour and role. It is not only non-gender-conforming people who have a gender, much as gender-conforming individuals may feel this is the case because the former stand out from the crowd. Many, if not most people, display a gender presentation, including all those GC women who choose to wear their hair long, and to wear dresses, make-up, skirts, high heels, jewellery or clothes that emphasize their breasts or hips. What motivates this of course is up for debate; GC activists would perhaps say it is just personality preference, or purely the patriarchal pressures of convention, and the associated penalties of not doing so. This does not explain, however, why many women, including those I shed light on in the next half of this book, express lifelong presentation the other way – masculine gender presentation – despite the penalties and pressures that result.

Gender-free trouble

As a masculine and masculine-presenting female person, I personally cannot help but bristle when feminine-presenting women argue passionately that everybody is gender-free and everyone is non-binary, while presumably not experiencing the sorts of gender policing and punishment that I and many other actually non-gender-normative people experience on a daily basis. Those who present themselves in line with current sex and gender norms will likely not experience being challenged by other women in public toilets, ejected from women's health clinics or laughed at by security guards who can't work out which line to send you to in order to be frisked. I accept that these sorts of incidences are minority concerns, and the philosopher Professor Kathleen Stock, writing with other GC activists and academics on Medium, suggests that occasional mis-sexing experiences such as these are just the price that has to be paid for protecting single-sex women-only spaces. Although this was widely critiqued, I actually can understand the point they are making here. The GC authors, Stock and her colleagues, describe such situations as 'a regrettable cost that has to be balanced against, and is nonetheless smaller than, the greater harms to females, should women-only space effectively become unisex via a policy of self-ID' (Allen et al., 2019). However rare they are overall, these incidences, that will be common knowledge to all of those who breach gender norms on a regular basis, highlight the very real impact of gender and gendering. They are examples of what the geographer of sexualities, Professor Kath Browne calls 'genderism' (2004). This term describes 'the hostile readings of, and reactions to, gender ambiguous bodies . . . instances of discrimination that are based on the discontinuities between the sex with which an individual identifies and how others, in a variety of spaces, read their sex' (2004: 331). This term is perhaps similar to an earlier one, coined in 1992 by the late author and activist, revolutionary communist Leslie Feinberg – the term 'genderphobia'. More recently, the academic, policy researcher and musician Dr Ruth Pearce also uses another more modern term 'cisgenderism', similar to terms like 'ableism' and 'heterosexism' (Lennon & Mistler, 2014). This term can describe the incidences we are discussing here; Pearce defines it as 'the structuring of social norms and institutions around the assumption that everyone has a cis experience of the world' (Pearce, 2018: 43). As I have explained elsewhere, the term 'cis' is used to describe non-trans.

Whatever we call these sorts of mis-sexing, cisgenderist or genderphobia incidents, the experience of them arguably highlights the powerful personal significance of gender identity. In the early, queer 1990s, the activist and academic Susan Stryker explained that those who are transgender, a term she identifies as first emerging in the 1970s, and she included butches in her definition, express a full-time commitment to their inner gender identity, which goes way beyond just the clothes they wear. While those who medically transitioned sex changed their bodies surgically, transgender individuals did not, but they did 'consistently and publicly express an ongoing commitment to their claimed gender identities through the same visual representational strategies used by others to signify that gender' (Stryker, 1994: 251). Again, whether it is innate or purely social, or a mixture of those forces, it is surely observable that gender identity is very important to most people, including gender-conforming people, and may well be experienced as a core part of identity and a deep-seated key part of selfhood. Some of us are motivated to follow long-held personal preferences for gender expression that result in mis-sexing, exclusion from places we should supposedly be safe and also in outright transphobic and homophobic physical violence and verbal assault. In addition, cumulative experiences of being challenged, mis-sexed and excluded can impact on a deeply personal level. It can lead to a general underlying sense of anxiety and heightened alert when in public spaces, acknowledging that obviously women of all kinds are no stranger to this. In the longer term, for non-conforming people it can also produce states of bodily dissatisfaction and unease, which revolve around one's sense and experience of sex and gender and can be profoundly shaming. As scholar Riki Wilchins explains in the 2002 edited collection *Genderqueer: Voices from Beyond the Sexual Binary*, we are well aware that when others cannot sex us at first glance, this is culturally taken to be our fault, rather than theirs, and it marks us out as deviant, and as some sort of gender freaks:

> As a system of meanings in which we participate each day, gender also feels exquisitely personal. So when someone gender-bashes or gender-baits us, we think, it's my own fault. If only I were more butch, if only I were more femme, if only I were taller, shorter, slimmer, heavier, had smaller breasts or larger muscles … if only I'd dressed or acted or felt differently, this never would have happened to me. We blame ourselves, and so we try to change ourselves. (2002c: 14)

Obviously, anyone who breaches gender norms will experience societal punishment and policing, this is by far from an experience unique to queer people or non-binary individuals. Women who do not play the game of femininity adequately will also be punished to varying degrees; likewise women who are feminine will probably receive routine sexual harassment and sexualized abuse from men, though they are doing gender 'correctly' for their sex. I am merely highlighting that women, or sexed as female NB individuals, who feel they have a masculine sense of self, or a masculine gender identity, will be punished if they pursue that identity, and there are a great many barriers to them doing so. The desire to overcome those barriers, and to carry on anyway, in spite of violence and prejudice, does arguably indicate a strong sense of self. Perhaps, for some people, it also indicates a strong sense of their gender identity – one that cannot be ignored or suppressed, no matter the social consequences. I suggest that to tell these people, to tell people like myself, that there is no such thing as gender identity and that everyone is non-binary, is thoughtless, demeaning and offensive, especially when that suggestion is made by sex and gender-conforming individuals; I wish those people would show some reflexivity around such a stance.

Tomboys that matter

The GC rejection of any possibility of gender identity also fuels the widely held GC standpoint, briefly addressed earlier in this chapter, that transgender or trans identification among female-born people is primarily due to a desire to escape the constraints of femininity and avoid the sexualized male violence that all women are subjected to and limited by. 'Being female means having a body that is seen as dirty, exploitable, penetrable: of course we want to run away from this', writes journalist Sarah Ditum (2018b). Professor Sheila Jeffreys generalizes that the majority of trans men transition due to childhood experiences of sexual abuse and internalized homophobia relating to lesbianism: 'The reasons given by FTMs relate straightforwardly to the oppression of women and lesbians and to child sexual abuse. The commonest reason given by FTMs for their decision to transition is discomfort with lesbianism' (2003: 137). In her book *Gender Hurts*, Sheila Jeffreys highlights the violence of beauty practices such as make-up, wearing tight and revealing clothing or high heels, and she notes the impact of the beauty industry on the mental health of girls and young women. For girls who want to escape this, and for young lesbian women who may be sick of being punished for not complying with femininity, Jeffreys argues that becoming trans men is being pushed as an alternative, as a get out clause or way of trading up, as she calls it: 'There is increasing evidence that woman-hating Western cultures are toxic to girls and very harmful to their mental health. It is, perhaps, not surprising, therefore, that there seem to be some girls bailing out and seeking to upgrade their status' (Jeffreys, 2014a: 112). Young lesbians who are tomboys as children are seen as particularly at risk of these pressures.

The psychotherapist Stella O'Malley describes herself as a tomboy as a child and, in a documentary for Channel 4 in the UK on young trans people which screened in 2018, explained that she probably would have transitioned when younger and gone on to identify as a trans man. Fortunately, she says, she then went through puberty, and although that wasn't an easy process, she found a new confidence eventually in being a woman, and is glad that she did. She is now heterosexual, married to a man and with children of her own and loves being a woman. Interviewed for *The Sunday Times* in 2018 she said, 'thank God they didn't make this tomboy trans' and recounts an experience when female friends took her in hand as a teen girl: 'My good friend was a hairdresser and she said, "Come round, we're going to do a job on you." She cut my hair and bobbed it and dyed it red. I came out and someone said "Gorgeous" to me and I cannot emphasise enough what that meant' (Kinchen, 2018). Frankly, I am disgusted by such comments and I am disgusted by the essentialist, heterosexist provocations that are overt between the lines of such speech. I am offended by the idea that femininity and heterosexuality will save tomboys from a presumably monstrous life of sex and gender nonconformity or that approval from the male gaze, and the pursuit of heterosexual marriage and children are all some sort of natural home destination that women will default to if we are only left to our own biological satnav devices like some sort of Stepford homing pigeon.

Anxiety about one's changing female body at puberty and understandable anger and fear in response to first experiencing sexual harassment from boys and men are unfortunately everyday female experiences, and most GC feminists are rightly quick to emphasize that none of this necessarily means that an individual is trans, as Kathleen Stock points out: 'Such feelings are not unusual. Many feminists would say they are an unconscious response to the social imposition of sexist and heteronormative stereotypes upon females' (Stock, 2018). As I have explained though, another common suggestion from GC activists is that young lesbians in particular, who are going through puberty and dealing with early experiences of objectification and other forms of male violence, are being put on a trans pathway just because they are masculine or gender non-conforming, for example – although obviously not all lesbians are masculine or gender non-conforming. These issues are taken up by the UK anti-trans-inclusion organizations like Get The L Out, Lesbian Rights Alliance and the LGB Alliance, for example, which I mentioned earlier in this chapter. In July 2019 the Lesbian Rights Alliance UK, along with other groups such as the feminist anti-pornography group Object, protested outside a Stonewall conference in London. The protestors carried huge banners with photographs of post-transition scars and healing tissue from the bodies of trans men, presumably lifted from the internet without permission. Their placards proclaimed that lesbians are being transed and that transition erases lesbians. Writing in *Vox* on the rise of GC feminism, journalist Katelyn Burns picks up on these connections that GC activists are keen to make between lesbian erasure and trans visibility: 'For anti-trans activists, establishing a narrative that trans men are really just lesbians attempting to identify out of womanhood is absolutely essential. By doing this, transitioning can be positioned as a form of "conversion therapy", whereby a lesbian is forced into a male identity and de facto heterosexuality' (Burns, 2019).

The symptoms of patriarchy, experienced by women of all sexual orientations, such as sexualized male violence, objectification and cultural shaming of the female body, GC activists then believe, are partly what lie behind the increasing numbers of young female-born individuals referred to the UK's Gender Identity Development Service (GIDS) Clinic at the Tavistock in London, or its satellite sites, which counsel children and young people who are too young to enter adult services. A report from the UK Government Equalities Office in July 2019 noted that in 2018–19, 2,590 children and young people were referred to GIDS, with three quarters of those being young people sexed as female at birth. 'Teenage girls don't want to identify as girls any more', writes journalist Helen Lewis, 'and who can blame them', she adds (Lewis, 2016). However, it is reductionist to suggest that the experiences of trans men, and young trans men, are simply a reaction to a misogynistic culture. After all, arguably every woman experiences a misogynistic culture, not every woman decides to pursue an identity as a trans man. Responding to comments by the author J. K. Rowling in the summer of 2020, journalist Evan Urquhart counters that it is sexist to assume that young sexed as female people who question their gender identity or go on to live as trans men do not know their own mind, or are brainwashed: 'It is unacceptable for us to be painted as victims led astray by trans ideology in this way' (Urquhart, 2020). Writing in *The Economist* in 2018, the author and activist Charlie Kiss also takes up this point, warning that too many people fall into this 'common misconception that trans men are "really women" who don't like their bodies and have been indoctrinated into a hatred of womanhood' (2018). As GC feminists may agree, for most women and for most young women, having breasts or hips is not a problem; it is the sexual harassment aimed at women's bodies which is a problem, not the body itself. Nobody likes the experience of sexual harassment, but this doesn't lead all girls to wish that they had a flat chest, pectoral muscles, facial hair, a penis and testicles, a deep voice and an Adam's apple. This is an important distinction that is often glossed over. It is glossed over partly because of the rampant unhelpful conflation of gender and sex. We cannot and should not reduce the experience of trans men to simply being a flight from sexism.

Sexism as well as resistance to sexism is a universal experience for sexed as female people; the desire to have a sexed as male body is not. I am not sure whether most GC activists can actually accept that the latter desire is even an experience; perhaps it is so outside their own life they cannot imagine what sex dysphoria would be like. Perhaps these activists are not really non-binary, as so many claim, because they are actually female women and their sense of self and embodiment has never contradicted that. Sex dysphoria, the sense, to varying degrees, that one's own body should have different primary and secondary sexed characteristics – those of the 'opposite' sex – is not the same as being disillusioned with experiences of sexism. Nor does being trans or transgender make one immune from sexism and sexual harassment anyway. It is actually outrageously naive that this claim is made so frequently, and it disavows, negates and ridicules the lives of trans men, transgender men, transgender butches and all female MOC individuals.

Queers can critique gender too

The gender-critical and/or gender-abolitionist position has not only been a stance of GC activists, Radical Feminists, or lesbian feminists (whether they actually do it in their own lives or not), because for decades this has also been a stance of many trans women and trans men too, especially those queer activists who are also intent on dismantling gender. Perhaps most famously, for example, in her posttranssexual manifesto, *The Empire Strikes Back*, from 1991, which was a reply to Janice Raymond's infamous *The Transsexual Empire* (1979), Sandy Stone critiques the pathologizing and medicalizing narratives that sought to construct what trans identities could be, and should not be. Pointing out the requirements of medical gatekeepers, she problematizes the 'wrong body' assertion that was necessary to access interventions at the gender clinics she was writing about in that period. She calls the 'wrong body' assertion 'a phrase whose lexicality suggests the phallocentric, binary character of gender differentiation should be examined with deepest suspicion' (2006: 231). Similarly to pathbreaking queer theorist Kate Bornstein, Stone asserts that to assimilate into the binary precludes a freedom to explore or pursue other possibilities and thus further erases what those other possibilities might even be: 'To attempt to occupy a place as a speaking subject within the traditional gender frame is to become complicit in the discourse which one wishes to deconstruct' (2006: 230). Self-described gender outlaw Kate Bornstein clarified in her work in the 1990s that once anyone takes on the label of man or woman and all the baggage that goes with that, they have bought into the harmful system of gender: 'Once we choose one or the other, we've bought into the system that perpetuates the binary' (Bornstein, 1994: 101).

In 2002, in an edited collection with Joan Nestle, trans theorist and activist Riki Wilchins pointed out that many trans and queer people do not believe that masculinity and femininity is innate or born either: 'when we equate transgenderism with those individuals who can claim their gender is a sign of an internal, binary essence, we privilege transsexuals over other genderqueers who cannot make similar claims. Moreover, we diminish those who conceptualise their transcending of narrow gender stereotypes as a matter of the right to self-expression' (Wilchins, 2002a: 61). Feminism was right, says Wilchins: 'gender is primarily a system of symbols and meanings – and the rules, privileges, and punishments pertaining to their use – for power and sexuality: masculinity and femininity, strength and vulnerability, action and passivity, dominance and weakness' (2002c: 14). More recently, the writer and critic Andrea Long Chu, who has been hailed by Sandy Stone for launching what she calls a second wave of trans studies, also attacks essentialism and applies this painfully honestly to her own life and transition. For her, there is no born, innate binary truth of gender; there is just the desire to be gendered in another way, and to have a body that is gendered in another way: 'This would require understanding transness as a matter not of who one *is*, but of what one *wants*' (2018). Chu covers the familiar terrain of both Raymond and Stone in her critiques of medical gatekeepers, arguing controversially that sex reassignment interventions are cosmetic surgeries: 'gender confirmation surgeries are aesthetic practices, continuous with rather than distinct from the so-called cosmetic surgeries. (No one goes into the operating room asking for an ugly cooch)' (2018).

She goes on to address the opposition I have discussed in this chapter, between gender-critical and gender-abolitionist positions; she acknowledges the praiseworthy stance of the latter, for its political consistency and logic: 'In this respect, someone like Ti-Grace Atkinson, a self-described radical feminist committed to the revolutionary dismantling of gender as a system of oppression, is not the dinosaur; I, who get my eyebrows threaded every two weeks, am' (2018). Her point is that consistent, pure political positions are not always personally desirable, and that people do not always want what is probably good for them in the long run. Chu points out that gender is implicated in such processes of desire, and it should need no biological justification or 'born this way' style apology; it just is, like any other desire. Her theory should, in theory, have much to appeal to GC and gender-abolitionist feminists alike. In its avowed anti-essentialism it has received much criticism from some trans activists, and due to the sharpness of the sides in the gender wars, it is unlikely to be read as closely as it deserves.

In conclusion, like many GC activists and queer activists, I believe gender is indeed a social construction. Masculinity, femininity, both, neither or something in between are not born; they are made. For me this is a primary part of my Radical Feminist politics. GC activists argue that only sex matters, as in the sex we were recorded at birth. I agree that sex matters; it affects our life trajectory and places us into one of two hierarchal sex classes. Our sexed bodies affect how we understand and experience our own bodies and the bodies of others. However, I disagree that gender identity is irrelevant. Gender too shapes how we understand and experience our bodies. This is intimately connected with sexuality too. Gender affects how we understand and experience our sexuality. Masculinity and femininity shape and construct heterosexuality; in fact, heterosexuality couldn't exist without them because heterosexuality is masculinity and femininity. While I believe that sexual orientation too is a social construction and is not born, but made, I can still acknowledge that sexual orientation forms a key part of most people's identity and sense of self, including my own.

Lesbian feminist Sheila Jeffreys also argues that sexuality, including lesbianism, is a social construction, but concludes that this does not mean it is not significant: 'Lesbian feminist identity is a social construction, I suggest, as is lesbian identity; but this does not mean that it needs to be abandoned' (2003: 39). This acknowledgement can surely extend to gender identity, even if some people feel that they have no inner sense of themselves as a woman or a man. Whether it is purely biological, social or a mixture of those things, everyone has a right to express themselves how they wish. If a non-normative individual has a sense of their gender identity as masculine, feminine or NB, it is important that they can express that without punishment or threat, let alone risk to life. We have as much of a right to express and have that identity recognized, as all those gender-conforming individuals who are male, masculine men or female, feminine women. As long as we live in the gendered context that we do, it is blatant discrimination to undermine, stigmatize and destabilize the gender expression of a minority, while overlooking the overt gender expression of the majority.

In the next half of this book I will move on to focus on those figures who have been mentioned in so many discourses so far, from Conservatives and feminists alike; these are the masculine females and queer subjects who are being claimed by all sides. Butch and masculine lesbians have been subjected to appalling stereotyping and scapegoating by some sections of feminism, for decades. As visible signifiers of lesbianism practically the world over, butches have also been subjected to public, private and state violence and control. Now, it seems, sections of feminism are offering an olive branch and suggesting that all is forgiven, if only the butches don't trans, or become too male-identified. At this time, to confuse and contradict such attacks with even more attacks, some feminists talk about saving butches in the same breath as saying that masculine females should carry identification with them and expect to be checked at women's toilets or changing rooms. Some suggest that such gender diversity is a form of disability or mental illness, and thus such individuals should use toilets rightly reserved for those with physical conditions that make accessing inaccessible, narrow stalls problematic or impossible.

Before exploring some of these charges and countering with the voices of butch and masculine queers themselves, I shall start by introducing and problematizing masculinity itself. This is a term that is often taken for granted; the gender wars are riddled with references to those who masculinize themselves too much, or are masculine identified or to those females who supposedly flee to masculinity to gain power under patriarchy. However, masculinity is a fluid concept, a descriptor that is hard to pin down and which has a multitude of understandings, not always associated with male bodies. Masculinity studies or men and masculinity studies is a huge area, and I will only give you a taste of it here. Alongside the variety of approaches in academia are the public understandings and usage of terms like 'toxic masculinity' and 'fragile masculinity' which are increasingly used in areas of life from adverts to education policies (Sundaram & Jackson, 2018). If we are to explore what masculinity means to female people, we need to look at some of the frameworks we have for masculinity in general, so that we can disentangle them from embodiment and bodily signifiers. Putting in female perspectives on masculinity is an important juncture into this field and, I would argue, is under researched. Such a move could backlight and perhaps expose just what masculinity is, or is not, and the threadbare thin myths that function to prop up some of the violent power relationships that too many of us write off as masculinity.

5

Butch/ering the 'real man'

What is masculinity anyway?

Defining masculinity is as difficult a question as defining female masculinity, or defining butch lesbian identity, for example – as will become clear in the chapters that follow in this half of this book. Received wisdom may instruct us that masculinity is just something men are, or something men do; but this is too simple an answer. In practice, we can see for ourselves that men are not a homogenous group, and what is considered appropriate manly behaviour, style and role for men changes depending on culture and historical time period, as well as what demands are put on to and expected of men from the economy for example, or for military requirements. Different cultures have different ideas of what is manly and womanly, what is masculine and feminine, and this extends to what jobs people should do or not do, what they should wear, how they should have their hair, how much they should be paid and all sorts of minutiae in everyday life. As I will outline in this chapter, defining masculinity is actually very complicated, and whole libraries have been written in the process of trying to do so. I will regularly refer throughout this book to masculinities, plural, rather than masculinity in the singular. This is to start right away from a position that acknowledges that there are so many different examples of masculinity, so it would not be appropriate to talk about just one kind or type. By masculinities, I mean all the many different examples of what is considered culturally and socially appropriate for (mainly) men, and for how (mainly) men should look and behave.

As I discussed in the Introduction to this book, all of us will be able to identify different examples of what we might understand as masculinity in the men from our own families and personal networks. These men were perhaps our first introduction to what men are supposed to be, and the options that were available to grow into and inhabit. If you think about representations of men and masculinities in the media too, you can see that there are many different recognizable types of men and masculinity. Taking mainstream Western films and TV for example, there are superhero men, there are nerds who win the day, there are sharp suited businessmen, there are tough cowboys, there are heartthrob sexy stars, and there are different representations again of gay men's masculinity, of Black men's masculinity, of urban young men and their masculinity, as well as of boys and their journeys into masculinity. There are many different visible images of what masculinity can look like in our media and culture. Well, many different examples of masculinity for men, that is. This gamut of representation of ways to do masculinity doesn't usually extend to female examples of masculinity, as I outline later in Chapter 8 on queering female masculinity. As Professor Jack Halberstam has always maintained, female masculinities are still treated as monstrous in popular culture, as somehow perverse and taboo (1998a). Such representations are still rare. Female, queer and lesbian masculinities are not given the attention they deserve; they are not seen as influences behind other types of masculinity, and they are more often seen as fakes or cheap copies of some supposed original manly male masculinity. This is just one of the false assumptions I hope to address with this book.

Sex not gender; male not masculine

In their 1994 collection on masculinities, anthropologists Andrea Cornwall and Nancy Lindisfarne note that the 1973 edition of the *Oxford English Dictionary* (*OED*) defined 'masculine' as 'having the appropriate excellence of the male sex; virile, vigorous and powerful' (1993: 1284). A glance at the 2000 edition of the *OED* still provides the exact same suggested definition, but most of the entries listed define masculinity as the male sex, and anything related to male humans or animals. Yet, there is already a word for the male sex, that is, 'male'. Male is the term used to refer to those humans or animals with genitalia commonly defined as male – penis and testicles – and with a reproductive system defined as male – the presumed capacity to produce (fertile) sperm. Masculinity therefore does not need to be and should not be a stand-in term to describe genital and reproductive bodily systems that are sexed as male. Masculinity is also not just another word for men, although it is often used to describe what are seen as commonalities between men, or common attributes that might link and therefore define all men. While male is a term to describe sexed features of the body, terms like 'man' and 'masculine' are terms to describe gendered features of the body and gendered presentations, expectations, ideals, behaviours and roles. As I have argued throughout this book, it is very important not to conflate sex and gender terms; there are two different words for a reason, and 'sex' and 'gender' are two very different things. Masculinity is not just another word for male bodies. Masculinity is not just another word for men. Masculinity is a gender, not a sex. In this chapter I will explore some of the different scholarly contributions to these starting points.

Masculinity is a serious business

So, if masculinity is not just something men are, or something men do that unites all male people, then what is it? In definitions like those quoted from the dictionary earlier (*OED*) masculinity is frequently related to attributes like virility, vigour and power. The dictionary definition advises that inanimate objects which are seen as essentially strong, superior or powerful in some way could also be defined as masculine. These are, in fact, some of the terms that crop up again and again if you go looking for definitions of masculinity. Many academic definitions of masculinity, from legacy-building scholars of masculinities such as Professor Raewyn Connell (1995), Jeff Hearn (1998), Stephen Whitehead (2002), John Stoltenberg (2000), Mairtin Mac an Ghaill (1994), Michael Messner (1997) and Michael Flood (2019), to name but a few in this field, underline that masculinity is often defined, symbolized and recognized in terms of power, control and dominance over self and others. Masculinity is a serious business, and achieving it can be a struggle and can involve great costs. The American essayist and novelist Norman Mailer wrote in his book *Cannibals and Christians* in 1966: 'Masculinity is not something given to you, something you're born with, but something you gain. And you gain it by winning small battles with honour' (1966: 242). This, like most of men's treatments of masculinity, is a rather romantic and esoteric definition. It also does not limit such displays to those defined as men; surely women too fight many battles in their life, and win them honourably.

Honour is a term that is regularly associated with masculinity, as are other human values such as loyalty, courage and strength. These are serious terms, for what is clearly meant to be seen as a serious identity, and this is just one reason why masculinity is not treated the same way as femininity in popular culture; where femininity can be funny, shallow and mockable, masculinity must be none of these things. Ricardo Ramirez, in his study of lesbian and gay characters in Chilean television soap operas, summarizes this aggrandizement of masculinity as serious and rational, defined against femininity which is constructed as frivolous, silly and vain, whether it is displayed by a sexed as female body, or a sexed as male body. 'Masculinity is a serious matter, a privilege that must only reside in the *macho*, avoiding its presence in any other body. Femininity, on the other hand, does not hold this privileged position; it is an unserious matter that can be ridiculed' (Ramirez, 2020: 6).

Masculinity is so serious that it is often a life and death matter, not only for men but for everyone else. Masculinity is regularly culturally attached to violence and aggression in particular ways, both in popular cultural understandings of what masculinity is or should be for men and, sadly, in practice, in terms of the higher rates of violence experienced by and perpetrated by men as opposed to women. This is an unarguable statistical fact, from the data we have in terms of conviction rates and from self-report surveys of crime, men are more likely to experience and perpetrate physical violence, and they are more likely to perpetrate sexual violence. In the first issue of the *Journal of Bodies, Sexualities and Masculinities*, the editors, Allan, Haywood and Karioris, caution, however, that the term 'masculinity' has wrongly become a catch-all for some men's violence and violent discrimination. 'Furthermore, we were aware of how "masculinity" itself has become shorthand for violence, misogyny, and homophobia, and of the importance of continually reflecting and challenging what is understood by the term' (Allan, Haywood & Karioris, 2020: 14). Not all men are violent and abusive, and most men do not abuse their partners and children; masculinity should not be used as some sort of excuse for some men's crimes, though it can contextualize them and point to paths to change.

Masculinity is deadly serious

It is important that we keep the focus on gendered socialization and gendered norms, rather than on the biological features of maleness, because there is nothing about a neutrally male body that predisposes one to battering intimate partners or raping children. The conflation of sex and gender actually hinders this vital feminist insight and reduces culturally constructed patterns of violence into the banal and uncontrollable fluctuations of nature. In turn, this passes onto men themselves, in the often repeated narratives that we hear about how men can't control themselves, or how they can't help but react when they are put down or how they are provoked by a female partner ending a relationship or how they lose it when they are angry. This enables the societal tendency to see men as victims of their provoked and wild emotions, with the woman who 'caused' such a response being the one to get the blame. It is a tendency that the philosopher Kate Manne has wonderfully titled 'himpathy' (2019). However, the important lesson from feminist theory on male violence against women is that these forms of violence are far from uncontrollable – both for the individual perpetrators and the society that excuses them. Not only does society often excuse such crimes but the link between masculinity and violence is actually aggrandized in culture, forming a staple in much film and literature, for example. This extends to sexual violence too, which is often eroticized and used in film as a titillation for the viewer; rape of women and sexual abuse of women sadly appear as a feature in many mainstream films.

Feminist sociologists had a vested interest in studying men and masculinity because they wanted to find out how to stop men's sexual violence against women and children. They were unusual in that, and they were even more unusual in assuming that these violent crimes were not natural, nor biological. As Black feminist theorist Professor bell hooks asserts in her fantastically illuminating and accessible book on men and masculinities, 'the will to use violence is really not linked to biology but to a set of expectations about the nature of power in a dominator culture' (hooks, 2004: 55). Thus, there must be something about the masculine gender role that has constructed, concretized and maintained dominating, controlling and aggressive behaviours over women, children and marginalized men. If we are to change this situation, then it is necessary to study and understand masculinities and their construction. The initial step towards that goal is believing the current situation can be changed in the first place, which requires the severing of the biological umbilical cord we have tied between maleness and masculinity. Feminist theorists like Professor Jalna Hanmer (1987), the late theorist and peace activist Cynthia Cockburn (1983), Professor Lynne Segal (1997) and Professor bell hooks (2004) have all contributed profound books on men and masculinities that put forward some answers to these challenges.

Enlightening masculinity

It is vital to emphasize just how radical this feminist work was. Studying men and masculinity as an object of scrutiny, as an object which could be problematized and analysed at all, was heresy to an ideology wherein the male subject is taken as the norm, the original and the superior to which all 'others' are defined. Within this ideology, what is constructed as deviant is to be pathologized, but the norm does not need to be questioned. As I outlined earlier in more detail in Chapter 1, on the construction of sex differences, this ideological framing is far from neutral; it is heavily raced, gendered and classed (Leek & Gerke, 2017; Innes & Anderson, 2015). Common gender stereotypes are rooted in dualistic discourses, not just of sex, but of race, class and sexuality too. As educationalist Stephen Whitehead underlines, these are 'dualisms such as passive/assertive, strong/weak, irrational/rational, gentle/forceful, emotional/distant', with female, women and femininity being firmly on the 'wrong', or powerless side of that dualism (Whitehead, 2002: 10). Western (un)enlightenment ideology put White European men at the top of a neat oil painted hierarchy, which it has then built upon and against the rest of the world, whitewashing over the cracks it created.

> A conception of humanity was consolidated according to which the world's population was differentiated in two groups: superior and inferior, rational and irrational, primitive and civilized, traditional and modern. 'Primitive' referred to a prior time in the history of the species, in terms of evolutionary time. Europe came to be mythically conceived as pre-existing colonial, global, capitalism and as having achieved a very advanced level in the continuous, linear, unidirectional path. (Lugones, 2008: 4)

Historically, the Western universities and academic disciplines were built by these men, and they were certainly not in the habit of othering themselves by putting themselves under the microscope.

As masculinities scholar Jeff Hearn (2004) points out, for millennia men in authoritative positions with the power to name, define and rank everyone and everything else have been busying themselves with men's studies that they falsely called universal history or politics. Those unfortunate enough to be not men or not White, were the objects of study in other disciplines like psychology, sexology and eugenics. The Western scientific revolution of the 1600s and 1700s was no revolution at all; it was a propaganda machine to justify and excuse socially constructed inequalities which those at the top were profiting from, and still are. Because there is no just reason to divide humans up into slave and owner, biology was brought in as the trump card, and science proved that those already at the top were superior in every way and thus that explained why they were at the top. As Professor Oyeronke Oyewumi, a scholar of gender studies, explains in her exciting book on the invention of the category of 'woman', 'Consequently, those in positions of power find it imperative to establish their superior biology as a way of affirming their privilege and dominance over "Others". Those who are different are seen as genetically inferior, and this, in turn, is used to account for their disadvantaged social positions' (1997: 1). This is clearly a circular argument; those in power get to define what powerful and superior is, they define themselves and their preferred ideal cultures and behaviours as naturally powerful and superior, and they define everyone else and their other cultures and behaviours as inferior. Those in power point to this constructed inferiority as the reason why those Other/ed people are not in power, and they use those biological reasonings to justify keeping them out of it. This brings us to power, and perhaps not early enough in this chapter, because power and the use of power is important in any study of masculinity; in fact, it is impossible to study masculinity without studying power.

Masculinity is the ideology of patriarchy

I am talking here about patriarchy, and patriarchal power. This has been defined by famous masculinities scholar Professor Raewyn Connell as follows: 'The main axis of power in the contemporary European/American gender order is the overall subordination of women and dominance of men – the structure Women's Liberation named patriarchy' (Connell, 1995: 74). Patriarchy is the term used to describe societies where all mainstream institutions of power are dominated overwhelmingly and disproportionately by particular kinds of men, institutions like politics, business, law, policing, military and cultural industries like the media and arts. These institutions are then sites of gender practice. Professor Connell explains that masculine practices, and feminine practices, are practices of gender or, what she calls, configurations of gender practice: 'when we speak of masculinity and femininity we are naming configurations of gender practice' (Connell, 1995: 72). All social patterns are gendered. Femininity and masculinity aren't just products of culture and society; they act on it and shape it as well. Gender thus needs to be considered as 'a product of history, and also as a producer of history' (1995: 81). These practices of gender bring gender into being and underpin what Connell calls the gender order. This is familiar territory to any readers of Professor Judith Butler, of course, who has done so much to popularize the idea of gender work – or, working at gender – as being what brings gender into being.

From this perspective there is no original gender, no inherently gendered soul that we are all born with. We don't 'do' gender because we are expressing a born, natural gender; we do it because we are schooled into it, and because it is all around us, it is part of what is seen to make people human. The more we do it, the more natural and seamless it becomes and the more we all expect and require it in ourselves and others; indeed, it becomes hard to understand people without it. This will become brutally clear when we explore the experiences of masculine queer female people, butch lesbians and masculine of centre queer people. The gender order, as Connell explains it, is made up of various localized gender regimes, that is, how gender relations between women and men, and between different kinds of men, are organized in any one given place and time period, such as in institutions, in a way that validates, reproduces and gives authority to the current overarching gender order. 'The patterning of all these relations within an institution (such as a school or a corporation) may be called its gender regime. The overall patterning of gender regimes, together with the gender patterning of culture and personal life, may be called the gender order of a society' (Connell, 2000: 29). Masculinity is then intrinsically linked to the construction and maintenance of patriarchal social governance (Millett, 1969). I make no apology for using the term 'patriarchy', while it may be considered out of date in some quarters; the global dominance of men in mainstream power shows no signs of diminishing.

Hegemonic masculinity is the poster boy for patriarchy

Professor Connell is known for establishing the influential theory of hegemonic masculinity, and this is a term that has journeyed from the academy and into popular mainstream usage. Whenever these sorts of journeys take place, the academic theories involved are always changed, stretched and expanded from their original meanings and intentions. 'Hegemonic masculinity' is a term now commonly used to describe powerful men, and the appearance, behaviour and roles of men in power. As the term has moved into the mainstream, it has also overlapped somewhat with another term in popular usage, that of 'toxic masculinity'. This is an unhelpful and problematic buzzword, from my feminist perspective, because it masks how gender roles of any kinds are all 'toxic' in a way, in that it is these that lead to more brutal or extreme behaviours we may then label as toxic. The behaviours or attitudes described by the term are certainly not anything to do with maleness, though they are often to do with what maleness is supposed to mean in any given context. 'When it comes to men, their bodies, and their sexualities, sweeping generalizations often premised on pop psychology come into play with self-explanatory terms such as "masculinities in crisis," "locker-room talk," and "toxic masculinity"' (Allan, Haywood & Karioris, 2020: 6). Both 'hegemonic masculinity' and 'toxic masculinity' are often currently used to describe a dominating, powerful, heterosexually sexually aggressive, bullish and bullying manner in powerful men who are at the top of whatever stage is set, be that business, politics, sport or the military. Professor Connell has taken pains to point out that this was not exactly what she meant though, and theorists of masculinities since have also spelled out the complexities of this concept, in contrast to the simplistic everyday way it has been used.

Hegemonic masculinity is political; it is the ways in which the patriarchal gender order is constructed, maintained and legitimated through what Professor Connell calls various configurations of gender practice in localized gender regimes – thus we return to the 'doing' of gender (West & Zimmerman, 1987) and the labour behind the gender labels. This labour is the practice of stylized cultural representations of gendered ways of being. The various ways that the patriarchal gender order is given authority and legitimation is the subject of much scholarship on hegemonic masculinity because hegemonic masculinity is all about political relations of power and the sort of appeals and claims made for that authority. In this reading, idealized types of powerful men, no matter that most men are not this type, and idealized behaviours of powerful men, no matter if most men do not conduct themselves in these ways (especially those actually in power), are held up to justify and legitimate male dominance by certain groups of men. 'At any given time, one form of masculinity rather than others is culturally exalted. Hegemonic masculinity can be defined as the configuration of gender practice which embodies the currently accepted answer to the problem of the legitimacy of patriarchy, which guarantees (or is taken to guarantee) the dominant position of men and the subordination of women' (Connell, 1995: 77). Male supremacy being entirely unnatural, Connell is pointing out the importance of understanding through what processes we are persuaded that it is, in fact, natural, just and right. If we want to identify what forms of masculinity are hegemonic in any culture, then we need to look at which configurations of gender practice are held up to define masculinity and are correspondingly aggrandized as proof of the natural dominance of mankind, or, at least, certain kinds of dominant men.

As noted earlier, these masculine examples may not be men in power, or men with power. They certainly may not be men in politics, as Professor Connell points out: 'This is not to say that the most visible bearers of hegemonic masculinity are always the most powerful people. They may be exemplars, such as film actors, or even fantasy figures, such as film characters. Individual holders of institutional power or great wealth may be far from the hegemonic pattern in their personal lives' (Connell, 1995: 77). What values should such exemplary characters be perceived to display and embody? Usually, we are back to the dictionary definitions we started with; they symbolize virility, honour, strength, leadership, power, dominance, control of self and others, rationality and the ability to utilize violence successfully, if or when needed, in order to maintain and defend all those aforementioned values and political positions. This is a kind of military masculinity almost, or rather, a stereotypical fantasy of military masculinity. It is a fantasy of the great leader strategically directing his men, or of the heroic soldier that is the first into battle and the last man standing, who can roll with the punches and keep going, carrying any wounded brethren on his back as he does so. When I think of what this kind of masculine fantasy looks like in the Western example, I always think of the White American actor Tom Cruise playing the character of real-life war veteran and peace activist Ron Kovic, in the 1989 film *Born on the Fourth of July* directed by Oliver Stone. This is a moving tale of the lies of hegemonic masculinity, and the suffering it brings when a mortal young man realizes he is not a superhero, he is not the fictional John Wayne, he will not in fact get up again and keep running when he is shot. Despite the fact that such idealized refrains about masculinity as immortal and all-powerful are well known and understood as lies, these narratives still have a powerful hold, and they play a part in maintaining the patriarchal gender order by setting up masculinity as leadership material, as naturally strong and superior, as innately able to command, strategize and win.

Professor Connell points out that hegemony – or, the dominant power of the gender order – will struggle to be maintained if there is not some crossover at least between idealized gender practices and the top of the current ruling institutions of that gender order. It is not therefore necessary for every man at the top of mainstream power to be a beacon of hegemonic masculinity, but their leadership and the leadership of the institution must be doing enough to be perceived as displaying some of these cultural ideals of masculinity.

> Nevertheless, hegemony is likely to be established only if there is some correspondence between cultural ideal and institutional power, collective if not individual. So, the top levels of business, the military and government provide a fairly convincing corporate display of masculinity, still very little shaken by feminist women or dissenting men. It is the successful claim to authority, more than direct violence, that is the mark of hegemony (though violence often underpins or supports authority). (Connell, 1995: 77)

While hegemonic masculinity may be mainly a mirage, a poster boy for patriarchy, these normative definitions of what masculinity could and should be, are widespread and provide a standard that all men are expected to measure up to, and women are meant to facilitate of course. Not all men will do, not all men want to, and not all men will be able to; some men will be actively excluded from doing so, despite their gender performances of any kind. Dominant ideals of masculine types actually depend on supposed inferior models that they can be defined in contrast to; those inferior types are obviously women of any kind, and femininities, particularly femininity in men.

Subordinated and marginalized masculinities

Feminine men are an example of what Connell has called in her four-part framing, subordinated masculinities. Subordinated masculinity, as Swedish scholars of gender and men's studies Lucas Gottzen and Wibke Straube summarize, 'is (together with "gayness"), the repository of whatever is symbolically expelled from hegemonic masculinity' (Gottzen & Straube, 2016: 219). In other words, not all masculinities, and certainly not all men, are equal. As masculinities scholar Michael Messner points out, 'Although it may be true that men, as a group, enjoy institutional privileges at the expense of women, as a group, men share very unequally in the fruits of these privileges' (Messner, 1997: 7). Some men are marginalized, and thus their stereotypical behaviours and values are marginalized also; this marginalization follows the socially constructed fault lines of race and class, for example. As James Messerschmidt defines, 'marginalised masculinities are trivialised and/or discriminated against because of unequal relations external to gender relations, such as class, race, ethnicity, and age' (2018: 29). Men as individuals will, of course, develop their own identities, and some will rebel against stereotypical expectations and develop and display their own alternative or new masculinities, or other gender displays altogether – such as, perhaps, some gay masculinities, egalitarian and pro-feminist masculinities – or also, what have been called protest masculinities.

Protest masculinities

Protest masculinities are claims to masculine power performed by those who are not in power and who do not benefit structurally from male supremacy and White supremacy, which go hand in interdependent hand in the Western model of hegemonic masculinity. Individuals may blend some of the mainstream models on offer and then make a masculinity of their own, perhaps a hyper masculine performance: 'protest masculinities are constructed as compensatory hypermasculinities that are formed in reaction to social positions lacking economic and political power' (Messerschmidt & Messner, 2018: 38). These exaggerated gender practices can garner degrees of respect and foster bonds of recognizable commonality within that group. Some scholars have suggested that some types of Black masculinities, or White working-class masculinities, could be seen as protest masculinities. Protest masculinity is defined by Connell and Messerschmidt, for example, as 'a pattern of masculinity constructed in local working-class settings, sometimes among ethnically marginalised men, which embodies the claim to power typical of regional hegemonic masculinities in Western countries, but which lacks the economic resources and institutional authority that underpins the regional and global patterns' (Connell & Messerschmidt, 2005: 848). It is sad and ironic that such claims to power do not result in mainstream power and in fact can be seen to only prop up and further entrench hegemonic masculinity, which remains and persists. There it is, always on top, reproducing itself, stubbornly symbolically, if not actually, at the pinnacle of all the major institutions of power in the global North and increasingly, worldwide. These are major global and globalized institutions which do not contain anywhere near any representative number of Black men or White working-class men and yet have a say over policies, laws and economic relationships that most profoundly negatively impact on the lives of marginalized people, including Black men and White working-class men.

The patriarchal dividend and complicit masculinities

Not all men perform the role of poster boy for patriarchy by displaying and embodying visible practices of hegemonic masculinity. However, while not all men are within the ranks of what counts as hegemonic masculinity, and do not perform these configurations of gender practice, Professor Connell argues that all men benefit from it because they benefit within a current gender order that, in the main, puts men above women. This is what Connell calls the patriarchal dividend, the varying degrees and scale of benefits that accrue to men within patriarchy, simply for being men and not being women.

> Normative definitions of masculinity, as I have noted, face the problem that not many men actually meet the normative standards. This point applies to hegemonic masculinity. The number of men rigorously practicing the hegemonic pattern in its entirety may be quite small. Yet the majority of men gain from its hegemony, since they benefit from the patriarchal dividend, the advantage men in general gain from the overall subordination of women. (Connell, 1995: 79)

Messerschmidt and Messner, in their book *Gender Reckonings*, suggest that these advantages are why some men's gender practices, performances of or buy-in to masculinities will go along with the cultural dominance of models of hegemonic masculinity. They call this a complicit masculinity – 'complicit masculinities do not actually embody hegemonic masculinity yet through practice realise some of the benefits of patriarchal relations' (Messerschmidt & Messner, 2018: 38).

Pro-feminist gender scholar, Jeff Hearn, in his nuanced and liberatory work, draws our attention back to the importance of structural power and how it operates. Hearn insists that we not lose sight of the operation of patriarchy, and warns that we not get enmeshed in some vague study of masculinity as an a-priori entity in itself, especially as there are so many different analyses, and so many different definitions and competing (how apt) examples offered of what masculinity even is or might be. Hegemonic masculinity has been used wrongly all too often, Hearn suggests, when it is mistakenly used to refer to a type of masculinity, or, perhaps, as I have suggested earlier, when it is used as synonymous with that toxic and misleading term 'toxic masculinity' (Morgan, 2019). It is also especially wrong to see hegemonic masculinity as a type of man. Patriarchy, of course, is a political system of power, which elite men have built and which they maintain (Carrigan, Connell & Lee, 1985).

Masculinity as political power

Hegemonic masculinity is not then a type of innate superior manliness or masculinity; it is a type of political power, a profoundly gendered, raced and classed political power that constructs and maintains those differentiations between White and not White, between men and not men, between heterosexual normal and not normal. This, of course, is the internal workings of patriarchy; this is how it maintains power, as Professor bell hooks (2004) explains: 'Patriarchy is a political-social system that insists that males are inherently dominating, superior to everything and everyone deemed weak, especially females, and endowed with the right to dominate and rule over the weak and to maintain that dominance through various forms of psychological terrorism and violence' (hooks, 2004: 18). Within this system of socially constructed differentials comes differential and unfair treatment. Within this gender order, the separate spheres for men and women are assumed as normal and natural, the domestic division of labour is assumed as normal and natural, heterosexism is assumed as normal and natural, the feminization of care and caring is assumed as normal and natural, the masculinization of wealth is assumed as normal and natural, men's superiority over women is assumed as natural and normal.

This ideology has engrained itself deeply, not just in men, but in women too, and all the rest of us. In 2018 the Pew Research Centre in the United States conducted a study on 'Women and Leadership', randomly surveying 4,587 adult Americans. While 59 per cent of Americans surveyed stated there were not enough women in senior roles currently, the research found that only 4 per cent of those surveyed felt positively about women outnumbering men in senior roles in business, and only 6 per cent would feel comfortable with this in politics (Parker, Horowitz & Igielnik, 2018). The majority of respondents were uncomfortable with the prospect of women outnumbering men in powerful institutions. Yet the status quo is one where men wildly outnumber women in all senior positions in all institutions of power, and this is rarely researched or scrutinized as a distasteful imbalance, or as proof of illegal positive discrimination, man-quotas and conscious bias. Constructs of masculinity are just a part of maintaining such an unequal gender order, albeit quite a key part. Education theorist Stephen Whitehead therefore reminds us again that masculinities are mainly a tool to maintain patriarchy, to serve the patriarchal gender order: 'masculinity becomes recognised as a vital, historical, component in the armoury of male dominance; informing the "gender system" while serving to validate and reinforce patriarchal power' (Whitehead, 2002: 89).

Complicity within this system can be rewarded by the prize of being seen as what queer scholar and Professor of Sociology Henry S Rubin calls 'real men'. Who gets to be a 'real man' is a serious question, because it does not contain all men. That, in fact, is the point. If all men were real men, then we wouldn't even have the concept of 'real men', which carries so much psychic and cultural weight that if you went up to most people in the streets of Europe or North America, and asked them what a 'real man' is, you would probably not get a blank response, as most people know only too well what this is supposed to symbolize – even if they know these are stereotypes. The pursuit of 'real manhood' is what necessitates the construction of, in turn, 'real' womanhood, of course, and the stereotypes that go along with that, visible in cultural standards for femininity, or in what Connell's taxonomy may call 'emphasised femininity' (Connell, 1987). Scholar of gender and masculinities John Stoltenberg explains this: 'Male supremacy is explicable not by biology but by belief in the delusion of "real manhood" and the concomitant insatiable urge to belong to it the only way one can: by committing acts that violate and subjugate others' (Stoltenberg, 2020). Henry Rubin, in his famous essay on trans men, argues that the measure of a 'real man' is the extent to which he will go along with legitimating and authorizing hegemonic models of masculinity. '"Real men" are typically defined by their willingness to participate in the cultural, economic, and political circulation of power. Real men do not activate their perverse identities. Real men are not gay, not black or brown or yellow. If they are, then they try to pass as real men' (Rubin, 1998: 305). As masculinity is about power and the maintenance of a particular political and economic system, it is not actually about biology, though biology is used to justify its authority, and male biology is imbibed and imbued with powerful gendered metaphors and meanings.

Masculinity without males

As Professor Raewyn Connell points out, gender exists 'precisely to the extent that biology does not determine the social' (1995: 71). It is because being born with a penis and testicles or a vagina or any combination of genitals and reproductive system does not make us behave in certain structural, public, private and interpersonal ways, that gender has to be created, taught and constantly maintained though repertoires of gender. There would be no need for such intense schooling in what is appropriately manly and womanly in different cultures, locations, groups and time periods, if it all just happened naturally because of what genitals one happened to be born with. Professor Judith Butler addresses this when discussing the crisis narratives that surround, and have always surrounded, understandings and definitions of masculinity. Butler underlines that most cultures have processes which symbolize boys becoming men, and manhood is not something that happens naturally at all; it is not chronological, it is not default (1995). In her work with boys in Scotland, feminist scholar McCarry finds in her research that 'normative masculinity was often discussed in an abstract, disembodied way and in relation to "others" rather than themselves', highlighting the role of other boys/men as external and internalized judges of appropriate gender compliance (McCarry, 2010: 28).

If a boy reaches sixteen or eighteen years old, or another arbitrarily socially significant age, and there is no other man around to see it and note it, we may ask if he becomes a man at all? Masculinity is fragile, like man's man Mailer reminded us at the start of this chapter; it can be gained, sometimes at great pains; but presumably if it can be gained, it can also be lost. It could be argued that such anxieties form the bedrock of much of men's novels, plays, films, music and great works. Men's cultural products are often concerned with men's search for manhood, or rather, the proving of it, to oneself and to other men who are nearly always the ultimate judge, with women as props to such journeys. Professor Butler suggests that there has perhaps never been an uncomplicated understanding of masculinity, because masculinity is complicated: 'masculinity appears transculturally as something to be acquired, achieved, initiated into – a process often involving painful or even mutilating rituals – there is ample evidence to suggest that there never is, never was, an unproblematic, a natural, or a crisis-free variant' (Butler, 1995: 71). If masculinity can be acquired, then even if this may be a difficult process, this begs the question as to why it couldn't be won and secured by those without sexed as male bodies. If masculinity is fragile and tenuous for men, then the male body is clearly no guarantee of achieving this elusive masculinity.

Connell points out that there is then no reason – other than, I would add, sexism, misogyny, lesbophobia and compulsory heterosexuality of course – to view masculinity as the property of male bodies only; especially when not all those with sexed as male bodies are considered to be, or treated as appropriately masculine, as I have discussed earlier. 'Masculinity refers to male bodies (sometimes directly, sometimes symbolically and indirectly), but it is not determined by male biology. It is thus perfectly logical to talk about masculine women or masculinity in women's lives, as well as masculinity in men's lives' (Connell, 2000: 29). As I set out at the start of this chapter, however, it is often a common-sense response to assume that masculinity is indeed about male bodies and maleness, and that it can only be about male bodies. Like the *Oxford English Dictionary*, many people might assume that masculinity and manliness are linked to the male body and especially that ultimate sign of maleness, masculinity and power – the penis, which Cheng (1999) calls, a cultural artefact of gender performance.

> The penis is the absolute insignia of the male sex . . . the penis validates men who are marginalized by class, e.g. the characters in the films Boogie Nights (1997) and The Full Monty (1997), and validates a woman who is attempting to join the hegemonically masculine group through symbolic appropriation of a penis, e.g., G.I. Jane (1997). The penis is then a cultural artefact of gender performance. (Cheng, 1999: 308)

Displaying their penis, in the first two films mentioned in this quotation, proves the maleness and therefore manliness and masculinity of marginalized male characters. The penis, in those two films, serves as a status symbol – the status being masculine. The presence of this bodily member compensates for lack in other defining features and requirements of hegemonic masculine membership, such as wealth, power, status, control and dominance over others.

Another film with a female hero as lead, in a male-dominated world, came out around the same time as Demi Moore's *GI Jane* was joining the US NAVY SEALS, and that is *The Long Kiss Goodnight*, starring Gina Davis in 1996. The character Davis plays is a female assassin, whose old friends and enemies are all out to kill her; in an entirely male-dominated field, she and her daughter actually end up escaping, and it is the enemies who wind up dead. In both these films the female characters invoke the symbolic power of the cultural artefact of gender performance. They validate their masculinity and their right to be equal players in a male field, by making reference to their symbolic penis power. There are strikingly similar scenes in both films, where in times of threat and danger the female characters overcome, and at the point of doing so, they both shout 'suck my dick'. The film directors, Renny Harlin of the latter, and Ridley Scott of the former, presumably assumed the audience would read these moments easily and without any interpretation. The female characters, as well as claiming their place, are making a statement about their masculinity, and they show they have the balls, and penis, to be able to prove it. While these are moments of resistance and female power, they are on and within classic male superhero scripts, and although the women use the language of the male body, this, in a way, only works as rebellious humour because the viewer assumes the hero, in this case, does not actually have a penis. Arguably then, such moments do not so much attach the validating penis to displays of female masculinity, as further highlight its lack. Representations of masculinity, and their use of and dependence on the male body, have changed over the years. From Greek statues with their big, hyper muscles and controlled, logical little penises, to the exaggerated physique of male body builders, manliness and thus, masculinity, has often been symbolized through the naked or semi-naked male body.

Masculine looks

What is considered masculine and suitable for men is historically, geographically and culturally specific. As Professor Aaron H Devor explored in his authoritative classic, *Gender Blending*: 'Standards of femininity and masculinity differ across class, age, race, ethnicity, and time, as well as with changing political and sexual persuasions' (Devor, 1989: 31). Masculinity changes over time and space; it looks different in different parts of the world, and it has looked different over the ages in Britain. In the so-called Renaissance period and the Elizabethan era (1300s–1600s) for example, men wore huge ruffs, velvet, lace and were not shy of bright colours. In the Victorian period (1830s–1900), however, men were to be physically tough and practical, and mainly not be feminine. In fact, masculinity is most often defined and recognized by not being feminine. As famous scholar Riki Wilchins summarizes: 'What is the meaning of masculinity? Mannish, not feminine, right?' (Wilchins, 2002: 43). This leads to a rather ironic dependency for masculinity, such a feminine position to be in, because it depends on femininity in order to define itself as the opposite. Masculinity is thus whatever femininity is not, and because women have always been on the wrong side of those Cartesian dualisms that I outlined in Chapter 1 on the construction of biological sex, femininity is defined as illogical, irrational, over-emotional, passive, weak, frivolous and object for the approving or disapproving male gaze (Mulvey, 1975). If women are supposed to be concerned with being beautiful objects to be gazed upon, then men are not supposed to be concerned with this. Men can just be, and get on with things they want to do, whereas women must be seen and looked at. As the famous John Berger summed up, 'men act and women appear' (1972: 42).

Of course, this depends on what type of woman one is seen as, and what type of man one is seen as. As I have asserted throughout, not all men are equal, thus not all masculinities are equal. Many Black men, or teenage boys, or working-class men cannot, of course, just be. They are hyper scrutinized, over policed, monitored, observed and pathologized; marginalized men are violently subjected to early criminalization and fatal racist and classed violence at the hands of the state, be it in police custody or the mental health system. In terms of the male bodies and displays of masculinity we see in media and advertising, these displays also shamelessly utilize and sometimes eroticize these very social inequalities between men. Reality TV shows like *Geordie Shore* in the UK make a spectacle of young working-class White male bodies, focussing on their muscular physique, for example, and emphasizing a predatory and dominant heterosexual sexuality. The BBC documentary *Models: Street to Catwalk*, which screened in 2020, focussed on the trend for the so-called Manchester Look, a working-class, laddish look now being sought worldwide. Black masculinity too is often fetishized in music, advertising and film as inherently violent, predatory and thuggish, which themselves are racialized and racist terms that have had deadly impact on Black men for centuries. Men are under scrutiny in popular media in ways not previously seen in recent years; their bodies are sexualized and eroticized, for a presumed audience of both male and female viewers.

From around the 1990s in the UK, there were changes in how men are displayed in advertising. The male body became much more of a feature than it had been before, by which I mean a naked or semi-naked sexed as male body that was buffed and oiled into beautiful idealized body types. Fashion models, sports and film stars were broken down into six packs and pecs; mainstream advertising started to show men in ways that previously women were commonly shown. In 1985 the fashion brand Levis screened its laundrette advert, with male model Nick Kamen stripping off to his perfect white boxers in a retro American laundrette, providing distraction to the women waiting for their loads. In 1988 men's lifestyle magazine *Men's Health* went into circulation and has sported semi-naked body beautifuls on its front cover ever since, alongside tips on how to achieve perfect stomach muscles or the best protein shakes for bulking up. In 1994 soft drinks company Coke introduced the hunky 'Diet Coke Man' to our screens, with a builder stripping off on his break to enjoy a drink of the finest brown stuff, while a gaggle of female office workers watch from the windows opposite. I grew up with the Gillette man on TV; beginning their campaign in 1989, their products were the best a man could get and the men who used them were the best a man can be. The Gillette man looked good on the football field with his mates, he looked good bossing up in his suit at work, he looked good cradling his baby like an Athena poster while his wife caressed his smooth face. The beauty industry was starting to cash in a bit more on the other half of the population.

Relatively suddenly it felt men were now shown as faceless and disembodied; they were not always looking in a manly way directly into the camera, they were looking down or away, and their mouths were open in a classic passive and receptive pose.

It is now quite normal for us to see male models and celebrities in nothing but tiny trunks, whether they are advertising a new product or just advertising themselves. The damaging effects of this trend can be witnessed in growing rates of eating disorders for men, dieting, extreme training or the risky use of illegal synthetic hormones as men struggle to look like the cover of *Men's Health* (Gill, Henwood & McLean, 2000; Grogan, 1999). As Allan, Haywood and Karioris address, 'pressures and unreal expectations about what it means to be a man may be introjected and then internalized' (2020: 7). What all this means for definitions of masculinity is that masculinity has become much more associated with the male body in popular culture, much more naked than before and less about the clothed male body. This has an effect on all masculine gender practices, and all claims to masculinity, especially by those men – arguably most – who are not shiny visions of airbrushed perfection. Some men try to measure up, evidenced in the damaging trends cited earlier, all of which is the grounds of much needed research.

Embodying masculinity

If not having the idealized masculine body type has negative effects for sexed as male men, then it is perhaps even more potentially negative for masculine people with sexed as female bodies. I will go on to discuss this in more depth in Chapter 8 on queering female masculinity. As I introduced earlier in this chapter, most scholars emphasize that masculinity is separate from the body, 'masculinity and femininity are not fixed properties of male and female bodies' (Schilt, 2009: 443). 'Gender is a social practice that constantly refers to bodies and what bodies do, it is not social practice reduced to the body' (Connell, 1995: 71). The body, however, can have an advantageous role in constructing expressions of gender, teaches Professor Judith Butler. The sexed body can help or aid in such expressions, but is not the total sum, nor guarantee of those expressions (Butler, 1995). Jamison Green underlines that judgements of masculinity can be based in readings of the body, meaning readable sexed as male bodies, but that the body is not the final say: 'masculinity is judged based on cultural understandings of maleness ascribed to male bodies, but the expression of masculinity is not solely the province of male bodies' (Green, 2005: 296). Yet scholars also acknowledge that, particularly currently, the sexed as male body is indeed one of the main cultural sites through which, and on which, masculinity is portrayed and displayed – as I have explained earlier.

Often such definitions refer to that presumed reliable membership card to maleness and therefore masculinity, the penis, as Green explains. 'While typically (though not always), maleness is conferred with the penis – an accident of birth – masculinity is often held to be "difficult to achieve". Rites of passage, behavioural conventions, social roles and political institutions have all been examined as sources for the production of masculinity' (Green, 2005: 291). Here we are returning to the analyses of masculinity as fragile, and as something that has to be gained, won or achieved by men. In any highly commodified, consumer society where the body is scrutinized and fashioned, trying to measure up to common coded masculine visuals will be more difficult when one is not starting off with a sexed as male body. The male body is not the only symbol of masculinity, as the scholarly quotes I have selected above maintain, but, as I have made clear, it is still one of them: 'masculinity is a socially negotiable quality that is understood through agreed-on symbols (such as the body and its secondary sex characteristics) and signals (such as clothing, behaviours, occupations, speech patterns etc, understood within a given cultural context) that together inform other people in that context concerning the individual person's status in a given group' (Green, 2005: 297).

As men are being dissected in advertising and media to within an inch of their lives, in similar ways to female bodies have endured, then not having the raw material, so to speak, of a flat chest, upper body muscle and a tidy penis package to display can make claims to masculinity more challenging; and, certainly, may result in those claims being more likely to be challenged by others and have their validity questioned. I was struck by a brief exchange in the 2015 documentary screened by Chanel 4 in the UK, titled 'Born in the Wrong Body: Girls to Men' where a young trans man converses with a non-trans man in a men's clothing store. The store owner asks questions about intentions, surgery and identity in an aggressive and demeaning way. At one point he offers the following sage advice: 'I know when you're standing in the urinal in your cubicle, and you're a man and you stand there and you've got that in your hand, that's what makes you feel like a man, in my eyes, 'cos I am a man, I was born one.' This, of course, is probably a common opinion; it is also not an attitude that trans and transgender people are unaware of, quite the contrary. Messerschmidt and Messner acknowledge this and suggest that sexed as female masculine people may experience not only external challenge from others but also an internal challenge, or a struggle with dissonance in an exceedingly binary sex-gender society that assumes the penis equals male for men and men equal masculine, and a vagina equals female for women and women equal feminine. 'Indeed, people assigned female at birth often experience a degree of bodily anxiety in constructing masculinities, especially when embedded in cultural conceptions of two and only two sexes and its accompanying discursive assertion that men have penises and women do not' (Messerschmidt & Messner, 2018: 45). Perhaps it is a case of – you don't have to have a male body to be masculine; but it can help.

Essentializing masculinity

To return to the two possible approaches to defining masculinity, which I began by setting out at the start of this chapter. If masculinity is viewed as what men just are, then this would indeed lead us to a more embodied but also a more essentialist or spiritual understanding of this particular gender. There are then questions over where this essence can be found; if the body is advantageous in claims to masculinity, does this mean that masculinity depends on having a sexed as male body from birth? If there is an inner masculine essence, then is this a property of all men, even if they don't have stereotypically idealized male body types? If we focus on essence, does this mean that anyone could have a masculine essence, regardless of their body and regardless of whether their body is sexed as male or female? This focus on a masculine essence has been the position at different times historically; also, economics and militarization certainly constructs and makes claim to the truth of a masculine essence when it suits. In the history of the West when men have been needed for war or for hard labour and industry, they are called to do so with liberal use of references to men's inheritance, natural place and natural warrior mentality. Scholars like Robert Bly, who wrote a seminal text called *Iron John* in 1990, are part of what is known as the mythopoetic men's movement. This is a movement that references psychoanalysis, New Age spirituality and uses Jungian archetypes to argue that there is an essential masculine essence or soul to all men. This masculinity is a warrior soul, forged in the hunt, genetically disposed to protect its mate and its young from other predators and driven to fight to the top, proving itself against and competing with other men, securing admiration from women and breeding rights in the process.

The ideology of masculine essence is not limited to such explicit men's movements; it can be found in other men's movements too, like evolutionary biology and psychology. It is a seductive ideology, unfortunately to women as well as men. These biological determinist beliefs construct a functional binary world, where roles are specialized based on natural skill sets and where women and men's roles, as the archetypal masculine and feminine, are complimentary and together form a balanced and harmonious world. This is not so much a separate spheres approach, as a separate species approach; it sets men and women up as different species. From this vantage springs much self-help literature, guides and toolkits on how women can tame men, how men can better understand women and how women can recognize when a man is not sexually interested in them. The essentialist position also brings forth policy in education and schooling, on the dangers of feminized schools, the need for boys to undergo military training if they are to become men, or the natural inabilities of boys to sit still long enough to write their own names. The relatively recent progress of girls and women in education and careers is framed as an attack on men's natural position and natural entitlement.

Masculinity is a crisis

This is actually what is behind a lot of the aforementioned narratives about a crisis in masculinity. I suggest there is actually no crisis in masculinity. In fact, masculinity itself is a crisis, and always has been. Entitlement scorned can be incredibly dangerous, and all too often fatal, as feminist theorist Professor Judith Gardiner asserts: 'Bly's writings help diagnose the popularly decried "crisis of masculinity" in contemporary US culture as in fact a crisis of patriarchal entitlement' (Gardiner, 2002: 91). There are stereotypes in many cultures about the dangers of a woman scorned, apparently hell hath no fury like it, yet surely, time and again, tragic cases of domestic homicide and family annihilation show that scorned men are the most dangerous and the most deadly. Such facts sit uncomfortably alongside the deep-seated UnEnlightenment stereotypes about men and masculinity as logical, rational and unemotional. There is also the fact that while not all men are in power, and not all men will feel powerful, as a group, men are still in power the world over. So, it would be an odd sort of crisis that did not even touch the sides of male supremacy. 'For how is it possible that men and masculinity are in "crisis" given the continued, worldwide, material inequalities that favour males and men?' (Whitehead, 2002: 47).

This crisis narrative is a product of a much wider zero-sum approach to equal rights; it is the assumption that there aren't enough rights to go around, thus if a new group is gaining rights, this must be at the expense of another group. All of these anxieties become ever more powerful at times of crisis, economic, environmental or political, as people look back to an imagined, rose tinted past, where society was stable and where that stability was signified most intimately of all in a visible gendered division of role and labour between women and men, at home, at work and in all arrangements including sexual and domestic power relationships. The current rise of racist right-wing nationalism across Europe, for example, invokes such essentialist gender discourse, with its concerns over foreign others taking the women and jobs of native White European men, constructing women and jobs as property to which particular types of men are entitled to. Alongside an emboldened, masculinist, racist right-wing in the United States comes an equally misguided movement for White women, called the Trad Wife phenomenon. This is women taking back control of their natural place in society by putting themselves firmly back into the domestic sphere and locking themselves up at home to reclaim the womanly arts of ironing and overnight oats. It is a return to the Western post-war ideal of separate spheres and a family wage, which would enable men of a certain race and class to sustain their household of wife and children on their one manly wage alone. It was a mirage even in the 1950s, as a life of leisure in between a quick run round with the carpet sweeper was not the reality for most women of the working classes, who, as the term suggests, had to work, formally or informally in homework and local economies. Biological essentialism has many homes in online communities too, where, combined with a discourse of entitlement lost/stolen, it plays into those narratives of a crisis in masculinity and monstrously morphs into anti-feminist men's rights activism like the radicalized Men Going Their Own Way giving up on revolting women altogether, or Incels, involuntary celibate men who also think women are revolting, especially the ones who won't have sex with them. Although different, these phenomena too depend on the ideology of a masculine essence, and the presumed natural hierarchy between masculinity and femininity.

Doing masculinity

If masculinity is not an innate essence, nor some warrior soul that all men share and must find and embrace, then what is it? If it is not the sexed as male body, what is it? Is it about the role of men and therefore the things that men are expected to do in any given culture? Some common-sense understandings would have us believe that masculinity is indeed what men do and suggest that commonalities can be identified the world over, usually around the provider and defender role, as well as stereotypes about sexual assertiveness. But, even this response is fraught with complications and contradictions. If masculinity is what men do, such as the jobs they do, the provider role they fulfil for a family, their willingness to use violence to defend their family, or, more frivolously perhaps, the sports they do, the hobbies they enjoy, the manners they have in terms of how they behave, interact, speak, walk or talk and all the rest, then this means that masculinity is an action, or a set of actions. This would lead us into the more philosophical understandings of gender that have been popularized in the work of famous queer theorist and philosopher Professor Judith Butler. It would lead us to ask whether, if masculinity is a set of actions, presumably it could be taken up by individuals regardless of their biological sexed body. Butler defines gender as a repeated set of stylized acts, not like drag or pretend, but rather ways of being that give off the appearance of natural. This is not to suggest a high degree of voluntarism here, as Butler has cautioned ever since the many simplifications and misreadings of the 1990 classic *Gender Trouble*: 'This is not freedom, but a question of how to work the trap that one is inevitably in' (Butler, 1992: 83). Babies are socialized into gender norms from before birth even, and then from birth are expected to comply with those gender norms – males are supposed to be masculine, females are supposed to be feminine. This is part of the regulatory regime that Butler calls the heterosexual matrix. The heterosexual matrix is a system of compulsory heterosexuality, brutally enforced from birth through the assumed natural and congruent triads of male, masculine and heterosexual or female, feminine and heterosexual, which are the only allowable identities for boys and girls. These routes are taken for granted, as Professor of Sociology Kristen Schilt explains: the 'taken for granted expectation that heterosexuality and gender identity follow from genitalia produces heteronormativity' (Schilt, 2009: 443). Professor Schilt goes on to point out the workings of what is called cultural sex, or cultural genitals, which I outlined in more detail in Chapter 1 on the construction of biological sex.

As a reminder, this theory refers to how social conventions assume that a sexed as male body will produce a masculine person with a heterosexual sex drive towards female feminine people. This belief is held so strongly that it works the other way too. That is to say a masculine person will be assumed to have sexed as male genitalia, 'even though in most social interactions genitals are not actually visible. People do not expect a mismatch between "biological" credentials and gender presentations but rather assume that gendered appearances reflect a biologically sexed reality' (Schilt, 2009: 443). This is a process of 'gender attribution' (Kessler & McKenna, 1978: 2). This is what cultural sex means; it is the cultural assumption that anyone feminine must likely have a female body and anyone masculine must likely have a male body. Schilt points out of course that this assumption is not always correct, and plenty of people are masculine or feminine but do not have the assumed binary requirement of a male body or a female body; they 'can successfully do masculinity or femininity without having the genitalia that are presumed to follow from their outward appearance' (Schilt, 2009: 443). Heterosexuality depends on these two polar opposites – masculine and feminine – to be constantly enacted, embodied and made visible so that it can function as a natural union between complimentary active and passive genders. There are very real punishments and negative consequences for refusing to comply with the demands of the heterosexual matrix; some of these consequences will be brought to light in the later chapter on queering female masculinities.

Famous social psychologists Suzanne Kessler and Wendy McKenna, in their 1978 classic, *Gender: An Ethnomethodological Approach*, defined gender, both masculinity and femininity, as something that one labours or works at to achieve and maintain. Sociologists Candace West and Don Zimmerman then developed this idea further in their much cited 1987 paper *Doing Gender*. West and Zimmerman also noted the lack of voluntarism in gendering, asking whether it is impossible not to do gender in such a heavily polarized gendered society. They defined doing gender as follows: 'Doing gender means creating differences between girls and boys and women and men, differences that are not natural, essential, or biological. Once the differences have been constructed, they are used to reinforce the "essentialness" of gender' (1987: 137). Gender is something that is created by society, but the differences are then enacted by the members; they do gender. 'We have claimed that a person's gender is not simply an aspect of what one is, but, more fundamentally, it is something that one does, and does recurrently, in interaction with others' (West & Zimmerman, 1987: 140). From this perspective, masculinity would indeed be about what one does then; it would be about what the doing of masculinity looks like, including how one inhabits one's body, moves physically and takes up space.

Raewyn Connell wrote in 1983 about the gendering of sexed as male bodies and the physical actions they are expected to take to show that they are masculine. She was writing here about the social construction of masculinity in the body and expressed through the body: 'the embedding of masculinity in the body is very much a social process, full of tensions and contradiction; that even physical masculinity is historical, rather than a biological fact . . . constantly in process, constantly being constituted in actions and relations, constantly implicated in historical change' (Connell, 1983: 30). Textbook definitions of masculinity often focus on gendered bodily narratives and comportments too, pointing to how men in many cultures take up more space and dominate space with their voices, manners and bodies and how this comes to define masculinity. Connell in her key 1995 text *Masculinities* underlined again that masculinity is partly about 'certain postures and ways of moving . . . to distinctly occupy space, to have a physical presence in the world' (1995: 53). The doing of masculine gender would then be to do these things; actions that are constructed as masculine, and which men are expected to do and when they do them, are seen as natural behaviours because they are male.

Of course, perhaps a more tempting answer to the question of what is masculinity is to suggest that it is probably a mixture of these two approaches; that is to say that masculinity is something men do, but also something that men are. This is a melding of biological and cultural or social perspectives; it is an approach of having it both ways and it is popular. Many people acknowledge societal stereotypes about what men are meant to be, which is masculinity, but they are also committed to the idea that men are just different to women, and do have some drives that make them drawn to what we would classify as masculine behaviours and roles. This would mean that men feel a certain degree of masculinity as an internal essence; they feel it is something that they just are. This sense of masculinity as what they are then drives them to do masculinity. The internal sense of oneself as masculine cannot exist outside society though, so that identity has been shaped by a society that teaches men to act in masculine-defined ways and suggests that these are natural ways for men to act. A self is formed by these lessons, but that does not mean the self is not then experienced as real. This sense of a masculine self fuels a drive to put what was taught into practice, and to act in the ways considered appropriate for masculine individuals. These successful adoptions and enactments of recognizable masculine ways of being then further entrench the belief that masculinity must, to some extent at least, be natural and innate. In turn, the belief that masculinity is internal and innate fuels the pressure to adopt and act in ways viewed as recognizably masculine in any given culture and time period. This is a circular perspective, but it is one that many people are comfortable with. When I discuss masculinities with students, or at public events on questions of gender, many will respond that while they understand that what a society defines as masculine is socially constructed, they nevertheless believe there is something a bit more to it as well.

What is this 'bit more'? It is the acknowledgement of a sense of self, an identity and a sense of inner character that drives one to follow, to varying degrees, different available socially constructed models of gender, blend them or refuse them. This is the approach I have come to see as the 'bit of both' approach. As Stephen Whitehead points out, this is a valid position to take; both nature and nurture are important considerations and influences and are mutually reinforcing. 'The individual is neither passive in the face of his/her genetic makeup, nor, indeed simply an empty vessel to be filled with ideological material' (Whitehead, 2002: 12). Professor Connell concludes the same: 'Masculinities are neither programmed in our genes, nor fixed by social structure, prior to social interaction. They come into existence as people act. They are actively produced, using the resources and strategies available in a given social setting' (Connell, 2000: 12). Masculinity has been studied mainly in relation to men, as we have seen from the brief tour through the literature; but if masculinity is a set of actions and roles, ways of bodily comportment and a particular experience of a sense of self, there is nothing in that understanding that requires a sexed as male body.

Contributing to a classic femme-butch text from America, Coyote and Sharman's (2011) *Persistence*, author and lecturer Anne Fleming writes about butch masculinity, and about an inner sense of this masculinity that persisted, even with a family and society that did not encourage it, precisely the opposite. 'I have what feels like a natural, in-born masculinity that even my mother's long, relentless siege could not vanquish or disguise' (Fleming, 2011: 48). In her moving documentation of her own queer motherhood, feminist scholar and theorist Cherrie Moraga recounts how masculinity can be taught and learnt, and it does not have to be taught by someone with a sexed as male body; in fact, it can be all the better for coming from someone else entirely.

A brilliant butch woman told me years ago about a boy she had raised with his mother for many years. One night her heart broke when, tucking in the bespectacled boy of ten, he wrapped his arms around her neck and called her daddy, with everything he had in him. When I finally met the boy, I saw that he shared Maria's poor eyesight, wit, and brainy humour. Most of all, he learned how to be a boy from Maria. He learned masculinity from Maria and she was a wonderful male role model; the best of fathers with a woman's compassion. (Moraga, 1997: 15)

Masculinity then is whatever we make it, and we can make it whatever our body type may be. I do not subscribe to essentialist notions of an innate and born gender, however. Gender is a social construction and varies from society to society, but I do believe that our early formations of self utilize those societal gender expressions to form our identity; it isn't all we are, but it's part of it. If people feel that a masculine gender identity, or a feminine gender identity, is part of their sense of self, then those feelings are no less valid whether they have a male or female body. Incidentally, they are no less questionable either. Acknowledging the production of a gendered sense of self does not have to ignore the political questions that surround masculinity and femininity, of which there are obviously many, because gender is the operating system of patriarchy. However, coming to realize and understand that a system is not about nature, but is about naturalizing an unequal system, does not mean that we don't all have our roots in that very system, and, in a myriad of contradictory and contrary ways, we have grown our selves in that ground. I will leave the last word on masculinity to king of queer masculine scholarship Professor Jack Halberstam. 'Masculinity in this context is of course what we make it. It has important relations to maleness, increasingly interesting relations to transexual maleness, and a historical debt to lesbian butchness' (Halberstam, 1998a: 288). In Chapter 6 then I will introduce and explore what lesbian butchness might be, what relationship it has to masculinity, if any, and what all of that means to those who claim it as their own.

6

Always endangered, never extinct

What is butch lesbian identity?

You were there, you were gay, you were queer and you were masculine.
(Sandy, 1950s American butch, interviewed in
Kennedy & Davis, 1993: 181)

Part of my motivation for writing this book was my sense that lesbian culture and spaces in general have been in decline since the 1980s in the UK. This has also been observed in the United States, in the work of Dr Bonnie J Morris, for example, and her historical research into the disappearing lesbian and lesbian feminist music genre, and other lesbian-only businesses; these are the sorts of examples of strategic tactical separatism that I described earlier in Chapters 2 and 3. Within lesbian culture there are many other cultures of course; there are different lesbian labels and identifiers, all with their own discrete communities and scenes. Just one of these is femme/butch identities and relationships, and I am interested whether, as lesbian spaces decrease in general, the niche communities within those will also be reduced. Added to this general trend of decline has, of course, been an explosion of new terms for female masculinities, lesbian and queer genders. These may perhaps, in some ways, eventually replace or surpass terms like 'butch' or become more popular due to being experienced as expansive and inclusive.

As I spelled out in the Introduction to this book, I have defined 'butch' as a label rooted in lesbian history, which refers to a sexed as female individual who identifies with and/or expresses culturally recognizable masculinities, and/or identifies as masculine. Professor Evelyn Blackwood affirms that butch is 'a proud marker of lesbian identity rather than an unreflective imitation of heterosexuality' (Blackwood, 2012: 92). I consider butch to be a gender identity expression, and it is a recognized lesbian gender expression in lesbian communities – although not all butches connect with the lesbian roots of the label, as I shall discuss later in Chapter 8 on queering female masculinities. With its association to lesbianism and its roots in lesbian communities, it is also of course a term to describe sexuality and sexual orientation, as well as being a term that holds meanings for gender. Star of butch scholarship, the trail blazing butch academic Esther Newton, defines butch as 'a gender expression that combines some version of the masculinity that you saw around you as a child with same-sex desire' (2018: 5). Here, Newton utilizes and combines the two most popular understandings of butch: (1) as a sexuality label for lesbianism and (2) a gender label for masculinity. As everyone who takes on the banner of butch will have a different relationship to it, my own perspective is, of course, just one. Labelling a lesbian identity as anything to do with masculinity is controversial in significant personal and political ways. For some, butch is a type of lesbian womanhood in its own right and not at all a subset of masculinity. Many respondents who took part in my research survey identified as butch, of various types, and they gave thoughtful definitions of what this term means to them, its many nuances, and how society responds – not always positively. I shall platform some of these varied and proud butch voices in Chapters 7 and 8.

What or who is butch?

Before exploring such issues though, it is important to discuss just what butch even means. This is not a simple task; there is disagreement over how to classify the term and how to recognize what butch is. In the 1994 book *Dagger: On Butch Women*, which itself is a play on a presumed slur for masculine lesbians, that of bull dagger, or bull dyke, the Editors, Burana, Due and Roxxie insist that the only thing that unites butches is their diversity and individuality, and that the identifier of butch just means a fulfilling of self, although one often not supported, validated or rewarded by society, far from it. 'For butches, being butch is about being yourself; for society, being butch is about slapping convention in the face' (1994: 10). Society has struck back of course, as it always does against difference, against what is perceived as other and therefore deviant. The label of butch and other terms for masculine lesbians have long been used as throwaway slurs and are known for this usage, perhaps more so than the identities they've been claimed and reclaimed to describe. Influential historians and ethnographers Elizabeth Lapovsky Kennedy and Madeline D Davis (1993) note that the term 'bull dagger', for example, was reclaimed from its hostile usage early on, particularly by Black lesbians in African American communities of the United States from around the 1940s onwards, where it was used to refer to tough, independent butches who were unafraid (Bogus, 1994). Hammer's article on the meanings of this term, bulldagger (BD), much earlier, in the Blues music business and scene, of the 1920s and 1930s, also explores the link to independence, for women regardless of their sexual orientation, to toughness and the useage of masculinity and challenge to Whiteness by Black women musicians and singers of that period (2019). On lesbian definitions, famous queer scholar Gayle Rubin characteristically gets to the point and acknowledges that what everyone knows about butches is that they are more masculine than feminine. 'Butch is the lesbian vernacular term for women who are more comfortable with masculine gender codes, styles, or identities than with feminine ones' (Rubin, 1992: 466). Like everything, though, it is a raced and classed term; it is, in the main, a Western label, associated with White, working-class, often American urban subcultures, and much literature on femme-butch identity and relationships has furthered this Americanization of the term; I shall explore this in more detail later in this chapter.

Readers may already be familiar with the term 'butch' and may have heard it used in wider, general usage, outside of academic gender studies or the queer scene. It has been a popular term to describe lesbians or women thought to be lesbians. It has been used as an insult to describe what are widely understood as negative stereotypes of lesbianism, such as being mannish, masculine, unattractive and unfeminine (Murphy, 2020). It has been a term put onto any women who are seen by others to not be complying, or not to be complying enough, with cultural expectations and requirements for femininity – women who may not be lesbians, let alone identify or understand themselves as butch lesbians. It is also of course a term long used in the gay male community too, where it is used to describe masculinity or perhaps an extreme of that, what could be called hypermasculinity. It arguably has a sense of the camp, theatrical and performative to it, being used to symbolize stereotypes, or parodies almost, of masculinity, whether in women or men. However, within many lesbian communities it is a serious term, often political, often one used reverently, and a name that has long been an important identifier, and a powerful label to describe sexuality, gender identity and relationships.

Climbing the butch family tree

Much of what is now seen as the classic literature and scholarship on femme-butch identities and relationships has come from the United States and emerged during the height of the 1990s queer zeitgeist. There is also a British history of butch, just as every country will have their own story to tell. A femme queen in the femme/butch field is Joan Nestle, founder of the Lesbian Herstory Archives in New York and editor of *The Persistent Desire: A Femme-Butch Reader* first published in 1992. This book is a mixture of queer theory, poems, photography, history, art and personal memoir; it has become somewhat of a sacred screed in femme-butch circles. A piece of fiction, rooted in history and personal experiences, has also become a classic; the late Leslie Feinberg's *Stone Butch Blues*, published in 1993, follows the fictional life of a White, butch lesbian in working-class America in New York throughout the 1960s and 1970s. Revolutionary communist Leslie Feinberg is a hero of transgender, trans and butch history, publishing several rallying calls for transgender rights and recognition, as well as being involved in the founding of Camp Trans opposite the Michigan Womyn's Music Festival in the 1990s, as I explained in Chapter 3 on the MichFest controversies. Tragically Feinberg died in 2014 and is a much-missed voice, often bringing nuance and empathy to some of the political horizontal hostilities at work today in LGBTQI+ organizing.

In 1991 the historian Professor Lillian Faderman published *Odd Girls and Twilight Lovers: A History of Lesbian Life in Twentieth-Century America*. This history covered the repressive 1950s in America, the spread of underground gay culture and within that subcultures such as lesbian bar life in particular and femme-butch identities and spaces. In 1993 Elizabeth Lapovsky Kennedy and Madeline Davis published their history on fem-butch identities, clubs and networks in working-class Buffalo, New York, from the 1930s through to the 1960s. *Boots of Leather, Slippers of Gold: The History of a Lesbian Community* contains responses from the oral histories exhaustively gathered by these scholars over a number of years. This book addresses class and race distinctions, including discussion on the solidarity and differences between fem and butch lesbians in White and Black working communities across these decades. They note the significance of the rise of an independent Black community in Buffalo in the period they studied, and the prominence of lesbians and lesbian life in Black communities and culture, including music. The blues song by early American blues artist Lucille Bogan, for example, 'BD Women Blues' from 1935, is a song about bull dagger women, who 'can lay their jive just like a natural man'! In her book on lesbian bars, Kelly Hankin (2002) also cites ethnographic work from the 1960s on working-class Black lesbian bars in America and the presence of fem-butch culture, where masculine lesbians were referred to as 'studs' rather than 'butches'.

There is also a British history of butch and femme/butch communities. England's capital city, London, was home to perhaps one of the most well-known femme/butch nightclubs. That was the Gateways Club in Chelsea, South West London, which operated from the 1930s and closed in 1985. Author Jill Gardiner published a history of the club in 2003, *From the Closet to the Screen: Women at the Gateways Club 1945-85*. The club is significant in lesbian history because it became famous due to it being the location for much of the filming of the early lesbian film *The Killing of Sister George* (1968), which starred well-known actress of the time, Beryl Reid, who won an award for her role in the film. Writing about the Gateways Club, lesbian feminist theorist Sheila Jeffreys documents with horror the acceptability of role playing as she calls it, suggesting that this was mainly because there were no other options at the time, until lesbian feminism emerged to provide more egalitarian choices. 'Prior to the 1970s, lesbians who used the club were likely to engage in role playing and even call themselves by male names' (Jeffreys, 2014a: 105). Contributing to the academic queer theory on femme-butch identities from the British corner is Professor Sally Munt, for example, and her 1998 book *Butch/Femme: Inside Lesbian Gender*. Professor Jack Halberstam, a Brit who has made America their home, is, of course, behind the canonical *Female Masculinity*, also published in 1998, which included exploration of butch lesbian identity and presentation. Published works then have included oral histories, cultural theory and gender studies, as well as art, erotica, photography, plays and poetry. For example, there is the work of artists and performers Peggy Shaw and Lois Weaver in Split Britches; there is the famous photographer of lesbian communities and subcultures, female masculinity appreciator and intersexy rights activist, Del LaGrace Volcano, who, among a veritable feast of a catalogue, produced *The Drag King Book* with Jack Halberstam in 1999.

Passing women and female husbands

Femme-butch and masculine lesbian genders and lives are not a new invention, and they have had many different names around the world and over time. Female masculinity and expressions of this are global, recorded in histories of passing women and female husbands, for example, women who lived as men and held careers as doctors, explorers, soldiers, farmers or artists, often marrying and raising children with their wives. Just a few of these lives are glimpsed in books such as *Female Husbands: A Trans History* by Jen Manion (2020), *Amazons and Military Maids* from Julie Wheelwright (1989), *The Lesbian History Sourcebook* (2001), from Alison Oram and Annmarie Turnbull, *Butch Heroes* by Ria Brodell (2018), or *Britannia's Glory: History of Twentieth-Century Lesbians in Britain* by Emily Hamer (1995). On passing and cross-dressing females there is also an early scholarly text from Rudolf Dekker and Lotte Van De Pol, *The Tradition of Female Transvestism in Early Modern Europe* (1997). It is perhaps unsurprising, in the current climate, that there is much debate over the identities that such individuals may have chosen for themselves, and whether their lives can be claimed now as examples of the adventures of trans men, or butch lesbians, or women usurping male power in patriarchal times to enter professions and gain privileges they would have been barred from due to their sex. Just one example of this sometimes fierce debate is in the positive and negative reaction to the announcement of a new book *The Cape Doctor* (2020) by author E. J. Levy, on the life of Victorian surgeon Dr James Barry, discovered and outed upon his death as being female bodied. As soon as the book was announced as a future publication, it was receiving one-star reviews and calls for it to be boycotted because the author was accused of mis-sexing Barry, referring to him as a woman and as 'she' in the version of history she would be presenting in her book. Prize-winning author Levy described the reaction as the actions of a 'troll mob' on social media platform Twitter in 2019. This row plays out today over the bodies of many such individuals from history, and it is proof of how fragile and tenuous various minority communities feel right now that such fights even take place, with different sides each claiming these historical figures as their own.

Embodied lives and deaths: Which morgue suits you sir

This happens with more recent cases too, and more recent bereavements. Philosophy Professor and Queer Studies Scholar Jacob Hale has written about this (1998) in response to the murder of Brandon Teena, for example, in 1993 in Falls City, Nebraska, America, as has Professor Jack Halberstam (2000). Brandon Teena was shot dead by two men, John Lotter and Marvin Thomas Nissen, who also fatally shot two of Brandon's friends, Phillip DeVine and Lisa Lambert. The deaths of these latter two young people have not been as well covered as the loss of Brandon Teena. In fact, scholar C Riley Snorton, in *Black on Both Sides: A Racial History of Trans Identity* (2017), explores the erasure of DeVine's murder in almost all of the news coverage and narratives in the LGBTQI+ press that followed. DeVine was a young twenty-two-year-old Black man, disabled since birth he used a prosthetic leg; he was a formidable athlete, he had begun a relationship with a young woman from Falls City, Nebraska, and he was staying in the Humbolt farmhouse at the time, where his life was taken that night on 31 December 1993. Lotter and Nissen had previously been questioned by the police after Brandon Teena had reported them for rape. Brandon Teena had a sexed as female body, and, depending on who you talk to, was either a trans man, or a transgendered female living as a man, or a transgender butch, or a butch or masculine lesbian passing as a man. Numerous accounts of his life have been given since (Minkowitz, 2018; Muska & Olafsdottir, 1998; Jones, 1996), not least in the award-winning mainstream hit film from director Kimberly Peirce 'Boy's Don't Cry' (1999), starring actor Hilary Swank, who won an Oscar for her portrayal of Brandon.

Arguably, it is impossible to say how someone who is no longer with us would choose to define themselves, let alone whether or not those that died hundreds of years ago would use such modern terms and labels only recently in use. 'The sexual and gender identities of people from the past cannot be unproblematically housed within newer identity categories' (Vincent, 2020:2). As Ben Vincent points out in their important book on non-binary lives, while there is a resonance and perhaps a sense of shared status with figures from the past, along with a joy at finding such examples in the first place, we cannot house them in today's categories. 'There is a shared history for anyone transgressive of "normal, proper" gendered or sexual behaviour, whereby their status as men or women could have been symbolically or literally called into question' (2020:2). It could have been that some such female husbands from history, passing women or soldier boys did consider themselves men and would have been trans men, or it could have been some were masculine lesbians finding a way to live out their life legitimately, or even, to live a life at all, in a world that made such relationships and families unimaginable and illegal. This was particularly the case for poorer, working-class individuals who would not have had the independent means enjoyed by wealthier classes, those who moved in high society, which gave them a degree of freedom about how they dressed, presented and whether or not they married men. Such degrees of freedom can be seen in British histories of brave souls like Anne Lister of eighteenth-century Yorkshire (Choma, 2019), or lesbian hero and literary giant Radclyffe Hall, who wrote *The Well of Loneliness* in 1928, or the speed demon boat racer Joe Carstairs in the 1930s (Summerscale, 1998). It could have been that some of the famous historical cases of passing women and female soldiers did not consider themselves masculine at all, nor lesbian, nor men, but were forced by patriarchal hand to pass as men in order to pursue education or professions that they were passionate about, and were willing to sacrifice their identity and future life as a woman in exchange for an entirely different destiny. Who knows? As more is uncovered about such lives, we find out new details and testimonies, but either way, putting labels from contemporary society onto those from the past often does not feel respectful or appropriate and that minority groups fight over such bodies is not a sign of strong and united communities. Perhaps we should focus on sustaining the life of these, now and in the present moment, and celebrate the fluidity and diversity of s/heroes past without needing to tag them for the attention of one morgue or another.

Global butch

Female masculinity is also not a purely Western phenomenon, let alone solely American or British, although my research was focused in the United Kingdom, and much English language literature on this topic is from the United States. Writing about the universality of butch identity in America, Esther Newton acknowledges that butch is a product of lesbian communities, not a copy of manhood or masculinity, and is one that 'fuses female masculinity with homosexual desire' (2018: 4), no matter what label is given to it. 'But whatever name they use, such women emerge from every American class, race, and subculture' (Newton, 2018: 4). In Japan, lesbian, queer and masculine of centre identities and expressions are known with terminology such as 'tombois', 'onabe' and 'boys' (Summerhawk et al., 1998; Blackwood & Johnson, 2012). Masculine and feminine lesbian gender identities in Thailand are the subject of Sinnott's anthropological study of toms and dees (2004). Cuba has a burgeoning Drag King scene, where masculine lesbians are finding a home to express their gender identities and sexualities (Santana, 2018). Chile's masculine or butch lesbians are known as 'camionas' (Ramirez, 2020). Indicating the fatal resistance to gender nonconformity that affects so many LGBTQI+ communities around the world, the BBC reported in June 2019 on a series of murders of masculine lesbians or camionas, in the mountainous Fifth Region of Chile along with reports of threats of corrective rape and beatings of visible camionas (Rest in Power: Nicole Saavedra Bahamondes; María Pía Castro; Susana Sanhueza). Lesbians in Chile call the Valparaíso region The Red Zone, due to the danger level for lesbians from male sexual violence against women, and the prevalence of lesbophobic harassment and violence (Mohan, 2019).

In Taiwan, masculine of centre lesbians or queer masculine females are known as 'zhongxing' or T's, for example (Hu, 2019), or as Ti, T or TB, with the latter standing for tomboy (Li & Lu, 2020). Scholar of gender and women's studies Anahi Russo Garrido notes that femme and butch lesbian couples used to be known in Mexico by the terms, 'azul' and 'rosas', meaning blue and pink, or by the terms, 'acti' and 'pastel', with 'acti' standing for active, and 'pastel' meaning passive (Garrido, 2020). Fem-butch or fem-stud identities are long-standing labels in Black queer communities, and in the United States butch or MOC individuals are also known by terms such as AG which stands for aggressive, and also by the label stud. The latter is usually used as a label for Black queer or lesbian masculine of centre individuals. It is often taken to be similar to 'butch', but 'butch' is largely understood as a term for White people, and to have come from White communities in the United States in particular (Cole, 2011; Lane-Steel, 2011; Wilson, 2009; Moore, 2006). Similarly to the accepted working definitions for butch, definitions for stud also emphasize that this is an individual who is more masculine than feminine. As scholar Laura Lane-Steele summarizes in her article on the protest masculinities of Black lesbian studs, 'to state it simply, a stud is a Black lesbian who embodies masculinity' (Lane-Steele, 2011: 480). Her article references discussions in Chapter 5 on the social construction of masculinities, and the classifications from Connell (1995). Lane-Steele suggests that hypermasculine performances by studs and butches could be seen as a form of protest masculinities, that is stylized displays of culturally recognizable masculine stereotypes, by marginalized groups who lack structural power.

As I outlined in the Introduction to this book, most of my respondents to my survey on lesbian and queer masculinities in the UK identified as White British and White European, with only a minority of Black and global majority respondents. This is obviously a weakness of the survey research. However, the complexities of the raced associations attached to different terms did arise as a topic in the responses people gave, and several individuals noted the raced elements of the term 'butch' and highlighted that 'stud' is a term reserved for Black queers. There is also a sense in queer communities, which respondents brought up in my survey too, that terms like 'butch' and 'stud' may have declined in usage, as newer and more fluid terms have become commonplace, but that this decline has mainly occurred in White communities, with voicing and recognition of identities like fem-stud and butch or stud much more strongly rooted still in Black queer communities. Meanwhile, ironically, 'butch' as a symbolic term continues to conjure images of White masculinity. This has been underlined by writers such as B Cole, activist and community organizer who actually coined the term 'masculine of centre' (MOC) and founded the Brown Boi Project in 2010. 'The deep irony is that historically butch identities have been more embraced among MoC womyn of colour than by white queer communities. Despite this rich history and legacy, the image of what butch looks like in popular media and academic writing is still overwhelmingly white' (Cole, 2011: 130). The nuance of such identities and terms, their raced and classed connotations and symbolic meanings and attachments are all important areas for further research in the UK.

Reclaiming butch

The queer explosion of relevant work in the 1990s was partly to reclaim femme-butch identities from what had been perceived as a previous attack or suppression, an attack fired from the political canons of lesbian feminist theory. This was the so-called lesbian sex wars of the 1980s in the United Kingdom and the United States, swimming in the legacy of the influence of lesbian feminism and lesbian separatism on femme-butch identities in the more androgynous 1970s. This was not the first feminist tension over lesbian identity, however, far from it. Lesbians of any visible kind had already been made to feel uncomfortable in feminism since the dawn of the Second Wave in the United States, where Betty Friedan of the National Organization of Women, 1966, infamously fretted over the so-called lavender menace. There was a fear that conventional society would be turned off from feminism if it was seen as a lesbian movement; thus it was thought better that lesbians not be seen. Prior to this, early homosexual or homophile rights movements, as they were known, often skirted (literally) around similar assimilationist concerns. Here in the UK the first magazine for lesbians, *Arena Three* (produced from 1964–71), founded by the Minorities Research Group (MRG), frequently covered how the image of lesbians could be improved, and how lesbians should dress (Hamer, 1995). The MRG was set up in 1963 by Esme Langley and Diana Chapman. There was overlap with American organizations and the American lesbian magazine, *The Ladder*, contained adverts for both the MRG and *Arena Three*.

The question of butch inclusion became an issue at social events for the MRG and *Arena Three*. At some of the early meetings, organized through the magazine, objections were raised to the presence of butch lesbians wearing masculine styles, men's fashions and haircuts, for example. At one of the meetings, held above the Shakespeare's Head pub on Carnaby Street in London, there was even a vote as to whether what was called male-attire should be allowed at MRG meetings; the vote against such attire was lost narrowly. Twenty-five voted for the motion, twenty-eight against, with six abstentions: 'On this occasion tolerance won (just)' (Gardiner, 2003: 119). The June 1964 issue of *Arena Three* editorial note reads: 'As the majority of women homosexuals are not "transvestites" we shall be glad if at further meetings there will be no further cause for wounded sensibilities.' Worries over public exposure and the public perception of lesbianism appear to be behind items in *Arena Three* on the 'exhibitionist tendency' to wear 'full drag'. 'For my money the Lesbian who errs a trifle on the conservative side looks a whole lot better than the one who goes about looking like a send-up of a male impersonator (if you get the idea)', advised an article in *Arena Three* in June 1964. Letters to the magazine also objected to a BBC 2 documentary series Man Alive, in 1967, which ran two episodes on homosexuality in the UK, one on men and one on women. However, one of the lesbians featured in the lesbian episode, 'Consenting Adults 2: The Women', called Stevie, spoke about living as a man and dating women as a man. Several readers of *Arena Three* saw this as male impersonation, rare transvestism and perhaps even transsexualism (Jennings, 2007; Hamer, 1995).

Surveys of MRG members found that most were in middle-class professions, with a majority in teaching and nursing. An interview with novelist Maureen Duffy, who wrote for *Arena Three* and who also wrote *The Microcosm* (1966), based on the Gateways Club, illustrates how concerns over how lesbians looked and were percieved were certainly not unfounded at the time, in the early 1960s, when exposure as a lesbian could have serious consequences. Duffy explains that she had to give up teaching because she had decided she would never wear skirts or dresses again, only trousers; this meant she had to leave her profession as female teachers were not allowed to wear trousers (British Library, LGBTQ Histories). Letters to the magazine also indicate that middle-class and professional women were very concerned about blackmail and exposure, furthering a classed link to butch lesbianism, in contrast, as being a preserve of those assumed to have nothing to lose, no profession, no property or family inheritance for example, as Hamer discusses: 'Butch lesbians were visible as lesbians, both to other lesbians and to the straight world, and much criticism of them seems to have been a result of other lesbians' anxiety about this visibility' (Hamer, 1995: 175). The novelist Maureen Duffy, quoted in Oram and Turnbull's British lesbian history, (2001) reported from the Gateways Club that professional women were less likely to become regulars, attempting more to fit in and be socially accepted, preferring 'select dinner parties, evenings at the theatre' (2001: 229). Duffy suggested that on the lesbian scene those in similar professions tended to socialize together, even if the pub or club itself was mixed: 'there is less mixing of the levels of society among female than among male homosexuals: teachers talk to other teachers, factory workers and petrol pump attendants clan together with lower-paid office workers and bus conductresses' (2001: 229).

However, the classed link to the pub and club scene is perhaps not so starkly noted in British lesbian history as it is in the United States. From the 1920s and 1930s the West End of London had been home to bars and clubs known for gay male clientele, arty and bohemian types, as well as women working in prostitution and lesbians too, all mixed together. In her British lesbian history of the post-war years, Rebecca Jennings notes that lesbians remained on the West End scene, but that the specific lesbian pubs and clubs that emerged from the 1950s, such as the Gateways, but also the Robin Hood in Bayswater, the Champion in Notting Hill and the Cricketers in Battersea thrived in areas a bit further afield, then known as high-rental areas, affordable areas and popular with immigrant communities to London. Jennings asserts that in the UK it was likely that classes were much more mixed together, with middle- and upper-class lesbians also regularly visiting the available pubs and clubs of the time, as well as private house parties being popular: 'it seems more probable that the lesbian clubs of this period catered to a cross-class clientele' (Jennings, 2007: 124).

In the United States, pioneering groups such as the organization the Daughters of Bilitis (DOB), founded in the 1950s, addressed similar issues in their magazine *The Ladder* (published from 1956 to 1972), such as the 'problem' of butch presentation, cross-dressing and mannish lesbians, who risked giving the homophile rights movement a bad name. In her history, Lillian Faderman notes that DOB emerged initially to provide a social alternative for lesbians who did not wish to frequent the bar scene. This could be partly due to class and a valid fear of being outed in their professions and losing independent livelihoods, as well as a rejection of the butch-femme scene so often perceived as role playing. DOB emerged 'to give middle-class lesbians an alternative to the gay bar scene' and for those interested in working on 'improving the lesbian image' (Faderman, 1991: 149). Joining this White middle-class, private party scene is what historian Elizabeth Smith refers to as entering 'the gold earing set' (Smith, 1989: 400).

As I have discussed in more detail in Chapter 2, lesbian feminism of the Second Wave and much Radical Feminist theory too observed femme-butch relationships as simply the continuation of masculine and feminine gender roles, roles which had already, by many schools of feminism in fact, been explained and understood convincingly as negative, harmful and the foundation of patriarchal societal arrangements and oppressions. 'This notion of "butch" and "femme" was a mirror of the power structures in the hegemonic discourse, heterosexist patriarchy, and it dominated lesbian relationships and hence spaces up until the late seventies' (Valentine, 1993: 245). The fact that it may be two women or two female individuals expressing elements of these roles was not seen to make this situation progressive or in any way outside the same critiques put upon it in male-female dynamics. Queer theory may have tried to see the progressive aspects of detaching gender assumptions from sex and celebrate the challenge that femme-butch identities presented to heteronormative relationships between the sexes. From a queer perspective such lives were also considered to threaten solid assumptions about a natural place for women and men and a natural or biological foundation to gender, gendered lives and relationships. However, none of this was convincing for the lesbian feminist and Radical Feminist theory that saw it all as just more of the same and therefore in no way inherently progressive. As butch theorist Esther Newton noted in her influential paper on the mythic mannish lesbian, 'thinking, acting, or looking like a man contradicts lesbian feminism's first principle: the lesbian is a woman-identified-woman' (Newton, 1984: 558).

The rise of Second Wave feminism in the 1960s and 1970s had a legacy effect that then played out into the sex wars of the 1980s in which femme-butch relationships were seen as the eroticization of male power, and the sexualization of dominance and submission, for example. Lesbian feminist Professor Sheila Jeffreys summarizes such a stance and has continued in her work to critique and condemn femme-butch individuals: 'Within lesbian culture, the practice of butch/femme role playing, in which the female partners in a relationship adopted the stereotyped roles provided in the foundation for heterosexuality, was common in some sections of the community before the advent of second wave feminism in the 1960s and has experienced a rebirth since the 1980s' (Jeffreys, 2014a: 103). What is clear then is that these labels, femme and butch, did not go away post-1970s feminism, but that community tensions were well known by those in them, and this was particularly likely to be the case for those who inhabited both feminist and lesbian and gay communities. Numerous contributors to Nestle's *The Persistent Desire* share memories of closeting themselves in a way during the 1970s, and of making themselves appear more androgynous than they would have preferred, as well as not being open about femme-butch identity or desires. 'Almost against my will, the early seventies turned me into a "lesbian feminist". Feminism tore apart my butch identity', writes butch journalist, historian and activist Jeanne Cordova, about her experiences in the United States at that time (1992: 283). I can recall myself in the mid to late 1990s being questioned at feminist conferences or lesbian events as to why I was wearing a suit or 'dressing like a man' among other such comments that have been a feature of my life in all circles, whether straight, feminist or gay.

All of this past no doubt had an effect on the presence, public face and reach of femme-butch communities in the United Kingdom and the United States. Writing about femmes in families, social worker and therapist Arlene Istar Lev suggests that these politics actually suppressed for a time the open expression of these elements of lesbian gender identity – femme and butch identities; closeting them, as the previous quote from Cordova suggests. 'The rise of lesbian-feminist politics in the 1970s effectively drove butch-femme identities, communities, and expression underground, silencing, and therefore historically distorting, discussions of gender expression in lesbian relationships' (Lev, 2008: 131). Added to this pressure was a decline perhaps in the perceived need for segregated lesbian and gay spaces in general, from the 1990s onwards, as laws in the UK, for example, gradually equalized the age of consent, lesbian and gay characters began appearing in mainstream television and culture and, significantly, an increasing corporatization of public space and the urban night-time economy also meant it was financially challenging to maintain the running of full-time lesbian and gay bars and clubs (Browne & Ferreira, 2015). Although, the work of geographers such as Gill Valentine points out the importance of lesbian and gay spaces as long as public spaces and institutions in general are still constructed as heterosexual. Valentine explores public space such as high streets and shopping centres as heterosexually coded, rather than neutral spaces. Adverts display images of heterosexual nuclear families and heterosexual couples; everything from clothes to holidays is sold using such imagery (Valentine, 1996).

Scholars such as Professor Surya Monro suggest that legal and policy changes on LGBT rights, like those in the UK, have created a more tolerant, though not liberated climate where increasing identity categories within lesbian and gay communities are also able to arise and flourish, adding new terms for lesbian identities, so that femme and butch are by no means now the only options. These are identities such as non-binary and genderqueer – NBGQ – for example: 'Arguably, the emergence of NBGQ in some northern anglophone countries is possible because of what is broadly termed "homonationalism"; the deployment of LGBT-friendly policies as part of the dominant national identities of countries' (Monro, 2019: 128). Playing a part in shaping the current context is also what scholars in gender and sexuality, such as Professor Jane Ward (2008), have seen as the assimilationist agendas of LGBTQ liberation movements, and what she calls increasing homonormativity against the backdrop of roaring neoliberalism. There are also the pertinent observations from academics such as Professor Amin Ghaziani on the decline of LGBTQ separatism and the end of what he cleverly calls the gayborhood (2014).

However, despite all this, following on from the trail blazed by the queer 1990s, moving into the mid-2000s there was another resurgent academic interest in documenting the survival, continuation and reclaiming of femme-butch labels. This resulted in work such as a revisiting of Nestle's classic, from two young writers, Ivan Coyote and Zena Sharman, in 2011 with *Persistence: All Ways Butch and Femme*. Another earlier collection also similarly brought together essays, art and personal memoir in *Femme/Butch: New Considerations of the Way We Want to Go* from academics Michelle Gibson and Deborah Meem (2002). Performance artist, activist and writer S Bear Bergman published *Butch Is a Noun* in 2006; and in the same year photographer Del LaGrace Volcano and Professor of Gender Studies Ulrika Dahl produced *Femmes of Power: Exploding Queer Femininities*. The history and labels of femme-butch that were being reclaimed in that moment, from the 1990s onwards, were often from a particular provenance. The heyday of the 1940s and 1950s bar culture in working-class, urban bars of America.

Butch: One origin story

This location provides a particularly popular and well-known origin story for this lesbian subculture. Post–Second World War in the United States there had been some quite radical emancipation of women; as a practical necessity for military production, women had legally and formally taken on jobs seen as men's jobs, and they were allowed to wear trousers and comfortable clothes, but it was still a time of exultant conservatism. Butch or masculine lesbians arguably had greater opportunity to use the workplace skills acquired and proven in order to continue in male-dominated jobs, and if necessary, where women were barred, passing as male if possible. Fashion trends changed as a result of wartime, creating a more dapper look for women, albeit a tailored and feminized one with high waists, for example, to accentuate a curvier rather than squarer more masculine look, but society was hardly gender revolutionizing. This moment was also the start of the Cold War and a period of McCarthyite repression, which included the seeking out and expelling of actual or suspected lesbian, gay and bisexual workers in the military and in state jobs, for example, as well as a push back on the lifting of limits during war time and a concern to make sure women and men returned to their presumed rightful roles. Historian of lesbian life Lillian Faderman labels this period as the 'military witch-hunts' noting how women serving in the military, as well as staff including chaplains and doctors, were urged to inform on each other for any suspected same-sex activity, which was treated as criminal behaviour by the military (1991: 150). Consensual same-sex sexual activity was still illegal under sodomy and moral misconduct laws, and homosexuality was highly pathologized and considered a form of mental illness, degeneracy and deviance. American gay bars and clubs of the 1950s and 1960s were subject to police raids; they were frequently owned and managed by organized crime and tenuous laws against cross-dressing for fraudulent purposes enabled police to violently harass, arrest, rob, assault and rape lesbian, gay and trans clientele of those clubs.

It is widely recorded in the histories cited earlier, such as those from Faderman (1991) and Kennedy and Davis (1993) that lesbian clubs had fairly strict conventions around presentation, with butch-femme couplings a cultural expectation, and little tolerance for anyone who could not be readily identified as one or the other, or for any expressions of butch-butch desire or femmes seeking relationships with other femmes. This was similar to the British scene in the same time period, as much oral histories attest, particularly at the often-cited Gateways Club in Chelsea, London, of course. 'There was role-playing and that was the way it was. If you weren't one way or the other, if you didn't conform, they derided you for it and said that you didn't know what you were' (Neild & Pearson, 1992: 60). Femme-butch then became established as a lesbian identity, and also as a symbolic lesbian identity, making lesbians visible to one another, and potentially, perhaps enabling femme-butch couples to pass as heterosexual some of the time in public space, potentially reducing levels of harassment. Although, it is unlikely that such heterosexual passing could operate on a more long-term basis, even if it provided some level of protection from hostile attention in fleeting glances.

In her book on UK lesbian history *Tomboys and Bachelor Girls*, Jennings recounts interviews with regulars of the Gateways who reported harassment received on public transport when on their way to the club. Some did not compromise and would shout back, whereas other butch regulars noted that they covered or softened their look a bit until they got to the club, to try to avoid too much negative public attention (Jennings, 2007). For masculine lesbians who were not prepared to feminize, economic survival may have depended on pursuing male-dominated jobs in factories and manual trades, for example, where butches would not have to feminize for work, or where it may have even been possible for some butch lesbians to pass as male for work in male-only environments. In turn, femme lesbians were also enabled economically by 'passing' as women assumed not to be lesbian, due to their feminine appearance; they may be assumed to be career girls, living without a man to focus on work. Historians like Jennings (2007) note that trends in the UK around the post-war period, for career girls and those living solo, made it slightly easier to live alone as a lesbian woman or with another woman. Although, writing in a guide to London in 1966, Maureen Duffy highlighted that it was still difficult to socialize or use public space, many restaurants barred women in trousers or slacks and going to pubs was risky for women on their own (Duffy, 1966). This does not mean that the repressive environment created or somehow birthed femme-butch identity, though; it is just to acknowledge how that environment shaped and gave rise to various opportunities for its expression. As addressed right at the start of this book, gender nonconformity and the crossing of cultural sex roles is as old as history itself. It is certainly arguable that masculine and feminine lesbian genders too have existed for just as long, finding expression in that sort of cross-gendered behaviour and same-sex relationships.

We're here, we're queer, we're White?

The Whiteness of the much-publicized American origin story is significant when considering the effect of Second Wave feminism and particularly the effects of lesbian feminist theory on lesbian communities. Often this was experienced and reported as an attack on femme-butch lesbians. Queen Nestle, for example, recalls 'the lesbian-feminists of the seventies who cried "traitor" into the faces of the few butch-femme couples who did cross over into the new world of cultural feminism' (1992: 14). Not only was the bar culture of that period largely, though not exclusively by any means, White, but feminism at that time was also White dominated. Indeed, as I have already discussed, racism within feminism as a social justice movement is a persistent feminist faultline and it remains so. Professor of Sociology, American scholar Mignon Moore, in her research into Black lesbian communities, suggests that the racism of mainstream feminism and lesbian feminism of the time meant Black lesbians and feminists were less likely to engage with lesbian feminist groups, and Black lesbian culture was also not so dependent on the underground bar scene of that era. Having private neighbourhood networks that did not utilize those underground gay bars so frequently also meant perhaps that Black lesbian communities were less easily identifiable and less public. This all meant that in those Black communities, masculine and feminine lesbian genders, fem-butch or fem-stud, were arguably less affected by the cultural onslaught from the late 1960s onwards in the United States, which attempted to define those relationships as backwards, sadomasochistic and anachronistic:

> As a group, black lesbians were less engaged in the public bar culture that defined many white working-class women's experiences; instead, they primarily socialised with one another at private house parties in their own racially segregated neighbourhoods. Black lesbians maintained a physical distance from white lesbian-feminists and were less often subjected to the assaults directed at gender presentation in their relationships. (Moore, 2006: 116)

There are then many complexities and questions around what has become received wisdom about the history and beginnings of femme-butch identity and culture.

This origin story is Americanized, White and urban, yet lives must also have been lived in rural settings, in Black communities and in other parts of the globe. Perhaps the racism of historical documentation plays out here, that is, the politics behind which stories get told and which don't. The cultural imaginary of 1950s gay America generally, and of places like the Stonewall Inn in New York, and the resistance of 1969 most famously, have been largely told by White people, and the figures photographed and made famous in film and fiction telling those stories are often also White men. I posit that while working-class, mainly White urban bar culture of the 1940s and 1950s in the United States is widely seen as a prime beginning for femme-butch, it might better be considered just one well-documented time and place when those identities became concretized in a semi-public underground gay scene and were thus given a physical home. With that physical space came boundaries, norms, trends and codes that went on to be widely and globally documented to this day. Those particular norms, trends and codes then came to represent femme-butch identity in general and have become universal references for femme-butch lesbian culture since. This reflects the cultural imperialism of the United States, of course, but also it is perhaps due to the overdue explosion of lesbian and gay liberation movements in the Western world, which famously emerged from those very spaces in the late 1960s. As the scholar Susan Stryker notes, resistance and organizing across communities of drag queens, gays, lesbians, trans women, trans men, 'gender nonconformists of many varieties' (Stryker, 2017: 106) and those working in prostitution had all been increasing in the United States. At Dewey's coffee house in Philadelphia in 1965, at Compton's Cafeteria in 1966 in San Francisco, for example, the progressive youth movements of the time were ready to march for gay liberation, 'primed for any event that would set such a movement off' (Stryker, 2017: 106). Marginalized LGBT people from various backgrounds, united in all being labelled as deviants, eventually fought back against the violent repression that shaped and limited their culture at that time, a resistance that, at the famous Stonewall Inn, included Black, Latino, Hispanic and White lesbians, gays and trans working-class people, including femmes and butches.

When you know, you know

It is ironic perhaps that although we have classic histories on the early and heydays of femme-butch, there is not an agreed definition of what femme-butch is, what a femme is or what a butch is. Indeed, acres of trees have provided the scratching posts onto which gender studies scholars have left their marks, arguing that these identities cannot be reduced, simplified or defined because they mean different things to different people. There is a reluctance to provide categorical definitions; as sexuality and gender scholar Gayle Rubin has highlighted, this is controversial terrain, with almost as many different additions to the spotter's guide as there are people who may take on these labels to varying degrees. 'Attempting to define terms such as butch and femme is one of the surest ways to incite volatile discussion among lesbians' (1992: 466). Much of the literature invokes spiritual references to internal essence and drives, basically underpinning, as Bear Bergman (2006) has asserted, that when one is femme or butch, one knows; and it can look, sound and act exactly how each individual wants it to. Butch identity and expression is something that may be formally hard to classify, and yet, as scholar and human rights activist Anthea Nguyen clarifies, it is often something widely understood as recognizable. 'Although there is no simple and easy definition of butch, much like masculinity, it is nonetheless still easily recognised' (Nguyen, 2008: 670). The reticence to limit and narrow expressions and self-definitions is understandable and admirable. All our identities are intersectional (Crenshaw, 1989; Combahee River Collective, 1977), that is to say that none of us are just one aspect of our selves; we are made up of overlapping and various recognized identities, some of which give us more access in our lives in terms of the matrix of power relationships we live in, and some of which may close down options, or even make us subject to marginalization and violence.

As I explored in Chapter 5, masculine identities too are not homogenous; there are so many different examples of masculinity for men (Messerschmidt, 2018), even if you think of men in your own family, or in film, music and television representations of men. There are arguably recognizable gay masculinities, Black masculinities, sporting masculinities and many, many more. Female, lesbian or queer masculine gender identities are also raced (Cole, 2011; Wilson, 2009; Moore, 2006), they are classed (Crawley, 2001: Case, 1989; Nestle, 1981), they are aged and they inhabit a body which is of varying shape, size and which is subject to strain, environment, illness and disability. Butches do masculinity in a variety of ways, which are recognizable, and therefore there are recognizable types of expression in this community. Subcategories within the butch gender identity illustrate this diversity, or possibly hierarchy, because as psychologists studying lesbian communities have documented, there is a spectrum of butch which is often commonly assumed to go from stone butch to soft butch (Levitt & Heistand, 2004).

This could be seen simplistically as a spectrum from more to less classically or stereotypically masculine, but it can also refer to sexual preferences and sexual relationships. 'Stone butch' is the term within lesbian communities to refer to a butch who does not wish to be a recipient of penetrative sex in particular, or perhaps of any sexual touch in general from their partners. This can be due to identity preference or due to sex dysphoria or a mixture of such influences. A soft butch is seen as a butch who is less stereotypically masculine, but still with a recognizable type or category of masculinity, a butch who might be more preppy in their clothing and style, or less focussed on acquiring a muscular physique to display, for example. As Gayle Rubin correctly observes, there are many types of butches:

> There are at least as many ways to be butch as there are ways for men to be masculine; actually, there are more ways to be butch, because when women appropriate masculine styles the element of travesty produces new significance and meaning. . . . Butches come in all the shapes and varieties and idioms of masculinity. there are butches who are tough street dudes, butches who are jocks, butches who are scholars, butches who are artists, rock-and-roll butches, butches who have motorcycles, and butches who have money. There are butches whose male role models are effeminate men, sissies, drag queens, and many different types of male homosexuals. There are butch nerds, butches with soft bodies and hard minds. (Rubin, 1992: 469–70)

Even in her introduction to what should surely be seen as one of the sacred books of femme-butch herstory, Joan Nestle (1992) does not define butch either; she makes references to erotic energies and self-fulfilment, just as much as she does short hair or starched collars. This notion of essence and internal drivers to butch identity is a common theme in literature within this field, from sociology and psychology too. There is discussion over whether butch identity is innate and sensed even before the descriptor term 'butch' is even known, or whether it is purely a product of social conditioning, or maybe a mixture of both. If butch is indeed more of a spiritual drive or internal essence, then perhaps this is what should define butch, and therefore could only be known by self-definition and known to others by self-declaration. 'The most common response was that butchness is a certain energy or essence. . . . For all participants, being butch was experienced as an unmalleable aspect of self, so essential that it even preceded their awareness of that label' (Levitt & Hiestand, 2004: 609–10). Professor Sally Munt also explored this question in her influential work on femme-butch identities: 'for many women their butch identity is felt to be their core identity (or one of their core identities), experienced as a deep self which is there to be expressed' (Munt, 2001: 100). Like their inspirational muse Joan Nestle, in their book, *Persistence*, Coyote and Sharman (2011) also do not define butch. They write that when they went looking for classic definitions, all they found were stereotypes of masculinity in terms of appearance, attitude and role. These were rejected then, in favour of acknowledging all the variety of butch expressions and embodiments, as Rubin has above. As Burana, Roxxie and Due (1994) explained in their collection, *Dagger: On Butch Women*, while Nestle states that for the butch, their/her identity is 'not a masquerade or a gender cliché, but her final and fullest expression of herself' (1992: 20), the rest of society often does indeed choose to see butch expression as an aping of male roles. Sometimes, as an affront or challenge to that natural order of male-masculine role and position.

Athena Nguyen, in her article on female masculinity, agrees that the butch identity 'can threaten the patriarchal status quo not only through her rejection of femininity but also through her severing the link between masculinity and men' (Nguyen, 2008: 681). Butch identity is, because of this, frequently associated with rebellion against such inscribed and expected sex, gender and sexuality norms, particularly the stifling and limiting requirements of femininity for those sexed as female at birth. It has also, by extension, been presented as a rebellion against sexist society more broadly and as a symbolic or real threat to male masculinity, as Professor of English and Theatre Alisa Solomon underlines: 'Adopting and often transforming traits traditionally associated with men, butches threaten masculinity more than they imitate it; they colonise it' (Solomon, 1993: 37). British scholar Dr Alison Eves, in her work on femme and butch lesbian identities, defines butch, as I do, as a form of lesbian gender, and notes that typographies and classifications are problematic because of the 'relative lack of language for lesbian genders' (2004: 483). Eves does go on though, to define butch, as most others have, as a term for lesbian gender preferences that reside on a spectrum of masculinity as it is commonly and culturally recognized and understood. It is perhaps unsurprising that this is the most prevalent definition of butch. As I started with at the beginning of this chapter, this is the common-sense understanding of what butch means. Not only is this true in lesbian and queer spaces but outside of them in mainstream culture as well, as Melinda Kanner asserts in her article on the semiotics of butch: 'The butch woman looks like who she is, to natives and non-natives alike' (Kanner, 2002: 28). Butch equals some degree of masculinity and the recognizable presentation of that by a sexed as female person who is assumed to pursue relationships with women.

Butch masculinity

Descriptions of what butch might be, unsurprisingly, given that butch equals masculinity, often fall back onto current culturally recognizable masculine signifiers for men (Weston, 1993), such as men's clothing and fashion, as American scholar of butch lesbian sexuality and identity, Sara L Crawley, observes in one of her articles on butch presentation and readings and how this is impacted by environment and location, as well as audience. 'Of course, a butch still wears men's clothes. There's no need for skimpy bathing suits or spaghetti-strap anything' (Crawley, 2008: 369). Styles and fashions such as men's short haircuts, or men's hairstyles, are often cited too, 'with haircuts, clothing, and ways of moving or being "comfortable" in one's body' (Levitt & Hiestand, 2004: 612). The latter point refers to the presumed masculinity of taking up space, and how masculinity is defined as dominant in voice, speech and movement, for example. This was briefly introduced earlier in Chapter 5 on the social construction of masculinity. Other psychologists studying femme-butch identity observed that butches would style themselves similarly to current cultural fashions for men in their communities, such that they would often be read as men: 'There are acknowledged differences in dress and hairstyle, such that some butch women are more likely to be mistaken for men' (Rosario et al., 2009: 35). Being butch is also sometimes associated with enjoying or pursuing male-dominated careers, hobbies or sports, such as being involved in construction jobs, taking up motorbiking or weight training 'dykes with such objects or attributes as motorcycles, cummerbunds, wingtips, money, pronounced biceps' (Solomon, 1993: 37). As well as, sometimes, also adopting attitudes and behaviours constructed as the domain of masculinity and as defining features of masculinity and manhood, not always seen positively to say the least, such as being competitive, being chivalrous or seen to be tough, having 'pride in toughness, out machoing men' (Crowder, 1998: 55) or being 'assertive and dominant' (Rosario et al., 2009: 35). While butch identity and presentation therefore utilize cultural tropes and displays of male masculinity, whether in mainstream culture or in raced or classed male subcultures, this is not to say that butch is just a stereotype of masculinity. Butches are no more stereotypes of masculinity than men are stereotypes of masculinity, and no less either.

The definition of butch as masculine to some degree is problematic if we take the decoupling of masculinity from male a bit further and see such identity preferences, styles and presentations as nothing to do with men or masculinity at all, but as simply ways of being women or ways of being a lesbian. This has been acknowledged by scholars on this subject too, who posit this question – why can't butch be seen as expanding different ways to be women, and perhaps, different ways to be men also? 'For some, the performance of a distinctive lesbian style allows for a kind of gender bending, a playfulness around traditional categories of "masculinity" and "femininity". . . . By playing on traditional formulations of masculinity, then, butch dykes enlarge the category "man" as well' (Esterberg, 1996: 276). These questions were also addressed by the butch and queer respondents who took part in my survey. For some individuals butch was a proud display of womanhood and lesbianism, while for others, as I discuss in depth in Chapter 8 on queering 'female' masculinity, it was an embodiment of their masculinity and manhood. Perhaps we have arrived where we began this chapter, with an almost clichéd acknowledgement of how complicated definitions are, and how controversial it is to try to come up with one totalizing category of butch. 'Despite the widespread discussion of butch and femme in various popular and academic works on lesbian and bisexual women, little consensus exists on the definition of what constitutes butch/femme identity' (Rosario et al., 2009: 35).

Butch on new terms

Further controversy abounds in discussions of the meaning and relevance of butch today, due to questions over whether this term is needed anymore anyway, due to the rise of more fluid terms such as MOC, NB, GNC, trans and transgender. Back in 1998 Professor Jack Halberstam presciently asked: 'As gender-queer practices and forms continue to emerge, presumably the definitions of gay, lesbian, transexual, and transgender will not remain static, and we will produce new terms to delineate what the current terms cannot' (1998a: 307). Indeed, the terms are far from static, but perhaps they are still and forever a work in progress, still in formulation and flux, rather than ever being fixed and agreed. It is true that new terms have emerged, as I have discussed throughout this book; there are many more terms for queer female masculinities, like 'MOC', 'NB', 'transmasculine', 'GNC', 'TG' and 'trans'. These have emerged in a landscape that is arguably more aware, though not necessarily well informed, about transgender lives, trans identities and the presence and contribution of trans women and trans men. This is what I have termed a post-trans landscape, with the qualifier that this is by no means to suggest that trans liberation has been won and is consequently over, because that is certainly far from the case. It is clear from British and American research at least that younger generations are increasingly choosing less binary and more fluid terms for sex, sexuality and gender, as the work in British schools by Professor Emma Renold and her team discovered in 2017, documenting an increasing lexicon or expanded vocabulary for sex and gender, with over twenty-three different terms in use for sex and gender identities (2017). The young students in school saw such a stance as contemporary and perhaps vanguardist almost. 'They often saw these rights as "modern" or "twenty-first century" and as important aspects of their sense of self and values, identifying themselves as more progressive than earlier generations' (Bragg et al., 2018: 4).

What will such shifts mean for fairly fixed terms such as butch lesbian then, which relies, traditionally, on binary sex categories; and will butch decline as an identity choice, becoming seen as backwards and out of date? Professor Halberstam has addressed such questions, being one of the most important voices to continue talking about butch lesbian identity and why it matters both as a descriptor for lived experiences and as an area of worthy scholarship. Halberstam examines the chicness of lesbian identities at different times and contexts, raising what they call the 'temporal paradox of the butch', being the fact that it seems to persist as a term, and as a reference point and it is widely understood, yet at the same time it is surrounded with crisis narratives about its imminent disappearance. Incidentally, this crisis narrative is one that it shares in common with masculinity too, as I explained in Chapter 5: 'Has butch been around long enough to become trendy? Or, in an era of unprecedented visibility for transgender embodiment, does butch represent an obstinate fragment of an older paradigm?' (Halberstam, 2015).

The increasing awareness and popularity of new terms for queer female masculinities also intersect with older concerns about what was called 'butch flight', as Bear Bergman reported in 2006: 'I hear from butches that they are saddened by what they think of as Butch Flight, that people who once might have lived as butches are now living as men, and it makes them sad. They want back the visibly queer phalanx of butches, and they want the kickass women butches sometimes embodied' (Bergman, 2006: 67). As I have explained previously, 'butch flight' is a term used to describe what is seen as an exodus from butchness to a trans identity instead and in replacement of butch, be that to take up the new identity of trans man, or transgender. Despite all such pressures though, as Halberstam continues to argue, the category of butch persists. For many of my respondents, who were all too aware of challenges to it, the label of butch still remained significant and was still the best term available to adequately define their identity. Thirty of my participants ticked the box to indicate their butch identity, and a further ten defined their identity themselves using a butch label, such as 'soft butch' and 'faggy butch'. In open text responses, these forty participants expounded on all the areas and questions I have introduced earlier. The sometimes rocky relationship to newer, queered terms for lesbian masculinities, for example, the origins of butchness and to what degree this is innate, as well as fears of a decline of butch identity and a concern that this was becoming seen as an outdated and old-fashioned identity. For most respondents, 'butch' was still a label with political and sentimental meaning. Many participants were keen that this identity not be lost and be included and distinguished within the contemporary rainbow of possibilities for sexuality and gender identities. In Chapter 7 I shall gladly platform some of these proud butch voices.

7

Butch voices and butch pride

In this chapter I will introduce voices from those we do not often hear from – proud, self-defined butch lesbians. The contemporary gender wars often stake claims to butch lesbians and use their name to justify concerns over trans rights and trans inclusion. The butch lesbian is invoked in debates over access to gender-affirming counselling, or puberty-blocking pharmaceutical interventions, the suggestion being that butch lesbians are being unwittingly set on a trans pathway, when they are not really trans. This premise is utilized to campaign for limiting access to such services, or even for removing them altogether. Fairly mainstream conversations are suddenly using terms and labels like 'butch' and GNC in parenting groups, in youth groups, in schools and in workplaces. While much anti-trans-inclusion and gender-critical discourse speaks for and about butch lesbians, these figures rarely get to speak for themselves, and even when they do, they are often ignored. After a history of being demonized by various political strands of feminist theory, the butch is back, and many different corners of this battlefield are now saying that they have her back. Meanwhile, faultlines and conflicts that have been present in the LGBTQI+ community for decades are not exactly something that butch lesbians are unable to talk about themselves and for themselves. As I briefly introduced in Chapter 6, numerous classic texts cover issues such as butch flight and the similarities and differences between butch lesbians and MOC, GNC or transgender identities. Older generations of butch lesbians have seen periods of interest in their communities come and go. They are sceptical of feminist supposed sympathies. They are also sceptical of conservative society and what some see as, controversial though it may be, a popular aggrandizement of trans identities at the expense of others. Younger butch lesbians have grown up with a background that some are calling a gender war or a culture war, which may just be their whole life, and one that they feel they have navigated and charted for themselves genuinely, rather than their life being a pawn in any warring side. Such lives are not aided by the screaming matches going on around them, and over them and in their name.

Butch lesbians are a minority community within a minority community, facing multiple discriminations from homophobia, sexism, racism and classism just for starters along with long-standing misunderstandings about who they even are, what they are, what they do and who they want to be. Butches have been told forever that they aren't real; they aren't woman enough, aren't man enough or are really trans. When butches do transition to a trans identity, they are told they need saving and that they are, ironically, not really trans. It is way past time that butch voices were heard in these mainstream conversations that concern our lives and our identities – conversations that often seek to define and limit those lives and identities, one way or another. In this chapter I shall platform just some of these butch voices. I will remind the reader that the survey was completed anonymously and thus I have given all participants pseudonyms. The self-identified butches who took part in my survey had different perspectives on the gender wars, butch flight, relationship of butch identity to masculinity and the impact of more recent terms for female queer masculinities. They had different perspectives on trans identities, sometimes positive, some negative, some cautious and unsure. The variety of views in one small community is huge, because not all butch lesbians are the same. I shall try to do justice to the variety of views and not hold back from diving into some of the points of disagreement and departure between those who have taken on and made the butch identity their home.

Butch = old skool and uncool?

First, before even getting started on the impact of the gender wars, many butch respondents, and other queer or lesbian respondents who commented on it, felt that attacks on the butch identity were far from a new phenomenon. These attacks came from various sides, from lesbian feminist theorizing and from sex and gender conservative society. Respondents frequently felt that their identity was misunderstood, misrepresented and shrouded in stereotypes functioning as received wisdom about the supposed truth of their lives, relationships, sex and desires. It was noted by queer, MOC, GNC, trans and lesbian participants in my survey that the label of butch is indeed, in their experience, less used today than in the past. This went along with a concern, from the butch respondents, as well as observers, that butch was seen by others as being somehow old fashioned and out of date, what several participants called old school, or old skool.

For example, one respondent, who was not butch herself, Roddy, gave her view of how the butch identity is seen today. She referred to butch as 'old school'. Roddy didn't give her age on the survey, but she did specify that she was queer and preferred to be identified as a gay woman; she identified as White British. Roddy said of the term 'butch':

> To me it seems more an old school term. Butch is used as a joke in my experience. (Roddy)

Malkie, a transmasculine trans man, aged in his early forties, also used this same term to describe the butch identity. Malkie specified their sexuality as queer, and their ethnic identity as Canadian. Malkie said the butch identity was still important to many, but for others they now had more various and accurate options to choose from. He defined butch as

> Old skool, but important! (Malkie)

Storm made the point that as butch was seen as uncool, femme-butch relationships in general were also often viewed as out of date, symbolizing lesbian history rather than present. Storm invoked some of the origin stories of femme-butch, making reference to butches in bars in badly fitting suits. Storm reported they were an NB genderqueer trans person. They reported their ethnic background as White English.

> I feel that the Butch/Femme identity is old fashioned and a bit 'uncool', it makes me think of people in bow ties and cummerbunds and badly fitting suits. (Storm)

This perspective was not demarcated by age, with younger respondents recounting similar experiences, even if they did not hold that perspective themselves. The first butch respondent I shall platform here is Lombard. She gave her background as White British, was aged in her late twenties, and she identified as a GNC or gender non-conforming woman and as a butch lesbian or butch dyke. Lombard explained that compared to newer terms like MOC or transmasculine, the label of butch

> is treated as the embarrassing archaic older cousin of most of the new terms . . . it is rarer to meet women/lesbians my age and younger using butch specifically as a descriptor. (Lombard)

Rohan, a butch aged in their early fifties, identified as MOC and as a lesbian. Rohan reported their ethnic background as White English and Irish. Rohan wrote about being stigmatized for their butch identity, but still felt it was significant to them. They said they kept the precious

> identity of Butch close to my heart, because historically butches shed a lot of blood, literally and metaphorically for me to be able to walk as freely as I do. (Rohan)

Rohan also reported that, from their experience, the butch identity is indeed seen as outdated and receives discrimination both within LGBTQI+ communities and outside.

> Outside of my communities I am still discriminated against in certain areas of society or in certain places that are not safe for people like me, like public bathrooms. Inside my communities, I am probably seen as somewhat outdated by many. (Rohan)

Dot responded similarly, a butch queer, aged in their late forties. Dot gave her ethnic identity as White English. Dot felt that new labels and identities had reduced the need for terms like 'butch' and that this added to the perception that butch was outdated and no longer necessary, although she did not agree herself that the category was outdated.

> I think butch is seen by some as old fashioned or traditional, when it absolutely isn't – it is varied, diverse and unique. (Dot)

Dot's view of the misunderstandings of butch individuals also related to the lesbian sex wars and assumptions about 'traditional' roles in femme-butch relationships, as I shall move on to discuss later in this chapter.

Transgender queer trans man, Caz, who was aged in his late forties, identified as White and Black Caribbean; Caz agreed that the term 'butch' had declined in usage, and they felt this was linked to general lesbophobia in the LGBTQI+ community, which they believed was fuelled by misogyny.

> Less used. There is a lot of lesbophobia in LGBTIQ culture and politics. Which is actually about misogyny. And maybe we should coin a new word, lesmisogyny or something. (Caz)

However, Caz pointed out that while the term 'butch' had decreased, this was mainly in White queer communities, and that it was still more used in Black queer communities by people of colour or POC. Caz stated, in response to the question of declining usage –

> Only by white people, it's still used by poc. (Caz)

Moving into discussing what the butch label means, Crieff responded to say that butch was less used, but when it was used, it was mainly to refer to outwards presentation or style, rather than any sort of identity marker or identity label. Crieff identified as a non-binary queer, aged in their late twenties and listed their ethnic identity as White and Asian.

> I hear butch used more as a descriptor or as a marker of style/dress more than an identity. Butch and stud are similar – masculine presenting or seeming in appearance. . . . Again it seems that butch has become more of a descriptor of gender performance rather than identity now. (Crieff)

Perhaps unsurprisingly, when respondents like Crieff did define butch, or give descriptions of what this identity looked like, they frequently made reference to masculinity and to masculine styles, clothing and presentation. As was indicated in the quote from Storm earlier, about cummerbunds and badly fitting suits, often the definitions given hinged on quite stereotypical or classic examples of masculinity and sartorial styles for men and menswear.

What is butch?

Clothing, body shape and hairstyles were mentioned frequently in definitions of butch, including by those who used the identity of butch for themselves. Joss, for example, was White British, aged in their late thirties and identified as butch and as a gay woman. They specified that butch equalled observable, outward styles to present the inner identity, such as haircuts and certain kinds of clothing, as well as the taking up of space and a confidence about bodily space.

> My personal view is this speaks only to appearance and not other characteristics. I guess, short hair, masculine clothing and the way we hold our bodies. (Joss)

Respondents noted that the term 'butch' was raced and classed, and more often used for White queers and lesbians, with 'stud' being a term only used for Black butch dykes or queers. Several participants also discussed the classed elements of the term, stating that perhaps butch carried connotations of being a solely working-class identity. This meant that sometimes it was considered difficult or contentious to claim as a label by those who were not working class, or those who preferred a sartorial expression that would not be linked with typical working-class masculine attire, being associated with workwear and speaking to the much-publicized origin stories of butches inhabiting working-class jobs. This was all explained by Laure, aged eighteen to twenty-five, a MOC lesbian or gay woman, who gave their ethnic identity as White, American and French.

> I kind of wish I could call myself butch but my hair isn't short enough and anytime I claim that identity, people always tell me that I don't look butch. I think that's probably just anti-butchness and old homophobia and misogyny. . . . I'm very educated and dress like a posh guy, and butch aesthetics seem more working class? So I would perhaps call myself dapper in dress sense. (Laure)

Idgie also invoked the classic origin story, but had no issues or insecurities in taking on the term of butch for themselves. They self-defined as an 'old fashioned butch dyke'; aged in their late forties, Idgie identified as White English and listed their sexuality as lesbian.

> For me, butch means a lesbian who is more stereotypically masculine than feminine. It has connotations of those lesbians who came before us, who dressed in suits and presented as male. (Idgie)

Several respondents pointed out in their definitions, which all used reference to masculinity, that there are, of course, as Laure raised in their response, many different masculine styles, and that butch could present or blend any number of these culturally available styles and markers. Raymondo, for example, a queer gay woman in their early thirties, White English, emphasized that there are many different ways to be masculine.

> Butch equals masculine of centre presentation, ranging from tough kinds of appearance through to quite effete dapper looks. (Raymondo)

Other respondents repeated this and also discussed the problems with using masculinity as a reference point; I pointed out earlier in this book that this conflict is a theme in the literature on femme-butch lives. Many respondents were aware of this association of butch = masculine as being problematic. They often underlined in their responses that there are many negative features of masculinities, ones that they did not want to be associated with or have to be compared to in order to describe their own identity. This was voiced by Tommi, for example, White British, a butch gay woman aged in her late fifties:

> I'm most definitely not male, and actually I don't much like a lot of heterosexual men. (Tommi)

Participants were also well aware of public debates around what has come to be called 'toxic masculinity' in the mainstream press, for example. This is an arguably unhelpful buzzword that I discussed in Chapter 5 on the social construction of masculinities. This sort of terminology and the debates around it just added to butches' stated dissatisfaction with even having to use reference to men and masculinity at all when talking about themselves. What many of the butch respondents actually believed was that butch identity and expression were very different to that of male men's masculinities. Jazza, White English, a queer in their late thirties, emphasized the differences of female masculinity for butch queers. Jazza saw female masculinity as a discrete, unique kind of masculinity in its own right, not reducible to men's masculinity.

> I don't believe in masculinity. I believe in masculinities and each would have its own definition, eg. toxic masculinity differs widely to my perception of female masculinity, which differs to my perception of faggy camp masculinity, which differs to butch masculinity etc. (Jazza)

Despite problems with the term though, masculinity was nevertheless relied upon in almost every response that offered a definition of butch. For example, to return to the voice of Laure, quoted earlier, a MOC lesbian respondent, who defined butch as follows:

> Butch is a term for masculine lesbians. (Laure)

Of course, as I have discussed throughout this book, there is a term well known in queer theory and LGBTQI+ communities for lesbian and queer masculinities. As raised by Jazza, quoted earlier, respondents were aware of the available descriptor of 'female masculinity', even though this may be considered by some to be a more Americanized term; it has undoubtably been popularized among queer communities in the UK too by Halberstam's 1998 classic text with that title. This term was often used or referred to in a context of reflecting on the utility or otherwise of referents like 'masculinity' and 'men'. Some respondents expressed a desire to recognize butch masculinity or female masculinity as its own category. There were suggestions that 'butch' could be seen as an additional masculine category in its own right, and therefore with a right to be a referent point for other multiple masculinities, including those of men, without the constant need to refer to male men's masculinity like some sort of original or master copy. Contrary to the queer butch or transgender butch respondents that I platform in Chapter 8 on queering female masculinity, many butch lesbian respondents were proud of their lesbian womanhood and/or their distinctly female masculinity; they saw it as an identity that should not be linked to men at all.

Butch masculinity or lesbian womanhood?

Although references to recognizable men's styles for masculinity were used in descriptions, this was theorized as being problematic and an undesirable situation that only came about because butch, lesbian or female expression of masculinity is not recognized. For many butches, their distinct lesbian style was something they were proud of. Leslie was just one such butch, for example. Leslie stated she was White English, was aged in her late forties, and she identified as butch and as a lesbian. For her, butch was just one way to be a woman.

My 'butchness' is one way of describing what type of woman I am. (Leslie)

Another proud butch, Minnie, was aged in their early forties, identified as White Jewish and defined as butch, MOC, queer and lesbian. Minnie raised problems with dominant or hegemonic masculinities, explaining that they had never been able to identify with these. Minnie echoed definitions outlined earlier, that link butch expression to a confidence in taking up space, and a confidence in the body in public space, as we also see in scholarly definitions of masculinity.

I have always identified as masculine but not with dominant masculinities. It's appearance, way of relating to the world, sense of body. (Minnie)

For these respondents, the identifier of woman, and womanhood, were sites of belonging, where they staked a claim. Even when, as was often the case, they were aware that they did not conform to most cultural expectations for womanhood and that this often caused them personal problems, for example the perennial toilet trouble as I have discussed elsewhere in this book. This point was illustrated by Gillespie, a Black British, masculine lesbian queer in their early forties. Gillespie said that society needed to recognize the expanse of the term 'woman' and all that it could contain.

I identified as trans for a while, not because I didn't want to be a woman, but because my womanhood did not conform with the conventional norms expected of womanhood. To 'society' I was too often not a woman. I feel I have and time has changed so that I'd rather force the word to adapt to be less rigid. (Gillespie)

Cleo also asserted her womanhood; she did not see being butch as related to men or maleness in any way at all and she also saw it as totally separate from being identified as trans or identifying as a trans man. She was Black British, aged in her early fifties and identified as androgynous, a gay woman, and she described herself as a femme-loving-butch, proud to be female and strong.

> I like the fact that I am a woman, I am not trying to be trans or masculine. I think it's important to recognise that being butch is about being a certain type of woman, not a woman who is trying to be a man or more masculine. (Cleo)

Similarly, DanC, who identified as White Welsh, and stated they were mostly butch lesbian, was aged in their early sixties. DanC argued as well that being butch is just one way of being a woman, and that womanhood can take a multitude of forms, even if these are not always recognized, respected, represented or seen as valid. Several butch respondents, like DanC, wrote about feeling comfortable with being female bodied; several were mothers and expressed that this was something they drew strength from, and they did not find it incongruent in any way.

> I identify as a woman because I feel comfortable in that role, even though I am a butch woman. I am also a mother. I have come to understand that being a woman can encompass many identities. (DanC)

However, for others, pregnancy and mothering had been a jolt to their sexual and gender identity and presentation. Raymondo, for example, wrote about previously looking forward to being able to queer pregnancy, but then finding the homogenous feminine environment overpowering. Raymondo identified as queer, a gay woman, butch dyke in various manifestations, and also as masculine of centre, they were in their early thirties and White English. Raymondo's responses also highlighted the symbolic power of the butch identity as a universally recognizable lesbian identity, and therefore a loud symbol of same-sex or lesbian desire.

> When I dress and present masculine, I feel more attractive to women – I think it's just because there's a swagger in it and it's a very visible way of saying whom I like. It feels powerful and sexy – even though I've also felt most vulnerable and had the most abuse looking that way too. I feel invisible as a queer woman when I dress feminine. My sexuality feels erased right now as I look so pregnant and people assume you are straight. (Raymondo)

Another out butch, Corrie, also mentioned how important it is to be proud of one's identity and butch womanhood, not least because this can act as a role model for other masculine, non-conforming women or butch lesbians. Corrie was aged in her early fifties and identified as White English, a butch dyke, and she also identified as queer.

> I am proud to be a big strong woman, positive role model for other women like myself. (Corrie)

For many of these proud butch respondents the label of butch was powerful and inspiring. For butches with this perspective, there was sometimes a degree of unease about the relationship of the identifier 'butch' to newer terms used to describe female masculinities or queer masculinities. There was seen to be a complex relationship between butch and terms like MOC, NB, GNC or transmasculine for example – not always a positive one.

Butch on whose terms – new terms

For some respondents there were clear differences between butch and these newer terms. Butch respondents were sometimes concerned that the newer terms would eclipse the label of butch, and this was partly fuelled by the previous observations of attitudes that see butch as outdated and backwards. It was stated that younger generations in particular favoured more fluid terms and did not like to be boxed into a rigid category, which butch may be seen to be. This was explored by Tundergarth for example, a Mixed/Dual Heritage butch lesbian in her early fifties.

> With greater acceptance of more fluid identities, Butch is being lost. (Tundergarth)

If newer terms are seen as modern and more progressive, then this could only further the perception of butch as an identity that has reached the end of its natural life course, being seen as 'old-school' as I explained earlier. Isambard experienced this perception of their butch identity, she identified as butch, as MOC and as a lesbian or gay woman as well as queer and she did not list her age or ethnicity.

> I find it hard now to have discussions about sexuality and gender as, being butch, I feel is seen as old fashioned, and not as cutting edge as being trans/genderqueer. So now I don't have those discussions with people, and distance myself. (Isambard)

Other respondents agreed there was a difference between the term 'butch' and the newer terms, but they thought that this just meant that individuals would have more accurate terms to describe themselves. This would mean that people who in the past may have identified as butch because they didn't have any other label might now feel that they were a better fit with one of these newer terms and be able to take a new label on instead. Stu made this point about trans men, for example. Stu was in their early forties, White English, and they identified as butch and as masculine:

> I think a lot of lesbians who have identified as Butch throughout history would probably have identified as Trans – if it had been an option. (Stu)

Della and Reggie also made this same point, asserting that maybe in the past some butch lesbians would have identified as trans men or as transmasculine for example, if those terms had been there and if they had been more readily available and widely represented. Reggie, aged in their early forties, identified as genderqueer; they listed their sexuality as pan or bi and they gave their ethnic heritage as White English, Scottish and Irish.

> Some people who in the past would have been butches are now probably trans. Others who simply dress in a boyish way without associated social expectations may not need labels. (Reggie)

White Swedish respondent, Della, a transmasculine queer aged in their late twenties agreed, and saw this shift as a generational change.

> I think the term butch is becoming less common because we have other words today. Some people would call themselves queer instead. I also think that many of the people who called themselves butch 40 years ago maybe today would call themselves transgender today. (Della)

Of course, none of this necessarily has to undermine the category of butch, it just acknowledges differences in what categories define and describe. By this reasoning there are more labels now, because there are more than one or two identities that need names, and probably always were. Yet, as indicated in their testimonies, for some respondents, newer terms presented a potential danger. Some respondents felt there was a danger that newer terms would subsume the identifier of butch, and maybe that this process or shift was motivated by lesbophobia. This was framed as part of a general decline of and distaste for specifically lesbian identities, relationships, spaces and communities. Lombard was a White British butch lesbian dyke, in her late twenties. Lombard spoke about what they saw as the elevation and aggrandizement of terms like MOC, GNC, transmasculine, NB or transgender in the LGBTQI+ community, an elevation they did not see occurring for the category of butch.

> 'Butch' has enjoyed no such reclamation, most probably because of lesbophobia in my opinion. People are still uncomfortable with masculine women. (Lombard)

This quote raises one of the key differences that respondents picked out between butch and the newer terms. Butch is a label that invokes an image of visible lesbian women, and/or of masculine women, which Lombard suggests is not a universally liked image. The other terms do not necessarily invoke similar images. Butch was therefore seen as a distinctly lesbian identity, one that emphasized a type of womanhood and/or femaleness; a feature which the newer terms do not include as they are not sexed and can be used by anyone of any sex identifier. Someone of any sexed bodily characteristics could be GNC or NB for example, trans and transgender also do not immediately symbolize that the bearer of that identity is of any particular sexed characteristics. This was spelt out clearly by Judith, a butch lesbian, in her early forties, who listed her ethnicity as White English.

> Butch to me, is of woman, of dyke. . . . Butch feels like it relates to women, the other's don't. (Judith)

Radclyffe also raised this same point, a White European butch lesbian in her late forties.

> For me butch and masculine of centre are very similar and do not imply that you don't identify with the term woman (which the other terms do imply). (Radclyffe)

Mo stated that in his opinion butch did share commonalities with GNC, NB, transmasculine and other newer terms, because they were all about some sort of masculinity, but that butch was unashamedly attached to womanhood and lesbianism, whereas the other terms were more comfortable for trans and transgender individuals. A trans man, Mo was aged in his early thirties; he identified his sexuality as pan and did not list his ethnic background.

> I think they have commonalities in that they are all referring to masculinity, usually in people assigned female at birth. I think butch was much more related to sexual orientation and lesbian culture and that the other terms fall more under the transgender spectrum and are more independent of sexual orientation. (Mo)

Dell felt that butch was just seen as uncool today, and that the new terms had indeed taken over for that reason. Dell identified as GNC, as a tomboy and a faggy butch. They listed their sexuality as lesbian dyke, and they specified their ethnic identity as White English and Gypsy/Traveller. Dell was aged in their late forties. Dell also thought it was partly due to misogyny that the use of the identifier butch was in decline, and that it was also due to lesbophobia and ageism that butch is seen as a hangover from an older time. Dell said people were less likely to use the term today, due to

> Fear of being uncool, fear of moving away from the herd, fear of being thought of as a 'dinosaur' and misogyny. (Dell)

Leslie, another butch lesbian, agreed with Dell, and thought that terms like MOC in particular, as well as other terms, had eclipsed butch, with butch consequently being a negative term today.

> I'm wondering if masculine of centre has become more common, at least among younger LGBT groups? Or queer/trans/nb? I just don't hear butch a lot anymore, and it almost feels like a slur in some contexts, although I don't think that it is at all. (Leslie)

Several respondents also raised dissatisfaction at the seemingly all-too-common assumption that individuals who identified as butch were actually MOC or transgender or on the road to pursuing a trans identity of some sort. Several respondents noted that this had been assumed of them, which they found frustrating. Lucy had observed this, White European, aged late fifties, and they were butch and queer. Of new terms, such as MOC, GNC and transmasculine, Lucy argued:

> I think that what they have in common is that people often mistake a butch for one of these other identities – one particular trend I have witnessed is that people assume you are somewhere en-route to transitioning, FTM. (Lucy)

It is impossible to talk about fears of butch erasure without talking about butch flight, and this issue was indeed articulated by many of the respondents to my survey. Many participants did perceive that butches were in decline, and that the ascendancy of terms like 'transmasculine', 'transgender' and 'trans' meant that these labels were viewed with higher status or currency in the LGBTQI+ community and therefore butch lesbians were perhaps being encouraged to take up these terms and leave the label of butch behind.

Butch flight and popular destinations

Not only did many respondents feel that butch flight was genuinely a pressing phenomenon in lesbian communities, they felt it was sometimes due to negative external pressures, rather than sincere personal motivations for a more accurate label. This was complex, because respondents also acknowledged that for some people, newer terms like transgender, MOC, GNC, transmasculine or trans man may just click and would have been adopted ages ago if they had been available. There was a logical reticence to question or disavow the validity of other people's identities; but this was alongside a sense that being butch was uncool and old school, as well as misunderstood, so there were therefore seen to be multiple incentives and rational reasons to prefer one of the newer terms instead, whether or not they fit better. Some more critical respondents openly stated that they felt the T in LGBTQI+ had been promoted above all others recently and this was having an effect in furthering and encouraging butch flight. Idgie, for example, was aged late forties, White English and identified as an old-fashioned butch dyke.

> This is a difficult subject I think. I feel like we're in a transition period of history and perhaps, in 100 years, gender and sexuality won't be an issue. Right now, it feels as though the transgender movement has become all-consuming in relation to political and social campaigns. But I notice this tends to be male tg trans, not female tg trans. I find it fascinating that the 'famous' transgender people are all transwomen. (Idgie)

Other respondents also addressed the invisibility of trans men in culture and the lack of any examples of transmasculinity or transmasculine role models; like Idgie argued, it was seen to be the case that trans women were much more central in media representations of trans lives. Bobby made this point too; they were aged eighteen to twenty-five, White English and identified as a butch lesbian. Bobby referenced debates about toxic masculinity too, and felt that analyses of men's masculinity could negatively influence how the masculinity of queer people was received too. What this meant was that masculine queer people could find themselves suspected of domineering or sexist behaviours, and so were hypervigilant to avoid such assumptions being made of them. Bobby felt this led to transmasculine people and butches not putting themselves or their concerns forward.

> The most awareness of trans politics is focussed around trans women and transfeminine. Which makes sense, as these people can be more visible, but

transmasculine is often excluded from discussion and spaces as we're told masculinity already takes over too much space, which lacks nuance. (Bobby)

Sometimes the responses given in the survey on butch flight were similar to some GC narratives. Similarly to what I outlined in Chapter 4, respondents at times suggested that there was some sort of trans agenda at work and that this was pressuring butch lesbians or GNC lesbians to become trans men where they would not have done so in different and less pressured circumstances. This is obviously a sensitive topic. Nobody lives in an objective bubble and the environment of increasing awareness about identity options, as well as long-standing negative stereotypes about butch lesbians, may well be influencing choices. However, some cases of butch flight may actually be cases of mistaken identity, as those individuals were trans men all along, and not in fact butch lesbians. The sensitivity of this whole discussion was acknowledged in the responses that participants gave, and how they gave them. They often began or bookended their accounts with phrases and qualifiers like, 'I have to say', or 'it's difficult, but' as Idgie did above, or 'in all honesty'. Valentine, for example, aged in her late thirties, identified as GNC and bisexual, White European. Valentine felt there was a cultural and social pressure on butch and GNC women to transition and identify as trans men instead.

Honestly, I think the term butch is being erased and GNC people are encouraged to transition. (Valentine)

Jender agreed, White Asian, aged in their early forties; she identified as a queer and NB, and stated her sexuality was lesbian.

Butch women are being encouraged to transition and become trans men. (Jender)

Some butch lesbians reported for themselves that they had indeed felt under pressure to transition, and this was put forward by Isambard and Bobby, for example. Isambard was butch, MOC and identified their sexuality as gay and queer; they recalled that many of their peers were transitioning and this made them wonder if they should do so as well.

In my late 20s I felt confused about my gender and thought I was trans. I think I was influenced by my peers that were boyish/butch and were transitioning into ftm. However, I did not want to be a man, but I wanted to be less female looking, and did not like my breasts. Now I would consider myself butch/masculine in presentation. (Isambard)

Bobby was aged between eighteen and twenty-five, White English and said although they had identified as a trans man in the past, they then started to use the term NB until eventually deciding on the category of butch and feeling comfortable in this identity. Bobby felt they had been pressured to transition and use the label of trans man, when it did not actually fit how they felt about themselves.

> Many butch people experiment with various terms when trying to navigate their gender identity. Society is confusing because it tells you if you want to be masculine then you can't be a woman, you must be in the wrong body. Now for many people this is true. However, when I was younger I felt forced to transition to a transman. (Bobby).

This is a case of a reversed flight path. Bobby found the identity of trans man first and thought that must be what they were, because they felt masculine, but after some time they became aware of other identities and realized that actually the label of butch fit them better. Some butch respondents expressed a sense of bitterness about the decline of butch identity, and the societal pressures that they saw to transition. Butch-esque, lesbian dyke Jenpen presented this view. Jenpen was aged in their late forties and listed their ethnicity as White and German. Like others have suggested, in earlier quotes, Jenpen felt that butches were seen as out of date and embarrassing; whereas being trans was, in their view, aggrandized and valorized, including in the media, in a way that butch lives were just not. This perception enabled Jenpen to speak of what they saw as trans privilege.

> Why be butch and get beaten up, looked down upon and die with the dinosaurs, when you can go trans and get you some real privileges? When butches are raped and murdered, Hollywood ain't coming. (Jenpen)

Several butches had also watched a lot of their friends transition, as Jez mentioned. Jez identified as MOC and had in the past started a transition to trans man, but had then realized they did not fit in this identity. Having taken testosterone for a time, they now felt they did not get read easily as any sex or gender, and that they had features that people would read as male and female. Jez described their sexuality as being emotionally attracted to women, and they listed their ethnic background as White, Mixed and European.

> over the last 20 years I've known so many butch lesbians who've transitioned FTM or decided to call themselves 'queer', MOC, transgendered etc. I can't keep up. (Jez).

Judith explicitly called this phenomena lesbian erasure. Judith was a butch lesbian, in her late forties, White English; she said that being female and a woman was a source of pride and power for her.

> I am increasingly troubled by what I can sense is an erasure of lesbians. I'm worried that young butch dykes are being persuaded that they need to transition to trans men. (Judith)

Several butches recounted for themselves that they did not necessarily feel pressured to transition, however, nor did they document peer pressure to follow this route. What many butch respondents had experienced was the assumption that they were trans men, or in the process of becoming trans men, and they had to be able to resist this sort of social pressure and keep asserting their own identity. I explore this experience more fully in Chapter 8 on queering female masculinities. Stu, for example, White English, was aged in their early forties, and identified as masculine, butch and specified their sexuality as gay.

> My girlfriend says that Butches are a dying breed, because everyone is transitioning. I have felt that sometimes I am judged by the queer community to be a trans man who just hasn't come out yet, a judgement I find a little offensive and a position that echoes my experience of patriarchy, like why would you choose to be a masculine woman when you could be a man?. (Stu)

Several respondents wrote about the negative connotations attached to the label of butch, such as Fred, a butch lesbian dyke in her early fifties who identified her ethnicity as Welsh.

> Negative connotations make it less attractive and younger people would rather not label at all, or prefer queer, and people are more movable in sexual orientations and expression. (Fred)

What were these negative connotations? Namely, respondents brought up the common assumption that these relationships are inherently sexist and that the butch identity is negatively masculine, in a way assumed to be domineering and sexist towards feminine partners. Lombard discussed this offensive stereotype about the butch identity and relationships; a White British, butch lesbian dyke, aged in her late twenties, she said butch was now being tied to notions of toxic masculinity.

> With 'butch' being tied to toxic notions of masculinity and dominant behaviour, its unsurprising that most younger women are choosing terms perceived as softer, and less confrontational, like transmasc or the suitably vague non-binary to describe themselves. (Lombard)

Butch battling the same old sex wars?

Respondents were all well aware of the history of the lesbian sex wars in LGBTQI+ communities; they felt these tensions had not necessarily gone away. Several times respondents gave personal reflections on experiences and encounters where they had observed or been subjected to assumptions that butches were all sexists who wanted sexist relationships with feminine partners based on some sort of heterosexual role playing. Shelley offered such observations for example; she was aged in her early thirties, a cis gay woman and a lesbian and she listed her ethnicity as Mixed/Dual Heritage.

> The term butch, even in the lesbian community, has been seen to have negative connotations. It is as if butch lesbians were seen to be mimicking men. . . . I have

seen butch identifying women being mocked on MANY occasions on the gay scene over the years, 'I want a woman, not some woman who looks like a bloke. If I wanted a bloke I'd go for one', is a direct quote that I have heard many times on the lesbian scene. Butch/femme are often ridiculed for mimicking heterosexuality too. (Shelley)

One respondent, Lois, had coined a term for their own identity, that of 'female man'. Lois described themselves as MOC and masculine, their sexuality as queer. They were aged in their early fifties and White English. Although Lois stated that they had long felt more male than female, they emphasized that they were not a butch in what they thought was the stereotypical sense, that is a sexually untouchable stone butch. For Lois, this was the main defining feature of stereotypical butch lesbians, and it was a feature that they did not relate to.

> I do know several butches, so they're definitely still around. Personally, I don't get it. I want to be egalitarian in my relationships, and if a woman wants to be a man, why doesn't she just become a man? I know it's not that simple – I've spent my whole life not becoming a man, but I've never wanted to be a butch. When I'm in bed, I want to use what I've got, and have an equal relationship. (Lois)

One of the younger butch respondents, Josh, German British, who was aged eighteen to twenty-five and also identified as MOC, GNC, transmasculine and listed their sexuality as poly and queer, was aware of the anti-egalitarian assumptions about femme-butch relationships, and also directly referenced the history of feminist critiques of these relationships. Josh dismissed these assumptions as unfair and also as factually incorrect, as they believed that femme-butch relationships are complex and do not seek to copy unequal heterosexual roles.

> Some feminists have too simplistically refuted it as adopting problematic masculine codes. Also assume it is part of a binary with femme which dictates a sexual exchange based on prescribed roles and inequalities. This is so not the case. (Josh)

Butch-identified respondents pointed out the inaccuracies in such stereotypes, emphasizing their own experiences of the variety and glorious mutuality of friendships and relationships between butches, femmes and between femmes and butches. The identity of butch, even if it was invoked via stereotypes, was still a well-recognized identity in the wider LGBTQI+ community, and for many, even with all the other identifiers on offer now, it was the one they chose and would still choose.

Butch pride

For many respondents, the butch label was the one that fits most comfortably. Some respondents had charted a journey to get there, including moving between different labels, before arriving at butch as the most accurate. Others had adopted it as soon as they had become aware of it and immediately resonated with the term and the meanings and characteristics it freighted. Bardle, for example, a butch lesbian who did not list their age or ethnicity, expressed that they had just always felt more drawn to men's clothes and styles, for as long as they could remember. Bardle wasn't sure whether or not this could be separated from their awareness of being a lesbian, or which came first.

> I'm not entirely sure, what came first, my hate of dresses or love for women? (Bardle)

Several respondents reported that their sense of butchness, and their preference for more masculine styles was a deeply felt part of their identity and one that they were aware of from a young age or for as long as they could remember. This relates to questions raised in the literature on femme-butch lives, and whether these identities are innate or experienced as if they are innate. Nell identified as masculine of centre, and also used butch sometimes and queer. Nell did not specify age group or ethnicity. Nell said that being masculine felt natural and they could not imagine being any other way.

> Only because I can't imagine being feminine any more than I can imagine being straight. (Nell)

Roddy agreed, they identified as queer, genderqueer and non-binary. They specified they were a gay woman, and listed their ethnicity as White British. Roddy had also felt masculine from a young age, and said this was a deep-rooted feeling.

> To me it is about simply not identifying as particularly feminine, something that from a very young age I have tried to do. I have identified more with masculinity than femininity my whole life, it has just been how I have felt, deep rooted inside. (Roddy)

Annan also reported that their gender identity was a part of themselves that they just had to express. They did not feel this was to do with expressing a lesbian sexual orientation, but about expressing their gender and that they would do that in their own way whether they were gay or straight. They asserted that gender identity is not dependent on sexual orientation. Annan used non-binary, genderqueer and tomboy to describe themselves. They were aged eighteen to twenty-five, White British and identified as a lesbian.

> I think regardless of my sexual identity I would always feel like this in my gender identity and expression. I think many assumptions are made about being a 'lesbian' and the code of how you dress, but I'd dress and express myself like this even if I was heterosexual. (Annan)

Many others emphasized that they too would always choose to be butch, and loved their own styles and presentation that went along with that. Respondents such as Elizabeth, White English, a butch dyke in her early fifties, acknowledged common perceptions of the butch identity as in decline, but for her, this scarcity narrative only made the butch label and community more powerful and important.

> I am who I am. Coming out as a lesbian brought me into a community which celebrates butchness (we are an endangered species after all). (Elizabeth)

Judith also celebrated being butch and expressed how proud it made her feel. She explained that, for her, butch is a visible assault against and defiance of societal expectations. Judith was aged in her late forties, White English, and she described herself as butch, lesbian and also as a powerful woman.

> I love being a butch lesbian – to me it forcefully presents another and alternative view of woman. . . . I can't tell you how much I love striding down the high street looking and feeling powerful, knowing that people have to reassess what they think a woman is. (Judith)

Hilary also saw being a butch as a powerful way of being a woman and being, as she saw it, passionately female. Hilary, a butch lesbian, White Irish, was aged in her late fifties. For her, being butch was brave and strong, it was a stand against patriarchal society and it was the most visible way of being a lesbian. This visibility brought danger but also wisdom and power.

> A butch woman is a very proud and out lesbian. A very very powerful force in the world, we threaten patriarchy massively. . . . I am powerful, strong, no men mess with me. I get things done. I don't play emotional games. I am able to relate to people of all races and social classes, being butch means NOT CONFORMING to male rules. It means being a very visible proud lesbian, we don't pass as straight, so we experience the world in a very real world. It takes a lot of courage to be a butch woman. I feel a solid sense of self respect and dignity, I do not sell out my body or my mind or my intellect to 'conform' to male dictates. (Hilary)

For many respondents, being butch was a source of pride; it brought them strength, and they believed it was a strong and powerful identity. This was for different reasons, as the accounts above make plain. For some it was about a sense of female masculinity, and staking a territory for a distinctly female or lesbian masculinity and sexuality. For others it was about expanding the bandwidth of womanhood, and pursuing different aspects of womanhood that were not masculine but womanly ways of being strong, capable, unashamed of sex and sexuality and refusing social feminine conventions.

Always endangered; never extinct

The narrative of impending extinction and crisis is one that seems to have followed butch identity almost as long as butch identity has been around. First it was under physical attack from a highly conservative, homophobic society as the archetypal bar dykes of the 1950s were harassed in public, arrested in their queer spaces, assaulted and raped by police. Temporary passing was fragile and was probably not a long-term defence for all butches against the hostile attitudes that considered their existence as deviance incarnate. Then the label came under attack again, less physically, but still effectively, with the assault from lesbian feminist theorizing and organizing that sought to rehabilitate femme and butch lesbians and provide a proliferation of lesbian spaces where what they saw as sadomasochistic role playing of heterosexual stereotypes was not present. More recently, new terms for lesbian subcultures and for female and lesbian masculinities have expanded and are added to each day. The post-trans landscape is one dominated by representations of trans femininities and trans women, much more than trans masculinities and trans men. There are almost certainly a lack of masculine female role models, and no positive representations of butch lesbians in the media – yes, even with Ellen DeGeneres as always the exception to the rule in her slightly more boxy suits and trendy trainers. As Jack Halberstam continues to argue in their invaluable scholarship though, rumours of the demise of the butch are overstated. Yet these panics continue, and in so doing they also seem to continue to point to, amplify and highlight the ever-present presence of the butch identity. If anything, perhaps the extinction narrative serves as a reminder of the butch existence, and its stoic determination, making it, arguably, an attractive label, despite the many misunderstandings and stereotypes wedded to it, as I have outlined earlier: 'Despite flannel shirt shortages, shifting fashion trends towards androgynous looks, the trendiness of transgenderism, a severe height disadvantage in relation to many femmes, and new levels of emotional sensitivity in queer communities, the butch has survived and lives to wear another ring of keys' (Halberstam, 2015).

The voices I have platformed here bring to light and give a weight of personal experience to long-standing and never-ending debates about butch flight and whether or not it is real. Many felt that their own butch identity had become seen as out of time, out of date, dinosaur-like and therefore old skool and uncool. The burgeoning of newer terms, less directly associated with lesbianism and femaleness, was viewed as just cooler, more attractive to younger generations who eschew fixed labels and narrow boxes. For some, this was part of a trans trend and an external pressure that may close down the possibility of the butch identity, before an individual has even had a chance to try it. Scholars such as the award-winning American journalist and femme theorist Victoria Brownworth raised the alarm in 2011, writing in *Persistence*.

> How many people will tell the budding butch that she really is transgender, born a man in a woman's body? But what if she's really just butch, that is, content with the confluence of her female body and masculine persona? Will her confusion lead her to hormone treatments and surgeries she will later regret when she realises what her true identity is? (Brownworth, 2011: 148)

Mirroring similar discussions in the scholarship I introduced in Chapter 6, respondents did indeed worry that some of the turn away from butch identity could be linked to plain old-fashioned homophobia and lesbophobia, not only from outside LGBTQI+ communities but from within too, and indeed from within our own psyches, even if this may be unconscious. Femme scholar Nairne Holtz raises this challenging point. She suggests that due to internalized misogyny and homophobia, butches who may indeed be butch and tick all the boxes in any spotter's guide for butches will be ever more increasingly reluctant to actually take the label on for themselves due to their awareness of the stereotypes that surround the term: 'When a masculine woman claims she's not butch, what she may be saying is: I'm not that stereotype; I'm not fat, I'm not ugly; I don't have a blue collar job; I don't hate men. I could point out that these attributes are nothing to be ashamed of' (Holtz, 2011: 116). In this extract, Holtz also references the classism attached to the butch label.

Brownworth (2011) also cautioned that quickness to jettison the butch identity could be fuelled by the homophobic and misogynist stereotypes that have been linked to that term by straight society. She poses an important question when she queries whether a flight towards LGBTQI+ assimilation within a grossly neoliberal backdrop requires ejecting the archetypal mannish lesbian: 'Is it our community now that disallows the male-centric butch because she fits a stereotype that assimilationists want straight society to either forget or ignore?' (Brownworth, 2011: 116). These referenced stereotypes are almost universal symbols of lesbian identity. They are used as slurs to police the sexuality of women, of course, by branding lesbianism as unattractive, mannish, undesirable, just a hollow copy of heterosexuality and harbinger of spinster loneliness. What's behind all such well-worn representations of lesbianism is of course the fact that lesbians reject men sexually. This is an un-saleable fact to straight, patriarchal society and will always be contentious. Part of the propaganda against any category of lesbianism is to define lesbianism as unattractive and lonely, meaning unattractive to men, unfeminine to men and thus in impending danger of not being in a relationship with a man. The latter is promoted as the most undesirable state. Such slurs are used then to reinforce that any distancing from men, sexually or otherwise, is an undesirable and monstrous state, inhabited by monsters. Thus, the fragile institution of heterosexuality is maintained.

Although prejudice towards the butch identity was acknowledged by my participants, the butch identity was considered readily identifiable. When summing it up, respondents, unsurprisingly, as all the available literature does too, linked the butch identity to some form and display of recognizable masculinity. Respondents referenced style and presentation, outward cultural codes that portrayed fashion and haircuts more commonly in usage for men. However, survey respondents like Jazza were completely aware of the irony of putting forward many critiques of normative heterosexual masculinities and men, while using quite stereotypical references to men and masculinity in order to describe how butches presented. Echoing common debates in the literature about the utility of this referent 'masculinity', respondents voiced concerns about whether another category is needed altogether, one separated from maleness, men and masculinity, which can more respectfully convey lesbian gender codes, female masculinity or butch expression.

Writing about tough bar dykes in 1950s America, historians Kennedy and Davis (1993) asserted throughout their pioneering text that being a butch was not about wanting to be male, no matter how masculine those women were. 'At the same time, they were not men, they were "queer". Throughout their life stories they counterpose acquiring masculine characteristics with not being male' (1992: 183). Respondents to my survey, such as Cleo and Leslie, certainly did not want to be associated with normative masculinity or with men or maleness. Several respondents identified with the label of 'dyke', an empowering reclaimed lesbian term, and referred to themselves as butch dykes. These women were unlikely to see their butchness as anything to do with men or masculinity; they saw it as butch expression. In this sense butch is indeed a noun (Bergman, 2006), and it was a useful descriptor that was immediately understandable and recognizable to those in lesbian communities. In a way, this label therefore conveniently stood in place of having to use other undesirable descriptors like masculine. As Kristen Esterberg observed in an article on lesbian identity, 'to present oneself as "butch" or "dykey" was an attempt to assert a distinctly lesbian presence that did not rely entirely on the language of "masculinity" and "femininity". Although the specific gestures draw more from traditional notions of masculinity, they are not identical' (Esterberg, 1996: 276).

In this citation Esterberg uses a reference to 'traditional' notions of masculinity. I have mentioned that respondents to my survey were aware of the raced and classed history of the origin story of butch. They were also aware that femme-butch identities and relationships were seen as traditional in a conservative and backwards sense. Sometimes, therefore, it was felt that newer terms like MOC, transmasc, GNC or transgender would be perceived as offering a more open, progressive and breathable space, free from some of those raced and classed assumptions and hangovers. Many of the newer terms are also not automatically associated with masculinity, or stereotypes of hegemonic masculinity, dominant White heterosexual masculinities or the behaviours of dominant men, which most respondents took care to point out they did not want to copy nor be assumed to be copying. This was behind the work of activist B Cole, of course, and the inspirational Brown Boi Project. Cole coined the term MOC to offer an alternative without historical baggage, and one that wasn't so tied in historical and contemporary representations to White masculinities only. 'Masculine of Centre recognises the cultural breadth and depth of identity for lesbian/ queer womyn who tilt toward the masculine side of the gender scale, and the term includes a wide range of identities such as butch, stud, aggressive/AG, tom, macha, boi, dom etc' (Cole, 2011: 128).

Terms like 'MOC', 'GNC', 'trans', 'NB' and 'transmasculine' are also not specifically attached to a sex; they are sex neutral terms. Newer terms are also sexuality neutral, and those taking them on may well be queer, may well be unboxed into any sexual orientation and could be in relationships with men, women or other NB or GNC identifying individuals. Whether respondents argued and saw this latter point positively or negatively, they all agreed, for better or worse, that butch is indeed wedded to lesbianism, to womanhood and to femaleness in a way that these newer terms are not. For respondents who found those elements problematic or uncomfortable, the sex and sexuality neutral feature of the newer terms made them more appealing and appropriate. On the other hand, the sexed and sexuality specific nature of the butch label was reclaimed by those who felt that being butch was just a part of their womanhood and their lesbianism. The history of butch in lesbian women's communities was a plus for many respondents and a heritage they did not want to see disappear. This was another reason behind a concern, from some quarters, at the ascendancy of newer terms and a fear that butch may decline in usage.

Although many respondents were positive then about the lesbian history of the butch label, this was noted as not always an easy relationship. Respondents, of all ages, were aware of the history of theoretical and real-life battles over what lesbian sexuality could and should be, in lesbian, feminist and lesbian feminist contexts. Butch was considered old fashioned not just because of its old origin stories, but because it was conceived as being sexist, retrograde and not egalitarian in its relationships. The fact that such conversations are still being had, and that people feel they still have to justify butch identity and femme-butch relationships against such stereotypes, shows just how much resonance these stereotypes still have in popular currency; and actually shows the mainstreaming and success, in a strange way, of lesbian feminist theorizing. A strand of feminism that was always niche and controversial has arguably punched way above its weight in this area; the question is who was getting hurt; and too often that was butch-identified women, femme-identified women, masculine-presenting women and feminine-presenting women. All of them minorities within minorities, too queer for straight society but too feminine or too masculine for some feminist spaces.

As I have discussed elsewhere in this book and in other publications (2015), this feminist fracture was just one of many in the Second Wave WLM of the 1970s and 1980s (Jeffreys, 2018; Rees, 2010). 'These tensions burst out in the "sex wars" of the early 1980s when one of the targets of the women's movement's antipornography forces became other feminists, the new "freaks" – primarily S/M and femme/butch lesbians, passing women, sex workers and, at times, sexually hungry straight women' (Nestle, 2002: 6). As I investigated in Chapter 4 dealing with cultural feminism, these fractures were constructed between, on the one side, lesbian feminists and also Radical Feminists who believed that lesbianism was wholly or mainly a political project of loving women and building women's community. On the other side, these standpoints were compared to those who saw lesbianism as a sexuality and a type of sexual practice and sexual relationship, no purer or more sacred or superior by default than any other type of sex or sexual relationship. Lesbian feminists such as Professor Sheila Jeffreys consider femme-butch identity and relationships to be simply the practice of another version of sadomasochism. 'Role playing, it became clear, offered the sexual satisfactions of a mild form of sadomasochism' (Jeffreys, 2014a: 43). For Professor Jeffreys femme-butch relationships are sadomasochistic because they are copying and eroticizing heterosexual dominance and submission. 'Butch/femme role playing recreates the roles of the heteropatriarchy' (Jeffreys, 2014a: 107). Respondents discussed how offensive such assumptions were and how they did not mirror reality – 'this is so not the case', said eighteen- to twenty-five-year-old Josh, quoted earlier.

For the butches who responded on this point, their relationships had an erotic life, like all sexual relationships, but this was not narrowly scripted as butch untouchability and femme submission, nor was it considered as default sadomasochistic. Respondents drew a picture of their lives and relationships which were forged precisely against social expectations for sex and gender norms, and which were not only critical of normative models of masculinity but actively working against them. Many respondents pointed out that although they may identify as masculine, they did not identify as a man, and did not much like what they saw in most men, or in most examples of manhood and masculinity. Tasks were arranged by preference, presence and skillset, and femme lesbians are not the gay branch of modern 'trad wives', for example. Theorists like Jeffreys are very concerned to present negative sexist role differentiation as a standard feature of femme-butch relationships. 'The femininity adopted by femmes involved an inequality – doing most of the housework – and an acquired powerlessness that would probably have no appeal for heterosexual women in the present' (2003: 127). This is a massive generalization, and was not a feature that my respondents noted as a prerequisite for their relationships. In my own domestic life, I have always been the cleaner, for example; I am the one vacuuming and washing the dishes. Like many contemporary couples, roles in my house are divided by skillset, preference and who has the time and opportunity to get on with the jobs that need doing.

For my respondents, their butch identity was far from heteropatriarchal, as some lesbian feminist theory would have us believe. Time and again butch respondents noted that they were also feminists, that being butch was a way, for them, to be a strong and powerful woman, that it was one part of their womanhood. They enjoyed subverting societal restrictions for women and the rules about femininity, like Judith, striding down the street taking up space and forcing onlookers to have to reassess what being a woman is capable of being. Or Hilary, proud of her femaleness, her lesbianism, her butch no-messing attitude. As Carol A Queen notes in her chapter on why she loves butch women, in the *Dagger* anthology, 'Butch is a giant fuck you to compulsory femininity' (Queen, 1994: 15). These were the butches for whom the association of butch with lesbian history, women's spaces and with feminism – albeit often troubled – was a relationship that, for their part at least, they embraced, and indeed it was partly why butch appealed to them. It is sad that in so many cases feminism has not embraced them in return.

Consider the widespread assumptions, stereotyping and rejections that butch women have faced, not only from straight society but from some elements of feminism and from other lesbians and LGBTQI+ people too; like the experiences I have shed light on in this chapter. For this branch of butch women, and butch dykes, the ascendancy of new terms like MOC, transmasculine and NB was problematic where it may erase those feminist and political histories, tense though they may be. They did not want an alternative butch identity that was separated from female signifiers or from the label of woman. The ongoing debates over butch flight raise questions as to whether these types of proud butch lesbian women, platformed in this chapter, are indeed going to reduce in number, as new identifiers are arguably in more common currency. Certainly, this was the perspective of many that took the time to share their views. However, as I showed with respondents such as Isambard and Bobby, butch flight can go the other way too. Perhaps this does not get enough attention, but Bobby and Isambard described how they had first found labels for their gender identity in queer discourses, labels such as MOC and transgender, and these proved to be popular and fit for many of their peers. As they continued to explore, however, they found the butch identity and felt that this was flexible and expansive enough for them to feel a sense of belonging there, and there they stayed. Yet, there are no community-wide narratives of queer flight to butch identities, not yet anyway – maybe this will change.

The responses to my survey suggest that butch flight is still a sensitive and delicate discussion, however, and one that has not gone away. If anything, many people perceive that in the contemporary context, there are just more departure destinations for butch flight to migrate off to. However, if the ones doing the migrating are the individuals who never felt that the butch label fitted them properly anyway, then perhaps this isn't actually a case of butch flight, as Stu, Della and Reggie highlighted. There are some butches who have probably always been transmasculine, or trans men, or GNC, but they just never had the language and the community to bring that to fruition. If one took this perspective, butch flight would not be butch flight. It would be trans man flight, GNC flight, NB flight, transmasculine flight. It would be viewed as setting off the ejector seat from a position in which they were never comfortable. As Hilary said, quoted earlier, butches are not trans, they never were, they never will be, they are proud and strong lesbian women who are unafraid to be proud and strong lesbian women. If this is so, one could ask, what's the problem? Why the ongoing decades-long concern over butch flight if all that's going on is a separation of the butches from the bois/boys/men. Of course, nothing is this simple.

These concerns are widespread, and they are not just being debated in the lesbian community, but in mainstream society in the context of the gender wars, as I have discussed throughout this book. Those seeking to speak for us may not always be from our communities, and for this and many other reasons it is vitally important, I would argue, that there should be no flight from our responsibilities to have these sensitive and painful discussions in our own communities, on and with our own terms, and together with each other. If we do not, there are plenty who will speak for us, and they have no idea about our lives, and no care for our needs or rights.

The gender wars are raging over the heads of individuals who are trying to find an identity that fits, and the public dissection, grading and approval rating of these identities is understandably exposing and often hurtful to those who have made certain identities home. Trans individuals resent the suggestion that they are not really trans and are fearful that support and medical interventions will be reduced even more than they already are, in case they encourage what others see as more reluctant transitions. In turn, butch individuals feel they are already experiencing the assumption that their identity is invalid and just a stopping point on the way to being a trans man – like Stu recounted earlier.

My motivation for writing this book is to keep highlighting that boundaries are not clean and clear, identities not only shift and change, but they also overlap and may inhabit several labels all at once. There are people who make their homes in these borderlands, as cultural theorist, poet and feminist scholar, the late Gloria Anzaldua, brought forth in her classic on racialized, sexed and gendered borders *Borderlands: The New Mestiza* (1987): 'A borderland is a vague and undetermined place created by the emotional residue of an unnatural boundary. It is in a constant state of transition. The prohibited and forbidden are its inhabitants' (Anzaldua, 1987: 3). In Chapter 8 I shall map some of these terrains for the borderers, the borderland dwellers who made a home between butch and trans, between lesbian and queer, and even between man and woman.

8

Queering 'female' masculinity

When I was beginning to plan my survey research, I struggled to find appropriate terms to use in the requests I was going to be distributing publicly calling for participants. I wanted to find out more about the identity of butch lesbian today, and how people expressed or understood masculinities in lesbian or queer communities. In the past, this is perhaps what would have been called 'female masculinity' (Halberstam, 1998a). However, using this term in the post-trans landscape today is not so seamless, nor so taken for granted, and it raises multiple questions. I did not want to exclude participants from taking part in my research, and I was aware that for some people the word 'female' in the term 'female masculinity' might be alienating. As would, potentially, the word 'lesbian', in the term 'lesbian masculinity', when, or if, 'lesbian' is seen as a term that emphasizes femaleness and womanhood, or the lesbian feminist definitions of lesbians as women-identified women, for example (Radicalesbians, 1970). Having been in lesbian, queer and femme-butch communities for decades, I know that many of us masculine-identified individuals in these spaces often use male pronouns for each other, and masculine friendship terms such as 'bro', 'brother' or 'dude'. For some people, the terms 'female' and 'lesbian' just do not fit, and I did not want to exclude these individuals from taking part in my research.

Despite the complexity, I partly wanted to explore this topic precisely because I believe it is important to keep shedding light on communities like these, and on these places and ways of belonging, which feel like second nature to me, but are unknown to most of those outside them. The existence and endurance of such communities trouble assumptions of clear lines and sides in the so-called border wars between trans and butch. In the current context of the gender wars, it seems that such ways of being are maybe even more unknowable today than they were in the past; but I am determined they should not be unspeakable. The glorious and realistic grey areas of life are too often being denied and disavowed as impossible, in an environment where everyone is called to pick sides, and where a non-normative gender identification or presentation is expected to be trans, or nothing. But, boundaries around sex, gender and sexuality identity have always been crossed and crossable; there are, and have always been, female-bodied masculine individuals who did not identify as trans men but who did not identify as or with womanhood or lesbianism either. There were, and still are, individuals who may identify as men or as male, and live their life in communities that affirm and recognize that, without any changes to the physicality of their sexed as female body. For some people, 'female' is a form-filling necessity, but doesn't go further than that; and 'woman' can feel inclusive as a political term, but highly exclusive and even alienating in other ways.

These concerns have been explored by a handful of academic researchers in the field of gender and sexualities research, such as the psychologists Levitt, Heistand and Horne who produce valuable and rare research into lesbian gender identity in femme-butch communities in the United States. However, it does often seem that lesbian communities are still treated as niche in academic research, and minority communities within them as even more niche. Research into lesbian gender and female masculinity has been taken up by those scholars who have questioned the expansion of terms like 'trans' and 'transgender' or 'queer'. Some have questioned these labels when those labels are taken as liberating terms that deconstruct and take apart binary sex/gender categories The assumption being that this deconstruction and un-coupling is always the intention or goal of subjects who may be assumed to be contained under those labels. Academics, especially trans men and trans women working in this field, rightly pointed out that for some people, there is no desire to 'queer' their sex and gender identity at all, and nor should there be pressure to do so. Some trans men, for example, identify as men, male and masculine.

Writers and academics like Jay Prosser (1995) and Jamison Green (2005), for example, highlighted that for some trans men the trans journey, homecoming or process can be one of coming to a conclusion where the sexed body affirms the sex and gender identity in a typical binary sense. As Green points out, some trans men do not wish to present as queer, fluid or in flux, but they wish to be seen as the men they are, full stop.

> Social validation of gender identity is important for people who may have been gender blending at some time in their lives but who found that landing firmly on one side of the fence rather than the other (in this case, the masculine side), at least in most social contexts, is important and meaningful for some people and that the task of doing so is neither trivial nor disordered nor unnatural, and it is a mistake of society not to recognise this. (Green, 2005: 292)

From perspectives and positions such as these, there may be little sign of overlap between trans and butch identities, in answer to Halberstam's question in 1998, for example, 'What is the relation, if any, of butch to FTM? How and where do lesbian and transexual definitions overlap?' (1998b: 288). This is still a live question though, perhaps increasingly so in the current context, and for many of the respondents in my research, it did not have a simple or straightforward answer.

Border wars

The so-called border wars between trans men and butch lesbians were much studied in the queer scholarship of the 1990s. As academic Bobby Noble asserts, this skirmish and the reconnaissance of it became, in fact, a well-worn platitude. 'That there are triangulated border wards between women's studies, lesbian butches and female to male transexual men (FTMs) is by now almost cliché' (Noble, 2004: 22). As the warlike language suggests, representations of this border were always focussed on disagreement and dispute over assumed natural territories that were supposedly the possession of one group over another. In reality there was never really a border, more a line that people drew for themselves and around themselves in different places every time, depending on the interaction, situation and other people around them. While lesbian, trans and queer communities overlapped, aired and worked out, or agreed to disagree on differences, including conflicts, around labels and identities ad-infinitum (believe me, I was there) in shared spaces and events, the public, and often the academic representation remained one of clear lines and warring sides. As scholars Beemyn and Eliason describe, 'The discourses around cis lesbian and trans identities and communities have been represented almost exclusively in negative terms – framed as border crossings, trespassing, battlegrounds, and conquests' (Beemyn & Eliason, 2016: 2).

Now, however, in the post-trans landscape, this border, as with other borders, is perhaps likely to be viewed and described publicly by activists, commentators and members of these communities themselves, as being far more fluid and porous. Or, even the very idea of a border may be seen as redundant, offensive and out of date. As Weiss asserted in 2007, 'the "Butch/FTM Borderlands", as a "real" line as written about by Hale and Halberstam in 1998, is now perceived as increasingly unstable and unreal by many in the younger generation' (Weiss, 2007: 209). Writing in *The New York Times T Magazine* in April 2020, photographer and editor Kerry Manders interviewed a veritable keyring of famous butches and studs from the arts, film, sports, literature and fashion. Manders noted that butches can be bois, that some butches might not be women and that, as ever thus, a million raindrops of shifting butch identities make up a whole rainbow of queer: 'Today, the interconnected spectrums of gender and queerness are as vibrant and diverse in language as they are in expression – genderqueer, transmasc, nonbinary, gender-nonconforming' (2020).

The limited literature concerning female masculinities and lesbian genders of the 2000s continues to expound on the topic of borders, however, and sometimes reflects a new concern over additional departures for butch flight – with the new added destinations being NB or enby, GNC, MOC, TG or genderfluid, for example. Addressing concerns around what some people see as increasing migration levels of butch flight in lesbian communities, Beemyn and Eliason acknowledge these tensions and fears that individuals hold, though they question the reasoning behind them. 'Their sense of invisibility needs to be acknowledged, as does their fear that they are disappearing in a world where some butch lesbians are transitioning to male identities and where many younger women are identifying as queer, pansexual, sexually fluid, or another non-binary sexual identity, rather than as lesbian' (Beemyn & Eliason, 2016: 6).

For some then, as this quote indicates, this contemporary shift is just further proof of what they see as ongoing lesbian erasure, and as the destabilization of a fragile and declining lesbian community. As the award-winning American journalist and human rights activist Victoria Brownworth argues, the decline of lesbian culture and the decline of lesbian as a unifying label are far from unrelated. That is to say, the more people who refuse, malign or just do not make a home in a lesbian identity or a lesbian gender identity like femme or butch, the smaller the lesbian community becomes. Thus, there are even fewer examples of habitable lesbian lives and gender identities that younger people could choose from in that environment: 'The marginalising of the butch women and femme men who once comprised a significant and vital demographic of queer society has forced many lesbians and gay men toward an alternative identification as transgender, even when they may not be. Many young butch lesbians, for example, say they feel pressured to claim a transgender identity' (Brownworth, 2011: 143).

Other scholars underline, however, as I stated at the start of this chapter, that it was ever thus. Many would argue that things have always been more complex, and therefore it is not new to attempt to inhabit both or many of these sorts of identities at once, with Halberstam writing in 1998 about the category of 'transgender butch', for example. In April 2020 the Olympian and menswear model Casey Legler identified themselves in *T Magazine* for *The New York Times* as a trans-butch-identified person, using they/them pronouns (Manders, 2020). The particular theorizing on the transgender elements of butch that appear in Halberstam's work reflected real lives and real communities that were already established at that time. This is worth emphasizing again; in the 1990s these debates about the fluidity of sex and gender, and the identification of male and masculine butch categories, were commonplace. For years, life experiences were discussed and compared and tossed back and forth across such borders, much like individuals themselves in many cases, often illustrating points of intersection. As Gayle Rubin noted back in 1992 in Nestle's classic collection *The Persistent Desire*,

> Although important discontinuities separate lesbian butch experience and female-to-male transexual experience, there are also significant points of connection. Some butches are psychologically indistinguishable from female-to-male transexuals, except for the identities they choose and the extent to which they are willing or able to alter their bodies. Many FTMs live as butches before adopting transexual or male identities. Some individuals explore each identity before choosing one that is more meaningful for them, and others use both categories to interpret and organise their experience. The boundaries between the categories of butch and transexual are permeable. (Rubin, 1992: 473)

In her research with masculine lesbians and trans men in the UK in 2001, Lee found more similarities than differences in the life histories and experiences of each group, also noting that several of the trans men had previously found a home in lesbian communities (Lee, 2001). In their research in the early 2000s with femme and butch communities in America, the psychologists Levitt and Heistand found butches in those communities who reported a masculine or transgender identification, as well as butch lesbians who had considered sex reassignment or gender affirming surgery at different points in their lives: 'Several respondents reported sometimes identifying as masculine, as "third sex", as transgendered, or as identifying more with men than women' (Levitt & Heistand, 2004: 610).

This disidentification with women, and identification with men, doesn't have to lead to an identification as a man, or as male, as the research by Levitt and Heistand pointed out. It can lead to a sense of belonging that has to wrestle with, and exist between, two categories – of being masculine but not male, of being female but not feminine, or perhaps, not identifying as a woman either, as butch academic Crawley acknowledges in her work on butch lives and labels: 'I recognise that not all butches (i.e particularly stone butches and trans men) define themselves as "women", opting instead to recognize their bodies as female but not their gender as "women"' (Crawley, 2001: 194). This is a common separation that is frequently made between the sexed characteristics of the body and gender identity. As I explored earlier in Chapter 7 on butch voices, for many self-identified butch lesbians there is no such incongruence. The female body and, in many cases, the identity of woman also is fundamental to their identification as a butch lesbian. Taking on the troublesome task of defining the undefinable, Gayle Rubin's influential submission to Nestle's classic at one point acknowledges this much repeated and presumed common-sense fact: 'Most butches enjoy combining expressions of masculinity with a female body. The coexistence of masculine traits with a female anatomy is a fundamental characteristic of "butch" and is a highly charged, eroticised and consequential lesbian signal' (Rubin, 1992: 468).

More recently, writing together in 2019 about their lesbian habitus, scholars Rachel E Silverman and Kristin Comeforo offer a new term, 'maskulinity', to describe the masculinity of butches. This, they argue, is an inherently subversive masculinity because it is mediated through and on a female body: 'Similarly, butch women, such as Kristin, while often mistaken for men, do not in fact want to be men. Theirs is a decidedly "female masculinity" that is inherent to being female bodied and it is this female body that not only attracts femmes, but also makes the masculinity performed by the butch transgressive' (2019: 2). They go on to note that 'we are both women who desire women and, as butch and femme lesbians, we manifest versions of gender against and within heteronormativity. We are both invisible, and yet our invisibility manifests in opposite ways – Rachel's as an unseen lesbian and Kristen's as an unseen woman' (Silverman & Comeforo, 2019: 2).

As is the problem with all definitions, it could be argued that this definition of butchness and butch masc(k)ulinity narrows down the possibilities within that identity and also reduces the number of individuals who may be included within its ranks. Certainly, it does not include those individuals who, as work by Halberstam and Crawley have highlighted, do not enjoy, celebrate or even experience such levels of congruence between their femaleness, womanhood and butch lesbian identity. Writer and activist Jan Brown, for example, in a collection from the 1990s, poetically and personally expresses the falsehood of assuming clear boundaries: 'Butch was not synonymous with male, we promised. Butches might look very masculine, but in reality we were butch women. There was, in fact, nothing male about us. Guess what? Right again. We lied. There is little "woman" left in us. . . . Still, we do not think of ourselves as women. Or, in fact, as lesbians' (Brown, 1992: 414). For many such individuals, even if they place themselves broadly within the identifier of 'butch', definitions such as the one above from the academics Silverman and Comeforo would be distasteful and impossible to inhabit or apply. For some butches their masculinity is not a parody or subversive political act; it just is. It is not defined by or made exciting by the fact of it inhabiting or blending with womanhood, femininity or femaleness, because they do not think of or present themselves as women, female or feminine.

Is woman home?

One question I asked the participants taking part in my research was whether they identified with the term 'woman'. The majority of respondents answered yes, but for seventy-five respondents it was not so simple, with some saying they used to, or that it was complicated, or that they did, but only on certain occasions. For many of my respondents, these were complex contours that shaped their identities and were sometimes rugged and challenging landscapes in which individuals attempted to form liveable and survivable homes.

Many participants made a distinction between identification with the category of 'woman' and with the category of 'female'. This distinction was one of the social or societal, compared to the bodily and biological experience. Sometimes, my participants explained that they did identify as female, or acknowledged their sexed as female bodies, but they did not feel that they fitted in, or fitted in comfortably, to the category of 'woman'. Cruise, for example, was aged between sixty-five and seventy years old, and they were White and identified as a non-sexual lesbian. Cruise mentioned that having a female body, and being a feminist, felt linked to being a woman, but they did not feel able to be a woman in the way they thought women are meant to be women.

> Apart from being a feminist (that took some doing), and having a female body, I don't feel just that one way. I don't present as female. . . . I'm a cis female, but never felt traditional. I tried for many years. I felt so conflicted so took to drugs and alcohol. (Cruise)

Ruith meanwhile was aged in their late thirties, and they identified as White and as Welsh. Ruith identified their sexuality as lesbian and gay and queer; they stated their gender as GNC and genderqueer. Ruith sometimes identified as a woman, but stated that it just never felt 100 per cent right for them. Being in queer communities allayed this sense of difference, because, as Ruith pointed out, queer communities are already apart and different to the mainstream, so this felt like a way to gain a feeling of fitting in for once.

> I was AFAB, so spent the first part of my life automatically identifying as a woman. It's never felt 100% right though, and I've always felt somewhat different to other women. For a time this was appeased by identifying as a lesbian, as queer women are often set apart from cis/straight women. (Ruith)

In this quote Ruith uses the term AFAB to describe being sexed as female at birth; this acronym stands for 'assigned female at birth'. Another respondent, Lucy, had actually adopted a similar strategy to Ruith, and also wrote about how being part of queer communities was a way to fit in and deal with a feeling of difference from women as a group. Lucy was aged forty-five to fifty years old, White European, and they identified as queer and as butch. Lucy replied that she used to identify as a woman, but did not now.

> I like being different most of the time. I feel like an outsider in most situations – over time, this has led me to feel most comfortable in the company of 'queers' (by which

I mean anyone who is non-conformist in some way, not based on sexual orientation but more a 'world view' which celebrates difference/oddity/weirdness). (Lucy)

Respondents who felt they were 'too big' or 'too tall' or too muscly or sporty also mentioned that this led to a feeling of being different and being at odds with what society told them women were meant to be like. Pier raised this issue; Pier identified as queer, but did not provide their age or ethnic identity. Pier replied that they identified as a woman sometimes:

I feel a bit rejected from the idea of being a cis woman. Being taller, bigger, it made it hard to feel my younger self's perceived idea of 'woman' being femme. Although I don't think that femme equates to women now. I do now feel strange about the idea of referring to myself as one. (Pier)

Even when respondents did not report feeling physically out of place, in terms of height or musculature, being different to most feminine women around them led to a feeling of difference from the category of woman overall. This was discussed by Minnie; they identified as White Jewish, were aged in their early forties and identified as butch, GNC, MOC and as queer and lesbian. Minnie had been pregnant and had a child and mentioned this experience as proof of having a female body, but this bodily feature was considered a different thing to being a woman. Answering the question of whether they identify as a woman, or not, Minnie responded:

Not really . . . I have a female body. I birthed a child. I am a feminist and I do appreciate women's spaces but can't help but feel deeply alienated from the category 'woman' itself. (Minnie)

This discomfort with the category 'woman' was raised by several respondents, and it was due to a variety of reasons. These reasons included a lack of identification with femininity and what femininity culturally is supposed to look like or be like. Reasons for discomfort included a lack of interest in clothes and styles considered feminine or appropriate womenswear; this was raised by many, many respondents and not only those who had difficulty identifying with terms like 'woman' and 'lesbian' but all those who identified as or with masculinity and queer masculinities. Steffan, for example, was aged in their early fifties, White English; they identified as an andro lesbian. Steffan did not identify as a woman, and they felt that they did not fit into what society expects a woman to look like, and they did not feel comfortable in clothes designated for women either.

Have many 'male' traits and behaviours as far as society is concerned. . . . If I ever wear 'women's clothing' I feel like a total fraud and could cry at how bad it makes me feel. (Steffan)

Storm described that they used to identify as a woman, but not anymore. Storm was aged forty-five to fifty years old, White British and identified as a non-binary, genderqueer trans person.

> I think that woman has become synonymous with feminine, as a person who never displayed feminine traits I always felt shoehorned into the label of woman. (Storm)

Another respondent who I have named Sol recounted their career experience of working professionally in women's organizations and how they constantly felt aware of their difference to other women, their colleagues, because of their more masculine style and appearance, compared to their colleagues' more feminine appearance and style. Sol did feel a similarity in terms of shared resistance to sexism, and being treated as a woman by society, but nothing much more than that. This political awareness also led Sol to be alert to any different or better treatment due to their more masculine appearance and mannerisms, and they were actively trying to avoid negative repercussions from this. Sol was in their late thirties and identified their ethnic identity as White and Asian. They identified as NB, butch, transmasculine, queer and genderqueer.

> I couldn't help but notice how my facial hair/clothes/body language would often have me feel at odds with the space that I was inhabiting. . . . For the last 15 years or so years I have felt able to remain active in anarcha-feminist spaces, but not in what I would call more 'straight' feminist spaces, I was aware that my lived experiences are so different from women around me, I do not identify as a woman (though definitely not as a man either), and I was acutely aware my embodied masculinity meant that there was a risk of me being more dominant or heard in those spaces. (Sol)

Obviously, it should not need stating but in the current climate it perhaps needs stating more than ever, that in a structural sense, femininity is not a choice for any women – just as masculinity is not a choice for men. In the vast majority of cases, it is forced upon, taught to and expected from girls from birth, if not before.

Being visibly different to the majority of women can lead to a sense of alienation and exclusion generally for butch or queer women, but particularly in those places presumed to be universally comfortable and welcoming for all women. Respondents frequently wrote about feeling excluded and out of place in these women's spaces. This was the case with Lois, aged fifty to fifty-five years old, White English; they identified as MOC. On everyday women-only spaces, such as changing rooms, Lois stated:

> Nowadays, when I'm in the female changing rooms, I look around and think: 'I shouldn't be here. I am not the same gender as these people'. But I can't use the male changing rooms. Most of my friends are women and on the whole I like women better than men because they're socialised to be in touch with their feelings, but I feel less and less like a woman myself. (Lois)

Bobby, a younger, White English butch lesbian aged eighteen to twenty-five years old, wrote about how difficult it was to be a butch lesbian in women's spaces. It felt to Bobby as if it was assumed that everyone in such spaces was comfortable with being a woman, and comfortable with their body – or, rather, as comfortable as any woman in this culture can possibly be with her body. Bobby mentioned how being visibly different from most women around them made them anxious that they wouldn't be welcomed or that they would never feel that they fitted in, within women's spaces. Although, this feeling did not last and once finding a home in the identity of butch, Bobby expressed how their sense of themselves became more secure and they were able to eventually feel at home in women's spaces.

> I found it hard to identify as a woman for a while, as I felt excluded from women's spaces for being butch, and also the awkwardness I felt around my butch body. (Bobby)

Another reason for a sense of exclusion was not only in appearance but also in beliefs about the possibility or impossibility of shared interests and concerns. This was often raised when respondents discussed being around non-queer women, or groups of women that were presumed to be heterosexual. Leslie mentioned this, Leslie was a butch lesbian, White English and in their late forties.

> Yes I was assigned female at birth, but no I don't feel a link to other cis women a lot of the time, particularly if they are heterosexual. (Leslie)

Another example was from Ivor, who was aged thirty to thirty-five years old and stated their ethnic identity as White and Canadian. Ivor wrote about feeling different from most women, and apart from what they assumed women's lives were concerned with in a general sense.

> I think it's because I feel outside of most female conversations and concerns. (Ivor)

There were several times while doing this research that I did encounter what I felt were quite stereotyped assumptions about non-masculine women's lives. This was not new to me, but I did experience uncertainty in how to document it; now that I was in charge of telling these stories second hand. I felt a sense of responsibility not to exacerbate well-worn stereotypes, which do exist in LGBTQI+ communities as well as outside. On the other hand, no community is an island, nor immune from the culture that surrounds it, and of which it is a part. It is true that some butches and transmasculine queers do indeed sometimes express sexist attitudes towards feminine women; I have heard this myself.

Such behaviours even featured in the 2005 book by journalist Ariel Levy, *Female Chauvinist Pigs*, in her chapter on boi culture and sexism towards femmes. It was interesting at that time in the early 2000s to be suddenly having conversations with people from outside queer culture about how true a reflection this book was and whether I had witnessed such behaviours. The book was widely read in mainstream feminist circles and reviewed in broadsheets and comment pieces. These discussion points were often raised with a quizzical and suspicious attitude from the questioner. This sort of critical attention and scrutiny is always the case when any marginalized community has a window opened into it from the mainstream culture and everyone looks in aghast, ready to critique from the outside.

Ivor went on to explain what they thought differentiated women's concerns from theirs, emphasizing their personal higher sex drive, lack of willingness to talk about emotions and a preference for physical and practical manual tasks.

> I have the empathy of growing up female, but a different mentality in my adult masculinity. Sure, as my ex says, I have man:fridge brain (still trying to figure out what it is), fits (get grumpy and go silent and just go fix stuff), and sex drive. But if you're crying, I'm comfortable reaching out, I'm comfortable and natural with babies, and I don't have a culture of machismo chasing me. (Ivor)

These could be seen as stereotypes of masculinity and masculine behaviour. Ironically, it is these sorts of expressions of masculinity which many non-trans men are starting to take apart, in the new wave of masculinity studies that is ongoing. For example, in books by British authors like the artist Grayson Perry (2016), and the comedian Robert Webb (2017) or in treatments in popular culture like the 2018 Gillette 'the best of men' advert or in *GQ*'s 'New Masculinity Issue' in October 2019. Despite my occasional discomfort, however, the responses I gathered from the data were real views and experiences expressed to me by individuals who took valuable time out of their lives to share them with me and I have to honour that. I also recognize some possible purposes behind such expressions of what could be seen as rather stereotypical masculinities. If you can recall the exploration of protest masculinities, for example, in Chapter 5 of this book, I would argue that similarly to why men use such tropes of masculinity, butches can use such stereotypes too, for very similar reasons as some men do. For example, as a bonding tool, and as a way to further one's collective identity and amplify one's difference to feminine women.

Men sometimes use negative behaviours which are often labelled as and read easily as masculinity, including 'banter' or 'locker room' talk as it is called, partly to emphasize their masculinity and their difference to women. Stereotypes of masculinity, being stereotypes, are usually quickly identifiable, for better or worse, and sometimes men will utilize these very obvious behaviours in order to define themselves firmly in reference to what they are not – feminine. In so doing, of course, they denigrate women and femininity as lesser in contrast to their assumed superior sex and gender. Too often, such displays of masculinity use stories of, or actual cases of, aggression and violence towards women, particularly reference to sexual violence and dominance, to prove levels of masculinity to other men and bond with them over that, receiving status and recognition from other men as reward. It is interesting that such masculine posturing is always for the approval of other men and to compete with other men. I think it is likely that butch and transmasculine individuals might sometimes do similar – though I have never encountered such behaviours as widespread and commitment to feminism is, I would suggest, a norm in these communities. I have also never witnessed or heard any butch or transmasculine individual bragging about physical or sexual violence towards women, although I have listened to femme-identified lesbian women when they have told me that this, sadly, is not unknown.

If men arguably rarely or never feel secure in their masculinity, as I analysed in Chapter 5, and yet their bodies and their embodied practices are what represents masculinity in many dominant areas of our culture, then of course butches and queers who are not male bodied, and who do not have their kinds of masculinity or cultures represented in media and culture at all, are perhaps unsurprisingly also going to look for ways to visibly express, solidify and cement their masculinity in the eyes of their peers. My discomfort at presenting negative conceptions of masculinity from within transgender, butch and transmasculine communities may also be due to a sense of dirty linen being laundered in public. This discomfort is in addition to a reluctance to only further the traditional charges I mentioned earlier, which are frequently aimed at butches and masculine queers: that such individuals benefit from male privilege, that we are sexist and oppressive to women who are feminine and that we copy the worst of masculine behaviours. These are old charges, but they are perpetually recycled.

Is female home?

For some of the individuals who took part in my research, the lack of identification with womanhood and with the word 'woman' extended to a sense of discomfort with the term 'female' as well. Some did not like to use sexed female pronouns for themselves like she/her and they did not like others referring to them by such pronouns or as 'Miss' or a 'lady', for example. This was explained by Stephen, aged twenty-five to thirty years old, White English and identifying as butch/soft butch, tomboi, boi and as queer or gay. Stephen did not use female pronouns for themselves.

> Female pronouns and titles don't fit for me. (Stephen)

Reggie also did not use female pronouns. They were in their early forties, and they identified their heritage as being English, Scottish and Irish. They identified as pan or bisexual and as genderqueer.

> The idea of non-binary gender is something I only became aware of two years ago and suddenly it made sense. . . . I lived as a woman for nearly 40 years, I carried a child. But I know these things are essentialist. . . . Inside there is something 'ajar'. I don't use she pronouns as they seem clunky to me. (Reggie)

Similarly, Radclyffe, a butch lesbian in their late thirties who identified as White European, noted that they were often read as male, and called 'sir' or 'mate' for example, and that this did not bother them. Radclyffe stated they were not very attached to the femaleness of their body, and it was not something that was important to them or which defined them.

> I'm not overly sensitive to being misgendered (which happens on a regular basis) and the femaleness of my body isn't something I'm very attached to, or that's very important to me. (Radclyffe)

Some masculine-identified respondents had devised new and novel ways of thinking about their identity; Lois, mentioned earlier, referred to themselves as a 'female man' for example. They acknowledged that their body was sexed as female, and they were not planning to alter their sexed characteristics, though Lois was thinking about taking hormones to masculinize the appearance of their body, and they regularly went to the gym to add to the muscularity of their body. Lois noted that they were often read as male in public.

> I've recently decided to call myself a female man. I have a female body but have always felt male. . . . Ever since I was three years old I've wanted to do what boys/men did. I am a man in my head. For a long time, I tried to deal with having a female body by being a man-hating radical lesbian, and then I identified as a woman, but it didn't last. I intend to keep my female body, but I'm considering maybe looking into taking hormones. I work out at the gym and look male enough that I regularly get hassled in female toilets. (Lois)

Toilet trouble was a frequent experience for many of my respondents, and not only for those who did not identify as female or as women; it was an often daily experience for those whose appearance is what society would see as more masculine. These sorts of experiences of hostility hardly add to such individuals' comfort with categories like female and 'woman'.

Is lesbian home?

Given that for several respondents the categories of 'woman' and female were not always inhabited with comfort or ease, either psychologically or in terms of the reactions of others based on their outward appearance, it was perhaps not unsurprising that the category of 'lesbian' also freighted similar problems. For some respondents, the common association of lesbianism with femaleness and with same-sex attraction between two women did not gel with their gendered sense of self and how they experienced their gender identity, sexuality and sexual orientation.

Eliza, for example, did not like the inherent femaleness of the term 'lesbian', so she preferred the labels queer and dyke. Although 'dyke' could be considered as inherently female and as uncomplicatedly applying to women, it was interesting that a few respondents actually stated they felt more comfortable with that term. Not necessarily because it wasn't sexed as female (which it arguably is) but because it sounded stronger and more political to them, like a political identifier rather than an identifier of sex or gender. Eliza identified as Jewish, aged in their late fifties and naming their sexuality as dyke and their gender as gender-neutral.

> I prefer queer or dyke. Lesbian is a little too female for my liking. (Eliza)

A few respondents reflected on how their sense of self could affect their partnerships and partners, especially if those partners expected a congruent lesbian identity in their partner that mirrored their own, even if that was within a butch lesbian. As Lois explained, the 'butch' part was, for some partners, only expected to go so far and when it crossed a line and became a more solid masculine, male or transmasculine identity then that was sometimes not so attractive, arguably understandably, to lesbian women who desired to be with similarly lesbian women.

> I'm a female man. A lot of lesbians don't appreciate my masculinity. Former girlfriends didn't want to know about my trans aspects. They wanted to be with a woman, not a trans man, so I had to hide parts of who I was. But I have a female body and I'm attracted to women, so most people see me as a lesbian. (Lois)

Tommi felt that the term 'gay' was more open and inclusive than lesbian. Tommi was White British, aged in their late fifties, and they identified as a butch and sometimes also as a gay woman. They preferred the identifier of 'gay' rather than lesbian, and this was raised by other respondents as well, perhaps because 'gay' does not equal female in the way that the word 'lesbian' does unequivocally. 'Gay' was seen as ungendered and unsexed by many of my respondents. Tommi speculated as to whether some of this was down to internalized homophobia.

> Oddly, I don't much like the word lesbian . . . (internalized homophobia?). (Tommi)

Perhaps such findings cannot be separated entirely from the background of sexist society and misogyny which exists in the LGBTQI+ community as in all communities. There are also the related and valid concerns about the decline of lesbian community – any kind of lesbian community, including queer, femme and butch or transgender lesbian communities. Another of my survey respondents, Josh, who was one of the younger participants, addressed this topic of sexism and internalized homophobia. Josh noted that there was stigma around the term 'lesbian' and that the flight from 'lesbian' as an identifier could well be due to sexism and the resulting internalized homophobia or lesbophobia. Josh was aged eighteen to twenty-five years old, German British, and identified as butch, masculine, NB, GNC, transmasculine, transgender, queer and androgynous, stating their sexuality as pan, poly and queer. Josh said identifying as a lesbian was complicated for them.

> Complicated – I feel like a lot of the rejection of lesbian for other categories is internalised homophobia. I am happy to embrace and subvert the label in certain settings where people do not have another language for people like me, so I am not afraid of the term, or the stigma. But I just don't identify with it. (Josh)

Stu highlighted that lesbian is a sexed term, sexed as female, and possibly to the outside world gendered as well, gendered as woman or womanly. Stu explained that they would tick 'lesbian' on a form if it was the only option for a sexuality descriptor, but they would prefer to use the word 'gay'.

> If it's the only option on forms; I prefer gay . . . I identify as GAY. I think I prefer GAY to lesbian as it less identifies me to a specific gender. (Stu)

Nell also did not like that 'lesbian' was seen to equal 'woman' in an uncomplicated way. Nell identified as MOC and as queer, but did not state their age or ethnic identity. They were glad to identify as queer because they felt it contained multitudes. Nell did not identify as a woman.

Lesbian depends a bit too much on 'woman'. I prefer 'queer'. (Nell)

Ruith agreed, acknowledging that the term was still important for political reasons, but because it was so profoundly sexed and gendered it wasn't going to fit for everyone sexed as female who desired sex and relationships with women.

As the term lesbian means a woman who likes women, if I no longer solely identify as a woman can it technically be applied to me? . . . you can't apply it to someone who doesn't identify as a woman (although as mentioned before, I still do identify as a woman in part). The short answer is, it's complex! (Ruith)

Picking up on the 'lesbian sex wars', addressed earlier in this book, and the simplistic and reductionist accounts of femme and butch identities and relationships that come from some sections of feminism, mainly from lesbian feminism, several of my respondents mentioned that they couldn't identify with the term 'lesbian'. They argued that they had been made to feel excluded or problematic in some lesbian spaces. In fact, many of my butch respondents felt that other lesbians, unless they were femme- or butch-identified themselves, did not understand them, and often had fairly backward and offensive ideas about their sexuality and relationships. This was discussed by Sasha, a butch and a queer who did not indicate their age or ethnic identity.

'I'm Butch, which to me is not lesbian . . . complicated huh. My experience is that lesbians are generally intolerant of the butch/femme dynamic and can be rigid and annoying. I'm not them' (Sasha).

This was also touched upon by Bobby, who did actually identify as a lesbian, because they felt it was important to do so, but they acknowledged that there were still very live stereotypes about butches that echoed those assumptions of male privilege and sexism from the days of the sex wars.

People are scared of being butch as 1. Society tells us we are ugly and unwanted and 2. LGBT politics says masculinity is evil and butches are controlling and femmes should reject butches for real women'. (Bobby)

The political is political – not necessarily personal

Despite all of the expressed discomfort, disidentification and alienation from the terms 'woman' and 'lesbian', it was interesting that most of my survey respondents underlined that they would always identify as women and as lesbians for political purposes. In this way, when the political stayed political, and did not reflect the personal, it was adoptable and inhabitable. For many of these respondents, this was the only way they could feel a sense of belonging with women as a group; it was the only way that 'woman' could be comfortable and claimable. Roddy expressed this point, for example, they were White British, they did not give their age but they identified as queer, genderqueer, non-binary and gay woman sometimes. Like many others, Roddy said they generally felt more comfortable around women rather than men, for a variety of reasons, and politically they could feel they shared things in common with those other women, thus overcoming other differences.

> I think I more politically identify as a woman/womyn and also just feel more comfortable around other women. I don't really identify with it much apart from that, I definitely feel more genderqueer/nonbinary. (Roddy)

When these terms were used as purely political statements, then butch and masculine-identified respondents were able to fly those flags. Leslie, for example, said that politically, they would also identify as a woman.

> Politically yes. Really I identify as anything that is not a cis man! It's political for me because I'm a feminist . . . when fighting for gender equality I feel a kinship with other women (including trans women), 'womyn' and non-binary identities. (Leslie).

Bobby agreed that the label was important to maintain politically and added that there are lesbian concerns and political causes which not all queer people share; it was thus seen as important to retain this term.

> I think it's very important to keep the identity of lesbian from a political standpoint as there's certain structural issues that only affect lesbians and not all queer people. . . . I say lesbian as I identify most with this label and see it as a political act to do so. (Bobby)

Jazza was aged in their late thirties, White English and identified their gender and sexuality as queer. They agreed on the political significance of the lesbian label.

> I will always choose and tick the box lesbian, as a political gesture on any tick box census style survey. To be counted. I know what has gone before. I do not wish to dishonour that or detract from it. (Jazza)

Many respondents agreed and pointed out that it was a feminist stance to identify as a woman, that it was political for those reasons and important to them to take this stand. This was the case with respondents like Rosa and Niamh, both of whom mentioned having been socialized as women being a good enough grounding on which to build a foundation of at least some sense of shared solidarity with women as a group. Niamh was aged in her late thirties, White English and identified as genderfluid, non-binary and queer. Rosa was in her early thirties, White Welsh and identified as queer, non-binary, androgynous and genderqueer.

'I feel both woman but also non-binary. I was socialised to be a woman and I have a lot of feelings associated with feminist struggles but my gender is more complicated. I don't feel completely female or male' (Niamh)

'I have been socialised and brought up as female, so yes, woman does form some of my identity, even though I know I am very different to most women' (Rosa).

Raymondo also raised shared solidarity with women as a reason for politically identifying as a woman. Raymondo was in their early thirties, White English and identified as queer, butch and gay.

For most of the last 4 years I felt uneasy about identifying as a 'woman', but I think it's important politically. Regardless of how complicated I find that label, as a political category, it expresses my experiences and my solidarity with other cis and trans women. (Raymondo)

These experiences and standpoints that vocalize discomfort with the labels of 'woman' and 'lesbian', and even 'female', may share some areas of overlap with the experiences and standpoints of individuals who may be trans men, or who may be transmasculine or transgender. In the current climate, such questions can become taboo. In a time where the mantra of 'with us or against us' seems to rule political debates of all kinds, the gender wars are no exception; in fact, they are perhaps a prime example. When marginalized communities are under attack, such as communities working for the rights and protection of trans men and trans women, this surrounding aggression does not produce a fertile environment for acknowledging the porous nature of some of the borders around those identity movements.

Identity movements, by definition, form around certain identities, and when rights are literally being taken away from those with that identity, priority is unlikely to be given to public discussions of how similar that identity might be to other identities, and how it might actually encapsulate lots of different and perhaps seemingly contradictory identities all at once. Judith Lorber discussed this fluidity that exists alongside the necessary assumptions of fixity.

In order to have a politics of identity, you have to know who is 'us' and who is 'them'. In many places, lesbians, gays, transvestites and transexuals have joined as one intellectual, political and social transgendered community. If they are quite avant-garde, they include self-identified 'queers' as well. However, they are quite different, and the differences frequently create tensions within the community. (Lorber, 1999: 360)

The gender wars have so much to answer for and one of those side effects is the decline of the past queer approach to including all those who were outsiders or who felt like outsiders, and then wrestling and flirting and fighting those differences out inside those shared spaces.

I do not wish to be guilty of aggrandizing or romanticizing the past, but I also am not going to pretend that I have not lived through this shift. I have recollections of so many discussions in shared queer spaces, from the mid-1990s onwards. Discussions about feminism, trans rights, the urgency of solidarity with trans women and trans men, the glorification of masculinity in the queer scene, the perceived benefits of transition for trans men as well as the raced consequences that Black queers faced, and the penalties sensed by butch and masculine people with sexed as female bodies who did not transition medically. We had these debates. But now, it often feels as if these conversations never happened. It feels like they are being shut down and silenced; in the past they were difficult and emotive, but now they seem impossible. One reason for the trickiness of these conversations is of course the perennial phenomenon I have addressed earlier, butch flight. Many of the masculine and trans-butch-identified respondents went on to talk about this as another side effect of the current polarized and binary gender wars.

Respondents asserted that, in their experience, the assumptions about butch flight have got more frequent, and with that, the assumption is laid onto masculine-identified people that they must be on that flight path themselves. As public awareness about the existence of trans men and trans women has grown, perhaps quite suddenly over the past few years, so it may happen more often that anyone who is not immediately perceptible as sex and gender normative may be assumed to be trans, often by well-meaning strangers or colleagues. This observation does not lay any blame at trans women and trans men for society finally representing their lives in media and culture, for better or worse, because that was long, long overdue. It is just a fact that with awareness can come backlash, as those working in the field of trans rights have acknowledged themselves. What I want to highlight is that this backlash does not only affect trans women and trans men, nor only those individuals who identify as trans. There are repercussions too for anyone who is not sex and gender normative, and, as I have argued throughout this book, this is just one reason why these lives need to be showcased and centred.

New destinations for the butch flight

Butch flight is perhaps stereotypically understood to mean a simple journey or crossing from point A, being a butch lesbian, to point B, being a trans man. As Halberstam defined in 2011, 'I was responding to community-based debates about the difference between gender variance in lesbian communities and the emergence of transgender identities. People were no longer calling themselves butches but were calling themselves transgender men. It's a thin line, but there were a lot of fights about it that I tried to respond to' (Halberstam, 2011: 377). Butch flight is often discussed using narratives of resignation and regret, as if those who do leave the identity of butch lesbian behind are our fallen soldiers, lost forever and leaving our side depleted.

Writing in 2011 in the edited collection by Ivan Coyote and Zena Sharman, which made an honourable nod to Nestle's classic in its title *Persistence*, Victoria Brownworth placed butch flight firmly in the context of neoliberal individualism. She blames this context, in part, for the rise of an assimilationist LGBTQI+ politics, one that is no longer focussed on gay liberation or on being different from the mainstream but is instead focussed on just joining the mainstream. In that landscape, she asserts, butch lesbians and perhaps particularly stone butches are more likely to be assumed to be 'really' men, because they certainly are not doing the label of 'woman' correctly. 'Severely butch? You must be transgender – born into the wrong body. That's okay, it's not your fault; it's a genetic mismatch. But severely butch and still think you are a lesbian? Rethink that, because we're all just like straight people now and we have to look the parts' (Brownworth, 2011: 144). She goes on to voice a common refrain, as I have discussed earlier in this book, the concern that butches are being 'transed'. This is a concern that butches are being forced to flee, when they might have actually just 'really' been butches and could have made a home here, all along, on our side.

> How many people will tell the budding butch that she really is transgender, born a man in a woman's body? But what if she's really just butch, that is, content with the confluence of her female body and masculine persona? Will her confusion lead her to hormone treatments and surgeries she will later regret when she realises what her true identity is? (Brownworth, 2011: 148)

Writing in the same 2011 collection, B Cole, who coined the term MOC, partly as a response to the Whiteness of terms like 'butch', acknowledges, as I have asserted also, that fears about butch flight are very live issues, and perhaps only growing in currency. 'For some, this raises the question: What is happening to all of our butches? I think this evolution highlights the fact that, for many of us who came of age ten or twenty years ago, and even called ourselves butches, we never felt fully rooted in that language and space' (Cole, 2011: 134). Here, Cole is pointing out what I have argued earlier that these were never stable categories in the first place, that there were always transgender or even trans and trans-man-identified butches who for lots of reasons stayed in what we would see as one place; that is, they did not medically transition. As one of my respondents, Jez pointed out though, that doesn't necessarily mean such chosen identities do not share life experiences with trans individuals, or share experiences of their body; it just means some have chosen to transition in those visible ways and some have not.

> I don't think all 'butches' are FTMs-in-waiting, but some are, some might've been under different circumstances and some aren't and perish the idea; it's taking T and/or having surgery that eventually makes the difference, not necessarily how we feel inside. (Jez)

Halberstam explained in 1998 the many reasons why a queer butch may not wish to medically transition and become a trans man, asserting that this does not mean they don't have similar ambivalence or even mismatch with their sexed as female body: 'There is little to no recognition here of the trials and tribulations that confront the butch who for whatever reasons (concerns about surgery/hormones, feminist scruples, desire to remain in a lesbian community, lack of successful phalloplasty models) decides to make a home in the body with which she was born' (Halberstam, 1998a: 305).

Concerns over butch flight only add to the scrutiny of butches and to those presumed to be butches, with the worry being that those butches will leave the ranks, as the activist, writer and poet Bear Bergman pointed out in 2006. He wrote that some butches worried they were going to be consigned to history, in the face of an exodus to seemingly more queer and modern destinations than 'butch'. 'They're fearful that soon, masculine women like them will be a more or less extinct species' (Bergman, 2006: 67). The increased awareness of trans and transgender identities, also means that, in turn, some individuals are worried others will assume they are trans men when they are not. Levitt and Hiestand assert that this is also the case in the academic field of psychology and perhaps also in therapeutic practice as well: 'Currently, however, much writing under the rubric of "transgender" is being focused on transsexualism so that, when it is discussed, butch gender often is cast as a precondition for women who later transition in to men' (Levitt & Hiestand, 2004: 620). It is perhaps a common experience for queer masculine butches or transmasculine people, to be seen by others as trans men who must be at the start of their transition. This was discussed by many of my respondents, not only those who were stone butches or those who did not identify with womanhood or femaleness, but by masculine-presenting queer females in general. For example, Bobby was frustrated that in public others rarely saw them as the queer masculine butch lesbian they were.

Many people assume I am trans, rather than a masculine woman. (Bobby)

Germaine was in her early sixties, White English, and she identified as a butch woman and as a lesbian. She recounted that people often mistake her as a man and as male; she also reported that, in addition to this, a newer, more recent occurrence has been people asking her if she is a trans man.

I have even been asked if I am trans recently, which really makes me unhappy as it's really taking a step back to what others think you should look like. (Germaine)

Lucy, a butch queer, added that the explosion of new terms to describe non-normative gender identities, such as MOC, NB, GNC and transmasculine, meant that butch lesbians were now assumed to be one of these and assumed to be a distinctly trans identity.

I think what they have in common is that people often mistake a butch for one of these identities – one particular trend I have witnessed is that people assume you are somewhere en-route to transitioning FTM. (Lucy)

Lucy voiced an argument here that scholarship from Halberstam and Hale has focussed on too, the argument that being a butch lesbian is not seen as, or treated as, stable, significant and important enough to endure in this new sea of available terms. Butch is the term that has been subsumed, rather than the other way round. Why is it that butch is the term to decline in use? Is this the case throughout all communities or do terms like stud or AG endure in Black and global majority communities? Why are the newer transmasculine, transgender and queer masculine terms emerging not just using 'butch' as a catch-all term? The obvious answer is perhaps the most likely answer here. Butch has declined, at least in certain communities, because it is explicitly sexed, and explicitly linked to the identity of lesbian, as I have discussed earlier. So much so that even those who are partially contained within its range, queer butches, transgender butches or transmasculine butches, for example, have to qualify the term too, and disentangle it from its female and lesbian roots. It is not therefore an easy term to use as a catch-all, because it has too much history, or herstory, and is too loaded with baggage.

Several of my respondents were aware of the prominence of trans identities rather than lesbian/butch gender identities and of the decline of lesbian communities from which to possibly observe such role models. One respondent, Josh, for example, suggested that this might be partly to do with the mainstream, public focus on a trans identity as being a painful pilgrimage, a process of journeying from one uncomfortable place to a true identity. This is perhaps a narrative that suits our current neoliberal, individualized and confessional backdrop. The narrative of transitioning from one point to another and finding home is certainly a common representation in the media of the lives of trans women and trans men.

Narratives such as this in the mainstream only added to the invisibility of the in-between identities I am discussing in this section of this book. These in-between identities were addressed by Jacob Hale back in 1998. Writing about the idea of competition between the two sides of the border wars, he cautions against butch or transmasculine masculinities being seen as less real, genuine or authentic when compared to the masculinities of trans men:

> The notion expressed was that the masculinities of non-FTMs with (varying degrees of) female embodiments are no more integral to their sense of self than an article of clothing and, hence, inauthentic – as if masculinities expressed differently from ours are less authentic aspects of the selves who express them merely because they are expressed differently, as if our FTM masculinities would be suspect if any other birth-assigned females were to don masculinities of their own, as if masculinity is a scarce commodity in a male-dominated economy. (Hale, 1998: 327)

My research participant Josh argued that when queer butches or trans butches do not actually medically transition, they are not seen as being so committed or 'true' in their masculine identity and are assumed to be therefore at ease and comfortable in their sexed as female bodies, when, as I've made clear above, this is often far from the case.

> I think butch is an identity, but we have been taught to think of trans as that big buzzword which comes with a whole accompanying narrative of tragedy, identity struggle, and existential crisis etc. So a lot of people might see butch as something surface-level, performed, and maybe even transient, taking place against a 'female body' with no accompanying identity crisis. (Josh)

It may be the case then that the category of butch is seen as less 'real' because it is assumed that this identity is not fought for, that it is not a place of pain and struggle, that it is not also a journey to forge such an identity and make it home. As I've hopefully introduced in this chapter, it is certainly not necessarily always a stable, comfortable and unquestioned identity position to live as a queer butch or transmasculine queer. As Halberstam has always argued so eloquently and clearly, 'it would not be accurate to make gender dysphoria the exclusive property of transexual bodies nor to surmise that the greater the gender dysphoria the likelier a transexual identification' (Halberstam, 1998a: 295). Halberstam has written extensively about this, and incidentally such communities owe Professor Halberstam a great debt in this area. Halberstam has addressed this, for example, in the influential exchange on this topic with fellow academic, Jacob Hale, in 'Butch/FTM Border Wars: A Note on Collaboration' in the journal of lesbian and gay studies, *GLQ*, in 1998.

Considerably more masculine than thou

Talking about and acknowledging borders, of course, also introduces the question of hierarchy or order. This is not new within butch lesbian gender identities, where there is already a commonly understood spectrum of expression from soft butch, for example, to stone butch. Around 2018 or thereabouts the term 'futch' circulated in social media too, used with a sense of irony in debates about scales from high femme to soft butch – with the term 'futch' functioning to describe the exact centre point between those two poles. With the assumption of such scales, humorous and creative though it may often be in our communities comes an invocation of rank or hierarchy. I think it is dishonest to pretend that a ranking system does not exist and doesn't affect many butch lesbians. Several of my respondents wrote about wondering whether they could legitimately claim the label of butch, for example. They worried whether they were butch or masculine enough.

The border wars can, likewise, also invoke ideas of scale or rank not just on the spectrum of butchness, but on a scale of masculinity. Are butches just failed trans men for example, who couldn't pull off masculinity; or are they just butches who couldn't go through with transition? As Bergman alerted us to, this kind of ranking has real effects. Discussing transmasculine or transgender butches and their problematic history and inclusion in lesbian and feminist space, Bergman points out that these identities are now being questioned, scrutinized and judged yet again, in this case because they haven't transitioned. 'Some of them, that after being thrown out of the women's movement for being too male-identified they are now being ridiculed or having their identities questioned for being not male-identified enough' (Bergman, 2006: 67). Are trans men always more masculine than butches? Are they trans men because they were better at masculinity? Those of us in these communities know that there are not simple answers to all these questions and that they reflect stereotypes and assumptions much more than they reflect reality. There are plenty of very feminine and camp trans men for example. As Halberstam rightly points out, these stereotypes and assumptions proceed on a belief that there is only one way to be masculine, or that certain expressions of masculinity are genuine and others are not. Basically, these assumptions flow from a sense that masculinity is gated and limited, echoing the earlier quote from Jacob Hale on masculinity as a finite resource. Therefore, this reasoning follows, the category of masculinity, if it is finite, should not and cannot contain just everyone and anyone: 'Some butches consider FTMs to be butches who "believe in anatomy" and some FTMs consider butches to be FTMs who are too afraid to transition. The border wars between transgender butches and FTMs seem to proceed on the assumption, shared by all sides, that masculinity is a limited resource, available to only a few in ever-decreasing quantities' (Halberstam, 1998a: 287).

I have lost count of the number of trans men I know who are very effeminate, many are gay and in gay relationships with non-trans men. In some cases it almost seems like once someone comes out about being a trans man and goes through a process of medical transition, in varying degrees, they are then liberated in a way to be less masculine in their appearance, style and mannerisms, than they were before, perhaps because there is less to prove and less to lose – while acknowledging the very real dangers to being seen as a feminine man under patriarchy. Non-trans men, as well as trans men, who are effeminate or camp are still men, but when someone is read as a masculine woman rather than a trans man, being camp or effeminate only adds to the public reception as the former (woman) rather than the latter (man). Gayle Rubin addressed this in her 1992 essay, pointing out that discussing any similarities between butch and trans identities can be construed as watering down both categories. Especially in a context where butches may be seen as failed trans men, and where trans men may wish to clearly demarcate their identity from that of a sexed as female embodiment of masculinity. 'Within the group of women labelled butch, there are many individuals who are gender dysphoric to varying degrees. Many butches have particularly male gender identities. Others border on being, and some are, female to male transsexuals (FTMs), although many lesbians and FTMs find the areas of overlap between butchness and transsexualism disturbing' (Rubin, 1992: 468). What does Rubin mean by this? I suggest that this relates to the arguments I have endeavoured to steer us through in this chapter. These are the arguments about whether butches are 'really' men or on the way to being so, whether butch flight is an offence to the Sisterhood and other such feminist arguments about butches being too male-centred, for example. But, there is another difficult issue here, and that is the issue introduced by Jacob Hale theorizing that masculinity is seen as some kind of zero-sum resource.

Who owns masculinity?

To put this plainly, what this is referring to is the worry that if butch lesbians can convincingly 'do' masculinity and be read and treated as men in much of their lives, this may endanger or threaten the clear recognition of the masculinity of trans men. Might trans men, early on in their medical transition or who have paused medical intervention for varying reasons, such as for health reasons, or to carry children, might they be wrongly assumed to 'just' be masculine women or stereotypical butch lesbians, rather than trans men? We may well ask why that term 'just' be put at the front of such a question in the first place. Most of us who have been on this scene for a while might remember in the early days of the internet, when guides on homemade binders did the rounds in our communities, often originating from the United States. These went along with tick lists for trans men who did not want to get mistaken as lesbians – leather jackets and buzz cuts were out, for example. Researching for this book I went through my archives to see if I still had any copies, and then I found that this advice is still actually circulating. On an archived site for FTM passing tips, which was cited in a recent support guide for trans youth, I found the following:

> Go for a short-back-n'-sides cut, but avoid getting an all-over crewcut or 'punk' style, as these are often sported by the butch lesbians who you are trying to distinguish yourself from. . . . If you live in a cosmopolitan area where there are a lot of butch lesbians then it's going to be much more difficult for you to pass. One way to help distinguish yourself from them is to dress more conservatively – you might want to leave the leather motorcycle jacket at home for a while. ('Andy', Geocitiesftmpass)

Sometimes there appears to be an assumption that transmasculine butches are encroaching on a category and blurring the boundaries for those that see the category as quite clear and wish to be clearly on one side of that boundary rather than the other. The scholar Bobby Noble, for example, argues explicitly that the masculinities of trans men and butches are completely different and should not be conflated: 'Certainly it would be unwise to presuppose lines of continuity between butch and ftm embodiment and sexual practice. Butch masculinity occupies a very different space of embodiment and engendering than ftm masculinity' (Noble, 2007: 17). In an academic article from 2007 on détente in the butch/FTM borderlands, Jillian T Weiss argues that the identities of trans men are always going to be intrinsically different to those of masculine-presenting queer female people or butch lesbians for example, because trans men have transitioned and are male, not female. 'The whole point of FTM identity, however, is that it is a male identity, *not* female' (Weiss, 2007: 206). This approach is therefore making a distinction between sexed characteristics and socially understood gender, and it focusses on the sexed body as the site of distinction and categorization. The latter is of course a commonplace and rather normative definition of masculinity in general, as I explored in Chapter 5. Some of those definitions of masculinity focus on the male body, particularly the penis, as being the ultimate and final symbol of masculinity. However, it is important to note that trans men are not the only ones who may use differing degrees of intervention to masculinize their bodies and their sexed bodily characteristics. As I've highlighted in this chapter, some individuals do not identify as trans men, but they may use testosterone to masculinize their bodies, or they may work out regularly to masculinize their bodies. Some may seek elective top surgery to remove their breasts and masculinize their chest, all while not identifying legally or socially as a trans man.

These bodies arguably cannot be set up as somehow 'cis' or 'gender normal' on the one side of a fence, in order that the bodies of trans men and trans women can be firmly set up on the opposite side of the fence as trans and transgressive. For a start, such a distinction only sets up yet another binary that assumes gender conformity on to everyone except trans men and trans women. It also privileges the medical and pharmaceutical industries and the scientific knowledge that diagnoses, names and affirms a trans status, denying the types of knowledges that people use to know themselves and identify themselves. As Professor Halberstam pointed out in the queer heyday of the 1990s, many bodies are 'gender strange' rather than gender normal; it is not only trans men or trans women who could be seen as transgressive in this way:

> There are many butches who pass as men and many transsexuals who present as gender ambiguous, as well as many bodies that cannot be classified as either transexual or butch. While I admit we are not all transexual, many bodies are gender strange to some degree or another. It is time to complicate the models that assign gender queerness only to transexual bodies and gender normativity to all others. (Halberstam, 1998a: 301)

Plus, as many trans writers have strongly and rightly underlined, trans men and trans women may well not consider themselves gender strange or transgressive at all, but, as the citations from Noble and Weiss hint at, some may consider themselves to be sex- and gender-normative women, or sex- and gender-normative men.

Home in between

The respondents I have platformed in this chapter represent the difficulty that many people live with, and within, which is the difficulty of penning themselves within any one identity category. In his 1995 essay, scholar Jay Prosser wrote about the trans journey as being possibly a homecoming. The fluid part, the crossing in the middle is a temporary state, which is inhabited along the way to reaching a stable point where the trans man or trans woman arrives at being legally, socially, medically and culturally recognized as the identity they are. Prosser uses the term 'home' to indicate a place of security, safety and refuge, connoting: 'familiarity, safety, fixity' as well as 'very powerful notions of belonging' (1995: 486). But there are, of course, those who do not reach a 'home' in this linear sense. There are those who, for a multitude of reasons, must bivouac in the shifting sands that they find themselves in, when they have not transitioned, as such, medically or legally, in a final or finalized way. For such individuals the process, or journey, can be ongoing, and thus the process of being and becoming can be ongoing. Several of my respondents did not really experience their body as 'home' in any fixed sense, or necessarily inhabit that location comfortably. They had made it their own though, sometimes coming up with new terms to describe their sex and their gender, and new ways to relate to their sexed as female body and their relationship with women as a group.

This gave them a rare and valuable standpoint, from which they could choose certain facets from dominant groups, men and women, and leave others behind. As the late Gloria Anzaldua has argued, it can be a blessing to be neither one thing nor the other, and to be a whole human instead. Anzaldua edited the feminist classic *This Bridge Called My Back*, along with Cherrie Moraga in 1981, an anthology of writings by radical Women of Colour. She also wrote in 1987, a monograph drawn from her own life experiences of growing up along the US/Mexico border, a book about borderlands and the new consciousness that can grow there. In *Borderlands/ La Frontera: The New Mestiza*, she delves through spiritual traditions from both countries, her family histories and her own gender and sexuality as what she calls half and half: 'I, like other queer people, am two in one body, both male and female. I am the embodiment of the hieros gamos: the coming together of opposite qualities within' (1987: 19). Writing about the paradoxes of identity politics, Judith Lorber in 1999 cautioned that sometimes trans men and trans women may, perhaps, struggle in some ways to belong in their status. She called this a kind of immigrant status, being 'immigrants, not natives' (1999: 359).

The transmasculine and butch individuals I have platformed in this chapter did not, or had not up until this point, transitioned to any new status as a trans man, but they certainly did not express feeling at home in their existing status either, and they did not feel like 'natives' in womanhood or femaleness. They did not experience womanhood as a 'home' if that means secure and familiar, not least due to the threats of homophobia and transphobia as they moved through the world. They had not found a stable home in terms of 'fixity', and they experienced varying and changing levels of sex dysphoria due to their sex and gender marked bodies, which they may well share in common with some trans men. As Hale pointed out, 'self-identification as butch or ftm is the only characteristic that distinguishes some butches from some ftms' (Hale, 1998: 325). They had not found a home where that means a powerful place of belonging, because the categories and communities that were often available to them, such as 'woman', 'man', 'lesbian' and 'trans', did not map neatly onto their lives, bodies, intimate relationships or personal self-definition. They traversed familiar territories, just as other queer individuals may do at different times, including transgender and trans individuals and perhaps trans men. As Jacob Hale surmises, it is often the case that 'borders between gender categories then, are zones of overlap, not lines' (1998: 323).

Many people survive and even thrive in these overlapping territories. Kate Bornstein wrote in her famous book *Gender Outlaw* in 1994: 'I love the idea of being without an identity, it gives me a lot of room to play around' (1994: 39). As Scheman has eloquently highlighted, there are numerous paths we could take in life, some go from A to B, but there are also 'an unlimited number of places in between – places where one might stop for a while or return to, places where people might even live' (Scheman, 2016: 214). It is these borderlands that many of my respondents inhabited. Some even wrote about how they had embraced living in the in-between categories, and they had got used to and reclaimed the fact of not being quite one identity or another. Jazza, for example, concluded their remarks by saying that although they were not sure about their identity or their relationship to the identity of woman anymore, they were trying to find freedom in that unmarked space:

I am no longer sure what is me, but the uncertainty feels ok. It feels like a space to breathe. (Jazza)

Tam, aged in their late forties, similarly emphasized this position. Tam identified as NB, but highlighted that this was in the absence of any other word they could find to describe themselves; they identified as feeling neither female or male:

I guess it's nice to be liminal. Liminal is a good word. I will describe myself as Liminal. I think it's hard for others to make assumptions about you when you're liminal (particularly straight people) as you're not fitting into expected norms; that can leave some space to manoeuvre. (Tam)

Ivor acknowledged being in a middle ground and being seen by others as occupying a middle ground too.

I think with the 'ease' of transitioning as compared to fifteen years ago, people can now become male. Butch can be hard because you constantly occupy a middle ground. (Ivor)

As Ivor notes here, it can be hard setting up camp in these disputed territories, like Hale points out: 'Living as a nearly unintelligible creature is no easy task' (1998: 337). For butches and MOC individuals our identities are not universally recognized, let alone understood. As Leslie Feinberg points out, having a label, a banner and a name that one can proudly wear is important: 'It's hard to fight oppression without a name connoting pride, a language that honours us' (1996: 206). There are few famous examples or role models; our terms are never used as catch-all containers for multitudes of expressions. We do not even have agreed upon definitions of butch, transgender butch or transmasculine. Yet all of us who take up such identities probably do share some knowledge of familiar journeys and familiar terrain, as well as shared obstacles. But these identities, without having any clear boundaries, are always harder to explain to others, and therefore hard to understand and recognize. Hale asserts that this makes it all the more important to elaborate on such lives, in their fullness and diversity and contradiction; otherwise, they will not be seen as lives at all. 'Only by speaking quite specifically about those located elements of our dislocatedness can we who dwell in border zones speak at all. Such lengthy, detailed specifications do not provide the discursive material for full occupancy of social existence, which at present requires more central, less multiple instantiations of social categories' (Hale, 1998: 336).

These identities matter, and the labels used to describe them matter. But that is not and does not have to be in exclusion of any other identities, as in the stereotypical case of butches being assumed to be 'really' trans men, or on the route to being so. The challenge we all face, in these communities and in the overlapping borderlands that we often all inhabit together, is to avoid a situation where identifications can only be made, or understood, against and in contrast to others. Too often, this is the main way that identities lay claim to their territories and provide a foundation for their existence. Too often identities, and the lives behind them, make cases for human rights and recognition based on their distinction and their difference or distance from the identities of others. This is a zero-sum game in which we are all bound to lose, and within such a competitive environment 'border wars' are perhaps inevitable and will fester. The challenge, then, is to take back our ground, but not out from under each other, our fellow travellers, but from the structures of power which make the journey so hard for everyone in the first place.

Conclusion

Together from here to where

This book has been a story of two halves: one looking back to make sense of the present, and one that might give us some indication of visions for the future. These visions have come not from binary positions but from those who are in between, from those who have a critical gaze in all directions, because they know what it is not to fit in. Those of us who live and have lived in multiple identities and communities can often see what unites and divides. This is a vital perspective, and, as I have argued in this book, it is one that is often missed, or wilfully erased. It is ignored and sidelined because nuance and shared interests are rejected in favour of simplistic, reductive headlines and social media soundbites. It used to be the case that people complained about the emergence of a twenty-four-hour news cycle, concerned that this diluted and abridged important political coverage and analysis; now we have a sixty-second news cycle in the palm of our hands. What gets traction is that which is clearly on one side or another of however an issue has been framed for us, thereby further entrenching binary bunkers into the wide field of possible speech and action. Meanwhile, the truth is that most people are not wedded firmly and immovably to any one side or another in the so-called gender wars because most people are in the middle. Many people are hearing about gender identity terms, trans and queer lives for the first time and most people don't feel well informed, but they usually know that they don't want to say or do the wrong thing. In my experience, most people are motivated not to upset or harass anyone, and nor do they want to be harassed for saying something that others object to.

The divisive with-us-or-against-us approach that saturates all of our society has silenced the majority of people on this topic, and continually recycles the false premise that everyone is either on one side or another and knows exactly what they think about sexed identities, gendered terms and the lives of trans and transgender people. The narrative goes that if you can't provide definitions for each of the fifty-two gender options on Facebook, then you should not speak at all. We are told this about all sorts of social issues of course, not just this one; and this stasis is actively designed to block solidarity and with it, change. All of us are learning all the time, and everyone has a right to ask questions, make mistakes and grow. I myself have still not worked out what I think about some of the questions that are asked in the various debates that circle around on gender identity and sports, for example, or appropriate healthcare responses for children exploring their gender identity. Because of this, many readers will no doubt have concerns for my own health, worrying about the side effects of sitting on the proverbial fence for a whole book. But this has really been my point all along; nothing is simple. There are areas of overlap, there are areas of conflict and this is real life. Not only are there different, competing accepted positions on political questions, but each of us has a unique standpoint from which we view those questions and most of the time we assume our own 'truth' is the truth. There are actually multiple truths; some may not look normal to us, and they may be outside our experience. Those are the very occasions we should open our eyes and ears, because learning how others see things helps us to better see the world.

Throughout the preceding chapters I have tried to empathize with the standpoints of different sides and contextualize the nuance of positions which are commonly presented as simplistically either/or. As a queer butch or masculine lesbian who has moved in and out of trans* identifications, I know that binaries cannot map onto the wonderful diversity of all our lives. I have knowledges of both women-only, lesbian feminist communities and queer communities. All these circles have genuine progressive hopes for a better and fairer world, sometimes they even overlap; in general their visions of the future may be very similar, but there are differences on how we get there. This is not a new situation; it has forever been the case for social justice movements. These are activist, largely voluntary movements, made up of disparate groups that have little time to focus on visionary plans because they are firefighting, because they are dealing with external opposition as well as trying to own and work with differences and power relationships in their own communities. As well as their sincere hopes for the future, all these communities also have real fears; and sometimes they are frightened of each other.

Trans men, trans women and transgender people are scared and angry that much public discourse, including language and campaigns from some GC activists and some feminist activists, presents them as perverts and sexual predators. Lesbians and gay men know the effects of such language too. It has long been the case that lesbian and gay people have been told they should not work with children, that they are not suitable parents, and treated like innate threats who should not be in shared spaces. There are many who seem to want trans men and trans women barred from public spaces also. In the summer of 2020, at the height of righteous Black Lives Matter protests the Conservative government in the UK announced that guidance would be clarified to ensure that trans women with sexed as male anatomy would be banned from women's public toilets. This was a bizarre announcement, which could never be policed in any way that was not a fundamental breach of privacy. Make no mistake, the effect of turning our binary society overnight into one that polices entry to public binary spaces based on birth sex alone, would be to severely limit and restrict the movement and participation of trans women, trans men and transgender people. Trans and transgender people already limit themselves, to manage the often hostile reactions of non-trans people, so to be told that they should use segregated toilets and changing rooms, or use public toilets based on their birth sex, amplifies the message that they are not welcome in public space. If someone doesn't have access to the basic facilities to move around for the day in their town or city or workplace, this is effectively a curfew or an outright bar.

Added to this, it is clear that some campaigners will not be happy until the Gender Recognition Act in the UK is altered or repealed so that trans women and trans men are no longer able to change their legal sex, or even update sex markers on personal identification like bank cards or utility bills. There are threats to counselling services for young trans people, threats to sex reassignment surgery provision, threats to provisions of hormone treatment. There are suggestions that trans women and trans men should be segregated and use segregated third spaces when it comes to places like toilets, changing rooms or gyms. Circulating behind such dictates is the suggestion that trans women are not 'real' women, and trans men are not 'real' men, ironically invoking the same traps of gender that prop up patriarchy and the division of men and women into predator and prey. These are real attacks on trans people, with very real consequences. Trans people can be forgiven for fearing that the language of anti-trans feminism from the 1970s is being brought into realization, with Raymondesque calls for trans people to be mandated out of existence by bans on treatment, bans on affirmative counselling, bans on updating of documents and bans on using facilities in public spaces which are overwhelmingly binary.

GC campaigners and anti-trans-inclusion feminists, meanwhile, fear that the legacy of precious and increasingly rare women-only political, cultural, social and healing spaces will be effectively turned unisex overnight. Pressures to be inclusive to all genders and all sex identities fuel concerns that those refuges, rape crisis centres or women's housing projects who have remained women-only will no longer be able to advertise themselves as such. There are questions around what this will mean too for places like women's prisons, where most of the women have histories shaped by male sexual violence; there are questions over consequences for women's sports, for scholarships or women-only prizes. Some feminists are asking whether calls to broaden the borders around such identity-based settings will mean that 52 per cent of the population, women sexed as female from birth, will end up getting left out, or pushed out. The sexist status quo that gives rise to the necessity of such provisions in the first place is not the fault of trans people though, who make up a marginalized minority in our society.

A much wider discourse also prevails in the mainstream media, often without any particular feminist mooring at all, which is about sharing public spaces with trans women. This unfolds despite the fact that trans women and trans men have been using binary provisions like anyone else for decades, and in fact it has long been a preference or requirement of securing any medical interventions or legal recognitions that trans people prove they are serious about who they are by evidencing 'living in role' for at least two years. It is likely that most people do not know any trans women or trans men, and very likely that most people would have no idea whether they had shared a public toilet with a trans man or trans woman. The never-ending toilet troubles and bathroom debates often descend into sheer conservative bigotry, with calls to police women's toilets or clothing store changing rooms based on how much one's appearance adheres to standards of femininity and to gendered norms about the sexed features of bodies.

As trans women are a tiny minority in society, the biggest group affected by such policing will be non-feminine or masculine non-trans women. Butch lesbians, studs, GNC, MOC and female masculine queers already know too well what it's like to be stared at, verbally abused, challenged, removed by security or assaulted by security staff, or harassed by passing men called upon by women to address the gender freak in the toilet. We already know what it is to be treated like deviants, where difference to mainstream ideas of what sex and gender should look like is seen to equal perversion and threat. There are so many sexist and homophobic assumptions here about the complementarity of masculinity and femininity and the presumption of default homing destinations to one or the other based on sex. As I have shown in this book, many people sexed as female at birth move through life being read as men; having sexed as female anatomy is no guarantee of occupying what mainstream society considers womanhood to look like. Butch lesbians are increasingly bored with constant challenge in the women's department store or gym when many just want their way of being a woman to be recognized and included like any other way of being a woman. Meanwhile some queer individuals who were sexed as female at birth would rather avoid women's spaces altogether, because of the hostility they receive and sometimes because they don't feel at home there.

Female people, as we have seen, can feel more at home in masculinity, and there make an identity category all of their own. Those are real identities too, just as real as your sex, gender and sexuality whatever that may be. They are identities which are loved, recognized and respected by other queer people who see them as female men, bois with different bodies, as real butches, or real studs. Trans men are seen and loved intimately as the men they are, by gay, bi or straight partners. Trans women are seen and loved intimately as the women they are, by lesbian, bi or straight partners. To non-queer readers some of this may be hard if not impossible to understand, and homophobia and heterosexism block any purview into how others may live their lives and conduct their relationships. But just because you cannot see them, it doesn't mean that they don't have a right to exist as they are. Imagine, there is a whole world out there, outside mainstream heterosexism and sex-gender-sexuality normativity. There are different rules, different recognized signs and different ways of belonging; I have tried to show you some of these in this book.

In the background, behind all these bathroom bills and toilet troubles is a universal fear of and necessity to control for the prevalence of sexualized male violence against women, children and marginalized men. It is often acknowledged therefore that trans women are not the problem in such spaces. There is no evidence to suggest that trans women are any more of a threat in women's toilets than any other woman is. Those of us queer people who regularly get homophobia or verbal abuse in women's toilets know only too well, of course, that not all women are nice; sometimes women are cruel, bigoted and violent. The anxiety, therefore, is often around opening up such spaces at all, and removing scrutiny in general. The scenario envisioned is that those in and around sex segregated toilets or changing rooms for example, will not feel comfortable policing entry, reluctant to misjudge someone else's sex identity. This reluctance to check out or ask people if they have a right to be in that space could then be abused by predatory men who will exploit this situation of uncertainty, to enter women's spaces. They could just declare themselves to identify as a woman if they are challenged, and then go into women's spaces to commit voyeurism or other forms of sexual violence. Having worked in domestic abuse prevention programmes, and having been in feminist activism for decades against male violence against women and children, I know only too well that there are indeed predatory men who will go to extremes to get access to women and children they desire to control and abuse. There is no point arguing that such a scenario could not happen. However, it is a sad fact that rates of sexualised male violence against women and children are already off the scale on the patriarchal geiger counter and too many men find facilitated ways to abuse and kill women every day without having to transition to live as trans women. Plus, many public women's spaces, like toilets to return to this perennial example, are already not safe. Men already wonder in and out as cleaning staff, many such spaces are down little staircases or corridors and are targeted by men who follow women inside, or wait outside. This is an argument to improve these spaces. And, once again, it is not acceptable to make trans women uniquely responsible for societal male violence, especially given that male violence is precisely what trans women fear most in their lives too, just like all women.

In this book I have argued that the normalized backdrop of such high levels of male sexualized violence against women, children and marginalized men, and the socialization of women in particular to take responsibility for it, is the biggest barrier to trans inclusion. Many women have good reason to be wary of people they think are men, whether those people are men or not. From a young age girls are taught to expect and manage sexual harassment and the threat of sexual violence; written down like this that sounds extreme, but think back to when you first experienced this, or ask the women in your life when they did. For lots of women this violation begins in their early teens, walking home in their school uniforms, swimming at the local pool, sunbathing in the park. The first lessons about bodily integrity and the right to personal boundaries are learnt via them being violently breached. This is not a healthy introduction to teenage years, to personhood, to sexual identity, and it instils harmful messages about what women should put up with, look out for and guard against. It is not, in the main, because of transphobia, homophobia or conservatism that a woman may look twice at a tall broad shouldered person in the women's store, or move to the other side of the changing room when someone with short hair and a baseball hat comes in. A lifetime of socialization into hypervigilance to potential threat cannot be shed away overnight. Double glances and checking out are kneejerk responses instilled into most women from childhood. It is not nice to be on the receiving end of those stares, whispers or challenges, and I am not saying this situation is ideal, but it is necessary, if we are to move on, that we contextualize where such anxieties are coming from in the first place. The problem with being told that there's nothing to talk about here, because supposedly we are going through a gender revolution now and everything is different, is that we haven't actually had a sex revolution. By that I mean a revolution between the sexes and an end to patriarchal violence. We will not and cannot achieve a gender revolution without a sex revolution, without ending patriarchy as our form of social governance.

As such a feminist revolution is unfortunately a long way off, we have to start where we are, and work with what we have. Trans inclusion, trans rights and trans individuals themselves cannot be made to pay the price for patriarchy, nor scapegoated for male violence which affects trans women and trans men too. If we are to progress forward, we need to acknowledge the anxieties that mobilize such visceral backlash to trans inclusion, and move away from shameful trans-panic discourse that is often nothing more than a desire on the part of normative society to point and laugh at trans women in particular. If all sides are to be heard and understood, then such sex and gender conservatism must not be tolerated or condoned. How then should we edge forward? If we are to make society more inclusive for all, we need to start dismantling sex-segregation overall, starting with the places and occasions where it is easiest and safest to do so first. We have to be realistic about where and why it may not immediately feel easy and safe to do so. Public toilets and store changing rooms could be the first and easiest places for desegregation; this may entail spending money on better facilities. Public toilets and debate around them have become a cliché and almost a joke, yet at the same time, GNC and trans people have real worries about using them and face real threats from hostile challenges, from being outed, from being targeted for homophobic and transphobic violence, none of which is a joke. Public toilets are essential in public space, if those spaces are to be open to everyone, and not only to non-disabled, non-carer, non-parent, sex- and gender-normative constituents. These facilities, or lack of them, tell us who is welcome in public space and who society would rather not have to see there. A revolution in public toilet provision is well overdue and the sixth richest country in the world has no excuse not to get on with it. Accessible, spacious, private, single-occupancy, unisex cubicles with sinks, mirrors and sanitary provision, with baby changing tables, with adult changing spaces available, all located from open communal areas, would be better for everyone. These could be the main provision, alongside a minority of single-sex options for those who would prefer them. This is actually an example of intersectionality in practice; start from the perspective of those people who have the most barriers put in their way, remove the barriers, and create a more comfortable world for everyone in the process.

Trans-inclusion challenges mainstream society because it calls into question a fundamental, normalized binary that we are told is natural – and that is not any divide or separation between trans and non-trans people – it is the constructed divide between women and men. Sex-segregation serves many different purposes, depending on historical time and place, and some of those purposes are and have been compulsory heterosexuality, the control of women's bodies and sexuality, the gendering of children and the policing or exclusion of women's participation in work and public places. For the feminist women's sector and women's liberation movement, the purpose of sex-segregation was, is, and has every right still to be – to provide respite and healing from the threat and reality of sexualized male violence, to facilitate women's leadership and opportunity, to foster solidarity between women and empower consciousness raising. It was not usually a long-term aim; in many ways it was and still is a response to patriarchy. All colleagues in the women's sector providing resources after male violence look forward to their jobs never being needed again. There is nothing inherently progressive about separating women and men. In fact, the assumption that such separation is natural and necessary only fuels essentialist beliefs about the potential and place of women and men, beliefs which were constructed in the first place to hold women back. Sexist language spills from the toilet debates like an unpleasant miasma, as we are called with familiar racialized and classed tropes to protect women's decency and dignity, when a cursory look at history would tell you this was never meant for all women in the first place. Woman has always been an unreliable category, simply being sexed female at birth was never a guarantee to entry into a protectorate of men, nor should such a destination ever appeal. Whether women are put on a pedestal or a pyre, it is the same old patriarchy instructing us that women are different, special cases that require different treatment.

Trans women are women is the answer to the question, are trans women women, but it isn't the only question we need to be asking, as I hope I have demonstrated in this book. Male violence against women and children is the main, foundational reason why so many women do not want unisex spaces. Essentialism is the main, foundational reason why so many women and men want to keep spaces segregated by sex in the first place. Let us talk about this honestly. The seperate spheres approach to women's role is built on the seperate species approach, and we have to start to chip away at this. We have to take down walls between women and men, including in spaces, where and when it feels safe to do so. Let us talk honestly too about sex and gender normativity and the gendered rules for passing as a man or a woman, which we are all encouraged to comply with and punished if we do not. Let us talk about queer lives and what joy and creativity exist outside normative rules. There is so much more we could be talking openly and honestly about and learning from each other in the process. All of this starts with our children, of course; it starts with raising humane humans rather than little women and little men. I am proud to work with organisations like Let Toys Be Toys, to try to raise small ideas for change, which could flow into paradigm shifts.

While the gender wars rumble on, there is a valid feminist question coming from some women's spaces about the right to self-organization. Some such spaces do wish to run as reserved for women sexed as female from birth. Opportunity to do this, whatever people think of it, has actually been included in guidance around the Equality Act 2010 in the UK, and there has always been acknowledgement that sometimes, spaces like rape crisis counselling groups or communal women's refuges may wish to exercise a right to use proportional means to exclude trans women in pursuit of a legitimate aim, which would be providing a safe space for women harmed by sexualized male violence and including women who do not wish to share that space with trans women. How can this request be managed? Trans women too are affected by intimate partner violence, rape and sexual assault. We can all surely imagine managing to escape such a situation, in a state of crisis, and then being turned away from somewhere because we are suspected of being a threat to other survivors in that setting. Most women know what it feels like to be disbelieved, to be shamed for the choices that others made to abuse them, and it is unfortunate that including one group of women is always a conscious choice to exclude others. Many providers of refuges meanwhile, without reporting any problems, have been running as trans-inclusive for years. Scottish Women's Aid make this clear in their position paper on trans inclusion. 'We believe that women are a diverse, not homogenous, group with trans women an important part of our rich and culturally diverse society and an important part of the women's rights movement of which we are proud to be part' (SWA). Women's Aid responded to the Westminster consultation on reforms to the GRA noting that their refuges already provided services to trans women and would continue to do so. Any clarification to the exemptions that enable the exclusion of trans women must also highlight the success of women-only services which have been providing inclusive provisions for years. We all understand that some organizations will sometimes provide separate services for different groups. For example, specialist services for groups of women who face additional barriers through being subjected to racism. Specialist women's services for Black women, or for women of particular religious faiths, for example, have over four decades of expertise; the model of self-organization is long-standing and embraced. This same model could perhaps be embraced so as to include the provision of services for women sexed as female from birth, alongside inclusive services for all women. The main aim being that all women have access to refuge and rape crisis provisions in their local area, or in a more anonymous area further afield if they need that. The ability to access any such services at all is the much more pressing issue following over ten years of ideological Conservative party cuts to the state under the banner of 'austerity'.

Being able to imagine getting excluded from a service or public space, and being told that you are, by nature of a part of your identity, an innate threat or unwelcome deviant, is not an abstract thought experiment. It is an important exercise. In fact, the ability to see the world from the perspective of someone different to ourselves is an urgent and visionary skill that could help us navigate not only the gender wars but all the other such wars that unfold around us. Radical empathy and real listening may sound like something from an embarassing inspirational meme on social media, but it is not shallow or tokenistic; it is a genuine revolutionary tool. Radical empathy is the basis of what is called an intersectional lens, that is, a lens through which to study the workings of power, both within and between groups. The term was coined in 1989 by inspirational Black feminist theorist and legal scholar, the sheroic Professor Kimberlé Crenshaw. It is a term that is now common on social media and has travelled into many mainstream debates, often used in a disparaging way. Written off by the same voices that complain about 'snowflakes', 'millennials' or 'keyboard warriors', it is widely misused. The point of an intersectional lens is to understand that power is complex, all of us have power in some areas and not in others. This is because none of us are ever just one status; for example, we move through age categories which bring different rights and responsibilities with them. When you were a teenager, I expect your concerns and demands of life were different to what they are now, or, if you are a teenager reading this, I expect when you were a child your needs and concerns were different.

We are also all racialized as whatever different options our employers, state or institutions provide on tick box forms. All of us have an ethnic background, White people included, because White is also a colour, and White is also a socially constructed racial category and deeply political. It is a category forged in the violence of European colonialism and which has no meaning outside of racism and the upholding of racism. All of us have a relationship too with sexuality and sexual identities; this may change over our lifetime, and we will likely move in and out of various intimate relationships. Everyone has a sexual orientation, heterosexual people included, because heterosexual is also a socially constructed category to describe social ideas about the form and function of sexual relationships. All of us have a relationship to religions and faiths, even if this was one of secularism and the rejection of religion. We may move in or out of different religions over our lifetimes. All of us will move through illness, or caring responsibilities, we may experience chronic illness or disability and many of us become parents. My point is that it is not only those people on some equal opportunities list who have a skin colour, or a sexuality, or a religion, or a gendered and sexed identity and we need to move away from this pathologising approach. It is common to consider heterosexuality normal, to the point that many people don't even think of it as a sexual orientation. It is common to consider only heterosexuality normal, to the point that many people don't even think of it as a sexual orientation. It is common to think that only trans or transgender people have a gender, while the majority of people conduct their sexed and gendered lives without scrutiny because they are seen as normal and thus everyone else as deviant.

Every one of these different status positions brings with it occasions where doors will be opened to us, and occasions where doors will be closed to us, purely because of one or some of these features of our personhood. None of us are ever a singular category; we are intersectional, and thus the socially constructed forces around us will act on us in different ways, and in a variety of ways at various points in our lives. In turn, we will have differing resources available to us at different times to interact with those forces, shape them and carve a trail for ourselves. Misunderstanding, and myths about who deserves what, or outright disbelief about the barriers faced by others who are categorized differently to ourselves can function as roadblocks, but through radical empathy we can turn those incidences into a bridge. Starting at different standpoints we can be brought together by putting ourselves in the position of another. This is the method of revolutionary change, because we can only take apart oppressive structures in society together with and led by those who see where the cracks in those structures are, because they've had those barriers shoved up against their faces every day of their lives. Politics is about seeing, and it is about seeing the world from many different vantage points, especially from those who have a much more restricted view than us, because, in a structural sense, we are standing on their heads.

Women's Liberation is one of the oldest and most powerful revolutionary movements in the world, and it can help open our eyes in so many ways. Radical Feminism has tried, tested, failed and succeeded in many different activist tactics and methods; there is much of value there in that body of theory and activism. It has been produced by women from all backgrounds, from women with differing levels of power and privilege, who forty years ago tried to address those differences and find ways to work together. They did not solve racism, transphobia, homophobia or classism in that movement, nor has any Wave of feminism since, nor has any other social justice movement so far; because those of us in movements addressing such constructed inequalities do not live outside the society that constructed them. Acknowledging that some strands of Radical Feminism have indeed bordered on essentialist, have homogenized trans women and trans men and promoted hateful stereotypes of trans women as sexual fetishists does not have to mean that whole school of feminism is redundant or should be jettisoned. I have also pointed out that much of these particular narratives owe a lot to lesbian feminism and lesbian separatism, yet the influence of those strands is rarely identified, if it is even understood at all in the simplified offerings that restrict these debates. As I have discussed in this book, there is not one story about Radical Feminism, much as some may wish this was the case. The very fact that the misused and overapplied term TERF exists in the first place is to distinguish between Radical Feminists who organized as trans-inclusive and those who did not.

The current so-called gender wars should therefore no longer be reduced to a battle between trans women and Radical Feminists. In fact, if Radical Feminists were all that trans men, trans women and transgender people had to worry about, then their worries would be greatly decreased. Radical Feminists are not in high political office; they are not the chairmen of insurance firms or health boards. Transphobia is unfortunately widespread, and it is hardly the preserve of Radical Feminism alone. The most transphobic voices, laws and policies are coming from sex and gender conservatives, most of whom are not feminist at all, let alone from any one particular school of feminism. Unless someone takes on the label of TERF for themselves, as an accurate descriptor of their feminist and trans-exclusive politics, we should stop using it. It is a reductive term, and it detracts from what is actually going on: the growth of illiberal populism (Graff & Korolczuk, 2018). While feminists aren't in charge of the world, increasingly, violently racist illiberal sex and gender conservatives are. They are unfortunately the heads of policy think tanks; they are funders of political candidates; they are the ones making decisions about healthcare, adoption, youth counselling, same-sex marriage, medical insurance, identity documentation, child custody, migrant rights, divorce law, reproductive rights, school curricula on sexuality, abortion provisions and much more. From my Western standpoint, I see such forces on the rise in North America and across much of Europe. Theirs is a nightmarish vision of patriarchal masculinity taken to its brutal, logical conclusion. If they win, it will not be a win for any women, or any minorities. They must not succeed.

This is the struggle we should all unite to face; and we have to do that together, facing each other, facing our received prejudices about one another and seeing each other as allies in a political dream much bigger than ourselves. A new generation is looking on at identity categories that were previously seen as fixed, and this new cohort of young people instead sees fluidity, flux, creativity and self-determination. This change is happening, and it will not go backwards. There is much positivity and potential here. This open-minded, critical thinking is to be welcomed. It is not only revolutionary considering how our restrictive education system taught young people to be, but it is also often in active and engaged opposition to it. This change, especially among younger generations, is rising against what our old system told young people they could be, do and were capable of. Feminists should welcome this, because feminism has always deconstructed labels put onto us, the labels of woman and man. In response, we said that we were always more complex than what you told us. We will be yet more complex still, in a changed world that we probably cannot imagine, but which is coming. The question has never been whether or not biology is real, because of course it is; the question is what does it mean, where does it matter and what should it mean in the future.

References

Allan, Jonathan A. Haywood, Chris & Karioris, Frank G. (2020) 'Introduction'. *Journal of Bodies, Sexualities and Masculinities*. Vol. 1 (March), pp. 6–17.

Allen, Sophie, Jones, Jane-Clare, Lawford-Smith, Holly, Leng, Mary, Reilly-Cooper, Rebecca & Stock, Kathleen (2019) 'Doing Better in Arguments about Sex, Gender and Trans Rights'. Medium. 23 May. Available at: https://medium.com/@kathleenstock/doing-better-in-arguments-about-sex-and-gender-3bec3fc4bdb6 [Accessed 11 August 2019].

Alpert, Jane (1973) 'Mother Right: A New Feminist Theory'. *Ms.* August.

Amadiume, Ifi (1987) *Male Daughters, Female Husbands: Gender and Sex in an African Society*. London: Zed Books.

'Andy' (ND) FTM Passing Guides. Available at: Geocitiesftmpass

Anick (2020) 'Caster Semenya Is a Woman Born with Natural Advantages – The World Cannot Be Allowed to Police Her Body'. *Attitude*. 9 September. Available at: https://www.attitude.co.uk/article/caster-semenya-is-a-woman-born-with-natural-advantages-the-world-cannot-be-allowed-to-police-her-body/23689/ [Accessed 15 September 2020].

Anzaldua, Gloria (1987) *Borderlands/La Frontera: The New Mestiza*. San Francisco: Aunt Lute Books.

Atkinson, Ti-Grace [1969] (2000) 'Radical Feminism'. In Barbara A. Crow (ed.), *Radical Feminism: A Documentary Reader*. New York: New York University Press, pp. 82–90.

Awkward-Rich, Cameron (2017) 'Trans, Feminism: Or, Reading like a Depressed Transsexual'. *Signs: Journal of Women in Culture and Society*. Vol. 42(4), pp. 819–41.

Barker, Joanne (ed.) (2009) *Critically Sovereign: Indigenous Gender, Sexuality, and Feminist Studies*. Durham: Duke University Press.

Barter, Christine, McCarry, Melanie, Berridge, D. & Evans, K. (2009) 'Partner Violence and Exploitation in Teenage Intimate Partner Relationships'. London: NSPCC.

Baumgardner & Richards (2000) *Manifesta*. New York: Farrar, Straus and Giroux.

Beemyn, Genny & Eliason, Mickey (2016) 'The Intersections of Trans Women and Lesbian Identities, Communities, and Movements' an Introduction'. *Journal of Lesbian Studies*. Vol. 20(1), pp. 1–7.

Bell, Diane & Klein, Renate (eds) (1996) *Radically Speaking: Feminism Reclaimed*. Melbourne, Victoria: Spinifex.

Bender-Baird, Kyla (2016) 'Peeing Under Surveillance: Bathrooms, Gender Policing, and Hate Violence'. *Gender, Place & Culture*. Vol. 23(7), pp. 983–8.

Bergdorf, Munroe (2017) 'Why I Talk About Being Raped'. BBC3. Health and Wellbeing. Available at: https://www.bbc.co.uk/bbcthree/article/a60e4103-97ab-4926-8022-7055df4d52de

Berger, John (1972) *Ways of Seeing*. London: Penguin.

Bergman, Bear S. (2006) *Butch Is a Noun*. Vancouver, CA: Arsenal Pulp Press.

Bettcher, Talia Mae (2016) 'Intersexuality, Transgender and Transsexuality'. In Disch Lisa & Hawkesworth Mary (eds), *The Oxford Handbook of Feminist Theory*. Oxford: Oxford University Press, pp. 407–28.

Blackwood, Evelyn (2012) 'From Butch-Femme to Female Masculinities: Elizabeth Kennedy and LGBT Anthropology'. *Feminist Formations*. Vol. 24(3), pp. 92–100.

Blackwood, Evelyn & Johnson, Mark (2012) 'Queer Asian Subjects: Transgressive Sexualities and Heteronormative Meanings'. *Asian Studies Review*. Vol. 36(4), pp. 441–51.

Bly, Robert (1990) *Iron John*. London: Rider Books.

Boellstorff, T., Cabral, M. & Cardenas, M. (2014) 'Decolonizing Transgender: A Roundtable Discussion'. *TSQ: Transgender Studies Quarterly*. Vol. 1(3), pp. 419–39.

Bogus, Diane A. (1994) 'The Myth and Tradition of the Black Bulldagger'. In Lily Burana, Linnea Due & Roxxie (eds), *Dagger: On Butch Women*. San Francisco: Cleiss Press.

Bornstein, Kate (1994) *Gender Outlaw: On Men, Women and the Rest of Us*. New York: Routledge.

Bowen, Gary (1998) 'An Entire Rainbow of Possibilities'. In Leslie Feinberg, *Trans Liberation: Beyond Pink or Blue*. Boston: Beacon Press, pp. 63–6.

Bragg, Sara, Renold, Emma, Ringrose, Jessica & Jackson, Carolyn (2018) 'More than Boy, Girl, Male Female': Exploring Young People's Views on Gender Diversity Within and Beyond School Contexts'. *Sex Education*. DOI: 10.1080/14681811.2018.1439373

Braidwood, Ella (2019) 'Trans Campaigner Sarah McBride Harassed by Anti-trans Feminists on Video'. *Pink News*. 31 January. Available at: https://www.pinknews.co.uk/2019/01/31/trans-sarah-mcbride-hrc-posie-parker/ [Accessed 5 January 2019].

British Library, LGBTQ Histories. Available at: https://www.bl.uk/lgbtq-histories.

Brodell, Ria (2018) *Butch Heroes*. Cambridge, MA: MIT Press.

Brown Boi Project. http://www.brownboiproject.org/.

Brown, Jan (1992) 'Sex, Lies, and Penetration: A Butch Finally "Fesses Up"'. In Joan Nestle (ed.), *The Persistent Desire: A Femme-Butch Reader*. Boston, MA: Alyson Publications Inc., pp. 410–15.

Browne, Kath & Ferreira, Eduarda (2015) *Lesbian Geographies: Gender, Place and Power*. Farnham: Ashgate.

Browne, Kath (2004) 'Genderism and the Bathroom Problem: (Re)Materialising Sexed Sites, (Re)Creating Sexed Bodies'. *Gender, Place & Culture*. Vol. 11(3), pp. 331–46.

Browne, Kath (2009) 'Womyn's Separatist Spaces: Rethinking Spaces of Difference and Exclusion'. *Transactions: Institute of British Geographers*, NS 34, pp. 541–56.

Browne, Kath (2010) 'Lesbian Separatist Feminism at Michigan Womyn's Music Festival'. *Feminism & Psychology*. Vol. 21(2), pp. 248–56.

Browne, Kath (2011) 'Beyond Rural Idylls: Imperfect Lesbian Utopias at Michigan Womyn's Music Festival'. *Journal of Rural Studies*. Vol. 27, pp. 13–23.

Brownworth, Victoria A. (2011) 'No Butches, No Femmes: The Mainstreaming of Queer Sexuality'. In Ivan E. Coyote & Zena Sharman (eds), *Persistence: All Ways Butch and Femme*. Vancouver: Arsenal Pulp Press, pp. 137–48.

Brusman, Liza (2019) 'Sex Isn't Binary, And We Should Stop Acting Like It Is'. *The Wire*. 25 June. Available at: https://thewire.in/the-sciences/sex-binary-science-spectrum [Accessed 17 August 2019].

Burana Lily, Due, Linnea & Roxxie (eds) (1994) *Dagger: On Butch Women*. San Francisco: Cleiss Press.

Burkholder, Nancy (2013) Interviewed by Cristan Williams. Michigan Womyn's Music Festival. *TransAdvocate*. Available at: https://www.transadvocate.com/michigan-womyns-music-festival_n_8943.htm

Burns, Christine (2018) *Trans Britain*. London: Unbound.

Burns, Katelyn (2019) 'The Rise of Anti-trans 'Radical' Feminists, Explained'. *Vox*. 5 September. Available at: https://www.vox.com/identities/2019/9/5/20840101/terfs -radical-feminists-gender-critical [Accessed 6 September 2019].

Burris, Barbara (1973) In Agreement with Barry Kathy, Parrent Joanne, Moore Terry, DeLor Joanne & Stadelman Cate. 'The Fourth World Manifesto'. In Koedt Anne, Levine Ellen & Rapone Anita (eds), *Radical Feminism*. New York: Quadrangle, pp. 322–57.

Burt, Callie H. (2020) 'Scrutinising Scrutinizing the U.S. Equality Act 2019: A Feminist Examination of Definitional Changes and Sociolegal Ramifications'. *Feminist Criminology*. (June). pp. 1–47. DOI: 10.1177/1557085120918667

Butler, Judith (1990) *Gender Trouble*. London: Routledge.

Butler, Judith (1992) Interviewed by Kotz, Liz 'The Body You Want'. *Artforum*, pp. 82–9.

Butler, Judith (1993) *Bodies That Matter*. London: Routledge.

Butler, Judith (1995) 'Melancholy Gender/Refused Identification'. In Maurice Berger, Brian Wallis & Simon Watson (eds), *Constructing Masculinity*. New York: Routledge, pp. 21–37.

Califia, Patrick (1997) *Sex Changes: The Politics of Transgenderism*. San Francisco: Cleiss Press.

Cameron, Deborah (2007) *The Myth of Mars and Venus*. Oxford: Oxford University Press.

Camp Trans (2000) camptrans.com. Personal archives

Carlson, Asa (2010) 'Gender and Sex: What Are They? Sally Haslanger's Debunking Social Constructivism'. *Distinktion: Scandinavian Journal of Social Theory*. Vol. 11(1), pp. 61–72.

Carrigan, Tim., Connell, R. W., & Lee, John. (1985). 'Toward a New Sociology of Masculinity'. *Theory and Society*. Vol. 14(5), pp. 551–604.

Case, Sue-Ellen (1989) 'Towards a Butch-Femme Aesthetic'. *Discourse*. Vol. 11(1), pp. 55–73.

Cheng, C. (1999) 'Marginalised Masculinities and Hegemonic Masculinity: An Introduction'. *Journal of Men's Studies*. Vol. 7, pp. 295–315.

Choma, Anne (2019) *Gentleman Jack*. London: BBC Books.

Chu, Andrea Long. (2018) 'My New Vagina Won't Make Me Happy'. *New York Times*. 24 November. Available at: https://www.nytimes.com/2018/11/24/opinion/sunday/ vaginoplasty-transgender-medicine.html [Accessed 20 January 2019].

Cockburn, Cynthia (1983) *Brothers*. London: Pluto Press.

Cole, B. (2011) 'Masculine of Centre, Seeks Her Refined Femme'. In Ivan E. Coyote & Zena Sharman (eds), *Persistence: All Ways Butch and Femme*. Vancouver: Arsenal Pulp Press, pp. 127–37.

Combahee River Collective (1977) Combahee River Collective Statement. Black Feminist Organising in the Seventies and Eighties. Kitchen Table Press. Available at: https:// americanstudies.yale.edu/sites/default/files/files/Keyword%20Coalition_Readings.pdf

Connell, R. W. (1983). *Which Way Is Up? Essays On Class, Sex and Culture*. Sydney: Alien & Unwin.

Connell, R. W. (1987) *Gender and Power*. Stanford: Stanford University Press.

Connell, R. W. (1995) *Masculinities*. California: University of California Press.

Connell, R. W. (2000) *The Men and The Boys*. Queensland: Allen and Unwin.

Connell, R. W. and Messerschmidt, James W. (2005) 'Hegemonic Masculinity: Rethinking the Concept'. *Gender & Society*. Vol. 19(6), pp. 829–59.

Cordova, Jeanne (1992) 'Butches, Lies, and Feminism'. In Joan Nestle (ed.), *The Persistent Desire: A Femme-Butch Reader*. Boston, MA: Alyson Publications Inc., pp. 272–92.

Cordova, Jeanne (2000) 'Radical Feminism? Dyke Separatism?' in Barbara A. Crow (ed.), *Radical Feminism A Documentary Reader*, pp. 358–64. New York University Press

Cornwall, Andrea & Lindisfarne, Nancy (1993) *Dislocating Masculinity*. London: Routledge.

Correa, Sonia (2017) 'Gender Ideology: Tracking Its Origins and Meanings in Current Gender Politics'. *LSE Blogs*.

Correa, Sonia, Paternotte, David & Kuhar, Roman (2018) 'The Globalisation of Anti-gender Campaigns'. *International Politics and Society*. May. Online.

Coveney, Lal (1979) 'Transexuals in the Women's Liberation Movement'. Rad/Rev conference papers. Leeds, Yorkshire, September. Available in The Feminist Archive South http://feministarchivesouth.org.uk/

Coyote, Ivan E. & Sharman, Zena (eds) (2011) *Persistence: All Ways Butch and Femme*. Vancouver: Arsenal Pulp Press.

Crawley, Sara (2001) 'Are Butch and Fem Working-Class and Antifeminist?'. *Gender & Society*. Vol. 15(2), pp. 175–96.

Crawley, Sara L. (2008) 'The Clothes Make the Trans: Region and Geography in Experiences of the Body'. *Journal of Lesbian Studies*. Vol. 12(4), pp. 365–79.

Crawley, Sara L. & Willman, Rebecca K. (2017) 'Heteronormativity Made Me Lesbian: Femme, Butch and the Production of Sexual Embodiment Projects'. *Sexualities*. 0(0), pp. 1–18.

Crenshaw, Kimberlé (1989) 'Demarginalizing the Intersection of Race and Sex: A Black Feminist Critique of Antidiscrimination Doctrine, Feminist Theory and Antiracist Politics'. *University of Chicago Legal Forum*. Vol. 1989(1), Article 8. Available at: http://chicagounbound.uchicago.edu/uclf/vol1989/iss1/8

Croson, Rachel (2001) 'Sex, Lies and Feminism'. *Off Our Backs*, June, pp. 6–9.

Crowder, Diane Griffin (1998) 'Lesbians and the (Re/De)Construction of the Female Body'. In Dawn Atkins (ed.), *Looking Queer: Body Image and Identity in Lesbian, Bisexual, Gay and Transgender Communities*. London: Routledge, pp. 47–68.

Dahl, Ulrika (2008) *Femmes of Power: Exploding Queer Femininities*. London: Serpent's Tail.

Daly, Mary (1973) *Beyond God the Father*. Boston: Beacon Press.

Darwin, Helana (2020) 'Challenging the Cisgender/Transgender Binary: Nonbinary People and the Transgender Label'. *Gender & Society*. Vol. 34(3), pp. 357–80.

Deerinwater, Jen (2017) 'Berdache, Two Spirit and the White Anthropologist'. *Medium*. October. Available at: https://medium.com/@JenDeerinwater/berdache-two-spirit-and -the-white-anthropologist-51edea0871bf [Accessed 8 February 2019].

Dekker, Rudolf M. & De Pol, Van Lotte C. (1997) *The Tradition of Female Transvestism in Early Modern Europe*. London: MacMillan Press.

Delphy, Christine (1984) *Close to Home: A Materialist Analysis of Women's Oppression*. London: Verso.

Delphy, Christine (1993) 'Rethinking Sex and Gender'. *Women's Studies International Forum*. Vol. 16(1), pp. 1–9.

Dennis, Riley J. (2016) 'Science Doesn't Support the Sex Binary. Psst: Not Everyone Is Male or Fmeale'. *Everyday Feminism*. 5 June. Available at: https://everydayfeminism .com/2016/06/science-doesnt-support-sex-binary/

Devor, Aaron (1989) *Gender Blending*. Indiana: Indiana University Press.

Devor, Aaron (1997) *FTM Female to Male Transexuals in Society*. Indiana University Press.

Ditum, Sarah (2018a) 'Trans Rights Should Not Come at the Cost of Women's Fragile Gains'. *The Economist*. 5 July. Available at: https://www.economist.com/open-future /2018/07/05/trans-rights-should-not-come-at-the-cost-of-womens-fragile-gains

Ditum, Sarah (2018b) 'Six Years in the Gender Wars'. 10 September. Available at: https://sarahditum.com/2018/09/10/six-years-in-the-gender-wars/

Ditum, Sarah (2018c) 'Why Were Lesbians Protesting at Pride? Because the LGBT Coalition Leaves Women Behind'. *New Statesman*. 11 July 2018. Available at: https://www.newstatesman.com/politics/feminism/2018/07/why-were-lesbians-protesting-pride-because-lgbt-coalition-leaves-women [Accessed 15 July 2018].

Duffy, Maureen [1966] (1990) *The Microcosm*. London: Penguin Books.

Dworkin, Andrea (1974) *Woman Hating*. New York: Plume.

Echols, Alice (1989) *Daring to Be Bad: Radical Feminism in America 1967 – 1975*. Minneapolis: University of Minnesota Press.

Egerton, Jayne (2020) 'There's more Than One Way to "Erase" Women – Women's Rights Under Attack in Victor Orban's Hungary'. Woman's Place UK. June. https://womansplaceuk.org/2020/06/18/womens-rights-under-attack-hungary/

Elliot, Lise (2012) *Pink Brain Blue Brain: How Small Differences Grow into Troublesome Gaps And What We Can Do About It*. London: Oneworld Publications.

Elliot, Patricia (2004) 'Who Gets to Be a Woman? Feminist Politics and the Question of Trans-inclusion'. *Atlantis*. Vol. 29(1), pp. 13–20.

Enke, Finn (2018) 'Collective Memory and the Transfeminist 1970s: Toward a Less Plausible History'. *Transgender Studies Quarterly TSQ*. Vol. 5(1), pp. 9–29.

Equality Act 2010 Statutory Code of Practice: Services, public functions and associations (2011).

Esterberg, Kristin (1996) 'A Certain Swagger When I Walk: Performing Lesbian Identity'. In Steven Seidman (ed.), *Queer Theory/Sociology*. London: Blackwell, pp. 259–79.

Eves, Alison (2004) 'Queer Theory, Butch/Femme Identities and Lesbian Space'. *Sexualities*. Vol 7(4), pp. 480–96.

Faderman, Lillian (1981) *Surpassing the Love of Men: Romantic Friendship and Love Between Women from the Renaissance to the Present*. London: Junction Books.

Faderman, Lillian (1991) *Odd Girls and Twilight Lovers: A History of Lesbian Life in Twentieth-Century America*. Columbia, NY: Columbia University Press.

Fausto-Sterling, Anne (2000) 'The Five Sexes Revisited'. *The Sciences*. (July/August), pp. 19–23.

Fausto-Sterling, Anne (2000) *Sexing The Body: Gender Politics and the Construction of Sexuality*. New York: Basic Books.

Fausto-Sterling, Anne (2018) 'Why Sex Is Not Binary'. *The New York Times*. 25 October.

Fausto-Sterling, Anne (2019) 'Gender/Sex, Sexual Orientation and Identity Are In the Body: How Did They Get There?'. *The Journal of Sex Research*. Vol. 56(4–5), pp. 529–55. DOI: 10.1080/00224499.2019.1581883

Feinberg, Leslie (1993) *Stone Butch Blues*. New York: Firebrand Books.

Feinberg, Leslie (1996) *Transgender Warriors*. Boston, MA: Beacon Press.

Feinberg, Leslie (1998) *Trans Liberation: Beyond Pink or Blue*. Boston: Beacon Press.

Fertig, Ruth (Dir.) (2009) *Two Spirits*. Film release 2009. www.twospirits.org

Ffiske, Caroline (2020) 'Women-Only Toilets – There Should Be a Law'. The Article. 4 March. Available at: https://www.thearticle.com/women-only-toilets-there-should-be-a-law

Fine, Cordelia (2012) *Delusions of Gender*. New York: W.W. Norton.

Fine, Cordelia (2017) *Testosterone Rex: Unmaking the Myths of Our Gendered Minds*. London: Icon Books.

Finlayson, Lorna., Jenkins, Katherine & Worsdale, Rosie (2018). '"I'm Not Transphobic, but . . .": A Feminist Case Against the Feminist Case Against Trans Inclusivity'. Verso Books. Available at: https://www.versobooks.com/blogs/4090-i-m-not-transphobic-but-a-feminist-case-against-the-feminist-case-against-trans-inclusivity.

Finley, Chris, Gilley Brian, Joseph and Morgensen Scott L (eds). (2011) *Introduction to Queer Indigenous Studies: Critical Interventions in Theory, Politics, and Literature.* Tucson: University of Arizona Press.

Firestone, Shulamith [1970] (1993) *The Dialectic of Sex: The Case for Feminist Revolution.* New York: Quill.

Fleming, Anne (2011) 'A Dad Called Mum'. In Ivan E. Coyote & Zena Sharman (eds), *Persistence: All Ways Butch and Femme.* Vancouver: Arsenal Pulp Press, pp. 43–52.

Flood, Michael (2019) *Engaging Men and Boys in Violence Prevention.* London: Palgrave.

Forstater, Maya (2019) 'Claimant's Witness Statement'. Medium. 22 November. Available at: https://medium.com/@MForstater/claimants-witness-statement-abe3e8073b41 [Accessed 22 November 2019].

Frosh, S., Phoenix, A. & Pattman, R. (2002). *Young Masculinities*, Basingstoke: Palgrave.

Gardiner, Jill (2003) *From the Closet to the Screen.* London: Rivers Oram Press.

Gardiner, Judith Keegan (ed.) (2002) *Masculinity Studies and Feminist Theory.* Columbia: Columbia University Press.

Garrido, Anahi Russo (2020) *Tortilleras Negotiating Intimacy.* Rutgers: Rutgers University Press.

Genderquake (2018) Chanel 4. https://www.channel4.com/programmes/genderquake

Ghaziani, Amin (2014) *There Goes the Gayborhood.* Princeton: Princeton University Press.

Gibson, Michelle & Meem, Deborah T. (eds) (2002) *Femme/Butch: New Considerations of the Way We Want to Go.* London: Harrington Park Press.

Gill, R., Henwood, K. & McLean, C. (2000) 'The Tyranny of the Sixpack: Men Talk About Idealised Images of the Male Body in Popular Culture'. In C. Squire (ed.), *Culture in Psychology.* London: Routledge.

Gottzen, Lucas & Straube, Wibke (2016) 'Trans Masculinities'. *NORMA.* Vol. 11(4), pp. 217–24.

Government Equalities Office (GEO) (2018) National LGBT Survey. July. Available at: https://assets.publishing.service.gov.uk/government/uploads/system/uploads/attachment_data/file/722314/GEO-LGBT-Survey-Report.pdf [Accessed 12 August 2018].

Graff, Agnieska & Korolczuk, Elzbieta (2017) 'Worse than Communism and Nazism Put Together: War on Gender in Poland'. In Roman Kuhar & David Paternotte (eds), *Anti-Gender Campaigns in Europe Mobilizing Against Equality.* London: Rowan and Littlefield.

Graff, Agnieszka & Korolczuk, Elzbieta (2018a) Interviewed by Karlberg Eva 'Is It the Swan Song of Patriarchy or the Beginning of a New Ice Age?'. *Baltic Worlds.* 7 March. Available at: http://balticworlds.com/is-it-the-swan-song-of-patriarchy-or-the-beginning-of-a-new-ice-age/

Graff, Agnieszka & Korolczuk, Elzbieta (2018b) 'Gender as "Ebola from Brussels": The Anti-colonial Frame and the Rise of Illiberal Populism'. *Signs: Journal of Women in Culture and Society.* Vol. 43(4), pp. 797–821.

Green, Jamison (2005) 'Part of the Package: Ideas of Masculinity among Male-Identified Transpeople'. *Men and Masculinities.* Vol. 7(3), pp. 291–9.

Grogan, S. (1999) *Body Image: Understanding Body Dissatisfaction in Men, Women and Children.* London: Routledge

Grosz, Elizabeth (1994) *Volatile Bodies.* Indiana: Indiana University Press.

Grzebalska, Weronika (2016) 'Why the War on "Gender Ideology" Matters — And Not JUST to Feminists. Anti-genderism and the Crisis of Neoliberal Democracy'. *Visegrad*

Insight. http://visegradinsight.eu/why-the-war-on-gender-ideology-matters-and-not-just-to-feminists/

Halberstam, Jack (1998a) *Female Masculinity*. Durham, NC: Duke University Press.

Halberstam, Jack (1998b) 'Transgender Butch: Butch/FTM Border Wars and the Masculine Continuum'. *GLQ: A Journal of Lesbian and Gay Studies*. Vol. 4(2), pp. 287–310.

Halberstam, Jack (2000) 'Telling Tales: Brandon Teena, Billy Tipton, and Transgender Biography'. *a/b Auto/Biography Studies*. Vol. 15(1), pp. 62–81.

Halberstam, Judith-Jack (2011) 'The Drag of Masculinity: An Interview with Judith Jack Halberstam by Jeffrey J Wiliams'. *Symploke*. Vol. 19(1–2), pp. 361–80

Halberstam, Jack (2015) 'From Sister George to Lonesome George? Or, Is The Butch Back?'. Bully Bloggers. 16 July. Available at: https://bullybloggers.wordpress.com/2015/07/16/from-sister-george-to-lonesome-george-or-is-the-butch-back/

Halberstam, Jack (2018) *Trans: A Quick and Quirky Account of Gender Variability*. California: University of California Press.

Hale, Jacob C. (1998) 'Consuming the Living, Dis(re)membering the Dead in the Butch/FTM Borderlands'. *GLQ: A Journal of Lesbian and Gay Studies*. Vol. 4(2), pp. 311–48.

Hamer, Emily (1995) *Brittania's Glory*. London: Continuum

Hammer, Allison K. (2019) '"Just Like a Natural Man": The BD Styles of Gertrude "Ma" Rainey and Bessie Smith'. *Journal of Lesbian Studies*. Vol. 23(2), pp. 279–93.

Hands Across the Aisle (2018) 'Mother Interrogated by the Police for Gender-Critical Tweets'. *Hands Across the Aisle News*. 14th March. Available at: https://handsacrosstheaislewomen.com/2018/03/14/mother-interrogated-by-the-police-for-gender-critical-tweets/

Hankin, Kelly (2002) *The Girls in the Back Room: Looking at the Lesbian Bar*. Minneapolis: University of Minnesota Press.

Hanmer, Jalna & Maynard, Mary (1987) *Women, Violence and Social Control: Explorations in Sociology*. London: Prometheus Books.

Hardy, Frances (2018) 'The Battle of Hampstead Ponds: Meet the Women Who Are Willing to Don Mankinis and Fake Beards to Protest Against Rules That Let Men Say They're Female and Use the Ladie's Changing Rooms'. *The Daily Mail*. 1 June. Available at: https://www.dailymail.co.uk/news/article-5796701/Hampstead-ponds-row-continues-transgender-demands-going-far.html

Hasenbush, Amira, Flores, Andrew R. & Herman, Jody L. (2019) 'Gender Identity Nondiscrimination Laws in Public Accommodations: A Review of Evidence Regarding Safety and Privacy in Public Restrooms, Locker Rooms and Changing Rooms'. *Sexuality Research and Social Policy*. Vol. 16, pp. 70–83.

Haslanger, Sally (2000) 'Gender and Race: (What) Are They? (What) Do We Want Them to Be?' *Nouis*. Vol. 34(r), pp. 31–55.

Hearn, Jeff (1998) *The Violences of Men*. London: Sage

Hearn, Jeff (2004) 'From Hegemonic Masculinity to the Hegemony of Men'. *Feminist Theory*. Vol. 5(1), pp. 49–72.

Heyes, Cressida J. & Latham, J. R. (2018) 'Trans Surgeries and Cosmetic Surgeries'. *TSQ Transgender Studies Quarterly*. Vol. 5(2), pp. 174–89.

Hiestand, Katherine R. & Levitt, Heidi (2005) 'Butch Identity Development: The Formation of an Authentic Gender'. *Feminism & Psychology*. Vol. 15(1), pp. 61–85.

Hill-Collins, Patricia (2000) *Black Feminist Thought*. Second edition. Routledge: London.

Hines, Sally (2017) 'The Feminist Frontier: On Trans and Feminism'. *Journal of Gender Studies.* DOI: 10.1080/09589236.2017.1411791

Hines, Sally (2019) 'On the Feminist Frontier – On Trans and Feminism'. In Tasha Oren & Andrea Press (eds), *The Routledge Handbook of Contemporary Feminism.* London: Routledge.

Hines, Sally (2020) 'Sex Wars and (Trans) Gender Panics: Identity and Body Politics in Contemporary UK Feminism'. *Sociological Review.* Vol. 68(4), pp. 699–717.

Holtz, Nairne (2011) 'Slide Rules'. In Ivan E. Coyote and Zena Sharman (eds), *Persistence: All Ways Butch and Femme.* Vancouver: Arsenal Pulp Press, pp. 113–18.

Hooks, bell (2004) *The Will to Change.* London: Simon & Schuster.

Hu, Yu-Ying (2019) 'Mainstreaming Female Masculinity, Signifying Lesbian Visibility: The Rise of the *Zhongxing* Phenomenon in Transnational Taiwan'. *Sexualities.* Vol. 22(1–2), pp. 182–202.

Innes, Robert Alexander, & Kim, Anderson (eds) (2015) *Indigenous Men and Masculinities: Legacies, Identities, Regeneration.* Winnipeg: University of Manitoba Press.

Innovation Group (2016) *Generation Z and Gender.* JWT Intelligence. www.jwt intelligence.com

Irving, Dan (2019) 'Trans/gender'. In Deborah Brock (eds), *Power and Everyday Practices,* Second Edition. Toronto: University of Toronto Press, pp. 101–25.

Jacques, Juliet (2020) 'Transphobia Is Everywhere in Britain'. *The New York Times.* 10 March.

Jeffreys, Sheila (2005) *Beauty and Misogyny.* London: Routledge.

Jeffreys, Sheila (2006) Andrea Dworkin Memorial Conference. 7 April. Oxford. Speeches available at: https://feminist-reprise.org/category/andrea-dworkin-commemorative -conference/

Jeffreys, Sheila (2014a) *Gender Hurts.* London: Routledge.

Jeffreys, Sheila (2014b) 'The Politics of the Toilet: A Feminist Response to the Campaign to 'Degender' a Women's Space'. *Women's Studies International Forum.* Vol. 45, pp. 42–51.

Jeffreys, Sheila (2018) *Lesbian Revolution.* London: Routledge.

Jeffreys, Sheila (1994) 'The Queer Disappearance of Lesbians: Sexuality in the Academy'. *Women's Studies International Forum.* Vol. 17(5), pp. 459–72.

Jeffreys, Sheila (2003) *Unpacking Queer Politics: A Lesbian Feminist Perspective.* London: Polity Press.

Jennings, Rebecca (2007) *Tomboys and Bachelor Girls.* Manchester: Manchester University Press

John, Tara (2020) The Quest for Trans Rights Has Exposed a Deep Divide in the UK. CNN. Available at: https://edition.cnn.com/2020/04/04/uk/trans-rights-reforms -scotland-gbr-intl/index.html

Jones, Aphrodite (1996) *All She Wanted.* London: Simon & Shchuster.

Jones, Jane Clare (2019) 'The Radical Notion That Women Are People'. Jane Clare Jones blog. 1 September. Available at: https://janeclarejones.com/2019/09/01/the-radical -notion-that-women-are-people/

Kanner, Melinda (2002) 'Towards a Semiotics of Butch'. *The Gay and Lesbian Review Worldwide.* Vol. 9(2), pp. 27–8.

Kaplan, R. D. (1996). 'Sex, Lies and Heteropatriarchy: The S/M Debate at the Michigan Womyn's Music Festival'. In P. Califia & R. Sweeney (eds), *The Second Coming: A Leatherdyke Reader.* Los Angeles, CA: Alyson Publications, pp. 123–30.

Karkazis, Katrina & Jordon-Young, Rebecca (2019) *Testosterone: An Unauthorized Biography*. Harvard: Harvard University Press.

Kaveney, Roz (2011) 'When a Writer's Words Have Unintended Consequences'. *The Guardian*. Comment is Free. 6 August. https://www.theguardian.com/commentisfree/belief/2011/aug/06/anders-behring-breivik-melanie-phillips

Kennedy, Elizabeth Lapovsky & Davis, Madeline D. (1993) *Boots of Leather, Slippers of Gold: The History of a Lesbian Community*. London: Penguin.

Kessler, Susanne (1998) *Lessons from the Intersexed*. New Brunswick: Rutgers University Press.

Kessler, Susanne J. and McKenna, Wendy (1978) *Gender: An Ethnomethodological Approach*. Chicago: University of Chicago Press.

Kilgannon, Meg (2017) 'Transgender Ideology in Public Schools: Parents and Educators Fight Back'. FRC Speaker Series. https://www.frc.org/events/transgender-ideology-in-public-schools-parents-fight-back

Kinchen, Rosie (2018) 'Thank God They Didn't Make This Tomboy Trans; The Psychotherapist Stella O'Malley Was Sure She Had Been Born in the Wrong Sex – Until She Hit 16. She Argues We Must Give Children Time to Decide'. *The Sunday Times*. 18 November.

King Daniel et al. (2020) Professor Daniel King, Professor Carrie Paechter and Dr Maranda Ridgway Reflect on Their Work as Analyst Team for the Gender Recognition Act consultation. NTU. https://www.ntu.ac.uk/about-us/news/news-articles/2020/09/expert-blog-analysing-the-gra-consultation-reflections-by-the-analysis-team

Kiss, Charlie (2018) 'The Idea That Trans Men Are "Lesbians in Denial" Is Demeaning and Wrong'. *The Economist*. 3 July. Available at: https://www.economist.com/open-future/2018/07/03/the-idea-that-trans-men-are-lesbians-in-denial-is-demeaning-and-wrong [Accessed 4 July 2018].

Knight, Marian, Bunch, Kathryn, Tuffnell, Derek, Jayakody, Hemali, Shakespeare, Judy, Kotnis, Rohit, Kenyon, Sara & Kurinczuk, Jennifer J. (eds) (2018) 'Saving Lives, Improving Mothers' Care: Lessons Learned to Inform Maternity Care from the UK and Ireland Confidential Enquiries into Maternal Deaths and Morbidity 2014–2016'. Embrace UK.

Koedt, Anne, Levine, Ellen & Rapone, Anita (1973) *Radical Feminism*. New York: Quadrangle.

Koyama, Emi (2003) 'Introduction to Intersex Activism'. Portland, OR: Intersex Initiative Portland. Available at: http://www.intersexinitiative.org/publications/pdf/intersex-activism2.pdf.

Koyama, Emi (2006) 'Whose Feminism Is It Anyway? The Unspoken Racism of the Trans Inclusion Debate'. In Susan Stryker & Stephen Whittle (eds), *The Transgender Studies Reader*. New York: Routledge, pp. 698–706.

Kuhar, Roman & Patternotte, David (eds) (2017) *Anti-Gender Campaigns in Europe Mobilizing Against Equality*. London: Rowan and Littlefield

Lane-Steele, Laura (2011) 'Studs and Protest-Hypermasculinity: The Tomboyism within Black Lesbian Female Masculinity'. *Journal of Lesbian Studies*. Vol. 15(4), pp. 480–92.

Lavizzari, Anna & Prearo, Massimo (2019) 'The Anti-gender Movement in Italy: Catholic Participation Between Electoral and Protest Politics'. *European Societies*. Vol. 21(3), pp. 422–42.

Lee, Tracey (2001) 'Trans(re)lations: Lesbian and Female to Male Transexual Accounts of Identity'. *Women's Studies International Forum*. Vol. 24(3–4), pp. 347–57.

Leek, Cliff, and Markus Gerke. (2017). 'Invisible and Unexamined: The State of Whiteness in Men's Studies Journals'. *International Journal of Gender Studies*. Vol. 6(11), pp. 29–44.

Lees, Paris (2013) 'At College, Most People Thought Feminist Meant Man-Hater'. *The Guardian*. 18 January. Available at: https://www.theguardian.com/commentisfree/2013/jan/18/trans-feminist-panel

Lennon, Erica & Mistler, Brian J. (2014) 'Cisgenderism'. *TSQ Transgender Studies Quarterly*. Vol. 1(1–2), pp. 63–4.

Lester CN (2017) *Trans Like Me*. London: Virago.

Lev, Arlene Istar (2008) 'More than Surface Tension: Femmes in Families'. *Journal of Lesbian Studies*. Vol. 12(2–3), pp. 127–44.

Levitt, Heidi M. & Hiestand, Katherine R. (2004) 'A Quest for Authenticity: Contemporary Butch Gender'. *Sex Roles*. Vol. 50(9/10)(May), pp. 605–21.

Levitt, Heidi M. & Horne, Sharon G. (2002) 'Explorations of Lesbian-Queer Genders'. *Journal of Lesbian Studies*. Vol. 6(2), pp. 25–39.

Levy, Ariel (2005) *Female Chauvinist Pigs*. London: Simon & Schuster

Levy, E. J. (2020) *The Cape Doctor* by author EJ Levy.

Lewis, Helen (2016) 'So Many Teenage Girls Don't Want to Identify as Girls Any More'. *New Statesman*. May. Available at: https://www.newstatesman.com/politics/feminism/2016/05/so-many-teenage-girls-don-t-want-identify-girls-any-more-and-who-can-blame

Lewis, Sophie (2019) 'How British Feminism Became Anti-Trans'. *New York Times*. 7 February.

Li, Po-Wei & Lu, Chia-Rung (2020) 'Articulating Sexuality, Desire, and Identity: A Keyword Analysis of Heteronormativity in Taiwanese Gay and Lesbian Dating Websites'. *Sexuality and Culture*. 14 February. https://link.springer.com/article/10.1007/s12119-020-09709-5

Lorber, Judith (1999) 'Crossing Borders and Erasing Boundaries: Paradoxes of Identity Politics'. *Sociological Focus*. Vol. 32(4), pp. 355–70.

Lugones, M. (2008). 'The Coloniality of Gender'. *Worlds & Knowledges Otherwise*. Vol. 2(Spring), pp. 1–17.

Mac an Ghaill, Mairtin (1994). *The Making of Men: Masculinities, Sexualities and Schooling*. Buckingham: Open University Press.

Mackay, Finn (2015) *Radical Feminism: Feminist Activism in Movement*. London: Palgrave.

Mackay, Kathryn (2020) 'The "Tyranny of Reproduction": Could Ectogenesis Further Women's Liberation?' *Bioethics*, pp. 1–8. https://doi.org/10.1111/bioe.12706

Mailer, Norman (1966) *Cannibals and Christians*. New York: Penguin Random House.

Manders, Kerry (2020) 'The Renegades. The Butches and Studs Who've Defied the Male Gaze and Redefined Culture'. *The New York Times*. T We Are Family. Chapter 3. (April) Available at: https://www.nytimes.com/interactive/2020/04/13/t-magazine/butch-stud-lesbian.html

Manion, Jen (2020) *Female Husbands: A Trans History*. Cambridge: Cambridge University Press.

Manne, Kate (2019) *Down Girl: The Logic of Misogyny*. Oxford: Oxford University Press.

Mantilla, Karla (2000) 'Men In Ewes Clothing: The Stealth Politics of the Transgender Movement'. *Off Our Backs*. Vol. 30(4) (April), pp. 5–12.

Martino, Wayne & Ingrey, Jennifer C. (2020) 'The Bathroom Polemic'. In Carol A. Taylor, Christina Hughes & Jasmine B. Ulmer (eds), *Transdisciplinary Feminist Research*. Abingdon: Routledge.

Maurice, Emma Powys (2021) 'Butch Lesbian Confronted 'Tens of Times' in Public Toilets as Anti-trans Hostility Spills Over'. *Pink News*. 19 January. Available at: Butch lesbian harassed 'tens of times' in public toilets by anti-trans people (pinknews.co.uk).

McCarry, Melanie (2010) 'Becoming a "Proper Man": Young People's Attitudes About Interpersonal Violence and Perceptions of Gender'. *Gender Education*. Vol. 22(1), pp. 17–30.

McKenna, Wendy and Kessler, Susanne (2000) 'Retrospective Response'. *Feminism & Psychology*. Vol. 10(1), pp. 66–72.

McLean, Barbara (1973) 'Diary of a Mad Organiser'. *The Lesbian Tide*. 30 June, pp. 36–8.

McRobbie, Angela (2018) 'Anti-feminism and Anti-gender Far Right Politics in Europe and Beyond'. *Open Democracy*. 18 January.

Messerschmidt, James W. (2018) *Hegemonic Masculinity: Formulation, Reformulation and Amplification*. London: Rowman and Littlefield.

Messerschmidt, James W. & Messner, Michael (2018) 'Hegemonic, Nonhegemonic, and "New" Masculinities'. In James W. Messerschmidt, Patricia Yancey Martin, Michael A. Messner & Raewyn Connell (eds), *Gender Reckonings: New Social Theory and Research*. New York: New York University Press, pp. 35–57.

Messner, Michael (1997) *Politics of Masculinities*. London: Rowman & Littlefield

Millett, Kate [1969] (1970) *Sexual Politics*. London: Abacus.

Minkowitz, Donna (2018) 'How I Broke, and Botched, The Brandon Teena Story'. *The Village Voice*. 20 June. Available at: https://www.villagevoice.com/2018/06/20/how-i-broke-and-botched-the-brandon-teena-story/

Miranda, A. Deborah (2010) 'Extermination of the Joyas: Gendercide in Spanish California'. *GLQ A Journal of Lesbian and Gay Studies*. Vol. 16(1–2), pp. 253–84.

Mohan, Megha (2019) 'The Red Zone: A Place Where Butch Lesbians Live in Fear'. *BBC*. Gender and Identity Report. 24 June. Available at: https://www.bbc.co.uk/news/stories-48719453

Monro, Surya (2019) 'Non-binary and Genderqueer: An Overview of the Field'. *International Journal of Transgenderism*. Vol. 20(2–3), pp. 126–31.

Moore, Mallory (2020) 'Female Embodiment Fantasies'. *Medium*. 15 August. Available at: https://medium.com/@Chican3ry/female-embodiment-fantasies-1e4bab7dc3f0

Moore Mallory & Greenesmith Heron (2021) 'Health Care for Trans Youth is Under Attack in UK and it's Impacting the US'. *Truthout*. 28th February. Available at: https://truthout.org/articles/health-care-for-trans-youth-is-under-attack-in-uk-and-its-impacting-the-us/

Moore, Mignon R. (2006) 'Lipstick or Timberlands? Meanings of Gender Presentation in Black Lesbian Communities'. *Signs*. Vol. 32(1), pp. 113–39.

Moraga, Cherrie (1997) *Waiting in the Wings: Portrait of a Queer Motherhood*. New York: Firebrand Books.

Moraga, Cherry (1983 [1981]) 'La Guera', in Moraga Cherrie, Anzaldua Gloria & Bambara Toni Cade (eds), *This Bridge Called My Back*. New York: Kitchen Table Press, pp. 27–34.

Moraga, Cherry, Anzaldua, Gloria & Bambara, Toni Cade [1981] (1983) *This Bridge Called My Back*. Kitchen Table Press.

Morgan, Ashley (2019) 'The Real Problem with Toxic Masculinity Is That It Assumes There Is Only One Way of Being a Man'. *The Conversation*. 7 February. Available at: https://theconversation.com/the-real-problem-with-toxic-masculinity-is-that-it-assumes-there-is-only-one-way-of-being-a-man-110305

Morgan, Nicky (2016) 'Government Response to the Women and Equalities Committee Report on Transgender Equality'. Government Equalities Office. Available at: https://assets.publishing.service.gov.uk/government/uploads/system/uploads/attachment_data/file/535764/Government_Response_to_the_Women_and_Equalities_Committee_Report_on_Transgender_Equality.pdf

Morgan, Robin (1977) *Going Too Far: The Personal Chronicle of a Feminist*. New York: Random House.

Morgan, Robin & Douglas Carol Anne (2001) 'Interview: Robin Morgan, Activist as Ever'. *Off Our Backs*. Vol. 31(2), pp. 4–14. Available at: http://jstor.org/stable/20836787

Morris, Bonnie (2015) 'Olivia Records: The Production of a Movement'. *Journal of Lesbian Studies*. Vol. 19(3), pp. 290–304.

Morris, Bonnie J. (1999) *Eden Built By Eves*. Boston, MA: Alyson Publications.

Morris, Bonnie J. (2016) *The Disappearing L: Erasure of Lesbian Spaces and Culture*. New York: SUNY Press.

Mulvey, Laura (1975) *Visual Pleasure and Narrative Cinema*. Munich: Grin Publishing.

Munt, Sally (1998) *Butch/Femme: Inside Lesbian Gender*. London: Cassell.

Munt, Sally (2001) 'The Butch Body'. In Ruth Holliday and John Hassard, *Contested Bodies*. London: Routledge, pp. 95–107.

Murphy, Meghan (2014) 'Why Has Drag Escaped Critique from Feminists and the LGBTQ Community?'. *Feminist Current*. 25 April. Available at: https://www.feministcurrent.com/2014/04/25/why-has-drag-escaped-critique-from-feminists-and-the-lgbtq-community/

Murphy Tooth, Amy (2020) 'Butch on the Streets: The Butch Flaneur and the Queering of the City'. In Berry Jess, Moore Timothy, Kalms Nicole & Bawden Gene (eds), *Contentious Cities: Design and the Gendered Production of Space*. Abingdon: Routledge, pp. 149–61.

Muska, Susan & Olafsdottir, Greta (1998) (Dir.) 'The Brandon Teena Story'. Bless Bless Productions.

Nataf, Zachary I. (1996) *Lesbians Talk Transgender*. London: Scarlet Press.

Neild, Suzanne & Pearson, Rosalind (1992) *Women Like Us*. London: Women's Press.

Nestle, Joan (1981) 'Butch-Fem Relationships: Sexual Courage in the 1950s'. *Heresies*. (12), pp. 21–4.

Nestle, Joan (1992) 'Flamboyance and Fortitude: An Introduction'. In Joan Nestle (ed.), *The Persistent Desire: A Femme-Butch Reader*. Boston, MA: Alyson Publications Inc., pp. 13–23.

Nestle, Joan (2002) 'Genders on My Mind'. In Joan Nestle, Clare Howell & Riki Wilchins (eds), *Genderqueer: Voices from Beyond the Sexual Binary*. New York: Alyson Books, pp. 3–11.

Nestle, Joan (1992) (ed.). *The Persistent Desire: A Femme-Butch Reader*. Boston, MA: Alyson Publications Inc.

Newton, Esther (1984) 'The Mythic Mannish Lesbian: Radclyffe Hall and the New Woman'. *Signs*. Vol. 9(4), pp. 557–75.

Newton, Esther (2018) *My Butch Career*. London: Duke University Press.

Nguyen, Athena (2008) 'Patriarchy, Power, and Female Masculinity'. *Journal of Homosexuality*. Vol. 55(4), pp. 665–83.

Noble Bobby, Jean (2004) 'Sons of the Movement: Feminism, Female Masculinity and Female to Male (FTM) Transexual Men'. *Atlantis*. Vol. 29(1), pp. 21–8.

Noble Bobby, Jean (2007) 'The P Word: Trans Men, Stone Butches and the Politics of Pentration'. *Atlantis*. Vol. 31(2): 16–23.

O'Leary, Dale & Sprigg, Peter (2015) 'Understanding and Responding to the Transgender Movement'. June. Family Research Council.

Oram, Alison & Turnbull, Annemarie (2001) *The Lesbian History Sourcebook*. London: Routledge.

Osobrn, Jan & Tyler, Robin (2016) Interviewed by Cristan Williams. 'Sex Essentialist Violence And Radical Inclusion: An Interview with Robin Tyler, Jan Osborn, and Michele Kammerer'. The Conversations Project. 1 February. Available at: http://radfem .transadvocate.com/sex-essentialist-violence-and-radical-inclusion-an-interview-with -robin-tyler-jan-osborn-and-michele-kammerer/

Owens, Glen & Heale, James (2020) 'At Last! Teachers Are Told to Stop Pushing Tomboys to Change Their Gender'. *The Daily Mail*. 26 September. Available at: https://www .dailymail.co.uk/news/article-8776765/Teachers-told-stop-pushing-tomboys-change -gender.html [Accessed 26 September].

Owens, Cooper & Benia, Deirdre (2017) *Medical Bondage: Race, Gender and the Origins of American Gynaecology*. Georgia: University of Georgia Press.

Oyewumi, Oyeronke (1997) *The Invention of Women: Making an African Sense of Western Gender Discourses*. Minneapolis: University of Minnesota Press.

Parker, Kim, Horowitz, Juliana & Igielnik, Ruth (2018) 'Women and Leadership'. Pew Research Centre. Available at: https://www.pewsocialtrends.org/2018/09/20/women -and-leadership-2018/

Pearce, Ruth (2018) *Understanding Trans Health*. Bristol: Policy Press.

Peirce, Kimberly (1999) (Dir.) 'Boys Don't Cry'.

Pence, Mike (2019) 'Vice President Mike Pence Speaks at Focus on the Family 40th Anniversary Celebration'. Available at: http://nrb.org/news-room/articles/nrbt/vice -president-mike-pence-speaks-focus-familys-40th-anniversary-celebration/

Perry, Grayson (2016) *The Descent of Man*. London: Penguin Random House.

Peterson, Jordan (2018) Interviewed by Cathy Newman for Channel 4 News. January. Available at: https://www.youtube.com/watch?v=aMcjxSThD54

Prosser, Jay (1995) 'No Place Like Home: The Transgendered Narrative of Leslie Feinberg's Stone Butch Blues'. *Modern Fiction Studies* (41), pp. 483–514.

Queen, Carol A. (1994) 'Why I Love Butch Women'. In Lily Burana, Linnea Due and Roxxie (eds), *Dagger: On Butch Women*. San Francisco: Cleiss Press, pp. 15–23.

Radicalesbians (1970) 'The Woman Identified Woman'. In Sarah Lucia Hoagland & Julia Penelope (1988) (eds), *For Lesbians Only: A Separatist Anthology*. London: Onlywomen Press, pp. 17–22.

Ramirez, Ricardo (2020) 'Simplified Identities: Four "Types" of Gays and Lesbians on Chilean Telenovelas'. *Sexualities*, pp. 1–9.

Raymond, Janice (1979) *The Transexual Empire*. Boston, MA: Beacon Press.

Raymond, Janice (1980) *The Transsexual Empire*. London: Women's Press.

Raymond, Janice (1986) *A Passion For Friends: Toward a Philosophy of Female Affection*. Boston: Beacon Press.

Raymond, Janice (1989) 'Putting the Politics Back Into Lesbianism'. *Women's Studies International Forum*. Vol. 12(2), pp. 149–56.

Raymond Janice (no date). 'Fictions and Facts About the Transexual Empire'. Janice Raymond Official Author Site. Available at: https://janiceraymond.com/fictions-and -facts-about-the-transsexual-empire/

Reddy-Best, Kelly. L. & Pederson, Elaine L. (2014). 'The Relationship of Gender Expression, Sexual Identity, Distress, Appearance, and Clothing Choices for Queer Women'. *International Journal of Fashion Design, Technology, and Education*. DOI: 10.1080/17543266.2014.958576.

Rees, Jeska (2010) 'A Look Back at Anger: The Women's Liberation Movement in 1978'. *Women's History Review*. Vol. 19(3), pp. 337–56.

Reilly-Cooper Rebecca (2015) 'Sex and Gender: A Beginner's Guide'. [online]. https://sexandgenderintro.com/how-did-we-get-here/

Relatio Finalis 2015 Synod of Bishops (2015). Final Report to the Holy Father, Pope Francis. The Vocation and Mission of the Family in The Church and in the Contemporary World. Vatican City. 24 October.

Renold, E. (2002) 'Presumed Innocence: (Hetero)Sexual, Homophobic and Heterosexist Harassment Amongst Primary School Girls and Boys'. *Childhood*. Vol. 9(4), pp. 415–34.

Renold, Emma, Sara, Bragg, Jackson, Carolyn & Jessica, Ringrose (2017) *How Gender Matters to Children and Young People Living in England*. Cardiff University, University of Brighton, University of Lancaster and University College London, Institute of Education. ISBN 978-1-908469-13-7.

Richardson, Diane (1996) '"Misguided, Dangerous and Wrong": On the maligning of Radical Feminism'. In Diane Bell & Renate Klein (eds), *Radically Speaking: Feminism Reclaimed*. Melbourne, Victoria: Spinifex, pp. 143–55.

Riddell, Carol. [1980] *Divided Sisterhood: A Critical Review of Janice Raymond's* The Transsexual Empire (Liverpool: News From Nowhere). In Susan Stryker and Stephen Whittle (2006) (eds), *The Transgender Studies Reader*. New York: Routledge, pp. 144–58.

Riggle, Ellen D. B. (2018) 'Experiences of a Gender Non-conforming Lesbian in the "Ladies" (Rest)Room'. *Journal of Lesbian Studies*. Vol. 22(4), pp. 1–14.

Rippon, Gina (2019) *The Gendered Brain*. London: Bodley Head

Roberts, Steven (2018) *Young Working-Class Men in Transition*. Abingdon: Routledge.

Rosario, Margaret, Schrimshaw, Eric W., Hunter, Joyce & Levy-Warren, Anna (2009) 'The Coming-Out Process of Young Lesbian and Bisexual Women: Are There Butch/Femme Differences in Sexual Identity Development?'. *Archives of Sexual Behaviour*. Vol. 38, pp. 34–49.

Rosario, Vernon A. (2009) 'Quantum Sex: Intersex and the Molecular Deconstruction of Sex'. *GLQ Journal of Lesbian and Gay Studies*. Vol. 15(2), pp. 267–84.

Rossiter, Hannah (2016) 'She's Always a Woman: Butch Lesbian Trans Women in the Lesbian Community'. *Journal of Lesbian Studies*. Vol. 20(1), pp. 87–96.

Rowling, J. K. (2020) 'JK Rowling Writes about Her Reasons for Speaking Out on Sex and Gender Issues'. JK Rowling personal website. Available at: https://www.jkrowling.com/opinions/j-k-rowling-writes-about-her-reasons-for-speaking-out-on-sex-and-gender-issues/ [Accessed 12 June 2020].

Rubin, Gayle (1992) 'Of Catamites and Kings: Reflections on Butch, Gender, and Boundaries'. In Joan Nestle (ed.), *The Persistent Desire: A Femme-Butch Reader*. Boston, MA: Alyson Publications Inc, pp. 466–82.

Rubin, Henry S. (1998) 'Reading Like A (Transexual) Man'. In Tom Digby (ed.), *Men Doing Feminism*. London: Routledge, pp. 305–25.

Santana, Matthew Leslie (2018) 'Transforming Havana's Gay Ambiente: Black Lesbian Gender Performers and Cuba's Sexual Revolution'. *ReVista: Harvard Review of Latin America* (Winter).

Sanz, Veronica (2017) 'No Way Out of the Binary: A Critical History of the Scientific Production of Sex'. *Signs*. Vol. 43(1), pp. 1–27.

Sax, Leonard (2002) 'How Common Is Intersex? A Response to Anne Fausto-Sterling'. *Journal of Sex Research*. Vol. 39(3), pp. 174–8.

Scheman, Naomi (1993) *Engenderings: Constructions of Knowledge, Authority and Privilege*. New York: Routledge.

Scheman, Naomi (2016) 'Looking Back on "Queering the Center"'. *TSQ: Transgender Studies Quarterly*. Vol. 3(1–2), pp. 212–19.

Schilt, Kristen (2009) 'Doing Gender, Doing Heteronormativity: "Gender Normals", Transgender People, and the Social Maintenance of Heterosexuality'. *Gender & Society*. Vol. 23(4), pp. 440–64.

Segal, Lynne (1997) *Slow Motion: Changing Masculinities; Changing Men*. London: Virago

Serano, Julia (2017) 'Transgender People and "Biological Sex" Myths'. Medium. 17 July. Available at: https://medium.com/@juliaserano/transgender-people-and-biological-sex-myths-c2a9bcdb4f4a

Serano, Julia (2020) 'Autogynophilia: A Scientific Review, Feminist Analysis and Alternative "Embodiment Fantasies" Model'. *Sociological Review*. Vol. 68(4). August, pp. 763–78.

Sharpe, Alex (2020) 'Will Gender Self-Declaration Undermine Women's Rights and Lead to an Increase in Harms?'. *Modern Law Review*. Vol. 83(3), pp. 539–57.

Shipman, Tim (2020) 'Boris Johnson Scraps Plans to Make Gender Change Easier'. *The Sunday Times*. 14 June. Available at: https://www.thetimes.co.uk/article/boris-johnson-scraps-plan-to-make-gender-change-easier-zs6lqfls0 [Accessed 15 June 2020].

Silverman, Rachel E. & Comeforo, Kristin (2019) 'Patriarchy Interrupted: Differential Realisations and Manifestations of Power in Butch/Femme Relationships'. *Cultural Studies Critical Methodologies*, pp. 1–13.

Sinnott, Megan (2004) *Toms and Dees: Transgender Identity and Female Same-Sex Relationships in Thailand*. Honolulu: University of Hawai'i Press.

Smith, Elizabeth A. (1989) 'Butches, Femmes and Feminists: The Politics of Lesbian Sexuality'. *NWSA Journal*. Vol. 1(3) (Spring), pp. 398–421.

Smythe, Viv (2018) 'I'm Credited with Having Coined the Word "Terf". Here's How It Happened'. *The Guardian*. 28 November. https://amp.theguardian.com/commentisfree/2018/nov/29/im-credited-with-having-coined-the-acronym-terf-heres-how-it-happened?__twitter_impression=true

Snorton, Riley C. (2017) *Black on Both Sides: A Racial History of Trans Identity*. Minnesota: University of Minnesota Press.

Solomon, Alisa (1993) 'Not Just a Passing Fancy: Notes on Butch'. *Theatre*. Vol. 24(2), pp. 35–46.

Stanley, Liz and Wise, Sue (1983) *Breaking Out: Feminist Consciousness and Feminist Research*. Abingdon, London: Routledge.

Steinem, Gloria (2013) 'On Working Together Over Time'. *The Advocate*. 2 October. https://www.advocate.com/commentary/2013/10/02/op-ed-working-together-over-time

Stock, Kathleen (2018) 'Stonewall's New Definition of 'Conversion Therapy' Raises a Few Questions'. The Article. 15 November. https://www.thearticle.com/stonewalls-new-definition-of-conversion-therapy-raises-a-few-questions/

Stock, Kathleen (2019a) 'Blackface Is Evil – Why Isn't Drag?'. *Standpoint*. 23 October. Available at: https://standpointmag.co.uk/issues/november-2019/blackface-is-evil-why-isnt-drag/

Stock, Kathleen (2019b) 'Are Academics Freely Able to Criticise the Idea of "Gender Identity" in UK Universities?'. *Medium*. 3 July. https://medium.com/@kathleenstock/are-academics-freely-able-to-criticise-the-idea-of-gender-identity-in-uk-universities-67b97c6e04be

Stock, Kathleen (2020) 'Transcript of Talk at Res Publica Event: Beyond the Failures of Liberal Feminism'. Available at: Transcript of talk at Res Publica event: Beyond the failures of liberal feminism (kathleenstock.com)

Stoltenberg, John (2000) *Refusing to Be a Man*. London: Routledge.

Stoltenberg, John (2020) 'Andrea Dworkin Was A Trans Ally'. *Boston Review*. 8 April. Available at: http://bostonreview.net/gender-sexuality/john-stoltenberg-andrea-dworkin-was-trans-ally

Stone, Sandy (1991) 'The Empire Strikes Back: A Posttransexual Manifesto'. In J. Epstein & K. Straub (eds), *Body Guards: The Cultural Politics of Gender Ambiguity*. London: Routledge, pp. 280–304.

Stone, Sandy (2006) 'The Empire Strikes Back', in S. Stryker and S. Whittle (eds), *The Transgender Studies Reader* (Volume 1). London and New York: Routledge: pp. 221–36.

Stone, Sandy (2018) Zachary Drucker interviews Sandy Stone. 'Sandy Stone on Living Among Lesbian Separatists as a Trans Woman in the 70s'. *Vice*. 19 September. Available at: https://www.vice.com/en_us/article/zmd5k5/sandy-stone-biography-transgender-history.

Stonewall. (2021) Glossary of Terms. Available at: https://www.stonewall.org.uk/help-advice/faqs-and-glossary/glossary-terms#s [Accessed 10 February 2021].

Strangio, Chase (2016) 'What Is A "Male Body"?' *Slate*. 19 July. Available at: https://slate.com/human-interest/2016/07/theres-no-such-thing-as-a-male-body.html [Accessed 20 July 2016].

Stryker, Susan (1994) 'My Words to Victor Frankenstein above the Village of Chamounix: Performing Transgender Rage'. *GLQ: Journal of Lesbian and Gay Studies*. Vol. 1(3), pp. 237–54.

Stryker, Susan (2017) *Transgender History*. New York: Seal Press.

Stryker, Susan & Whittle, Stephen (2006) (eds) *The Transgender Studies Reader*. New York: Routledge.

Summerhawk, B., McMahill, C., & McDonald, D. (eds). (1998). *Queer Japan: Personal Stories of Japanese Lesbians, Gays, Transexuals and Bisexuals*. Norwich, VT: NewVictoria Publishers.

Summerscale, Kate (1998) *The Queen of Whale Cay*. London: Bloomsbury

Sundaram, V. & Jackson, C. P. (2018) '"Monstrous Men" and "Sex Scandals": The Myth of Exceptional Deviance in Sexual Harassment and Violence in Education'. *Palgrave Communications*. Vol. 4, p. 147. https://doi.org/10.1057/s41599-018-0202-9

SWA Scottish Women's Aid (no date) 'Position Statement on Transgender Women'. Available at: https://womensaid.scot/wp-content/uploads/2017/11/SWA-position-on-trans-women.pdf

Sweeney, Nick (Dir.) (2015) Born in the Wrong Body: Girls to Men. Channel 4. 13 October 2015.

Swerling, Gabriella (2019) 'Trans Dispute Prompts New Gay Faction to Break With Stonewall'. *The Telegraph*. 23 October. Available at: https://www.telegraph.co.uk/news/2019/10/23/stonewall-splits-accused-promoting-trans-agenda-expense-gay/

Triller Kaeley (2019) 'Women Won't Be Liberated Until We're Free From Abortion'. *The Federalist*. 16th January. Available at: https://thefederalist.com/2019/01/16/women-wont-liberated-free-abortion/

Truss Liz & Government Equalities Office (2020) 'Government Responds to Gender Recognition Act Consultation'. GEO Press Release. 22 September. Available at: https://www.gov.uk/government/news/government-responds-to-gender-recognition-act-consultation [Accessed 22 September 2020].

Tubb Rosalind, A. (1985) 'Are You a Real Woman?'. *Spare Rib*. (161), p. 8.

Turner, Janice (2019) 'Lesbians Face a Fight for Their Very Existence'. *The Times*. 13 July. Available at: https://www.thetimes.co.uk/article/lesbians-face-a-fight-for-their-very-existence-v97mswc0p [Accessed 14 July 2019].

Tyler, Robin (2014) Interviewed by Cristan Williams 'A TERF's Fist Gave Rise to Trans-Inclusive Women's Music Festivals'. *TransAdvocate*. 17 August. Available at: https://www.transadvocate.com/a-terfs-fist-gave-rise-to-trans-inclusive-womens-music-festivals_n_14390.htm

Urquhart, Evan (2020) 'JK Rowling and the Echo Chamber of TERFs'. *Slate*. 12 June. Available at: https://slate.com/human-interest/2020/06/jk-rowling-trans-men-terf.html

Valentine, Gill (1993) 'Negotiating and Managing Multiple Sexual Identities: Lesbian Time-Space Strategies'. *Transactions of the Institute of British Geographers*. Vol. 18(2), pp. 237–48.

Valentine, Gill (1996) '(Re)negotiating the "Heterosexual Street": Lesbian Productions of Space'. In Nancy Duncan (ed.), *Body Space: Destabilising Geographies of Gender and Sexuality*. London: Routledge, pp. 146–55.

Vera-Gray, Fiona (2018) *The Right Amount of Panic*. Bristol: Policy Press.

Verloo, Mieke (2013) 'Intersectional and Cross-Movement Politics and Policies: Reflections on Current Practices and Debates'. *Signs: Journal of Women in Culture and Society*. Vol. 38(4), pp. 893–915.

Vincent Ben (2020) *Non-Binary Genders*. Bristol: Policy Press.

Vogel, Lisa (2018) Letter to Jonathan Best 'The Truth about Michigan Womyn's Music Festival and Trans Women – A Correction'. *Medium*. Available at: https://medium.com/@JonnnyBest/the-truth-about-michigan-womyns-festival-and-trans-women-a-correction-899d8e49f655

Walworth, Janis (2014) Interviewed by Cristan Williams. 'How TERF Violence Inspired Camp Trans'. *TransAdvocate*. Available at: https://www.transadvocate.com/how-terf-violence-inspired-camp-trans_n_14413.htm

Ward, Jane (2008) *Respectably Queer*. Nashville, TN: Vanderbilt University Press.

Watson, Lori (2016) 'The Woman Question'. *Transgender Studies Quarterly TSQ*. Vol. 3(1–2), pp. 246–53.

Webb, Robert (2017) *How Not to Be a Boy*. Edinburgh: Canongate.

Webb, Sam (2016) 'McDonalds Boots Out Teenage Girl "Who Used Women's Toilet Because Staff Thought She Was a boy"'. *The Mirror*. 7 April.

Weiss, Jillian T. (2007) 'The Lesbian Community and FTMs: Détente in the Butch/FTM Borderlands'. *Journal of Lesbian Studies*. Vol. 11(3–4), pp. 203–11.

West, Candace and Zimmerman, Don (1987) 'Doing Gender'. *Gender and Society*. Vol. 1(2), pp. 12–551.

West, Celeste R. (2013) 'Trans Women in Feminism: Nothing About Us Without Us'. Open Democracy. 29 April. Available at: https://www.opendemocracy.net/en/5050/trans-women-in-feminism-nothing-about-us-without-us/

Weston, Kate (1993) 'Do Clothes Maketh the Woman? Gender, Performance Theory and Lesbian Eroticism'. *Genders*. Vol. 17(Fall), pp. 1–21.

Wheelwright, Julie (1989) *Amazons and Military Maids*. New York: Rivers Oram Press.

Whitehead, Stephen M. (2002) *Men and Masculinities*. Cambridge: Polity Press.

Whittle Stephen (2020) 'Women and Equalities Committee Oral evidence: Reform of the Gender Recognition Act, HC 884'. Wednesday 9 December 2020. London. House of Commons. Available at: https://committees.parliament.uk/oralevidence/1394/default/

Wilchins, Riki (2002a) 'Deconstructing Trans'. In Joan Nestle, Clare Howell & Riki Wilchins (eds), *Genderqueer: Voices from Beyond the Sexual Binary*. New York: Alyson Books, pp 55–67.

Wilchins, Riki (2002b) 'Queerer Bodies'. In Joan Nestle, Clare Howell & Riki Wilchins (eds), *Genderqueer: Voices from Beyond the Sexual Binary*. New York: Alyson Books, pp 33–46.

Wilchins, Riki (2002c) 'A Continuous Non Verbal Communication'. In Joan Nestle, Clare Howell & Riki Wilchins (eds), *Genderqueer: Voices from Beyond the Sexual Binary*. New York: Alyson Books, pp. 11–17.

Williams, Cristan (2015) 'Sex, Gender, and Sexuality: An Interview with Catharine A. MacKinnon'. Interview by Cristan Williams for The Conversation Project in the *TransAdvocate*.

Williams, Cristan (2016) 'Radical Inclusion: Recounting the Trans Inclusive History of Radical Feminism'. *TSQ: Transgender Studies Quarterly*. Vol. 3(1–2), pp. 254–9.

Williams, Cristan (2020) 'The Ontological Woman: A History of Deauthentification, Dehumanisation and Violence'. *Sociological Review*. Vol. 68(4), pp. 718–34.

Willis, Ellen (1984) 'Radical Feminism and Feminist Radicalism'. *Social Text*. 9/10(Spring/Summer), pp. 91–118.

Wilson, Bianca D. M. (2009) 'Black Lesbian Gender and Sexual Culture: Celebration and Resistance'. *Culture, Health and Sexuality*. Vol. 11(3), pp. 297–313.

Wittig, Monique (1992) *The Straight Mind and Other Essays*. London: Prentice-Hall.

Wodak, Ruth (2015) *The Politics of Fear: What Right-Wing Populist Discourses Mean*. London: Sage.

WPUK Woman's Place UK (2018) 'Gender Neutral Toilets Don't Work for Women'. Available at: https://womansplaceuk.org/gender-neutral-toilets-dont-work-for-women-2/

WWTLC (2018) We Want the Land Coalition. Available at: https://wwtlc.org/

Young, Antonia (1999) *Women Who Become Men*. Oxford: Berg Press.

Zanghellini, Aleardo (2020) 'Philosophical Problems with the Gender-Critical Feminist Argument Against Trans Inclusion'. *Sage Open*. May. Available at: https://journals-sagepub-com.ezproxy.uwe.ac.uk/doi/10.1177/2158244020927029

Index